An Introduction to Language and Linguistics

Breaking the Language Spell

Christopher J. Hall

continuum

Continuum

The Tower Building
11 York Road
London SE1 7NX

15 East 26th Street
New York
NY 10010

First published 2005

British Library Cataloguing-in-Publication Data
A catalogue record for this book is available from the British Library.

ISBN 0-8264-87335 (hardback)
    0-8264-87343 (paperback)

Library of Congress Cataloging-in-Publication Data
To come

Typeset by BookEns Ltd, Royston, Herts
Printed and bound in Great Britain by MPG Books Ltd, Bodmin, Cornwall

Anda pensamiento mío
(Go ahead, thought of mine)

> From the song *Pensamiento*
> ('Thought') by R. Gómez

In memory of my Dad
John Mortimer Hall
(1930–2004)

and for
Juan Gustavo Galindo González
εις αιωνα

Acknowledgements

We are grateful to the original publishers for permission to reprint the following extracts in this book.

'The Language Issue' by Nuala Ní Dhomhnaill, translated by Paul Muldoon, by kind permission of the author and The Gallery Press, Loughcrew, Oldcastle, County Meath, Ireland, from *Pharaoh's Daughter* (1990).

The Clouds, from *Four Plays by Aristophanes*, translated by William Arrowsmith, copyright © 1962 by William Arrowsmith. Used by permission of Dutton Signet, a division of Penguin Group (USA) Inc.

Contents

Preface

Over breakfast the other morning I read the following sentence in the newspaper:

> With so many vehicles on the road, traffic on principle streets moves between 7 and 15 kilometres per hour (4 to 9 miles per hour) during the periods of heaviest use.

That was the second time I'd seen *principal* confused with *principle* in a major newspaper within the space of a month, and it upset me. The article was about traffic congestion in Mexico City, where I drive home to every weekend, so it was a topic that directly concerned me. Now if it wasn't for the spelling error, I probably wouldn't have paid any conscious attention at all to the language used in the article. What was important was the traffic problem itself. Instead of fuming over orthography, maybe I would have recalled my own lost hours trying to get home on a Friday evening, or on the improvement I witnessed in London's traffic flow on a recent trip back to the UK. Like all language users, I would have digested the information in the sentence without a thought for the series of little miracles which caused the writer's intended message to escape from the physical confines of his brain and register itself in my own. But instead, I got upset by the misplacement of two miserable letters. Why did I find the writer's error so annoying? He had a clear meaning to impart, and I understood it perfectly. So what was the problem? Isn't that just what language is for?

The thing is, language isn't just a way of transmitting meaning. Whether we like it or not, it's also perceived as a reflection of our education and social identity. The language we speak, the accent and dialect we speak it with, whether we can spell correctly, or can write at all – these facts all contribute to the formulation of strong judgements of who we are and how we should treat each other. That morning over breakfast I judged the writer of the sentence not on what he said, but on the way he said it. I am, like all of us, a hostage to what I call *the Language Spell*. This spell generally works extremely well, keeping most of the extraordinary nature of human language tidily in the background as we concentrate on the messages it conveys. Once we reflect on the aspects of the medium that we typically *do* tend to notice (spelling errors, foreign accents, 'bad' grammar, plummy tones, etc.), we are immediately struck by their fierce social significance. And yet a moment's further thought reveals their utter insignificance in the light of the overall scheme of human language as a shared property of the species.

This book is about human beings' natural inability to penetrate beyond the surface of language, and the consequences this has for our individual and communal beliefs and practices. It's as though we're under a spell, which hides from us the essential biological reality of the language faculty, and throws to the fore its social purposes. The magic is prodigious, yet it can have pernicious effects. It makes verbal communication seem uncomplicated and instantaneous, the next best thing to telepathy. But by so doing, it also tempts us to confuse people's inner thoughts and feelings with the words that express them, and, conversely, to treat languages and dialects as external, social objects, handed down to us as children by our parents and, if necessary, corrected by schooling and exposure to good usage. In adulthood we are constantly judged for what we say and how we say it, even when this doesn't truly mirror what we think or how we act.

This is a serious matter, because language is power: indeed, it's the principal resource we use to know ourselves and others. Mastery of language is the key to knowledge, self-identity, and the benefits and trials of group membership. In Shakespeare's *The Tempest*, the magician Prospero tells his slave Caliban:

> [. . .] I pitied thee,
> Took pains to make thee speak, taught thee each hour
> One thing or other: when thou didst not, savage,
> Know thine own meaning, but wouldst gabble like
> A thing most brutish, I endow'd thy purposes
> With words that made them known [. . .]

Through the extraordinary power of language, Caliban can in turn express his contempt for this new skill, responding:

> You taught me language; and my profit on't
> Is, I know how to curse: the red plague rid you,
> For learning me your language!

Caliban's development of speech has turned him from brute into human being. He gives external expression to highly abstract thoughts, thoughts that may well be self-contradictory, but which once said, allow us to judge who he is. By making his thoughts public, his words make him a person in our eyes: whether we see him as vile rapist or oppressed slave, his use of language shows us that he is one of us.

Inevitably, this book is about linguistics, the scientific discipline which studies the nature of human language, as well as the social and psychological contexts in which it's used. But it's not a conventional textbook, and neither is it an academic treatise. It's too selective and idiosyncratic in coverage to provide the kind of rigorous survey needed by students in linguistics courses (although students might read it as a preview or complement to their formal studies). And it's too reliant on the scholarly work of a host of fellow linguists to constitute a new theory or a profound departure from prevailing wisdom (although my professional colleagues will maybe find in it some novel spins on their work). In fact, the purpose of the book is to appeal to as many ordinary readers as possible, to share with them a broad vision of the wonders of human language and the peril of taking them for granted. Unlike many introductory books on language and linguistics, I have written this book in a way that embraces and integrates the social and the psychological aspects of language, using the spell metaphor to bridge the gap. I have simplified complex aspects of current linguistic theory without 'dumbing down', because I believe non-specialists should have access to the knowledge they need in order to formulate their own informed judgements on the vast range of language-related issues which confront us all. These issues include bilingual education policies, literacy rates, job discrimination based on the way you speak, the loss of minority languages and the ubiquitous problem of just saying what you mean and understanding the meanings of others. In accord with this goal, I also connect what linguists do with real problems and issues in people's lives. This is the province of the flourishing sister discipline of applied linguistics, a field that has helped to frame many of my own research interests over the last decade or so.

Given my objectives, I knew at the beginning of this project that I had two major ground plans to choose from: I could go for either depth or breadth. I decided on breadth of coverage, and in a big way. What you'll experience in the following chapters is a roller-coaster ride through the labyrinth of human language. Like a textbook, we cover a lot of ground, and so inevitably we move quickly over much of the terrain. But I want readers to enjoy the ride, and so I try to provide the maximum amount of intellectual thrills along the way. In this sense, the book is more like a week's tour of the major European capitals than a month-long sojourn in a Tuscan villa. For those who wish to know more about a topic, each chapter has a 'More information' section of websites and books (referenced in the Bibliography), and at the end there is an extensive glossary of the **boldfaced** terms in the text. I also indulge myself a bit, by freely quoting from the novels (and occasional poems) that have accompanied me over the last few years. In so doing, I also have two less selfish purposes: to illuminate the ideas presented with the unique visions of some of the world's finest philosophers of human nature; and also to pay homage to literature itself, that supreme manifestation of the magic we all possess.

The organization of the chapters, and the selection of topics discussed in each one, is far from traditional for a book on language. Textbooks often take the anatomist's route, dissecting our linguistic capacity according to the components of grammar and their relation to sound and meaning, and then explaining how they develop in the individual and the species, how they are represented and processed in the mind and brain, how they vary across groups of speakers and are employed for distinct purposes. The result, though clear and orderly, can often be fragmentary, like a description of the parts needed to assemble a bookcase, rather than of the bookcase itself. As a student, I used books like these, and couldn't see the forest for the trees.

As a reaction to my youthful myopia, I have designed this book so that it presents different aspects of the big picture simultaneously but gradually – a fade-in approach that permits the reader to see the language system in its social and psychological context from the outset. Part I, *Magic*, presents the over-arching metaphor of the Spell and the role of linguistics in helping us to look behind it. Chapter 1 defines the borders of the language faculty, describes the nature of the evolutionary magic which hides it from view, and sketches some of the social consequences of its near-invisibility. Chapter 2 sets out the major professional goals and activities of linguistics and applied linguistics, and introduces the reader to the essential components of language identified by linguistic theory.

Part II, *Words*, explores the nature of meaning and its linguistic expression by taking a close look at wordhood. Chapter 3 tackles the thorny issue of what a word is, and in so doing explains how we use language to share the contents of our minds with others. Chapter 4 begins to reveal the biological reality of language, by showing how vocabulary knowledge emerges in individual children, changes across the generations, and yet paradoxically, must be seen as a property of groups if it is to perform its social function. In Chapter 5, the focus is on how words come to be: from the micro perspective of their physical expression as strings of phonemes or letters, and from the broader viewpoint of how languages adopt new words, especially when speakers of one language come into contact with speakers of another.

In Part III, *Grammar*, we go beyond the word level to examine in some depth the key to the magic of linguistic communication: our capacity to express complex new thoughts through the combination of a finite number of smaller memorized units. Chapter 6 deals with morphology, the component of grammar which governs how prefixes, suffixes and roots are combined together to make new words and perform different grammatical functions. This discussion allows us to appreciate how grammatical systems change through time and vary across communities. Chapter 7, on syntax, sketches the basic machinery underlying the ways in which languages channel non-linear thought into hierarchically-structured linear strings of words. To make the hidden secrets of syntax more accessible, the chapter also shows how sentences are actually used in communication, the province of the often disconnected field of pragmatics. Chapter 8 then situates grammatical knowledge at the two poles of language development: at one end infant language acquirers, who come into the world already biologically prepared for the task; and at the other end *us*: mature language users whose linguistic knowledge is seamlessly interwoven with other sociocognitive capacities so that we can participate in culturally-embedded discourse.

Having now exposed much of the workings of the Language Spell, Part IV, *Babel*, brings us back to the paradox which underlies it all: the fact that language is socially motivated, spread across a culturally diverse world of different mother tongues and ways of speaking, but is ultimately a property of the human brain, and is therefore common to the species. Chapter 9 confronts the apparent problem of linguistic diversity across the human population and through history, reporting the typological facts and exposing untenable monolingual views of the world's multilingual heritage. Then Chapter 10 takes a different vantage point on diversity, looking at the interaction of groups of speakers of the same language, and at the different ways individual speakers use their language according to their distinct needs and circumstances. The chapter closes with a discussion of how this diversity affects educational and political policy-making, and returns to the issue of language and its intimate relationship with power.

The final chapter, Chapter 11, evaluates the power of the Language Spell and provides the basis for a resolution of the social-biological paradox which underlies it. The chapter demonstrates how language evolved in the human brain as a key component of our cultural development and as our principal means of freeing ourselves from the genetic programmes that build us. This allows us to conclude that although the Spell will remain unbroken, a glimpse of what's behind the magic can help us to better understand the dynamic nature of the human condition, and so remind us that we have the power to challenge some of the damaging effects of the Spell, if we so wish.

I hope you enjoy this book. It took me longer than I expected to plan and write, but I wouldn't have got very far at all without the support and feedback of many people, and without the knowledge acquired from countless classes, conversations, books, articles, talks and conferences. In the text I have mentioned by name some of the key influences on my thought over the years, and the sources of some of the major ideas I use. This book represents the distillation and extension of the scholarship of a very large number of individual linguists, some of whose work is also mentioned in the 'More information' sections following each chapter and in the Sources section at the end. The majority, however, remain anonymous. Many linguists reading this will recognize the fruits of their intellectual labours reflected in the text: my greatest debt is clearly to you.

I thank the authorities of the Universidad de las Américas, Puebla, for granting me a sabbatical year for this project in 2001–2002, as well as for financial support, student aids, and all-important class-release time. I am especially grateful to research dean Marco Rosales and to my head of department Pat McCoy, for their unquestioning support. To my research assistants and student aids Lisa Hayes, Gerardo Ortega, Juan Carlos Ortiz and Cynthia Prado: ¡muchisimas gracias! Thanks also to Noël Burton-Roberts and colleagues at the University of Newcastle upon Tyne for providing me with office space, library access, and stimulating academic encounters during my sabbatical year. Maggie Tallerman, S. J. Hannahs, and their colleagues at the University of Durham furnished additional intellectual support, friendship and great conviviality. As always, I am especially indebted to my Mum, Joan Hall, who apart from her perennial emotional support, also let me use her flat in Tynemouth, where most of this book was written. Thanks also to Jonathan Price for his good-natured encouragement throughout.

I am extremely grateful to the following linguists, colleagues and friends for reading and commenting on previous versions of different chapters: Jean Aitchison, John Ayto, Ginger Clarkson, Ed Finegan, S. J. Hannahs, Stephanie Lindemann, Virginia LoCastro, Gayle Nelson, Fritz Newmeyer and Ashley Withers. I benefited greatly also from comments provided by anonymous reviewers of earlier versions of some of the material. I offer my sincere thanks to the graduate students who read versions of the manuscript as part of my Linguistics for Language Professionals course, and particularly the generation which gave me such thoughtful suggestions in the Fall of 2003: Dyann Gregg, Rebeca Martínez, Denise Newbrand, Erin Quirk, Svetlana Sokolova, Brent Tieber and Christopher Vance. I owe a great debt to Patrick Smith for his careful reading of, and reactions to, the entire manuscript. His input helped me enormously and led to significant improvements, as did the many marathon, tequila-oiled discussions we have had on language and linguistics over the years: ¡*Salud compadre*! I thank also my principal co-researcher Peter Ecke, as well as UDLA colleagues Roberto Herrera, Mandy Holzrichter, Tom Hunsberger, Luz Murillo and Vanessa Marchand for their friendship, wild conversation and stimulating debate over the time of writing – at conferences, at the Colloquium Club and at uncountable parties. Jennifer Lovel, my editor at Continuum, has given me extremely prompt and sound advice, for which I'm most grateful.

Unsurprisingly, not everyone mentioned here has agreed with all my arguments or the way I have presented them, but on the other hand, some have liked much more of it than I expected. All their observations and suggestions have made the book a better one; the many shortcomings that remain are all my own fault.

Finally, I thank my partner Juan for his unceasing belief in this book and for the emotional, intellectual and gastronomical support he has given me over the years of its writing.

Part I: Magic

1 The Spell

> By means of inking symbols onto a page, she was able to send thoughts
> and feelings from her mind to her reader's. It was a magical process, so
> commonplace that no one stopped to wonder at it. Reading a sentence
> and understanding it were the same thing; [...], nothing lay between
> them. There was no gap during which the symbols were unravelled.
> You saw the word *castle*, and it was there, seen from some distance, with
> woods in high summer spread before it, the air bluish and soft with
> smoke rising from the blacksmith's forge, and a cobbled road twisting
> away into the green shade ...
>
> (Ian McEwan, *Atonement*)

The 'commonplace magic' of human language may not be as
spectacular as the spells of Harry Potter or Gandalf the Grey. There
are no pyrotechnic flashes, bangs or disappearing acts. But, believe
me, it's hugely potent stuff. Think about it: language provides the
essential social energy that powers most of our cultural processes,
from breeding livestock to trading on the stock exchange, from pillow
talk to political propaganda. At the same time it allows us to define
and project our own personalities in the social world, to seek freedom
and exercise individual will, by knowing something about how others
think and so more able to understand ourselves. Yet for us, its
complacent users, the way it works is magical and mysterious, as
incomprehensible as the way TV shows flash through a cable or
bounce off a satellite dish.

Just as we take our TV sets for granted, few of us look beyond the
exterior packaging of language. When we do, we often see things that
aren't there, and miss or misread a great deal of what is. Even after
centuries of enquiry and reflection undertaken by a host of
philosophers and scientists, and the musings of countless generations
of amateur dabblers, the precise nature of language and how it works
are still elusive. Those professionals whose jobs involve providing
linguistic services or services in language – from linguists, language
teachers and translators, to journalists, copy editors and poets – have

greater insights into language than many users, ... but we still get easily lost in its enchanted domain.

Somehow, language allows us to produce patterns of sound (i.e. speech) and light (text) which have the potential to change in an infinity of ways the mental states of fellow human beings. Millions of times a day throughout the planet – when people tell jokes in Nairobi, listen to the radio in Jakarta, fill out a form in Perth, or read an email in Moscow – these modest sound and light shows affect us in very specific ways, by causing modifications to the internal record we have constructed of the physical, social, intellectual and emotional worlds we inhabit. In countless scenarios, the use of language yields new states of affairs in the world. Words literally have the power to change the way the world is. The utterance of certain words by certain people can directly result in the bombing of an Arab republic or the cessation of hostilities in a cluster of West African states, but a slightly different linguistic act can lead to the election of a new local government, the booking of a holiday for two, or the breakdown of a marriage.

The extraordinary agents through which all these events come to pass are words and sentences, in their external guise of air molecules rippling through space from mouth to eardrum, or of contrasting patterns of light created by human hands and hitting a retina from page or screen. But what kinds of things are words and sentences? We can *think* them, and see and hear their physical manifestations out in the world. But it's very hard to think *about* them. Are they really there as separate 'objects' in our minds? Or are *word* and *sentence* just the names we give to thoughts when we wrap them up in speech sounds, ink or pixels? Is language in essence no more than meanings represented as external physical energy? I will be arguing in this book that in fact language is an entity in its own right, lying *between* the two: that words and sentences are generated by an internal mental code which serves as an *intermediary* between thought and its physical expression, i.e. a hidden agent that is independent of them both.

Thought and sound ... with language in between

Let's take a first cursory glance at these three components of the language process, to set the scene for the pages to come. What I'm claiming is that language is separate from the thoughts it expresses and the sounds (or written text) which give it external expression. The diagram in Figure 1 provides a simplified visual sketch of the process. (In Chapter 2 I'll argue that in addition to speech and text, we'll need to add handsigns for users of sign languages.)

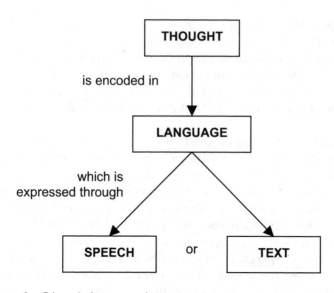

Figure 1 Linguistic expression

Think of the concept of colour. How would you communicate this disembodied thought to your neighbour, best friend or boss? Well, most probably through the word *colour*. The word becomes a sound sequence when it's spoken (rhyming with *duller*), and a pattern of light when written (with five or six letters, depending on whether you use British or US spelling conventions). But can 'colour' be all things at once? A thought, a word and a sequence of sounds or printed characters? According to one view, associated with the early twentieth century linguist Ferdinand de Saussure, the answer is *yes*: a word is like a coin, with meaning on one face and sound/print on the other. The answer I give in this book is a little different: that we think the thought before we select the word, and we select the word before we utter it or write it down. Words – or indeed longer stretches of language, like sentences – constitute links between the concepts, intentions and meanings we communicate, and special kinds of sound and light patterns that carry them from one person to another, called speech and text.

Let's unpack these three fundamental elements even further. Our *concept* of colour is the permanent thought which we invoke when we reflect on the effect different wavelengths of light particles have on our visual system. But this is not the same thing as the *word* we use if we decide to express the thought. We could use different linguistic resources to express the same thought, for example. Orhan Pamuk, in his novel *My Name is Red*, valiantly invokes the concept using a string of other words (his originals are in Turkish). For him, colour is 'the touch of the eye, music to the deaf, a word out of the darkness'. More mundanely, when I ask for my bathroom to be painted in a different *shade*, when I make cruel comments about the *tint* of a colleague's hair, or wax lyrical about the autumnal *hues* of the surrounding landscape – my concept of colour is active, but the word *colour* goes unsaid and unheard.

Language is not the complex network of meaning it represents, but neither is it the external manifestation it assumes as sound or light. Text without a reader is not language: it has no meaning until it is transformed into thought by a reader. Pamuk's manuscript, in an envelope on its way to his publishers, contained neither language nor thought, only lots of black marks on a series of white pages. Only when the package arrived, was opened, and read, were language and meaning restored. Speech is the same: between speaker's mouth and hearer's ear, it is just sound. If the publisher read aloud Pamuk's wonderful description of colour to a colleague, then it was transformed from text to speech, and only became meaning again when the colleague heard and understood it. Language is neither the thought, nor its physical expression: it's the marvellous engine we use to transform one into the other.

But despite its ubiquity and utility in our lives, it seems to fall into a gap in our consciousness, and remains largely invisible to us. As protagonists of each daily language scenario – insincerely complimenting a neighbour, complaining to the local council, planning a holiday in Ibiza or Acapulco, regretting our choice of life partner over a beer with a friend, ordering an air strike on a foreign state – we concentrate on the business at hand: the *thoughts*, not the way they are dressed for conversational outings. Meanwhile, busily working behind the scenes, the words through which these thoughts, actions and transactions are momentarily clothed insinuate themselves into other people's brains through ears and eyes. How we express thoughts as speech sounds or writing symbols, and how they actually impinge on interlocutors' brains, is not something we are normally aware of at the moment of language use, nor are we prone to reflect upon them much when the linguistic act is done. We are interested in the results of the act, the newly acquired brain state, not how it came about. Indeed, the fact that language was involved at all may go completely unnoticed.

Don't take my word for it. Think back to the last time you exploited your language faculty before opening this book. Maybe you had just got off the phone with a trying relative, or finished watching a TV sitcom, inanities still ringing in your ears. Perhaps you just loudly reprimanded your son, your lover, or your dog. Were you reading your email and wishing there was much less of it (or much more)? Or maybe you just wrote some feverish comments in the margins of a volume of poetry you've been finding hard to put down? ... Whatever you were doing, I'd like to bet you weren't aware of any cognitive effort as you deployed your linguistic powers. If you happened to be speaking, do you remember pursing your lips for 'p's and 'b's or raising the back of your tongue to your palate for 'k's and 'g's? If you were listening, were you aware of the words sounding familiar, and did you feel their senses emerge as the sound of each fell on your eardrums? If writing, do you remember looking for the right endings to put on the verbs or the correct side of the noun to place your adjectives? And if you were reading, do you remember patiently looking at each letter and skipping over each space, moving your eyes inexorably from left to right?

Odd questions indeed. But as you exercised your workaday abilities to speak, listen, read or write, you were in fact taking the principal role in the most amazing sociocognitive performance, involving a set of complex mental computations, an array of subtle social judgements and, when writing or speaking, a display of spectacular muscular choreography. It is, however, a performance without spectators, without applause: all human beings stage it many times a day. It's a brilliant routine that has been designed to play behind closed curtains and with the spotlights turned off. Language has us under a spell, and the magic is powerful and mysterious.

Under the spell of language

It was probably the invisibility of language, its impenetrable *modus operandi*, that led our preliterate ancestors to associate it with magic and supernatural forces. Significantly, magic in all cultural traditions is practised in large part through spoken or written incantations and spells. And in all the religions of the world, there are chants, mantras or litanies which are used to invoke deities, enter into spiritual states, or seek the revelation of eternal mysteries. The strong connection between language and magic in the perceptions of our forebears is attested in the histories of words associated with both domains. The Latinate word *grammar*, for example, is related to *glamour*, in its original magical sense, as the following etymologies from the *Shorter Oxford English Dictionary* attest:

Glamour ... 1720. [Alteration of GRAMMAR with the sense of GRAMARYE; introduced by Scott. For the form with *gl-* cf. med.L. *glomeria* grammar, *glomerellus* schoolboy learning grammar.] **1**. Magic, enchantment, spell. **2**. A magical or fictitious beauty attaching to any person or object; a delusive or alluring charm 1840.

Gramarye ... [– AFr. *gramarie* = OFr. *gramaire* GRAMMAR; cf. Fr. *grimoire* book of magic, earlier *gramoire* (dial. var. of *gramaire*) † Latin grammar.] † **1**. Grammar; learning – 1483. **2**. Occult learning, magic, necromancy. (Revived by Scott.) 1470.

We see a similar shift from the domain of language to that of magic with the Germanic word *spell* itself:

Spell ... [OE. *spel(l)* = OS., OHG. *spel*, ON. *Spjall*, Goth. *spill* recital, tale :- Gmc. **spellam*. Cf. GOSPEL.] **1**. Without article: Discourse, narration, speech; occas. idle talk, fable. -late ME. **2**. A discourse or sermon; a narrative or tale -1653. **3**. A set of words, a formula or verse, supposed to possess occult or magical powers; a charm or incantation 1579. b. *transf.* and *fig.* An occult or mysterious power or influence; a fascinating or enthralling charm 1592.

Once human beings learnt to devise visual representations of the spoken word, in the form of writing systems, the magical power of speech was fused with similar powers ascribed to concrete objects that could be seen with the eye, like fetishes and idols. Visual symbols representing speech – runes and sacred texts, inscriptions and cabalistic formulae – were thought to possess mysterious powers which were independent of those whose hands carved or wrote them. The runes of the ancient Germanic and Nordic cultures, for example, were both identified with deities and used to make spells. Runic stones cast on the ground in certain combinations could release prisoners from their chains.

We live now in a more enlightened world, where *grammar* is the bane of foreign language learners, *spells* are the province of children's books and video games, and *glamour* is the near monopoly of Hollywood. But language is still implicitly viewed as a magical device. Let me show you what I mean.

Language design

At some stage in our much more distant past, probably hundreds of thousands of years before the first alphabet, human beings developed the extraordinary ability to clothe parts of thought with sound so that we could share it with others of our species. Maybe it all started with the spontaneous sounds which accompany raw sensations and emotions: grunts of pain or pleasure which slowly were transformed into words, the prehistoric equivalents of *ouch* and *yummy*. We don't know much yet about what precursors language evolved from, but we do know what it has evolved into: a device so intricate, polished and fine-tuned that its design and functioning lie largely beyond our ability to fathom. Like a sixth sense, it does its job so rapidly and efficiently that we're seldom aware of its operation. Indeed, it seems instantaneous: Briony, the young character in Ian McEwan's novel, assumed that when she read a sentence, 'there was no gap during which the symbols were unravelled'. But there is indeed a gap, and lying within it is language. It's just that language events happen so fast and so easily for their users that we are unaware of them. In the absence of telepathy, this is an optimal arrangement. Sharing thoughts through language has given us a remarkable adaptive tool for survival, allowing us to pool individual resources into richly-textured social groups, cultures and civilizations.

When early humans descended from the trees to the savannahs, they left behind the fruits and berries which were so easy to gather, and were forced instead to confront a far more extensive and complicated ecosystem, in which the highest-yielding food sources moved on four legs and had to be hunted and trapped. This new theatre of action, coupled with the lack of tree-top refuge from predators, ensured that those members of the species who could cooperate in groups, over large distances, were much more likely to propagate and leave behind copies of their genes. The emergence of human language must have given them a special advantage here. Like the five senses, it provided the species with an automatic and extremely rapid information-processing system, a mechanism for getting data from the environment into the mind, so it could be reasoned about and acted upon. But unlike the senses, it could also provide knowledge about states of affairs which were displaced in time and space: that a rich food source was located by the lake over the hill behind them; that a predator had been spotted coming their way along the river; that they had better not pass through the valley they normally took to reach higher ground, because the way was blocked by melting ice ...

For language to be optimally efficient, it must, like the senses, do its job in the background, without detracting from the business at hand, be it avoiding a predator or avoiding paying a parking ticket. As we speak, some part of our brain is planning the order of the words we use, adding articles, prepositions, suffixes and pronouns. Another bit of cerebral cortex is sending messages to the muscles of our vocal tract, telling the lips to purse, the tongue to raise and the larynx to hum. As we listen to words racing into our ears at an average rate of around four per second, our brain's speech detectors identify the sounds they are made up of, allowing other bits of grey matter to look them up in our mental dictionaries, work out how they combine with each other, and then integrate them with general knowledge and the current context, to finally deliver a meaning. There's a lot going on, all at once, but the mental hullabaloo goes unwitnessed by that executive part of our minds which gets to engage consciously with the outside world.

Like the heart or the liver, language is part of us, but its operation must remain hidden from our immediate practical concerns. Yet unlike our senses and vital organs, it plays an obvious and apparent social role, so that although we don't know how it works, we think and talk *about* it, and are aware of its power and utility. Hence we operate as though under a spell, content to know that language is there, but not being able to see it plainly or penetrate its mystery. This paradox of the invisibility of language and yet its palpable presence in our lives, is what I am calling the Language Spell.

Cognitive processes

The Language Spell can be seen as part of a larger pattern of evolutionary 'magic' which ensures that the human machine is optimally user-friendly to the mind that is housed within it. Consider, for example, locomotion and motor coordination: our ability to move our bodies from one place to another and to employ arms, hands and legs as tools to get things done with. When we go to a supermarket, our principal objective is usually to buy groceries. On entering the store, however, the motor programme in our brains has other, more pressing, objectives: to navigate us through the aisles without colliding with shelves, product displays and fellow shoppers; to slow us down and stop us when we are beckoned by required or attractive articles; and to deliver us safely to the check-out when our shopping list (or budget) is exhausted.

This is no easy task, as robotic scientists and engineers will tell you, after decades trying to build machines which can move around with human grace and can pick things up without breaking or dropping them. The human brain (our own organic supercomputer) has evolved more successful supermarket navigation circuitry than any existing C3PO or Terminator prototype. When shopping, our motor programmes send instructions to the muscles on the basis of data processed further back in the brain, coordinating sensory input from the visual system with the shopping list data and spontaneous impulses to buy. In a constant cycle of voluntary and involuntary nerve impulses and interpretation of visual feedback, resulting in muscular activity, our lower limbs are able to propel us through the appropriate trajectories. Luckily, we don't need to worry ourselves with these minutiae as we cruise the breakfast cereals or slalom through the fruit and vegetable stands. Neural circuits throughout the brain do the calculations for us, but the fact that we're moving at all is not at the forefront of our minds.

... Unless something goes wrong, that is, and we stumble into the canned soups or collide with an oncoming shopper. Even here our attempts to explain the mishap would appeal to the fact that 'our attention was elsewhere', or 'we weren't looking where we were going', without being able to say much, if anything, about how the retinal input we needed was lacking or inadequately processed, or how the appropriate motor instructions failed to get sent from our brain to our legs in time. The point here is that although our conscious minds can operate quite comfortably with vague concepts like 'attention' and 'walking', there has to be *some* part of our minds that is doing the nuts-and-bolts work of actually 'paying attention', so that we can engage in the highly choreographed spatiotemporal planning and patterns of muscle contractions which we call *walking without bumping into things*.

Shopping at the supermarket is not one of the most complex of human actions, but neither is it simple from the perspective of mind: we have said nothing about the way in which we make decisions about which brands to purchase, how we keep a running count of the approximate final cost, how we steer the shopping trolley, how we reach for, grasp and deposit in the trolley the products we choose, how we unload and pay for them once they're safely at the check-out, etc. The miracle is that, happily for us, most of this series of highly coordinated mechanical and computational events is controlled below the level of consciousness.

Sociocognitive processes

Now imagine extending this cognitive perspective to procedures which more directly involve other human beings (and therefore, notice, require language to a greater extent). Like getting someone to dance with us at a party, going to the hairdresser's, playing football, or going on strike for better pay. On top of managing purely selfish events like lone voyages through the supermarket aisles (compensating for the wonky wheel on the trolley or agonizing over whether we can afford that bottle of cognac), we also have to negotiate *social* situations, which might involve judging the set of values, beliefs and attitudes of the other participants, their ages and relative power and prestige and their immediate and future needs, intentions and actions. We must now coordinate our expectations and actions with those of others.

Quite a feat! And yet, if we fall within the normal bounds of human paranoia, our experience is that we conduct these everyday activities without having to attempt conscious control of all the tiny sociocognitive moves from which they are built. The perceived smoothness and effortlessness of most of our actions belie the frenetic activity that underlies them in the brain and the rest of the body. It is this wired-in deception that allows us to get on with the real purposes of life (like dancing at parties), and it is largely a product of biological evolution. So if we are designed not to be aware of an awful lot of what we are doing, both physically and mentally, in vast areas of human action and interaction, why should we be surprised if we are similarly deceived in the realm of language, the Olympic Stadium or Grand Opera House of human social and cognitive performance?

The spell is cast: linguistic awareness and linguistic belief

... And yet of course we *are* quite aware of being users of language. We are all conscious, for example, that the words we use and the way we speak is one of the strongest factors linking us with other individuals who are 'like us', at the level of community, profession, subculture or ethnic group: Geordies in Newcastle upon Tyne, lawyers in their chambers, gangs on the streets of East LA, or Kurdish women in Turkey and Iraq, for example. And this means we're also very much aware that other people speak *differently*, using a dialect which differs from ours, or another language entirely. Hence language is a powerful marker of social identity, and is the source of pride to many, especially members of minority groups. Listen to some of the voices of speakers from marginalized groups around the world:

> Our language is one of God's blessings that our forefathers received thousands of years ago. Our parents have conserved Kaqchikel, and we cannot simply cast it off now as if it were worth nothing. God gave us talent through Kaqchikel; either we bury it or we make it multiply.
>
> Kaqchikel speaker from Guatemala

I had been robbed of my language, my own history and my own culture. The school had substituted something that was now well known to me. What was foreign to me was I, myself. I felt cheated.

Sámi (Lapp) speaker from Sweden

I left Moshiri, the land of the Ainu. Life was hard. But then I started to think of the Ainu language. I am one of the Ainu people. I feel my ethnicity. I began to notice that the Ainu language reflects the Ainu ways and now know that it is my obligation to recall and regain this precious language.

Ainu speaker from Japan

The same language pride, intimately connected with pride in group membership, is present too among speakers of dominant languages, like English or Spanish. Sometimes this is at the level of the language itself, seen in speakers' reverence for their grand dictionaries, their deification of literary heroes like Shakespeare and Cervantes, ... or their arrogant tendency to travel abroad without a phrase-book. But given the geographical and cultural diversity of dominant languages, people often consciously identify to a greater extent with a more localized variety, celebrating its distinctiveness through folk songs, dialect poems and those enthusiastic explanations of words and phrases you get as a visitor from out of town.

This conscious linguistic awareness is used also as a political tool by the powerful, leading to the English-Only movement and attacks on bilingual education in the United States, or to historical reinterpretations of colonialism, reflected in this 2001 claim by King Juan Carlos of Spain:

Ours was never a language of imposition, but rather of encounter, no-one was ever obliged to speak in Spanish: it was a diverse group of peoples who, through their free will, made the language of Cervantes their own.

The hurtful effects of language awareness also lead sometimes to language *shame*. The Sámi speaker quoted above writes further:

Once I saw some Sámi youths purposely avoiding their parents in order not to demonstrate their Sámi origin. It hurt me unbelievably and filled me with feelings of shame. To be absolutely honest, it could have been me, who felt forced to act the same way!

Similarly, speakers of non-prestige dialects in some countries take elocution courses, or respond to newspaper adverts which promise to 'eliminate' their 'embarrassing' accents, and second language learners fret that that they'll never sound like a native.

These are all examples of people's consciousness that the languages or dialects they speak define, in part, who they are, how they are perceived, and how they are different from others outside their group. But despite our conscious feelings about the importance of language in moulding our identities, I hope to show that the Spell wields such power that it obliges us to think of language *most* of the time as a hollow conduit for thought, no more. In order to appreciate this, we must distinguish three mental domains in which language figures, and see how the Spell affects them all. The most fundamental, where the Spell is actually encoded, is the domain of **linguistic knowledge**. This is our language software, stored in human brain circuitry, which encodes the grammar and stores the words necessary for transforming sound into meaning and meaning into sound (I'll introduce the major components of this knowledge in the next chapter).

The second domain is that of **linguistic awareness**. Some of our knowledge and aspects of its deployment can percolate up into consciousness, and we 'know' at a higher level that we are using language. This is the case, for example, when we notice the accent or tone of voice of an interlocutor, experience trouble trying to say what we mean, or realize we're not understanding what someone else is trying to convey. Although these sensations are real ones, and can provoke strong emotional reactions and intellectual responses, the Spell ensures that introspection won't reveal much about the basis for them.

The third mental domain concerning language is that of **linguistic belief**. Many, perhaps all, human beings possess a powerful set of beliefs about the language(s) we speak and about language in general. These beliefs emerge from linguistic awareness, but may or may not be borne out by linguistic knowledge, in the sense of the term used here. A major subset of linguistic beliefs are normative or evaluative, and underlie our attitudes to speakers of other languages or other varieties of our own language. They constitute a 'folk knowledge' or 'popular culture' of language, and are a direct effect of the Spell's concealment of its inner workings. Although the cognitive magic ensures that linguistic knowledge doesn't normally get in the way of human communication, it can't completely switch off linguistic awareness (since language is not telepathy). The formation and cultural dissemination of linguistic folk beliefs are an inevitable result.

Here are some common linguistic beliefs, so strong that they often subvert linguists as well as laypeople:

- some versions of languages are better (more correct) than others;
- languages used to be better (purer) than they are now;
- some languages are better (more logical) than others.

These beliefs reflect a deeper, general assumption that language is a purely social artefact, motivated largely by social factors, played out uniquely in the social domain, and thus co-varying with the social factors which characterize different groups of speakers. This assumption in itself is clearly very practical. Conceiving of human language as a biological or mental faculty will not provide any immediate benefits to its users, whereas recognition of its social role can lead to its more effective deployment as a tool to achieve a variety of goals. At least part of the general assumption is supported by the actual facts, too: sociolinguists, ethnographers and linguistic anthropologists in the universities have amassed impressive amounts of data and theoretical insights about the correlations between language use and social functions, and the vital role language plays in the forging of sociocultural identities, practices and beliefs.

Language 'happens' in communicative events, not just in minds, and communicative events unfold in the ways that they do partly because of the ways in which the participants in those events construe them. Dell Hymes pioneered an anthropological approach to such events using ethnographic methods, which seek to understand ways of speaking by understanding what speakers *believe* about their speaking. William Labov and others have sought to identify the social variables which inevitably play a role in language use, variation and change. Clearly language *is* a social mechanism – perhaps *the* social mechanism – and it makes little sense to pretend that it isn't, even for linguists only interested in describing abstract grammatical rules. We shall return to some of this work later in the book, but in the meantime let's explore a little further the consequences of this overriding social conception of language in the collective minds of speakers.

Linguistic differences

Viewing language as a purely social phenomenon may be functional and inevitable, but it does not of course guarantee that our beliefs about language will lead to benign social attitudes and behaviours. The three specific beliefs listed earlier, for example, can lead to attitudes which can damage or disempower whole groups of language users. Take the first belief: it is a commonplace assumption that some groups of speakers make more 'grammatical errors' than others, and that this has to do with the amount of education they have received and the type of homes they come from (i.e. social factors). For many, the same social factors that cause 'grammatical errors' also determine the kinds of hairstyles we might wear or the way we use a knife and fork. It is true that we learn social behaviours from the people that live around us (especially family members and age-group peers). And these behaviours include the characteristic patterns in which we use our language. But what is completely untenable is the belief that *one* group has a monopoly on using the language correctly and well, that their version of the language is somehow purer than others, and that access to this correct code can only be attained through upbringing or education. Take a look at the following newspaper report, which appeared in the *Guardian* in 1999:

> The Queen's grammar [. . .] has slipped so far that she has started 'talking common'. [A] linguistics professor even insists the monarch is the victim of 'American vowel play'. Erik Wensberg, who has revised Wilson Follett's Modern American Usage, says that the Queen's use of language [is] 'at best colloquial and at worst, simply wrong'. He singles out a sentence from her Christmas message, in which she observed: 'The young can sometimes be wiser than us.'
>
> Mr Wensberg asks, 'Is than a conjunction that must be followed by a pronoun in the nominative case (I, we, they), or is it a preposition that must take a pronoun in the objective? . . . Than us is wrong. But, as she rightly sensed, than we is annoyingly starchy. The answer? Than we are.'
>
> Kevin Botting, who heads the Queen's English Society, said: 'It pains me to say it, but Mr. Wensberg is absolutely correct: the Queen has made a frightful howler.'

Oh dear. It appears that not even the Queen's English is immune to deviations from the 'correct' patterns of the language (known in the UK as 'The Queen's English' – perhaps anachronistically in the light of the *Guardian*'s revelation). Who, then, is the arbiter of this pure version of English? Where are its correct rules inscribed? What makes it better than the colloquial English of Manchester, Milwaukee, Manitoba or Melbourne? In the absence of an Academy of the English Language, most people assume that 'good English' is enshrined in good literature, and by that they mean the hallowed works of the past, rather than the more irreverent and linguistically adventurous novels of our age, the age of the Internet, globalization, lifestyle choices and multi-ethnic communities. If you believe the pundits and angry letter-writers, we're all gradually deviating further and further from the golden language norm.

Sociolinguists have shown convincingly that no matter how appealing and intuitively obvious this story of a 'correct' or 'purer' way of speaking might be, it is not borne out by the linguistic facts. Look at the following pair of sentences. Which one uses the negative 'correctly'?

(1) It ain't no cat can't get in no coop
(2) There isn't a single cat that can get into any coop at all

Sentence (1) was spoken by Speedy, a black gang leader from New York studied by Labov in the 1970s, and sentence (2) is its closest equivalent in the dialect I am using in this book. Most people would have no doubts in judging Speedy's sentence as incorrect and, indeed, illogical. But Labov's ground-breaking research showed that Speedy's use of the negative just follows different *rules* from his and mine (and perhaps yours). No-one has accused Chaucer of being illogical or incorrect when he wrote sentences like (3):

(3) He **nevere** yet **no** vileynye **ne** sayde in al his lyf unto **no** maner wight
'In his whole life he has never said anything wicked to anyone'

And no-one would accuse Montserrat Caballé, Gabriel García Marquez, or their three-and-a-half million fellow Spanish speakers, of grammatical sloppiness when they say sentences like (4):

(4) **No** tengo **ningún** problema con eso
(Literally: I do not have no problem with that)

Clearly our judgement of Speedy's use of the negative is socially, rather than linguistically, based. He was using the rules of *his* dialect. I am writing using the rules of *mine*. Mine happens to be the dialect which is used for writing books, since it's a '**standard**' (mainstream) dialect. And, oversimplifying just a bit, it's a 'standard' dialect because when the Normans invaded England in 1066, the court moved from Winchester to London and gradually assumed that city's way of speaking. People may not like the way Speedy speaks, but they should be clear that the *reason* they don't like it has little to do with his accent and grammar and a great deal to do with who they think he is.

At a more global level of linguistic awareness and belief, probably few English speakers would bridle at the claim that English is more complex than the languages of Borneo or Papua New Guinea, and they might readily agree that English is less logical than Latin or Sanskrit. In exactly the same way, an untrained and relatively ignorant oenologist like me might swear that Spanish wine is more complex than Chilean, but that still there's no beating French (I may not be right here, but the point is about standards of evidence and argumentation, not strength of opinion). People's impressions of language complexity, and even whether a language can be said to be a real language or not, are generally guided by their knowledge of the levels of education, culture, and industrialization of its speakers, and almost never by the linguistic facts themselves. Even a socially liberal publication like *The Economist* magazine unwittingly betrayed such a prejudice when it referred recently to the principal language of Rwanda, spoken by over nine million people, as *kinyarwanda*, italicized and in lower case. (They would never dream of rendering European languages as *english, french, german*, etc.)

From this folk perspective, human language is viewed solely as a shared convention, a cultural standard, a learned practical skill, a set of external facts or a grand public enterprise. Hence it is narrowly defined at the level of groups such as nations, gangs, literary movements or academies, and is viewed as naturally subject to teaching, authority, principles of usage and cases of abusage. But in order to fully understand the nature of human language, we must, I think, formulate a broader and richer perspective. Such a view, once in focus, would reveal a mental faculty common to all members of the species, a sociocognitive programme, located in the brain, determined by biological and social factors, with vast effects on our lives in society, and yet without meaning if divorced from the minds of individual users.

The Fundamental Paradox

The broad view is missed, or remains out of focus, for most language users as a result of the 'fundamental paradox' underlying the Language Spell: that *languages exist only in individual human minds, but can only work if they are perceived as shared by social groups*. Language in one sense *is* a public property, a shared ability, designed for interaction between speakers and hearers in social contexts. And yet at the same time it really only exists and functions in millions of separate minds, human islands in society's ocean: to get out of individual heads, language surfs on sound and light waves, which ebb and flow independently of it. When we hear the sounds and see the light, however, we're not seeing or hearing language. Like many other mental phenomena, like our neural supermarket-navigation programmes or visual apparatus, language is 'designed' to seem invisible, even though its effects pervade society and, indeed, have played a leading role in making us the social species we are. We don't 'see' language happening because language events happen at extraordinary speeds and, normally, below the level of human awareness. These properties are essential if language is to fulfil its principal role: to enable speakers to activate target thoughts in the minds of hearers, by mimicking telepathy as closely as possible within the limitations of our physical world.

Metalinguistic knowledge

Language as a mental faculty does appear to come into focus when it is used to talk about itself, i.e. when the target concepts are linguistic or language-related. Such **metalinguistic** events (using language to talk *about* language) are relatively rare in the multiplex daily unfolding of human interactions outside of university linguistics departments. But they are common enough to have given rise to their own specialized folk vocabulary. Language also emerges into conscious awareness when aspects of its external channels (speech, writing or sign for the hearing-impaired) call attention to themselves, or when it is observed that the linguistic expressions of one person differ from those of another. Here are some of the occasions on which language can become an apparent end as well as the hidden means in the process of sharing mental states:

- when language doesn't work, and hearers seek clarification ('What do you mean?' 'Did you say *caps* or *cats*?' '*Funny* "ha-ha" or *funny* "peculiar"?');
- when individuals speaking different dialects or languages come into contact, or attempt to learn foreign languages;
- when people play with the language, using puns and double meanings, doing crosswords, or playing Scrabble;
- when people exploit language consciously – creatively or artistically – to rap, tell stories, write poetry, or prepare a witty speech for a wedding;
- when parents observe their children rushing headlong from babbling into incessant discourse ...;
- ... and when those children take their turn in adulthood to watch their parents *lose* language as the result of strokes or dementia.

Such contexts will involve different degrees of conscious awareness of the components and mechanisms of language. A slip of the tongue, a lapse in attention, or a momentary ambiguity will normally lead to automatic 'repair' by the speaker, with little extra thought on the part of either interlocutor. The composition of a sonnet, however, or Laotian students' attempts to translate Beatles lyrics, will require deliberate metalinguistic thought and analysis. Somewhere in between, perhaps, will be fond parents' wondrous speculation about their baby's first words, or their awkward mimicking of teenage offspring's latest street-cred vocabulary.

But in all these cases, users needn't worry too much about subtle details of linguistic knowledge: indeed, the Spell prevents us from doing so even if we want to (without having studied some linguistics). A rough and ready 'folk theory' of language is all that is necessary (and all we normally have available). For most of us, our language probably appears to constitute a fuzzy collection of grammar, spelling and pronunciation rules, together with a long list of words. This general view, in fact, entails an enormous act of faith: few language users can list more than a handful of superficial rules, though it's believed by most that they all must be written down somewhere. Many English speakers would accept the claim that a word not in the *Oxford English Dictionary* or *Webster's* cannot be said to be a real English word at all. The folk theory requires that language be publicly available, open to conscious awareness, and relatively simple, with a right way and wrong way of doing things. Our faith is constantly tested, but seldom vanquished, despite overwhelming evidence that things are not quite as they appear.

Our effective blindness (or at least short-sightedness) regarding the mental reality of language is akin to our ever-increasing faith in technologies that most of us can't hope to fully understand. Take computers: we know that when we double-click on a desktop icon it will open a folder or launch an application. Of course it is neither the finger-clicking nor the icon that actually launches the application or reveals the contents of the folder: the technical reality lies beyond most of us, and is irrelevant to our immediate needs, until something goes wrong or we dare to do some programming of our own. The aspects of human-computer interaction that non-experts are normally aware of are limited to a visual layout of images and text, which we modify by moving a mouse, pressing keys, tapping on a trackpad, or whatever. We don't need to know the binary code underlying the surface magic in order to import snapshots from a digital camera, do our accounts in Excel, or surf the Internet.

We can clearly have more subtle metalinguistic knowledge than I'm suggesting here, especially if we have been exposed to English grammar or a foreign language at school, and perhaps even more so if we are part of the language professions. But this kind of attention to things linguistic is not pervasive in the social lives of most human beings, being restricted as it is mostly to pockets of the world's educated elites. And even (perhaps especially) here the Spell is cast, leaving our linguistic awareness attenuated. As we've seen, the reduced kind of linguistic awareness humans typically experience, and the largely unexamined linguistic beliefs that we construct as a result, can lead to undesirable consequences. In the remainder of this chapter, we'll explore a series of domains in which linguistic beliefs influence our social interactions, with progressively more disturbing results.

The downside of linguistic awareness

Mild problems can arise when we invest language with too much power, because the Spell leads us to view language essentially as telepathy, transferring the contents of one mind into another. Consider the following (invented, but probably familiar) dialogue between a couple:

Sam: So, we're going to the cinema tonight, right?
Jo: Well, I'm feeling a bit tired actually. Why don't you go without me? I'd rather just stay at home and rest for a while.
Sam: But didn't we agree last night?
Jo: Yes, but I've had a hard day at work.
Sam: So you don't want to be with me?
Jo: You know that's not what I meant.
Sam: But that's what you said – you said I should go on my own!

Now in a way, Sam is right: if Jo prefers to stay at home while Sam is at the cinema, then Jo prefers not to be with Sam. If we watch a lot of soap operas, perhaps we will be naturally inclined to accuse Sam of wilful misinterpretation, as part of an attempt to prompt a showdown that will end the relationship. Or maybe Jo is really guilty of deceit, but wants to cast Sam as the initiator of an eventual separation. Either way, there are currents of meaning which flow below the surface discourse, and they are different for each participant. The references to 'saying' and 'meaning' in the last two utterances show the couple exploiting the fragility of the exchange's linguistic surface to accomplish their aims.

If we recast Sam and Jo as loving partners, on the other hand, a more benign interpretation is available: that the dispute is caused by an innocent confusion between words and thoughts. A case of temporary miscommunication, but equally the product of an implicit linguistic belief, holding that people say what they mean, and that they mean what their interlocutor assumes they mean on the basis of what they say! Such miscommunications occur very frequently, and are the natural consequence of the interaction of two minds, containing two independent sets of linguistic knowledge, deployed in two non-identical emotional, intellectual, social and cognitive contexts, whatever the depth of intimacy between them.

This irritatingly common phenomenon arises because we fail to appreciate the fact that an utterance does not serve up the whole intended message on a platter: it loosely clothes parts of thought into communicable sound, and leaves the hearer to reconstruct the original intention. Language does not transfer thoughts from one place to another, like a fork moving pasta from plate to mouth. As we've seen, all it can do is cause speakers and writers to produce energy patterns of sound or light. It is the experience of these patterns that is transferred, and on receiving them, other human beings can use *their* language faculty to reconstruct as best they can the meanings intended. This is achieved on the basis of linguistic and other kinds of knowledge – of the speaker, the immediate context, the conventions of social interaction, and the way the world is. The unfortunate 'transfer of meaning' metaphor does little to help us in our efforts to break the Language Spell, and its use is a hard habit to break (even for linguists). We are all unavoidably lax in our efforts to delve deeper than the words we hear, tending instead to filter what we hear through our own expectations of what was meant. We assume that all that can be thought can be communicated in an utterance: that what is said is all that is meant, and what is meant is all that is said.

Here's another mild example of the Spell at work, showing what can happen when linguistic form is muddled up with the thoughts it is used to convey. At a planning meeting a few years ago, I came upon two of my colleagues – one from the Design department, the other from the Architecture department – engaged in a lively dispute about the boundaries of their respective disciplines. Having failed to reach agreement on the basis of a brief exchange on the objectives, methodologies and traditions of their two fields, they quite naturally began to reflect on the meanings of the words themselves: *architecture* and *design*. In order to establish the 'true' meaning of these words, they turned unhesitatingly to their *etymologies*, and rightly established that *design* comes from the Latin 'mark down (as in "sketch") thoroughly, completely'. (The roots of *architecture*, from the Greek word for 'chief, principal builder', eluded both them and me at the time.)

The discussion then resumed, this time taking the etymology of *design* as the basis for subsequent claims, for example that architecture was the mere instrumentation of design in the sphere of building, or alternatively that design was the simple realization of the architect's higher purpose (guess who said which). As I listened, I was struck by the fact that by now it was no longer the current, living *concepts* of design and architecture which were under discussion, but the history and tradition of *naming* certain activities as one or the other, and whether this was justified given what the words had meant in other languages millennia before.

Language as a barrier to thought

At the levels of science and academic enquiry, politics and rational debate, the opacity of language has, inevitably, hindered our ability to understand ourselves and the universe in which we live. Wittgenstein, echoing Bacon and Locke centuries earlier, claimed that '[p]hilosophy is a battle against the bewitchment of our intelligence by means of language' and that '[t]he results of philosophy are the uncovering of one or another piece of plain nonsense and of bumps the understanding has got by running its head up against the limits of language'. Because we cannot 'transfer' complete thoughts and meanings from one mind to another using the language faculty, and have no other means of doing so, we are constrained in our abilities to understand each other and therefore to work together in the search for knowledge. We are further constrained because the invisibility of language ensures that we only appreciate this fact with difficulty and, indeed, behave mostly as though it isn't true.

This second layer of self-deceit imposed by the Language Spell often condemns us, therefore, to participate in endless 'semantic debates', in which disagreement about word meanings can often mask fundamental coincidence of ideas. Although for the most part the Spell keeps language tidily in the background, its strength is such that, whenever we want to get directly to our thoughts, bypassing language, it inevitably gets invoked anew. In this sense, language assumes the role of minder, blocking our access to the boss, instead of acting as faithful messenger, broadcasting ideas to the outside world.

The Spell can wield more immediate and more insidious power, however. Political leaders (and now their spin doctors) are often accused of consciously exploiting language to mislead us or constrain our understanding. We are told that choice of words and style of discourse can conceal brute facts of corruption, manipulation, oppression, torture and genocide. George Orwell and others, also falling under the Spell in subtle ways, have argued that word and thought are so inextricably bound up together that changes in the language will lead to changes in the ways we think. In his novel *1984*, Orwell pushed the idea to its limit, exploring the possibility that governments can remould language in order to control the thoughts of the governed, eliminating resistance to the authoritarian regime, for example, by abolishing the word *freedom*, and by so doing making the concept itself unthinkable.

Whether language can in fact beguile us in this way is not as obvious as many people think. Is it really the case that the words produced by spin doctors and salespeople can mesmerize us into changing the way we think and behave? Or is it rather that our own predispositions, patterns of belief and undeveloped critical powers invite manipulation, and the words used merely encourage us to overlook other aspects of the speaker's agenda? If language does have the power to impose thoughts upon us, is this yet another aspect of the Spell, adding to the hidden repertoire of language the role of thug in addition to messenger and minder? It's clearly part of our folk linguistic beliefs that language can determine the way we think, but we'll see later on, I hope, that this view endows words with more power than they have, and underestimates the critical potential of the minds that hear and read them.

Linguistic discrimination

Throughout history, languages and language varieties have been associated not only with local, regional, national and ethnic identity, but also with age, social class, sex, sexuality, level of education and the perceived degree of 'civilization' of their speakers. A result of this is that language has always been an icon of inequality, often leading to discrimination and frequently also to persecution. Deborah Cameron has pointed out that '[l]inguistic bigotry is among the last publicly expressible prejudices left to the members of the western intelligentsia. Intellectuals who would find it unthinkable to sneer at a beggar or someone in a wheelchair will sneer without compunction at linguistic "solecisms".' Up until recently, a regional accent would render you ineligible for a job reading the news on British TV and radio. Boys still get beaten up in school playgrounds for sounding effeminate. And it wasn't wise to speak Arabic too loudly in some quarters of the USA in the days after 11 September 2001. Similar examples could fill a series of books.

As though such scenarios were not scary enough, they are still mild in comparison with more global results of the dark side of our linguistic awareness. In past centuries, the old European empires imposed their cultures, and with them inevitably their languages, on large parts of the planet. Ngugi wa Thiong'o, a Kenyan writer, tells how in the colonization of his country, '[t]he bullet was the means of physical subjugation' but '[l]anguage was the means of the spiritual subjugation.' So too, the Sámi (Lapps) in northern Scandinavia and Russia, Latin American immigrants in the USA, Roma travellers (gypsies) throughout continental Europe, Zapotecs in Mexico, the Manyjily-jarra in Australia, ... and countless other groups across the globe, have had their traditional languages taken away from them. Thus, many of them have been effectively deprived of a role in the governance of their lands and peoples, and a chance at inheriting and evolving their linguistically-transmitted cultural practices and beliefs.

And linguistic genocide continues, resulting in such barbarities as the imprisonment without trial of minority language activists in Nepal, the Zimbabwean President's imposition of fellow Shona-speaking bureaucrats on less favoured tribes speaking other languages, and the torture and killing of Kurds for speaking their own native tongue in the north of Saddam's Iraq. For a human faculty that according to my thesis is invisible, it does seem to cause a lot of deliberate, visible damage in our world. But if we stop to think for just one moment, it's not language itself that causes the heartache – it's the awful consequences of what linguistic differences are seen to represent. The Spell ensures that we notice only the external emblems of language, which divide humanity into regions, nations, tribes, clans, insiders, outsiders, etc. – just as much as skin colour, creed, musical taste and choice (or lack) of daily footwear. The role of language in underlining such divisions is compounded as we have seen by the fact that the principal way to understand the thoughts of others, and often to clarify our own, is through language. So we are led to confuse the two. Different languages and different ways of speaking are thus seen to point firmly to different ways of *meaning*, and in consequence to deep and inevitable chasms of human misunderstanding.

The few books written by linguists for the non-specialist which, like this one, attempt to debunk popular myths and explain language from a scientific point of view, have had little impact on the world's population. Only one or two have approached best-seller status, and no movie deals are being negotiated as far as I know. In the universities, linguistics as a field of study has not yet attracted vast numbers of eager undergraduates, and in the schools, it is still absent from most curriculums. The marginal status of linguistics is hardly surprising, given the success of the Spell and the benefits we derive from it. Most people are quite happy with what they know about language, and for the most part, they are right to be so: that's the way the Spell has made it, and it has made it so because language does its job best by staying hidden from conscious view most of the time.

But there must be a way to break the Language Spell when it hurts in some of the ways we've seen in the latter part of this chapter. Philosophy, religion and pure common sense tell us that through knowledge, empathy and good will, we can better see each other for what we are, rather than for what we wear, where we come from, or how we speak. Since language is our principal means of knowing others, then an ability to break the Spell, in the sense of creating more general awareness of what language is, should help us in a small way to develop more empathy with the people we live among.

Now that's as bold as I'm going to get here (although I'm tempted to claim that linguistics can create good will too, but I don't want to push my luck so far so soon). Even *contemplating* such a monumental challenge may strike some as absurdly naive, given the depth of the chasms which have separated human societies for millennia. But I hope to convince you that the path is worth treading, and that it's linguistics which provides the clearest map.

More information

 Daniel Osherson (1995–1998) has edited a comprehensive introductory series on **cognitive science** covering *Language* (Vol. 1), *Visual Cognition* (Vol. 2), *Thinking* (Vol. 3), and *Conceptual Foundations* (Vol. 4). Look out for William Labov's chapter on African-American English grammar from a cognitive perspective, in Vol. 1.

Information and action on **endangered languages** may be found at Terralingua (www.terralingua.org), dedicated to understanding and preserving the planet's biocultural diversity.

Popular views about language are discussed with humour and intelligence in Ronald Wardhaugh's (1999) book. Deborah Cameron's enthralling discussion (1995) is a less 'orthodox' linguistic response to public myths: she takes speakers' attitudes seriously, and critically addresses the roles they play in society.

Dell Hymes (1996) collects together a series of essays on the interconnection between linguistics, education, anthropology and ethnography. The second and third sections, on linguistic inequality and the role of narrative in social life, are particularly relevant to some of the issues discussed in this chapter.

To see a very different view of language from that provided by linguists, visit the site of the **Queen's English Society** at www.queens-english-society.com. I recommend that you revisit the site after you have read this book, to see whether you still agree with anything it says there.

The **Wittgenstein** quote is from aphorism 119 of his penetrating *Philosophical Investigations* (Wittgenstein 2002 [1953]). The edition I give in the Bibliography comes in the original German, together with the latest version of its most celebrated English translation.

To read more about George Orwell's views on **language and power**, just type 'Politics and the English Language' into any search engine on the Internet and you'll be given dozens of sites which contain the full text of this famous 1946 essay.

2 Linguistics

> It is difficult to imagine a profession which by definition commits its practitioners to any greater degree of abstraction or detachment from the world. To people who have been drawn to such a profession, however practical and rugged they may be, the idea that language is an object in its own right rather than an utterly transparent and permeable window to the movements of the soul is a professional cliché.
>
> (John Haiman, *Talk Is Cheap*)

Within linguistics, it is indeed a cliché that language is, at some level, independent of the thoughts it communicates, the sounds and light patterns that afford it external expression, the motives that cause it to be engaged, the functions it performs, and the ways its users think about it. But there are very few linguists in the world, and their work is unknown to most people. This is partly because, practical and rugged though some of them may be, their detachment from the world has made them a rather inward-looking lot. But I think linguistics' lack of penetration in the marketplace of popular ideas has more to do with the fact that what is a cliché to the linguist is completely unintuitive to the non-specialist.

The opacity of language as an object in its own right filters the beliefs of linguists and laypeople alike, of course. Linguists are also language users, and can't abandon this status when they put on their professional hats. They have no X-ray vision into syntax, no quantum semantics, no phonological equivalent of $E = mc^2$. But the array of methods and approaches they and allied scientists have designed over the years have led them to some significant conclusions about the nature of language and its place in our lives. These findings have had a greater impact on other scientific fields and on the language professions than on the public at large. Haiman's cliché still ensures that, for the most part, the intellectual treasures of linguistics have remained locked in one of the more obscure turrets of academe's ivory tower.

Unlike the rest of the book, the first part of this chapter deals specifically with **linguistics**, the discipline, rather than language, the phenomenon, trying to situate it within its academic and professional context. I then go on to sketch how theoretical linguists have divided up and labelled the basic components of the machinery of linguistic knowledge, how these components work and why we need them.

Linguistics, applied linguistics and the language professions

An awareness of language unfiltered by the Spell, that is, a *linguistic view* of language, should provide additional intellectual empowerment for those in the language professions. Whether they teach, translate, work with the speech-impaired or use language for other purposes (such as journalism, the law or advertising), a broad understanding of how the language system works and how it interacts with the rest of mind and society should provide valuable insights into, and tools for, their professional practice. Before delving deeper into the doings of linguists, therefore, let me present a few brief comments on these professions.

Language, as we have seen, plays a major role in our collective existence, pervading all our activities, not least our working lives. Certain professions require their practitioners to pay special attention to language, whereas others use language simply because they are involved in human activity. While dentists, pilots, accountants and engineers need language to exercise their skills, they no doubt attach greater value to their drills, cabin instruments, spreadsheet programs and design software. On the other hand, for other professionals the vocal tract and computer keyboard are among their principal tools. Lawyers, priests, journalists, advertisers, politicians, spin doctors, psychiatrists, social workers, teachers, broadcasters – all get paid for addressing other people using the spoken or written word (some need to *listen*, too).

Now, although sermons, newspaper columns, lectures and advertising blurb are examples of language in use, it is not normally language which is the point of the exercise: lawyers wish to win cases, priests souls and advertisers sales. Another set of language professionals, who we might think of as 'language purveyors', see language *itself* as a primary goal. These include novelists, playwrights, poets, lexicographers, translators, language teachers, language therapists and pathologists, language planners, copy editors and also some computer scientists and software developers. Among the language purveyors, a small number (especially teachers, translators and lexicographers) have been enthusiastic collaborators with scholars in the interdisciplinary field of **applied linguistics**. For many working in this field, the relationship with 'mainstream' linguistics is as remote as that between business administration and economic theory.

Linguistics and applied linguistics

So what is it that linguists do? For a relatively small group of scholars they manage to cover a lot of territory. If you browse through a dictionary of linguistics, or look at the programme of the annual meeting of the Linguistic Society of America, you'll see a range of specialist sub-disciplines to rival the panoply of fantastic creatures in a set of Pokemon cards. Here are some of the major players. **Theoretical linguists** study the overall structure of the human language faculty, and **descriptive linguists** the specific languages (Finnish, French, Farsi, etc.) that give it group expression. **Socio-linguists** and **psycholinguists** are interested in how these structured systems are represented, acquired, and put to use, and how they interface with the non-linguistic world, at the levels of social groups (sociolinguistics) and individual minds (psycholinguistics). **Historical linguists** address the issue of how these systems change through time, **neurolinguists** explore the location and organization of the brain tissue in which they are embodied, **anthropological linguists** the role of language in cultural behaviours and practices, **computational linguists** the interface between language and machine, and the list could go on. (We'll add to it in the chapters to come.)

Applied linguists, on the other hand, are experts who develop theories *and* practices for the solution of language *problems*, combining resources from several academic disciplines. One of the principal fields tapped (not surprisingly) is linguistics, but also involved are ideas from education, anthropology, sociology, psychology, public policy, cultural theory, pathology and others. The problems addressed are equally varied, even though most of those who would call themselves applied linguists concentrate on issues in foreign language learning and teaching.

A representative selection of some of the activities applied linguists get involved in is given in Table 1. In very few instances are theories from their sister discipline of linguistics directly applied to the solution of 'real world' problems like these, but their influence is clear, especially in the development of language teaching methods, dictionary compilation, national language policy-making and the diagnosis of language disorders. Sometimes even theoretical linguistics,

Table 1 Some areas and activities of Applied Linguistics

Field	Selection of problems addressed
Discourse Analysis	• developing strategies for the negotiation of disputes • safeguarding consumer rights in doctor-patient or lawyer-client interaction • designing strategies for effective intercultural communication
First Language Education and Literacy	• developing strategies for adult literacy programmes • teaching academic writing skills • raising awareness of 'non-standard' dialects
Forensic Linguistics	• authenticating voice recordings • analysing the interpretation of linguistic evidence in court cases
Language Pathology and Therapy	• helping the deaf and hearing-impaired understand spoken language • providing therapy for people with speech and language disorders • advising on alternative learning strategies for dyslexics
Language Policy and Planning	• drafting national language policies • implementing bilingual education systems • devising alphabets or other writing systems • promoting universal literacy • defining, promoting and defending linguistic rights
Lexicography	• writing dictionaries and thesauri • establishing international terminology banks • developing tools for word-processing packages
Literary Linguistics	• identifying authorship of texts where disputed or unknown • contributing to an understanding of stylistic choices • teaching creative writing
Rhetoric	• writing advertising copy • advising politicians and lobbyists • speech writing
Second Language Teaching	• designing curricula and materials • creating valid testing and evaluation instruments • examining the effectiveness of teaching methodologies
Translation	• translating written text • interpreting spoken discourse

analysing the structural system of language and languages, has immediate impact on practical concerns, by providing tools for describing the human genome at one extreme, to assisting in the preservation of marginalized cultures at the other.

Perhaps inevitably, given the effects of the Spell we discussed in the first chapter, most language problems are of a social and psychological order, and so understanding the abstract 'computational' nature of linguistic knowledge is not going to be of much immediate practical help, without good accounts of the way this knowledge is used in the social and psychological space we inhabit. For this reason, the fields of psycholinguistics, and especially sociolinguistics, have provided more useful insights for applied linguists. Yet even here (and particularly with psycholinguistics) there are limits on both the usefulness of the knowledge yielded by research and applied linguists' inclination to consider it.

Different perspectives in linguistics

There is often considerable tension in linguistics departments between those who study linguistic knowledge as an abstract 'computational' system, ultimately embedded in the human brain, and those who are more concerned with language as a social system played out in human interactional patterns and networks of beliefs. Underlying these tensions there are often some fundamental differences of opinion about questions of philosophy and methodology, which give rise to what appear to be, in some cases, irreconcilable linguistic world views. Although most theoretical linguists are reasonable types, they are sometimes accused of seeing human language as *purely* a formal, abstract system, and of marginalizing the importance of sociolinguistic research. It is true that some 'formalists', notably in the tradition of Noam Chomsky, take Haiman's cliché a step further than most, and argue that language may be *studied* without taking into account any of the other spheres of human reality with which it interacts. Other linguists believe that it is impossible to divorce structure from use, and some rail passionately against those, like Chomsky, who they believe *refuse* to see the users behind the system. (This is a source of particular frustration for those who happen to applaud Chomsky's very separate work on the duplicity of Western governments and media.)

Theoretical linguists who ignore work on the sociology and psychology of language have been likened to pre-Reformation catholic priests who said mass only in Latin to prevent uninformed popular engagement in the mysteries of their art. The impression that they oppose attempts to link the internal and external realities of language has encouraged others, including applied linguists and laypeople, to question their entire enterprise or ignore it completely. Equally, sociolinguists and others have been seen by formalists as disdaining attempts to crack the underlying mental code of language, and thus surrendering to the power of the Spell. I'm not sure how many linguists working in the 'formalist' or 'functionalist' camps of linguistics actually hold such limiting views. Most, I imagine, adopt a more reasonable approach, deciding to use their finite research time and resources to focus on a manageable and personally appealing aspect of the linguistic conundrum, without explicitly rejecting what their colleagues are doing down the corridor.

And in any case, despite these contretemps, linguistics has been stunningly successful over the last 50 years in its attempts to account for the full splendour of human language phenomena: what its basic formal properties might be, to what extent it can vary across different groups of speakers, how it changes through time, how it is acquired and lost, where it is stored in the brain, how it is used to perform social acts. There are even good guesses about how it connects with concepts and intentions, how it evolved in the species, and how it's handled in the minds of bilinguals. It's often hard, however, to step back, appreciate these advances and see how they might fit together. Students of linguistics and applied linguistics are not always invited to assume this vantage point, and disenchantment often results. Linguists, like most academics, become more focused on their own speciality and often don't find time to *talk* to their colleagues down the corridor, let alone to applied linguists. Many applied linguists, in turn, restrict their limited theory-time to the more accessible and potentially practical fruits of linguistic research, or ignore linguistics entirely. This is quite understandable, and even justifiable, much of the time. But all too often such selectivity can prove risky, even reckless.

Consequently, some 'clients' of applied linguistics – those 'language purveyors' who confront linguistic problems first-hand, like foreign language teachers, translators and speech therapists – tend to use linguistic research only sporadically and indirectly, if at all. Probably, there are large numbers of practising language teachers and translators around the globe who have never *heard* of applied linguistics, or have only a vague notion of what it's for. And if we step past the 'language purveyors' altogether, to confront the typical 'civilian' language user, we'll be faced with, at most, undetectable levels of awareness of what linguists and applied linguists do for a living.

This, in my view, is a regrettable state of affairs, but not a hopeless one. There have been encouraging signs in recent years that more linguists are at least seeing the need to air their views in the public domain, and to engage the non-expert in the debates that were earlier confined to the scientific journals and the academic conference halls. The Linguistic Society of America, for example, is at the time of writing planning a Language Summit with the US Center for Applied Linguistics and the Modern Language Association, to address the public perception of language and linguistics. And in the last decade or so, dozens of excellent new books on language for the general reader have been published. This new openness is in part due to external events, like the English-only and Ebonics debates in the USA, the national curriculum debate in the UK, the increased ecological anxiety of ordinary people over the extinction of species and cultures, the advent of the Internet, and public interest in the cognitive sciences. But for linguists and applied linguists to contribute more fully and effectively to public life, I think we need to find ways of presenting a view of language which unifies its mental and social reality, by attempting to resolve what I've been calling the Fundamental Paradox. I hope that the ideas I connect up in this book are of some help in this endeavour. In the meantime let's press on, and start to see what the linguists have achieved.

Breaking the spell: linguistic knowledge

We'll begin our brief introduction to the linguistic view of language with a very basic question. When a person knows a language, what is it that they know, and what are the kinds of knowledge involved? Consider Angela, an English speaker. Does it make sense to start by saying that Angela knows how to speak English, listen to English, and, assuming she's literate, read and write English? Well, yes, this is *part* of what she knows but it's perhaps the wrong place to start, since it assumes we know what English is in the first place, so that we can understand what it means for Angela to be able to speak it, listen to it, read it and write it. What, then *is* this 'English' that Angela knows?

Declarative knowledge of language

From the perspective of linguistic theory, English is: (a) a set of speech sounds; (b) a set of principles for how to put them together in meaningful ways; and (c) a set of principles for how to interpret the meanings they express.

The set of speech sounds (consonants and vowels) that Angela knows is called her **phoneme inventory**. The principles she knows for combining them into English words and sentences are contained in three systems:

- the **phonology**, which stipulates the ways in which the phonemes can be strung together into longer sequences, like words (e.g. *complete*), prefixes (e.g. *in-*), and suffixes (e.g. *-ness*);
- the **morphology**, which states how these phonological units can be combined together to create complex words (e.g. *in-complete-ness*);
- the **syntax**, which governs the ways in which words can be arranged together to form phrases and sentences (e.g. *A certain incompleteness;* and *She sensed a certain incompleteness in her life*).

The words that Angela knows, built out of bits of phonology, morphology and syntax, are stored as entries in her **lexicon**. Each word's entry will include a representation of its form, as a string of phonemes (and letters), and its grammatical properties (for instance, whether it's a noun or a verb). Her lexicon will also contain prefixes like *in-* and suffixes like-*ness*, and also longer bits of language which she has memorized as wholes, as though they were very long words, like *There you go!*, *Speak of the devil!* and *Touch wood!*

The principles for associating meanings and intentions with the strings of phonemes stored in the lexicon and the strings of words built by the syntax, are contained in her **semantics** of English. Using her semantic knowledge of how English expresses meaning, she connects **concepts** to words, parts of words, phrases, sentences and whole discourses.

Philosophers and psychologists call this kind of knowledge **declarative knowledge**: it is knowledge of *what*, rather than knowledge of *how to*. Viewed this way, English is a set of facts, not a set of procedures: when Angela knows English, she still knows it when she's not *using* it. When she goes to bed after a night on the town and spends it in dreamless sleep, she is not *doing* anything. Her body and mind have shut down for a while, but when she wakes up again in the morning, she still knows English and can read what's on the back of the cornflakes packet: Angela is an English speaker even while she's not using English, and this is because she carries English around in her head, as a **mental lexicon** and a **mental grammar**, ready to be called upon when necessary.

Figure 1 is a diagram of how the different bits of her linguistic knowledge fit together and connect up with what she can say (meanings) and how she says it (through speech or writing):

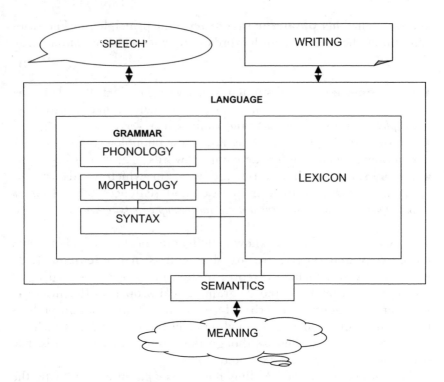

Figure 1   Angela's knowledge of language

In Chapters 3 and 4 we'll take a closer look at linguistic meaning and the lexicon, and in Chapter 5 we'll focus in on speech and writing. Chapters 6 and 7 will outline our knowledge of morphology and syntax, respectively.

Procedural knowledge of language

Knowledge of the phonemes of English and the rules for arranging them and interpreting them is not all that makes Angela an English speaker. Unless she knows how to *use* the knowledge in actual speaking and listening, that knowledge is not going to be of much value to her in the real world of social action and interaction. Noam Chomsky, the leading scholar in modern theoretical linguistics, has dedicated a lot of thought and effort to characterizing the system of declarative knowledge of human language: the grammar and lexicon. He is not terribly interested in how the knowledge is used, and has demonstrated (to many convincingly, to others not) that language *can* be studied independently of use. He has used the term **competence** to refer to *knowing what* and **performance** to refer to *knowing how* and *actually doing it*. (His research is restricted uniquely to the former.)

But if you want a complete account of human language, you have to read beyond Chomsky, to see how psycholinguists like Steven Pinker or Jean Aitchison explain the processes by which individual minds acquire, store and use the abstract principles of language to turn them into actual sounds or meanings; and sociolinguists like Deborah Tannen or Deborah Cameron, to marvel at how members of language groups plug the products of their mental grammars into social routines, to construct their identities, shoot the breeze, and get things done together.

Outside of the universities, it is the sociolinguistic message which has tended to penetrate more readily than Chomsky's or the psycholinguists' (who rarely risk ridicule, opprobrium, or incredulity at the hairdresser's or in the pub by talking shop). As I stressed in Chapter 1, language is rarely thought about by the layperson as a set of declarative knowledge encoded in a mental computer program. Non-linguists are aware of *using* it, to *perform*: to tell jokes, get the latest gossip, ask for directions, make speeches, understand pop song lyrics, read novels, pray for peace in the world, etc. But we'll have to leave discussion of the social uses of languages for later, though, since in order to understand how language has effects in (and on) society, we first need to appreciate how it gets meanings out of speakers' heads and into those of listeners.

For this to happen, language users like Angela need what's called **procedural knowledge** as well as declarative knowledge, and this is part of what psycholinguists are interested in exploring and explaining. In Chomsky's terminology, psycholinguists are trying to build theories of mental performance. Apart from being an unconscious grammarian, then, Angela also 'knows' a lot of procedural tricks.

Speech sounds

At the level of sound, she knows how to transform stored phonemes into actual speech. This is called **speech production**, and is explored by students of **articulatory phonetics**. This 'how-to' knowledge tells Angela which arrays of muscle movements need to be played out in order to produce the air molecule vibrations which her interlocutors hear as words rather than as mere noise. So she knows to spread her lips for the initial consonant of the word *sip*, in anticipation of the vowel that follows it, but to purse them on the same consonant for the word *soup*. She also knows how to decode the speech sounds produced by others: this is the area of **speech perception** (the domain of **acoustic phonetics**), and is concerned with how she extracts sounds matching her stored phonemes from the brain impulses stimulated by vibration patterns in her ear drums. Here she applies her implicit knowledge at spectacular speeds, normally matching the acoustic input with her stored representations of word forms within a fifth of a second.

These two sets of procedural knowledge define the difference between speaking and listening, but there's much more to deploying our grammatical and lexical knowledge than producing and hearing sounds.

Words

At the level of words, Angela knows how to choose the ones she needs from the dictionary she carries around in her head: this is knowledge of **lexical selection**, and involves mechanisms which take the thought she wishes to communicate and lead her to the relevant entries in her mental lexicon. Thinking about dogs, for example, doesn't necessarily take her directly to the word *dog*, which is a part of her declarative (vocabulary) knowledge. Say she's remembering when she tried to stroke a Chihuahua that was yapping at her ankles in the street the previous day. If she's alone, her thoughts about the incident will consist of memories of textures, visual images, and sounds, but probably not words – and even then not necessarily the word *dog* itself: if she decides to *talk* about the incident, she might use the words *little beast* instead. Choosing the word (lexical selection), is obviously not the same as knowing the word (vocabulary knowledge).

She also knows how to identify the words she *hears* on the basis of the phonemes she's recognized and the accumulating context of the utterance she's been listening to: this is the process of **word recognition**, invoking a variety of cues which take her to entries in her mental lexicon. For example, how does Angela distinguish between *Don't take offence* and *Don't take a fence*; *illegal operations* and *ill eagle operations*; *superficial dream* and *super fish'll dream*?

Sentences

At the level of sentence structure, Angela knows how to group together the words she's activated in the mental lexicon as she's speaking: this is called **syntactic planning**, and involves distinguishing alternatives of grammatical expression, for example whether to say:

(1) (a) Sal ate the squid this morning   or
     (b) The squid was eaten by Sal this morning   or
     (c) This morning Sal ate the squid   or
     (d) This morning the squid was eaten by Sal   etc.

She also knows how to group together the words she's recognizing as she *hears* or *reads* a sentence: this is the process called **parsing**, which helps her to know who is doing what to whom (whether Sal is eating the squid or the squid is eating Sal).

Meanings

Unsurprisingly, our English speaker knows how to encode her thoughts into language in the first place, when she has something to say. This, the **semantic planning** stage, is the starting point of any verbal act and requires her to decide (unconsciously, of course) how much of the message she can and should express. (Not all speakers appear to obey this golden rule. In Tolstoy's *War and Peace*, the unfortunate Prince Hippolyte speaks 'in a tone which showed that he only understood the meaning of his words after he had uttered them'. I'm sure we all know people who give the same impression!)

Imagine, for example, that Angela is in the middle of describing to someone a car accident she's just witnessed. She knows how to judge her interlocutor's current state of knowledge so she can choose how to package the information appropriately. Unlike the Sal and squid sentences, each of the following expresses different bits of meaning associated with her mental representation of the incident, and each one may be appropriate, depending on the circumstances of the exchange:

(2) (a) The driver missed the Ford, but hit the Volkswagen
     (b) He missed the Ford, but hit the Volkswagen
     (c) The driver hit the Volkswagen
     (d) The Volkswagen was hit
     (e) He missed one, but hit the other
     (f) And then that one got hit

As if that wasn't enough, she also knows how to get from the sentence to what it means when someone says something to her. This is the stage of **semantic interpretation**. Knowing the words and the order they come in does not necessarily give her the meaning intended: If she had been around when my friend asked her colleagues:

(3)   Who has a car that doesn't work on Wednesday?

she would, like us, have had to do some fancy interpretative processing. Despite recognizing all the words, it was tough for us to work out that Rosa wished to borrow a functioning car from someone who wouldn't need it on Wednesday since they wouldn't be teaching that day. (... At least, I *think* that's what she meant.)

Intentions

Since language use is embedded in a wide variety of contexts and serves innumerable functions, its expressions are very often intended and interpreted in ways that don't correspond to the literal linguistic meanings they conventionally encode. Angela, at times, will want to express benevolent (and sometimes malevolent) deception, solidarity or distance with her interlocutors, or barely camouflaged anger. She can say:

(4)   Darling, what an interesting combination of colours!

when her new boyfriend shows up wearing a turquoise tie with a red and brown checked shirt. And:

(5)   Might I suggest we open a window?

when her boss makes to light up a cigarette in her small office. Or:

(6)   Thank you for your consideration!

when the boss leaves mid-sentence, slamming the door behind him.

She will also want to extend and embellish her language use with metaphors, calling her boss a *child* (when he's 40) and her boyfriend *colour-blind* (when he isn't). To produce these kinds of expressions she needs more than a grammar, a lexicon and semantics. She needs integrated knowledge of a set of conventional social and cognitive routines which allow her to go beyond the literal meanings of expressions, within limits which permit her interlocutor to recover her intentions (except when deception is the goal, of course). Such knowledge provides an interface level between grammar and other kinds of knowledge. Angela has, then, what is called **pragmatic competence**, which she also uses to make inferences in comprehension when others use non-literal language to her. More on this in Chapter 8.

Communicative competence

Of course, language use is inextricably bound up with social convention, action and belief, and groups of speakers grow up expecting language to be used in certain ways for certain purposes. If Angela has all the grammatical machinery of English in place, has stored tens of thousands of words in her lexicon, and knows how to conventionally map between linguistic expressions and contextualized intentions (both hers and her interlocutors), she still needs to have all this embedded in a more general sociocultural competence in order to use it appropriately to communicate with other members of the communities she interacts with. If she and her boyfriend are lawyers, and face each other in court, then she knows not to call him *darling* in that context. And when a client arrives for an interview, she knows they will probably go through a greeting and small-talk ritual before getting down to the details of the case.

This broader notion of what Angela knows as an English speaker has been termed **communicative competence** by Dell Hymes. It includes not just the language system itself, but also the ability to use it appropriately and effectively, given the social norms and cultural traditions of the speech community. From this perspective, we can appreciate how language is a tool of social meaning, with sets of norms and conventions which correlate with other domains, like style of dress, degree of physical contact, gift-giving and expectations of deference. Chapter 11 will explore this in more detail.

Input, output and modality

Notice that at each 'level' of linguistic expression, there are two ways in which Angela accesses the knowledge she needs: for *production*, when she's speaking, or for *comprehension*, when she's listening. The levels of declarative knowledge that make up Angela's lexical, grammatical and pragmatic competence are thus databases and routines in long-term memory that she consults during performance: procedural knowledge acts on declarative knowledge to put her language to work in actual instances of language use (and, remember, she won't normally be aware of any of it happening).

Now that we are beginning to understand what Angela's English is and how she puts it to use, we can turn again to the issue of what it means for her to speak it, listen to it, read it and write it. In the above account of what psycholinguists call **language processing**, the psychological mechanisms involved were all exemplified from the perspective of spoken language. Speech, though, as we've already noted, is only one of the modalities of language use. The most common alternative **modality** is that of written text, and another is the manual signing used by and with the deaf. Writing and signing share the property that instead of relying on the vocal tract and the ear as transmission channels, they employ the hands and the eyes. Spoken language requires hearers to activate meaning on the basis of incoming sound, and speakers to produce sounds which allow others to activate the meanings they want to share. When people read, or understand signing, however, they process patterns of light, and when they write or sign, they are producing visual symbols with the hands. Remember: a book doesn't contain language or meaning, only black marks on a white background. Equally, a recording of speech is only noise if it's played where there's no-one to hear it. Language and meaning reside uniquely in human minds. Text, sign and speech are the external signs that language has been in action, like fingerprints betraying the presence of a criminal at the scene of the crime.

A difference between speech and text is that speech comes naturally to all normal human beings and, in fact, its building blocks are programmed into our genetic code, whereas writing is an invented device which is learnt by conscious intent and is not common to all members of the species. Unlike speech and sign, it is a derivative modality which originally 'mimicked' a given spoken language in the visual plane, even though it has developed intellectual light years beyond the mimicking stage in modern literate societies (see Chapter 5). Signing, on the other hand, is a modality that may be acquired by infants naturally, the same way as speech, in order to externalize the grammar of a **sign language**. American Sign Language, for example, has nothing to do with English, and is incomprehensible to users of British Sign Language. Sign languages have lexicons, morphologies and syntax. They also have phonologies, although the basic units are handshapes, rather than phonemes. Children exposed to sign as infants acquire such languages in the same way and in the same developmental sequence as spoken languages. Sign can express the same range of concepts and functions as any language that relies on speech. They even have babbling, whispering, shouting, poetry and foreign accents. In short, they are complete human languages, with native speakers who have 'mother hands' instead of mother tongues.

We can now appreciate that, in literate societies at least, most language users have four ways of accessing the grammar and using language, depending on modality and processing direction:

	comprehension	production
speech	LISTENING	SPEAKING
text	READING	WRITING

A point which is often overlooked (especially in language teaching) is that the 'four skills', if indeed they are 'skills', are not derived from separate or independent sets of knowledge. First of all from the perspective of modality: every time you engage in linguistic activity, whether it involves the *spoken* or the *written* word, you are employing essentially the same declarative and procedural knowledge of semantics, syntax and lexicon: only the surface realization (through phonology or **orthography**) is different. And from the perspective of processing direction: whether you are *producing* language or *comprehending* language, in either modality, you are still consulting essentially the same grammatical and lexical databases in your journey from meaning to sound or sound to meaning. The differences between the 'skills' are therefore pretty superficial when one considers the entire amount of knowledge it takes to use a language.

But the differences become much richer and deeper if we correlate them with the kinds of *uses* to which the modalities are put. And this kind of sensitivity must be fostered in second language learners and infant acquirers if we want them to perform appropriately in real sociocultural contexts. As we'll see in Chapters 5, 8 and 10, spoken discourse is often very different from written discourse, in terms of the grammatical and lexical choices that tend to get made, as well as the social functions they typically serve.

So this is some of what Angela knows as an English speaker. At its core, her language is a powerful set of grammatical rules and a memorized list of phoneme combinations. But it also contains an associated suite of processors and is deftly interwoven with pragmatic and sociocultural systems and mechanisms which put it to work. Figure 2 sketches this procedural view.

In this first couple of chapters I've introduced the notion that human language is a powerful human endowment, encoded in the mind, but which largely operates below the level of consciousness, and therefore seems to us to be a uniquely social, rather than a sociocognitive, phenomenon. This is the Language Spell, woven to keep us concentrated on what we do with language, rather than on language itself. We saw that our limited awareness of the internal nature and

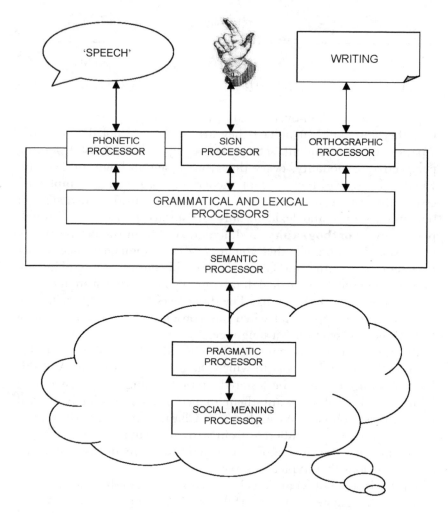

Figure 2   Angela's knowledge of how to use language

functioning of language (declarative and procedural linguistic knowledge) leads to a variety of other consequences, however, some encoded in folk linguistic beliefs, others in the confounding of the form and content of linguistic expressions. Some of these consequences are positive (indeed they motivated the evolutionary Spell in the first place), whereas others are of a less salutary nature.

In the following chapters we start to unpack linguistic knowledge further, showing how linguists approach it from various directions, bombarding language with the counter-spells of science. We begin with perhaps the most fundamental and intuitive level: associating sounds with meanings or, sacrificing accuracy to intuitive appeal, the possibility of *naming things*.

More information

The **Linguistic Society of America**'s website is at www.lsadc.org. Look for the FAQs at the 'About Linguistics' link.

The 'What is linguistics?' link at the **Linguistics Association of Great Britain** website (www.lagb.org) provides a set of Language Facts Sheets (maintained by Dick Hudson) and a number of interesting links.

The **Ask-A-Linguist** service offered by the Linguist List at http://linguistlist.org/ask-ling provides readers with the opportunity to follow up on doubts or interests raised in this book by asking an expert (he or she may tell you a different story from the one provided here!).

The **Center for Applied Linguistics** website at www.cal.org provides information about language, literacy, education and culture from an applied linguistics viewpoint. It also has FAQs and an 'Ask the Language Experts' service.

Noam **Chomsky**'s work on linguistics is notoriously difficult for the non-syntactician. His two most accessible books both contain 'oral' material, one in the form of lecture notes, the other an interview transcript. The first, Chomsky (1988), presents a clear description of the generative enterprise and linguistic argumentation. The second, Chomsky (2002), discusses language as a cognitive and biological faculty, and also introduces the reader to some of the latest developments in thinking on generative grammar.

A solid introduction to **psycholinguistics** is Jean Aitchison's (1996) *The articulate mammal*. A briefer introduction is John Field's (2002) resource book which, through innovative sequencing of chapter topics, provides a thought-provoking, interactive approach, and includes abridged excerpts from primary research articles. Steven Pinker's 1994 best-seller *The language instinct* showcases psycholinguistic thinking in an extremely readable account of the innate human language faculty.

Elaine Chaika's (1994) book on **sociolinguistics**, although over 10 years old, remains one of the best introductions to the field. Ronald Wardhaugh's introduction (2001) is wide-ranging and authoritative, especially on the social aspects of multilingualism.

Guy Cook (2003) presents a brief and readable review of issues in **applied linguistics**, especially those concerning language learning and teaching. It includes a series of abridged excerpts from the specialist literature. Norbert Schmitt's (2002) collection offers introductory articles by some of the best known names in the field, many of them presenting an applied linguistic view of some of the central areas of linguistics itself.

The **British Deaf Association** has a superb website (well worth waiting for it to load!) at www.signcommunity.org.uk. There is a text version for those of us who don't know British Sign Language.

The Clerc Center at Gallaudet University (a college run principally by and for the deaf) has a website with **information on deafness** at http://clerccenter.gallaudet.edu/infotogo.

Karen Nakamura's Deaf Resource Library provides information about **American Sign Language** at www.deaflibrary.org/asl.html.

Part II: Words

3 Names, Words and Things

The spoken word is silver but the unspoken is golden.

(Tolstoy, *War and Peace*)

Most introductory linguistics books move on to phonology or morphology after a general introduction to the field. This book, however, is about language, and the ways we normally think (or don't think) about it, so my strategy is going to be a little different (rather unorthodox, in fact). The next three chapters are about *words*, and only then do I move on to morphology and syntax. (Phonology, as the grammatical level closest to the physical surface, doesn't get its own chapter, but is discussed in some detail in Chapter 5.) The reason for arranging things thus is that words are what language users are most aware of, and through them we can explore all sorts of other aspects of language, including semantics (a major focus of this chapter), language acquisition and change (discussed in the next chapter), and language form (the topic of the chapter after that). So let's start at the very beginning, and try to define what words are, and what they are not.

Problems with names

An essential part of the success of the Language Spell is our everyday assumption that things and categories of things have individual and unambiguous names. If one day we ceased to believe that words and meanings were in stable, monogamous relationships, then disorientation and social chaos would ensue. We'd no doubt reach the conclusion that our languages were completely unsuited for the no-nonsense job of transferring the intended contents of one person's mind into the mind of another. Luckily, language appears, at least on the face of it, to provide neat, clear labels for everything we might want to talk about (even *think* about). Take some of the physical objects in my immediate vicinity. The contraption I am using to write these words is called in

English a *computer*, and it's sitting on what we call a *table*. The two organic protuberances I am employing to operate the computer are called *fingers*. My fingers are themselves components of larger entities called *hands*, and these in turn are part of the entire physical mass of me called a *body*, covered in *clothes*. The parts of the computer I am touching with my fingers are called a *mouse* and *keys*. How simple! It seems like every thing around me, and every part of it, has a name: a string of speech sounds (and of letters) which allows me to refer to it and distinguish it from other 'things'.

Adamic naming

It is part of our folk linguistic knowledge that human language arose through a process of naming things, right back to the original grunts of our prehistoric ancestors. We imagine one of them (like the original tool-user from Kubrick's *2001: A Space Odyssey*) pointing at the flames of the camp fire one day and roaring *Garghhhhhh!*, then changing the roar-initial consonant to coin *Darghhhhhh!* to baptise the nearby river, *Barghhhhhh!* for the sky, and so on. Unlikely, maybe, but it may not be *that* far from the truth (we'll see in the final chapter that linguists haven't come up with hard evidence for a much more elaborate account yet). Most educated language users do know that each name has an **etymology**, its own personal history. So might we assume that such histories do lead back to the 'original' names, to the distant past in which language was born in our species? Perhaps the first human talkers convened an 'Adamic Convention' to distribute names to the things around them, maybe starting with important, universal concepts like 'earth', 'sky', 'man', 'woman', 'food', 'predator', 'fire', 'water' (... and probably 'cockroach').

If the representatives at the Convention were methodical, systematic folk, they would probably have started with the simplest sounds, the vowels: perhaps *uh* for 'earth', *ee* for 'sky', *ey* for 'man', *ah* for 'woman', *oh* for 'tree' and *oo* for 'predator'. When they had run out of vowels, they might have tried obstructing the air flow at the beginnings of these simple words, bringing their lips together and rapidly releasing them to produce a consonant-vowel sequence like *buh* for 'fire', or briefly touching the back of the tongue to the roof of the mouth to make *gah* for 'water'. Then perhaps they would try the same kind of thing *after* vowels, maybe by bringing the tip of the tongue up behind the teeth to get *ud* for 'chief', or making a hissing noise by forcing the air from the lungs through a narrow central channel formed by the curled tongue, to produce, say, *ez* for 'berry'. With those combinations exhausted they could create new kinds of consonants, for example by momentarily stopping the vibration of their vocal chords, deriving *p* from *b*, *k* from *g*, *t* from *d*, and *s* from *z*. Forming less radical obstructions with the tongue and lips they could get the 'liquid' *r*, *l*, and *w* sounds.

The Conventioneers could now feel quite pleased with themselves, having developed a phoneme inventory capable of naming hundreds of things through monosyllabic pairings of consonants and vowels. But there still wouldn't be anywhere near enough names to cover even a fraction of the concrete objects in their environment – let alone to name all their abstract ideas: of kinship, spirit powers, tastes, time, distance, tool use, emotions, goals, group identity, territorial limits, dreams ... and so much more. So, to further expand their lexical repertoire, they might have decided in a subsequent session to recycle the phonological materials already deployed, adding consonants at *both* ends of each vowel, then doubling up the consonants, and finally stringing together vowels and consonants in sequences of syllables. With this kind of imaginative use and reuse of a finite phoneme inventory, they'd have enough names for everything.

The arbitrary linking of sound sequences with meanings is a fundamental part of the way human languages work, and a human being's linguistic knowledge includes a long list of such correspondences between sound and meaning (stored in the lexicon). But thinking of words in terms of conscious *naming* invites frivolous flights of fancy like the story I have just told. More subtly, it implies a belief that words and meanings are two sides of a single coin, one **word form** for each **word meaning**. The Spell bewitches us into thinking that names are linked with things *isomorphically*, in a one-to-one fashion, like the picture-word pairings in children's vocabulary books: on page 1, a picture of an apple with its name ('apple') below it; on page 2, a picture of a ball with its name ('ball') below it; etc. This 'alphabet book' view of words also illustrates our tendency to equate 'meanings' with 'concrete things' or visual images of them. We take for granted that the 'things' named have sharply defined boundaries, and may be pointed to or depicted visually, or defined using other words (as in dictionaries). But it is not quite so simple. There are various glitches in this ideal naming system, which don't occur to us unless we reflect upon them, or they surface due to some metalinguistic trigger, like a pun or a book on linguistics (i.e. until the Spell receives a dent or two).

Polysemy and metaphor

Let's start with the examples I gave at the beginning of the chapter. What picture would you pair with *hand*, *body*, *mouse* or *key*? If we use pictures of a human hand, a human body, a computer mouse and a keyboard, then how do we account for the following uses of these 'names'?

(1) (a) The second **hand** had long since fallen off the clock face.
     (b) They decided to play poker, and Gianni was dealt a good **hand**.

(2) (a) Jessica's car needed urgent **body** repairs.
     (b) The **body** of evidence was clearly against him.

(3) (a) The **mouse** ran up the clock.
     (b) Are you a man or a **mouse**?

(4) (a) Karim closed the door and put the **key** safely in his pocket.
     (b) The **key** to the mystery obviously lay in the vault below.

One apparent problem here is that English seems to be giving the same name to different things, a phenomenon known technically as **homonymy**, very common in the world's languages. But are they really such different things? Could they not be just different examples of the same category of thing, named at different levels of abstraction? It *is* possible to view a human body, the body of a car, and a body of evidence as the same kind of 'thing': a 'mass' of some sort. In which case we could talk of a single word form expressing a series of meanings which share a common core (a phenomenon called **polysemy**). But outside the lexicon these meanings do look highly dissimilar: my body and the body of my car look and feel very different, being made from very different materials and serving very different purposes. Even further away in semantic space is the *body* of evidence against Saddam Hussein presented at the UN Security Council.

The very *distinctness* of the meanings shared by the word form *body* make it seem highly unlikely that our minds will be thrown into semantic confusion when we encounter it in a real life situation. Words are not normally used in isolation of a communicative context, unaccompanied by extralinguistic cues to their meaning. In other words, we don't read (2a) and entertain the possibility that Jessica's car is made of flesh and blood, or read (2b) and wonder whether the metallic shell of a car might have been marked as Exhibit A in some court case.

It remains true, though, that if we take a *conscious* look at word forms like *body*, *key*, *hand*, and *mouse* in isolation from context, we can detect strands of meaning which connect together their different readings. The general concept of 'abstract mass' does seem to unite in a plausible semantic grouping the multiple meanings of *body*, and it is not too hard to see the common sense of a 'means of achieving something' in *key*, the shape or the function of the body part in *hand*, and the physical or psychological properties of tiny rodents in *mouse*. This is because all these meanings derive historically from an earlier, more limited, use of the word, and have been extended through what we call **metaphor**. In his novel *The Inheritors*, about the last days of our cousins the Neanderthals, William Golding records the moment when Lok, one of the last of the species, realizes the power of metaphor:

> Lok discovered 'Like'. He had used likeness all his life without being aware of it. Fungi on a tree were ears, the word was the same but acquired a distinction by circumstances that could never apply to the sensitive things on the side of his head. Now, in a convulsion of the understanding Lok found himself using likeness as a tool as surely as ever he had used a stone to hack at sticks or meat.

This is a poignant moment, coming just as the rudimentary speech of the Neanderthals was about to become silent for ever. Metaphor continues to be a driving force in the language of our own species, and yet the part it has played in the history of our vocabularies is almost as obscure as our knowledge of Lok and his kindred. Sensitivity to the metaphorical sources of current word meanings is probably part of the linguistic awareness of only some (educated or highly reflective) individuals, not part of the linguistic knowledge of all language users.

And yet metaphor is also employed on a spontaneous, *ad hoc* basis, especially in the written modality, to communicate thoughts for which existing options of lexical expression may be either too parochial or trite – for novelists and poets, for example. In other cases the words just don't exist, either in the lexicons of most people (if they are very technical) or in any language at all (because the concepts are just too amorphous or hard to grasp). This is the typical case of science, and especially popular science (like this book). This latter phenomenon is perhaps under-appreciated, given the dominant literary connotations of metaphor in the minds of most speakers. But it's rife in classrooms, lecture theatres, textbooks, and documentaries. Richard Dawkins' popular science book *The Selfish Gene*, for example, simply *oozes* metaphor. Here's a passage, explaining aspects of the evolution of an altruistic behavioural strategy he calls 'Tit for Tat' (I've put the most obvious metaphors in boldface):

> In a **climate** entirely dominated by **Tit for Tat**, **Suspicious** Tit for Tat does not **prosper**, because its initial **defection triggers** an **unbroken run** of mutual **recrimination**. When it **meets** a Tit for Two Tats **player**, on the other **hand**, Tit for Two Tats's greater **forgivingness nips** this recrimination in the **bud**.

Lok would be in his element!

Abstract words

Another problem area for Adamic naming thrown to the fore by examples such as those in (1) to (4) is that many of the things we give 'names' to cannot be pointed at or pictured, because they are abstract: ideas, rather than entities with extensions in space and time. Metaphor is one of the processes by which we give names to abstract concepts, by extending a label for something concrete to an abstract domain with which it shares some dimension of meaning. We talk about the *head* of an organization, for example, because we perceive him or her as being located at the 'top' of the organization and as constituting the part of the organization which takes the decisions. And it follows from this that the organization itself can be thought of as a 'body', and can therefore be labelled as such. But many abstract words do not originate in metaphor. Some can still be named with concrete nouns (like *hobbits*, *angels* and *pokemon*) or proper names (like *Godzilla*, *Excalibur*, or *Puck*), because they refer to imaginary concrete objects, which can only be seen or touched in our dreams. These, however, are insignificant in comparison with the many tens of thousands of non-metaphorical words which name not material entities but rather qualities, relationships, processes, properties and other abstract concepts.

Arundhati Roy's novel *The God of Small Things* opens with a very vivid description of the lusciousness of life in an Indian province in the month of May (Ms Roy, please forgive the typographical butchery!):

> MAY in **Ayemenem** IS a [hot], [brooding] MONTH. The DAYS ARE [long] and [humid]. The **river** SHRINKS and [black] **crows** GORGE on [bright] **mangoes** in [still], [dustgreen] **trees**. [Red] **bananas** RIPEN. **Jackfruits** BURST. [Dissolute] **bluebottles** HUM [vacuously] in the [fruity] AIR. Then they STUN themselves against [clear] **windowpanes** and DIE, [fatly] BAFFLED in the **sun**.

Of the 55 words in this passage, only 10 (marked in boldface) correspond to concrete nouns (and in fact, the concreteness of one of these, the proper noun *Ayemenem*, is questionable). Of the remaining 45, 4 (marked in small capitals) name abstract entities, 10 (in large capitals) label processes or states, 14 (in square brackets) name properties of these entities, states and processes, and a further 17 (underlined) seem not to name things at all, but rather to have linguistic roles or relational functions which operate on the things named in the passage. What possible sense can it make to say that these 45 non-concrete words are *naming things*?

Homonyms, synonyms and hyponyms

The one-to-one meaning-to-form idea of names breaks down for reasons other than polysemy, metaphor and abstractness. There are word forms, for example, which are used to signify two or more entirely different meanings (that is, they are homonymous, not polysemous). Looking at the top right-hand corner of my computer screen I could tell you that 'I can see the date in the menu bar'. Aside from two metaphors (*menu* and *bar*), this simple declaration has three other lexical ambiguities: *can*, which is a modal verb here, but also has the sense of a container for baked beans or beer; *see*, which can refer to the office or area of jurisdiction of a bishop as well as what we use our eyes for; and *dates*, which apart from labelling calendar entries and romantic assignations can also name dried fruits from a type of palm tree. It just happens that the same phonological sequences got used twice in these cases. Their etymologies tell us so: modal verb *can* is from Old English *kunnan*, tin *can* from Old English *canne*; to *see* with the eyes is from Old English *seon*, whereas the 'Holy' version was borrowed from French *sied*; finally, today's *date* comes ultimately from Latin *datum*, while the *dates* scoffed at Christmas are from French *datte*.

Maybe the Adamic Conventioneers ran out of phoneme sequences after a while and started to cheat? But no, it can't be the case that there aren't enough word forms to go round, since yet another problem for the one-to-one matching of names to things is that most things can be referred to by more than one name. This can happen via **synonymy**, when the relationship is one of (near) identity of meaning, like *football* and *soccer* for speakers of British English, or *settee* and *sofa*, *jump* and *leap*; but more often it's through **hyponymy**, when the relationship is one of sets and subsets of meaning, like *activity/sport/ soccer*, *thing/furniture/sofa*, *act/move/jump*.

Some linguists have argued that synonyms don't exist, since

differences between the use and/or users of the pair of items in question can always be detected. For example, *tin* and *can* belong to different dialects of English (British and American respectively), so to say they are synonyms is as absurd as saying that French *chien* is a synonym of English *dog*. But if you consider that the greater part of the world's population is bilingual (see Chapter 9), and that perhaps most of the monolinguals are **bidialectal** (see Chapter 10), then the argument loses its apparent psychological weight, for clearly many individual lexicons *do* contain different word forms expressing an identical meaning. My lexicon, for example, contains both *tin* and *can*, *lorry* and *truck*, *lift* and *elevator*, etc. as I have lived and had to make myself understood in both the USA and the UK (which means I also have bidialectal homonyms like *pissed*, meaning either 'drunk' or 'angry', and sometimes both at the same time).

Other arguments against synonymy have pointed to differences in the appropriate contexts of use for the items in the pair, so that *father* is more formal than *dad*, *hackney carriage* more quaint than *taxi*, *posterior* more subtle than *ass*. But it's not the *meaning* that changes from word to word, only the ranges of appropriate contexts for their use. If you tell your partner you're taking the *kids* to the park, you can't promise to leave the *children* at home in the same breath. A final argument levelled against synonymy is that purported synonyms often have different **connotations** (i.e. semantic, cultural or affective implications), so that a *politician* is not the same as a *statesman*, and being *firm* is not the same as being *obstinate*. (A letter to the *Guardian Weekly* a few years ago asked: 'Why are *rings* (paedophile, drug) nasty, but *circles* (family, friends) nice?') This I accept, but only for those cases for which it is true, which still leaves all the others ...

Proper names

The unpredictability and instability of word-meaning relations is, then, an inescapable fact. (Or at least it would be inescapable were it not warded off so effectively by the Language Spell.) And even the empire of *proper* names is not immune to this hidden semantic tangle. Names, in this narrower sense, are used in cases where the individuality of members of certain categories of things is important to us, like people, pets, places or works of art. It is useful, for example, for me to have a proper name, *Chris*, in addition to the myriad other common names which I might share with countless others (*partner, son, brother, teacher, smoker, neighbour, tourist, friend, taxpayer, passenger, atheist, European, fool, ...*). But of course, other people bear my name, and even my full name, *Christopher John Hall*, can probably be found on electoral rolls or birth registers in several parts of the English-speaking world. (In Mexico, much to my Mum's pleasure and amusement, both paternal and maternal names are used, so here my university ID calls me *Christopher John Hall Sim*, and I'm almost certainly the only individual who has ever lived that goes by that name: a bottle of champagne to anyone who proves me wrong.)

So even with proper names, it appears that the one-to-one ideal breaks down. Some unique individual things have more than one proper name, for example. The *Mona Lisa* is also called *La Giaconda*, and the *Rio Grande* is also the *Rio Bravo*. The author of *Silas Marner* is known to us as *George Eliot*, but was named *Mary Ann Evans* by her parents. *Benedict XVI* was born *Joseph Ratzinger*, and the painter *Domenikos Theotokopoulos* is better known to us by the name *El Greco*. Some things change their names with time: *Cassius Clay* became *Muhammad Ali* when he joined the Black Muslim movement, and *Rhodesia* changed its name to *Zimbabwe* when it finally gained formal independence from Britain in 1980. The time and place of utterance can also affect the interpretation of a name and what it names: *Jethro Tull* was the name of an agricultural reformer in the eighteenth century, but is associated more often now with an ageing band of rock and rollers. *Mérida* is the name of the capital of Yucatán State in Mexico, but is the capital of Extremadura in Spain, and of the state of the same name in Venezuela.

Words, meanings and thought

If you can't even trust a proper name to stay still, then perhaps, after all, the ideal design for language would have been for everything to have an exclusive right to one and only one name, as our fictional Adamic Conventioneers intended. Then there'd be no ambiguity, and everyone would know exactly where they were. ... Or perhaps not. The two body parts I'm using to type these words are called *fingers*. But there are ten of them all together, and what about the ones on my partner's hands, my next door neighbour's, the US president's and everyone else's? In our ideal Adamic world, we'd need different names for all the millions of other things in the world called *finger*: perhaps, *binger, zinger, hinger*, etc. for mine, *bonger, zonger, honger*, etc. for my partner's, and *benger, zenger, henger*, etc. for my neighbour's? I'm afraid we'd soon run out of memory and patience.

Word meanings in context

It is clearly the case that we don't need or can't use individual, *proper* names for most things in the world. Words share out the work of reference between them, and also, crucially, leave their owners (us) to do some of the work, by getting us to pay close attention to the linguistic and non-linguistic environments in which they are deployed. In this way we can talk about millions of things without using millions of names for them:

- If you're getting married and the priest whispers *Place the ring on his finger*, it's your knowledge of weddings, not the words of the priest, which tells you *which* ring to put on *which* finger.
- We understand that the word *for* serves different functions in *a shampoo for greasy hair* and *a shampoo for beautiful hair*, only because we know something about the before-and-after effects of shampoo.
- You know the word *you* refers to me when you say it to me, but to you when I say it to you.
- A security guard at Heathrow airport knows that a *suspicious package* might blow up, but that the *suspicious passenger* who reported it will not.

Indeed, one may speculate (as some experts in linguistic meaning have done) that the meaning of a word *is* its use in context. According to such a view, *body*, for example, would mean whatever it contributes to a successful communicative event. But there are serious problems with this argument. One is that we must store in our minds a meaning for *body* even when we're not using the word or thinking of its meaning (it's part of our *declarative* linguistic knowledge). No-one would argue that speakers forget the phonological form corresponding to *body* in between uses of it. Once it's learnt by a child and placed in their internal vocabulary list, it stays there. But also, crucially, *it must stay linked to conceptual memory*, rather than being severed from meaning once it's been heard or read, spoken or written. Otherwise how would we reconnect word and meaning the next time we wanted to use it? It can't be uniquely reconstructed through context, because context is always ambiguous to some degree. Imagine you spend the night with a friend and the next morning read the following on the back of a tube you find in your host's bathroom:

(5) An invigorating, fragranced foaming gel **body** wash. TO USE: Dispense a small amount of gel into your hand or onto your **body**. Massage foam over your **body**, then rinse.

Even if we somehow worked out the meaning of the other words, how would we know the product wasn't just for our scalp, our face, or our feet?

Another problem with the 'meaning is use' theory is that use is always a two-way street: when a word is used, there is a producer and a (real or implied) comprehender, i.e. a speaker with listener(s), a writer with reader(s). Mismatches between the producer's intended meaning and the comprehender's interpreted meaning *do* arise, as we saw in Chapter 1. Imagine you're still in the bathroom, courageously doing semantic battle in your efforts to get yourself clean. You pick up another tube and read:

(6)   Hold at least 12 inches from palm and spray liberally

Quite reasonably, you assume it's a skin moisturiser and apply it to your hands, until you notice in the corner of your eye an exotic potted plant and realize that the lotion is for getting that extra-shiny look on indoor palm fronds. The writer of the instructions clearly intended one meaning, but temporarily you interpreted quite another. The 'meaning is use' theory fails, since although a word (a homonymous word form) can have two meanings, a *meaning* can't have two meanings, by definition!

This is perhaps a little unfair, I suppose, since a meaning-is-use account would require the communicative event to be *successful*. But if we define success here as a linguistic exchange which results, in part, in the activation of the *same* concept(s) in the minds of speaker and hearer, then language will rarely achieve it, even when used between inseparable identical twins. This is especially true of writing, when shared context can often be minimal. Readers are seldom in the same physical location as the writer at the time of writing, and they often approach the text from within vastly different contexts (see Chapters 8 and 10).

Even concrete physical objects for which there are unambiguous words will provoke trouble, as A. S. Byatt makes abundantly clear in this passage from her novel *Still Life*. The writer Alexander, working on a project about Van Gogh, is musing on the difficulties of communicating in words the 'plumness' of a particular plum:

A writer aiming for unadorned immediacy might say a plum [. . .], and by naming [it] evoke in every reader's mind a different plum, a dull tomato-and-green speckled Victoria, a yellow-buff globular plum, a tight, black-purple damson. If he wishes to share a vision of a specific plum he must exclude and evoke: a matte, oval, purple-black plum, with a pronounced cleft.

You may use the word 'bloom' for the haze on this plum, and it will call up in the mind of any competent reader the idea that the plum is glistening, overlaid with a matte softness. You may talk about the firm texture of the flesh, and these words will not be metaphors, bloom and flesh, as the earlier 'cleft' was certainly not a metaphor but a description of a grown declivity. But you cannot exclude from the busy automatically connecting mind possible metaphors, human flesh for fruit flesh, flower bloom, skin bloom, bloom of bright youth for this powdery haze, human clefts, declivities, cleavages for that plain noun.

Which all leads us to the inevitable conclusion that we must store word forms with permanent word meanings attached, such that when we encounter them in situations of use we have a basis for employing the context to get as close as possible to the original concept the speaker or writer intends. The meanings stored must, of course, be as free as possible of contextually-supplied elements, otherwise we would be lost when context was absent or ambiguous. There are therefore two components to word meaning: the part that is stored permanently in our minds, and the part that is supplied by the context in which the word is used.

Core meanings

So when we're asleep at night, with our grammar turned off and our lexicon dormant, what is the nature of our knowledge of the ways we can use the word *body*? Is it the core meaning, the *essence* of the word, that sense of 'abstract mass' that we distilled from the metaphorical extensions it has undergone? If so, this would suggest that we can break down word meanings into parts, some of which may be more central than others (and also that the basis for metaphor could be part of our unconscious linguistic knowledge, and not just an epiphenomenon of conscious linguistic belief). This does seem reasonable for words with more transparent meanings, like *cow* or *gas*, and is the way dictionaries often approach the problem of meaning. Included in the core meaning of *cow* might be elements like {MATURE, FEMALE, BOVINE} and for *gas* the elements {NONSOLID, FORMLESS}. This would also allow us to account for our ability to group words into families, which themselves can be named, as in hypernyms like *fish*, which names things sharing the core meaning elements {COLD-BLOODED, AQUATIC, VERTEBRATE, WITH-GILLS, WITH-SCALES}. Similarly, we can class together words like *man, boy, father, uncle, pimp, pope,* and *prince* because they share the meaning elements {HUMAN, MALE}.

An immediate problem here, however, is that 'NONSOLID',

'AQUATIC', 'MALE', etc. are patently words themselves, and so have their *own* meanings. We are thus thrust back unceremoniously onto the horns of the original Language Spell dilemma: the main way we gain conscious access to linguistic meaning is through language, i.e. precisely the linguistic meaning we're trying to gain access to. The human mental lexicon is not the same as a printed dictionary, providing meanings for words in terms of the words it's providing meanings for. In the human mind there has to be an end point, a point where language stops and meaning starts.

How might these 'core meaning elements' or 'lexical essences' be represented in the mind? We know they can't be visual images, since many words represent abstract concepts that can't be seen, and even concrete things with the same name can differ enormously (what image would we store for *furniture* such that it covered glass-topped coffee table, comfy old sofa, elegant writing bureau and Scandinavian pine bookcase?). Furthermore, a stored image in the mind is as much a *representation* of something as a word is. Unlike a word, a visual image is not an arbitrary representation, but it is still not the same thing as what it depicts (as Magritte's paintings wittily attest). A picture of a plum is not a plum, it's a picture. There is no miniature person ('homunculus') in our brains looking at the images we have stored there and telling us what they are images of. But maybe this is a clue. Maybe the 'meaning' of a mentally represented visual image (our knowledge of what it's an image of) is the same thing as the 'meaning' of a word (our knowledge of what it's the word for)? The Language Spell makes this seem a surprising conclusion, as Byatt's character Alexander again perceptively observes, as he compares a painting of a plum with a linguistic description of one:

> We know that paint is not plum flesh. We do not know with the same certainty that our language does not simply, mimetically, coincide with our world. There was a cultural shock when painters shifted their attention from imitating apples to describing the nature of vision, paint, canvas. But the nausea Jean Paul Sartre felt on discovering that he could not, with language, adequately describe a chestnut tree root is a shock of another kind.

Up to now, the Language Spell has prevented us from getting very far when we start with the word form and try to follow it into the mind to see what's attached at the other end. So let's change perspective and look out from the mind to the actual physical world beyond, using as lenses the word forms in the mental lexicon and the images in our mental picture gallery. Don't forget that the external world happens to contain, among many other things, potential interlocutors with their own minds and the meanings they store there: How can words and images possibly bridge the chasm between us?

Meanings and concepts

In the darkest depths of our brooding minds, we all have knowledge of things for which there are no names. ... But don't worry, we don't need to unearth hidden secrets and fears to illustrate the point. Here are some decidedly unspooky examples. The vast majority of us have no name for the rolls of plastic which stop our shoe laces from fraying at the ends (Lisa Hayes, my assiduous research assistant, informs me that they are called *aglets*). To my knowledge, there is no name for the pesky nodes of plastic which are supposed to hold a CD in place in its case but all too often become detached and fall out, together with the disk, when the case is opened. Iris Murdoch's character Charles in *The Sea, The Sea* asks 'Is there any language in which there is a word for that tender runnel that joins the mouth and the nose?' This is significant. We know these things exist, but we don't necessarily have names for them. In a sense, they are word meanings without word forms, *half* of the lexical equation.

Even more significant, however, are bits of knowledge that not only lack names, but that we can't even describe using circumlocution or by painting a picture, and for which coining a new word (a **neologism**) wouldn't help. We probably all know the first four notes of Beethoven's Fifth or the theme music from *The Godfather*. We know what a rose smells like, or burning toast. We know what it feels like to love someone (or hate them), to feel sad (or deliriously happy). Music, odour and emotion are all represented in our minds, and we can 'think' them without invoking our faculties of language and vision: indeed, doing so would not do us much good at all, since the concepts in question are virtually *unrepresentable* in terms of language or vision. Of course we can attempt to *evoke* them, in painting or sculpture for example, or to describe them in sentences and well-chosen words, but we will never be able to conventionally represent them in the same way that the word *cat* or a remembered visual image of a cat neatly represents our concept of the domestic feline. Word meanings, then, are concepts for which we happen to have word forms, just as images represent concepts that we happen to be able to see.

Language and thought

This 'conceptualist' view of meaning, presented most coherently in the work of the linguist Ray Jackendoff, seems to suggest that another of our folk linguistic beliefs is a spurious effect of the Language Spell. Most people tend to assume that they think in language, that thought is just silent speech. The behaviourist psychologist John B. Watson believed that 'thought processes are really motor habits in the larynx'! This is perhaps the most extreme statement to the effect that language and thought are identical. A weaker version would hold that in the mind (which is in the brain, not the neck) we think using our linguistic system, i.e. in words and sentences, but *not* in speech (i.e. muscular gestures in the lungs and vocal tract). Proof (as though it were really needed) has been provided in experiments where subjects under the effects of muscle-paralysing drugs (like *curare*) were found to be able to think without any impediment.

As we saw in Chapter 1, George Orwell argued that language can confine our thoughts, by imposing a single way of talking about the world, and thus, a single way of thinking about it. How far this rather depressing claim might turn out to be true depends in large part on the extent to which we 'think in language'. So, we need to ask some pretty basic questions:

- Do we have more complicated minds than other species because we think using our large vocabularies and sophisticated ways of combining words?
- Are we circumscribed in the way we think about the world by the expressive power of the particular language we acquired as infants?

Well, we *can* think in language and often do, but then it is a *conscious* process – indeed all conscious thought (i.e. when we are thinking about thinking) seems to be linguistically modulated, hence our impression that we *always* think in language. So, although language is often used as a tool of conscious introspection (as a channel for thinking about thinking), the answer to these questions appears to be *no*. In fact, many cognitive scientists have argued that we have an internal 'second' language, the 'language of thought,' often referred to as **mentalese**, which is shared by all human beings, and although it may be influenced to a greater or lesser degree by the 'linguistic' language we speak and understand, it is not the same thing. The evidence for this separation is strong, if not immediately obvious.

First, recall those times when you have had a thought or meaning in your mind, clear as crystal, but have not been able to access the linguistic expression (word or string of words) to communicate it to an interlocutor. This absence of linguistic expression can be temporary, as in the so-called 'tip-of-the-tongue' phenomenon, when you know what you want to say but just can't find the word for it, showing some sort of obstruction in the connections between thought (word meaning) and language (word form). Or it can be permanent, when you never learned the word for a particular concept, or the language itself doesn't provide the equipment necessary for talking about it. For example, I have knowledge (i.e. permanent thoughts) about many of the trees to be found in an English forest, in that I can recognize leaf shapes, branch structure, colour variation, etc. and can make gross divisions such as deciduous versus coniferous, sapling versus fully-grown, etc. I even have feelings (like Tolkien) about which trees appear evil, and which benevolent. What I cannot do, however, is give the conventional English *name* to more than a handful of tree types (like *oak*, *birch*, *willow*, and *poplar*), and I can't satisfactorily express the differences between the others, even through extensive circumlocution. But this lack of *linguistic* expressivity does not truly reflect my (albeit limited) knowledge of trees: I still have tree knowledge, in the form of disembodied thoughts in mentalese – or, put more simply, I (like Sartre) know more about trees than I can say.

Often it is the language itself which is restricted, rather than an individual speaker's knowledge of vocabulary. There's the problem of 'lexical gaps' like the un-nameable plastic CD spindles and facial runnels. And there's the problem of 'non-lexical concepts': as I have already suggested, most of us would have no trouble recalling exactly how we felt the last time we experienced a deep emotional state (love, hatred, joy, bitterness, rage, etc.), and yet none of us would conceptualize this state of mind using the tools provided by human language. Similarly, faith, music, memories of flavours, textures and sounds, together with a host of other complex thoughts and concepts, are not adequately representable using the linguistic system. And yet we have no problem in thinking them. Patently, on the basis of anecdotal evidence such as this, language would seem to be uninvolved in large areas of our mental life, thus demonstrating that language cannot be the same thing as thought.

More rigorous evidence for the separation between language and thought, and thus for the separate existence of mentalese, is forthcoming from studies of populations other than normally functioning monolingual human adults. The most obvious case, perhaps, is that of very young children, who can perform quite complex mental feats before they utter their first words. They have a basic conceptualization of addition and subtraction by the age of five months, they have the animate/inanimate distinction by the age of one, and can tell the difference between artificial and natural objects by the time they go to kindergarten. Clearly, infants are not thoughtless zombies before they learn their language: indeed, maybe the greatest mental feat of all times is mastery of that first language, and yet by definition it occurs without the assistance of a full lexicon and a mature syntax. Similarly, non-human animals can think without the benefit of language, with many species displaying complex mental capacities. And humans with acquired or inherited language impairments (aphasics), often show perfectly healthy and intact mental life outside the realm of language (see Chapter 11). Finally, and closer to home for language teachers and translators reading this, we know that learning a second language does not lead to schizophrenia: even balanced bilinguals think of what they want to say only once, regardless of which language they may choose to express themselves in for external reasons.

The fact that we all do think of what we want to say prior to saying it shows the weakness of the 'thought = language' argument. Psycholinguists studying the production and comprehension of language have shown that speaking involves the encoding of a message from mentalese into language, and that listening involves the reverse (i.e. decoding of language into mentalese). Listeners, for example, have been shown to be unable to accurately recall the form of a sentence they have heard only a minute or two before, but to be spot-on when asked to report the *information* expressed. Studies of speakers, meanwhile, have yielded extensive collections of speech errors ('slips of the tongue' like saying *bobby* for *body*, or *toes* for *fingers*), where the wrong word is chosen purely because an entry in the mental dictionary is somehow misread or mistargeted. If thought is performed *in* language, then the former type of evidence is unexpected: the precise words used and their syntactic arrangements should be *identical with* the thoughts expressed, and should not fade any more rapidly than the meaning of the utterance. In the second case, if thoughts *are* the words that label them, then production of the 'wrong word' would imply the wrong initial thought, and in the absence of an Orwellian 'Thought Police', such an idea remains highly bizarre, if not totally meaningless.

Language as a sixth sense

The evidence for mentalese, the 'language of thought', is strong. In order to understand the nature of mentalese and to conceptualize it as distinct from language, it is useful to think of language as a 'sixth sense', along with vision, hearing, smell, touch and taste. The psychologist Jerry Fodor resurrected the term **faculties** for these sensory abilities, and claimed that they (together with some others) constitute **input systems**, which serve to 'translate' information from outside in the world into mentalese, so that we can think about them. For example, a prelinguistic infant can think about a novel object that she can see, smell, touch and taste, such as an egg, without being able to say anything about it, or understand anything said about it. Infants construct their primary knowledge of the world in this way, and adults, throughout their lives, learn about and reflect on the world (i.e. build an understanding of it) using information delivered by the entire battery of input systems. Language can thus be seen as one more, very special, channel through which we build memory representations of what we perceive in our minds as reality (and unreality).

Figure 1 provides a (rather frightening-looking) schematic representation of the major human input systems, how they relate to each other, and how they connect the outside world, via physical organs, to the inner mental sanctuary of **conceptual systems**. At the bottom of the figure is the outside world, containing objects that we can perceive with the five senses. Among the perceivable objects are solid three-dimensional entities, such as eggs (... which I chose for their multisensory status: they have a unique feel and shape, let off a dreadful smell when they're rotten, make a distinctive sound when they're cracked and fried, and taste pretty good in a Spanish Tortilla). The word *egg* printed in a recipe book and the word *egg* spoken by a grocer are very different objects (the former is a pattern of light and the latter a noise). And yet these three objects in the world – the egg itself, and the written and spoken words – can, on perception by human beings, lead us to recognize the single concept of 'egg' in the mind. For the senses to do their job of identifying concepts, they need input from physical organs which can detect different kinds of energy patterns in the environment: that's why we've evolved eyes and ears, an aroma-sensitive nose, touch-sensitive cells in the skin (especially on the fingertips) and taste buds in the mouth. In the figure, the route taken from incoming energy patterns to decodification by the senses is indicated by dotted lines.

The external triggering of our internal 'egg' concept can happen only on the basis of input from one of the five senses. We must remember that until the auditory input system (our sense of hearing) identifies the acoustic input corresponding to *egg* as linguistically

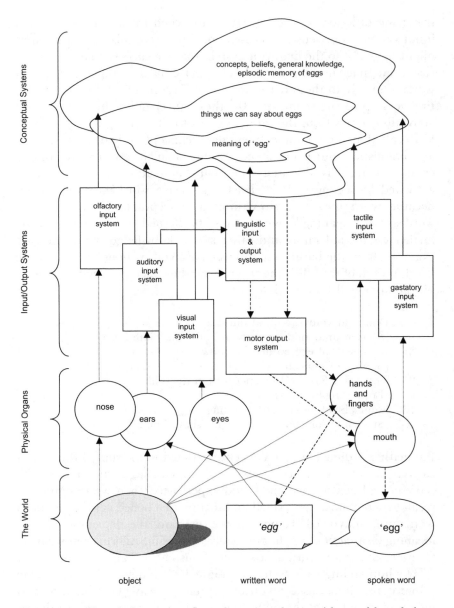

Figure 1 How information flows between the outside world and the human mind

relevant (i.e. as speech and not just a hiccup), the sound sequence has the same sensory status as the sound of the egg cracking or frying in a pan (i.e. they're both noises). The same goes for the photic (light) energy from the black lines on a white background that correspond to the string of letters 'e', 'g', 'g'. It's only when the auditory or visual input systems (our senses of hearing or sight) recognize that the input might be useful to the linguistic system that we can say that we have a case of language use. But once that happens, the linguistic input system works similarly to the other senses, decoding the input and activating the corresponding concept. In the figure, solid lines represent activation routes from the input systems to the conceptual systems.

Recall that the common 'mentalese' concept activated by sensory and linguistic input is not a picture, nor a smell, nor a word: in our example here, it is ultimately the neural activation pattern uniquely activated by 'eggness'. It is clearly not just a word meaning, partly because word meanings store limited conceptual information (the word's 'core meaning'), which must be fleshed out in actuality by further contextual input and other stored knowledge (as in the *body* examples from the bathroom, discussed above). Although it's the same word in each of the following utterances, the concept of 'egg' activated by each one will be very different:

(7)   Don't eat your egg all at once!
       [Spoken to a child by a parent, of a chocolate Easter egg.]
(8)   Etienne's got egg on her face now!
       [Spoken of someone who just made a fool of herself.]
(9)   The egg is fertilized by sperm from the male.
       [From a biology textbook.]
(10)   Knut's head looks just like a huge egg.
       [Spoken of someone who has just shaved off all his hair.]

But neither is the whole egg concept restricted to the sum of things you can *say* about eggs, since, as we've seen, language cannot faithfully represent all of what we know and experience: when we recognize or recall the combined taste, smell and texture of a boiled egg at breakfast, words are uninvolved. Hence, in the diagram, the depiction of word meaning as a *subset* of the linguistically expressible information we have for eggs, and this in turn as a subset of our entire 'egg database'.

The human linguistic system is unique for a number of reasons. One is that it also functions as an output system – a way of getting intended information out from the mind and into the external world, so that it can be picked up by potential hearers and readers who dwell there. (If we emit smells, it doesn't happen via the nose, and if we make a sound, it doesn't come out of our ears.) For this reason, I have included the motor output system in the diagram, since it's only through muscular contractions in the arms, hands and vocal tract that we can produce spoken, written or signed language.

The meaning of a word, then, can be seen as the *concept*, encoded in mentalese, with which the word form is conventionally associated. The meaning of the linguistic string *egg*, for example, is part of the mentalese concept which also allows us to recognize an egg when we see one, smell one when it's rotten, or hear one flapping in a frying pan. The meaning of the word is a permanent thought in long-term memory, accessed by any of the input systems separately or together, depending, in this case, on whether we see a photo of an egg (yielding visual input), break open a rotten one by accident (visual, olfactory and tactile), break it open in the dark (olfactory and tactile only), or encounter the spoken or written word form (i.e. linguistic input only).

Abstract words again

Now what about abstract words? Word forms like *lesson*, *cruelty* or *syntax* do not have unique visual images associated with them, nor representations of what they feel like, or how they smell, taste or sound. Since they generally lack support from the other input systems, abstract words tend to have 'harder' meanings: studies by psycholinguists have shown them to be more difficult to understand, slower to be recalled from memory, and learnt later than concrete words by children. This last point is particularly interesting. You might think it a relatively straightforward job for children to learn words like *dog*, *apple* and *chair*, since adults and older kids can point at them, providing visual evidence for the meaning to be associated with the new word form (though we'll see in the next chapter that the Spell makes even this look much easier than it is). For concrete words, there's often a whole host of sensory information to help children establish the right meanings for the phoneme strings they derive from the acoustic input around them: they can stroke the dog and hear it bark; they can shine apples on their sweaters, hear them crunch as they sink their teeth into them and taste their juices; they can sit on chairs, hide underneath them, or hurt their toes when they stub them against a leg ... Not so with *lessons*, *cruelty* and *syntax*. (Indeed, one would hope that children could remain blissfully unaware of all these concepts for as long as possible.)

How, then, do we acquire the meanings of abstract words? Well, whether the concept develops first and then a linguistic label gets attached, or we hear an abstract word and then have to construct a new concept for it, it's clear that the five senses are not going to be of much help. If we're not born already knowing the concept, and can't easily infer it from existing knowledge, then that leaves only one other possibility: that the form-meaning relation must be established on the basis of what we are *told* or understand from what we *hear* from utterances in particular contexts, i.e. principally through *linguistic* input. We can begin to see, therefore, why concrete words are 'easier' (because they label things we can see with our own eyes) and why abstract words are 'harder' (because we have to rely on sociocultural convention, acquired largely through language). A Berber in North Africa and an Inuit in Alaska have the same sensory input systems, seeing colours, shapes, edges and sizes of three-dimensional objects the same way. They also appear to categorize objects in universal ways. But they speak different languages, and different languages can express different aspects of conceptual systems in different ways. It follows from this, therefore, that across languages, concrete words should have better translation equivalents than abstract words, since the former rely to a greater extent on universally available, external cues, whereas the latter are mediated more by the expressive resources of the language one happens to speak. I'm sure that translators reading will broadly concur with this intuition.

Evidence from bilinguals

The prediction turns out to be well supported in research on how bilinguals manage words in their two languages. Psycholinguists have devised ingenious ways of exploring how words might be connected up with each other in the minds of speakers of more than one language. There are at least three possibilities for words perceived to be translation equivalents, as described in the 1950s by Uriel Weinreich, and illustrated in Figure 2.

In the **compound** type of representation, the word forms from languages 'a' and 'b' share an identical meaning, whereas in the **coordinate** representation, the translation equivalents in the two languages are connected to separate, potentially overlapping concepts. In the third kind, as suggested by the term **subordinate**, the word form in language 'b' is connected with the word form in language 'a', and thence only indirectly with *its* meaning representation. The subordinate case has been shown to hold for incipient bilinguals (second language learners), who still rely on their first language (L1) to store and use words in the language they are learning (L2). More balanced bilinguals, i.e. learners who have attained more autonomous control over their L2, or speakers who acquired two languages more or less simultaneously, as a natural process in infancy, are likely to have a greater number of compound or coordinate lexical representations.

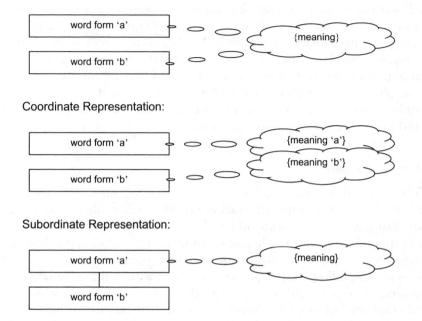

Figure 2 Three possibilities for the representation of translation equivalents in bilinguals

As we have noted, bilinguals are not schizophrenic, so it would be absurd to imagine that they have two completely separate, coordinate meaning representations for the same concept, just because they have two different ways of labelling it linguistically (i.e. a different word in each of their two languages). When the translation equivalents are not identical, however, i.e. when they label slightly different aspects of a concept, then we can imagine coordinate representations which closely overlap in conceptual space. Take the word *Christmas*, for example, and its Spanish translation *Navidad*. The festive season labelled by these two words is the same, in that it occurs in December, celebrates (for Christian believers) the birth of Christ, is characterized by gift-giving, feasting and self-indulgence, decorations and carol-singing. But there are clearly cultural differences too: for *Navidad* the main celebration is on the evening of 24 December, not 25 December, and gifts are brought by the three kings on 6 January, not by Santa Claus on Christmas Day.

A tree for English-speakers, on the other hand, is much the same as a tree for Spanish-speakers. Although the 'prototypical' tree might not be the same for an English-speaking Londoner and a Spanish-speaking Majorcan, it's equally true that an Australian's ideal tree will differ from a New Yorker's, despite their common English mother tongue. So too, of course, for an Asturian and a Bogotan, despite their shared *lengua materna*. It is what people see around them, not how it is talked about, that accounts for any superficial difference in prototypical concrete objects. Notice, then, a correlation between concrete words and compound representations on the one hand, and abstract words and overlapping coordinate representations on the other.

Priming experiments

The correlation is not absolute, of course, but it is enough to show up in psycholinguistic experimentation on bilingual speakers, conducted by Annette de Groot and others. One technique used in dozens of experiments, on various language combinations, and in many different laboratories, is called **priming**. In one version of this kind of experiment, bilingual speakers are presented with strings of letters on a computer screen, and have to decide as fast as they possibly can whether the letters spell a word in one of their languages. The letter strings used are actual words, like *tree* in English or *plátano* ('banana') in Spanish; or they are *nonwords*: potential word forms that have gone unused in the language, like *pree* in English, or *clátano* in Spanish. In order to know whether the letter string is a word in your language, you need to look it up in your mental lexicon (if it's there, it's a word; if it's not, it's not). The long-suffering participants in these experiments are presented with hundreds of words and nonwords, in random order, and for each one they have to press a button marked 'YES' for a real word or 'NO' for a nonword, as fast as possible, like a reflex test. The experimenter uses a sophisticated chronometer to see how long it takes for participants to look up the words in their mental lexicon and then respond. The experiment is repeated on maybe 40 or 50 speakers, and then the results (recorded in milliseconds, or thousandths of a second) are crunched through the computer to give estimations of the average **recognition time** for each word. This has proved to be a very reliable way of finding out how long it takes people to recognize different kinds of words, and it's accurate down to tenths of a second.

Then the fun starts. The participants are aware of only the individual letter strings, one on each session, but the crafty researchers have hidden a second letter string before the first, such that it appears for a fraction of a second, too little time for the participants to be consciously aware of it. (Just like subliminal advertising, but surely more ethical, since the participants are informed volunteers.) Now we're getting closer to the point of it all. For the characteristics of the hidden word (the 'prime') can be varied to see whether it has an effect on the recognition time for the following 'target' word (the one consciously seen and responded to by the participant). In one interesting variation on this experimental theme, bilinguals are shown target words in one of their languages, primed by translation equivalents from the other language in hidden mode. The studies show that primes for concrete words (e.g. *árbol* for *tree* in Spanish/ English bilinguals) result in faster recognition times than primes for abstract words (like *Navidad* for *Christmas*, or more usually common nouns like *creencia* for *belief*).

How do we interpret these findings? Why should subliminal exposure to a concrete word in one of your languages help you recognize its equivalent in your other language, faster than pairs of abstract words? To answer this question, we need to take a trip along the nerve fibres that carry messages from our visual input system to our linguistic input system, and thence to conceptual systems.

The story starts with light energy from the letters on the computer screen hitting the retina and stimulating the optical nerve. The patterns received are recognized as linguistically significant, and are shunted off for special processing in the linguistic input system. If the priming word is *árbol*, then even if you're not consciously aware of having seen it, the corresponding orthographic word form stored in your lexicon will be activated by the incoming signal from the visual system, and it in turn will activate the associated concept in conceptual systems. Activation of elements in memory is not like an on/off switch, but more like the warming up and cooling down of an oven. So when the target word *tree* is seen just after the subliminal presentation of *árbol*, it first activates its own represented word form in the lexicon (i.e. gets its shape recognized), and then finds that its meaning (identical with that of *árbol*) has already been activated by the prior presentation of the prime. It's like switching off the oven after roasting your joint of beef, and then remembering just after that you wanted Yorkshire puddings or roasted parsnips: the oven will still be at a high temperature and it won't take as long to heat up a second time.

Hence for Spanish-English bilinguals, *tree* will be faster to recognize when preceded by *árbol* than when it's preceded by nothing, or an unrelated word like *hombre*, because it still maintains high levels of activation from the priming event. The case with *creencia* and *belief* is similar, but the effect is attenuated. If you work in a restaurant and roast your beef in one of a bank of ovens, the oven next door to yours will still heat up faster for the puddings or parsnips if yours has been on full power for a few hours, but not as fast as if you'd thrown them into the *same* oven. This is essentially the difference between compound representations (for concrete words) and coordinate representations (for abstract words). What we are seeing, then, is that abstract words differ from concrete words in the ways in which they are acquired and the variability of their meanings across cultures, because they are unanchored in sensory perceptual experience.

Context again

So far, we've been trying to grapple with the outrageously difficult notions of the meanings of isolated words. This is an important first step in breaking the spell of lexical semantics, since we *do* store and carry around word meanings in our heads even when we're not using them. But when we actually put them to use in communicative scenarios, then all sorts of other inputs, outputs and knowledge bases have to get involved. Take our example word form *body* again. One way to see how it gets deployed in real linguistic contexts is to consult a **concordancer**, a computer program which is used to scan massive files of real text and speech collected from different genres of use (a **corpus**) for an input word form, and yield as output a list of all instances found, with part of the preceding and following context. One of the most important corpora of English is the COBUILD corpus, with 45 million words. Figure 3 is a random sample concordance of 40 items for the word form *body*.

The bits of surrounding context for the word form *body* in Figure 3 show that it's being used with at least four major core meanings: (a) 'human body'; (b) 'organization, institution, group'; (c) 'thickness, substance' (in example 31); and (d) 'main part of vehicle'. Inspection of the contexts, however, reveals lots of different shades of meaning that are recoverable on the fly from conceptual systems, but do not need to be (and possibly can't be) permanently linked to the word's entry in the mental lexicon. The most common core meaning in the sample is 'human body', but in many different senses. Here are some of them:

- 'torso' (example 4);
- 'physical well-being' (example 6);
- 'whole physical mass' (examples 8 and 9);
- 'corpse' (examples 10 and 18);
- 'sexual functions' (examples 16 and 23);
- 'external physical image' (examples 25 and 33);
- 'physical system' (examples 22 and 39).

1.	...letters he wrote with his whole	body.	In enlightenment, the knower and...
2.	...in the IRB to be the global governing	body.	If we don't, I fear that...
3.	...of routes, we've replaced some wide-	body	aircraft with narrow-body aircraft...
4.	...elsewhere were beaten around the	body	and shoulders with truncheons. A...
5.	...him, he abruptly saw her slender	body	as a shaft of granite, hard and cold...
6.	...assumes that others are minding her	body	as closely as she is minding it...
7.	...Franjo Seper, accepted the new	body	because the Holy Father wanted it. ...
8.	...with his hands, sank into a seat; his	body	began to tremble. He was suffering, ...
9.	...Yoga, stretching and energizing the	body,	calming and focusing the mind, ...
10.	...look at the bedrooms when she saw the	body	dangling through the trap door to...
11.	...your silhouette and knowing your	body	enough to flatter its good points. ...
12.	...can only have been possible if his	body	had first been dehydrated by a warm...
13.	...with Haig as Grand President (the	body	has since become the British...
14.	...so far the General Synod - the	body	in the Church which decides these...
15.	...all the time watching my eyes. His	body	is so thick, his skin cool and moist...
16.	...adolescence. Learning about one's	body	occurs not only when teenagers are...
17.	...they were a closely knit, experienced	body	of 60 battle-hardened men, most of...
18.	...body; Susan Griffiths. THE	body	of Susan Griffiths, 31, whose BMW...
19.	...know if the blood came from their own	body	or from someone else. During each...
20.	...Harshly, ironically, it was about the	body	parts of a man who goes into...
21.	...in fact use thicker gauge metal for	body	pressings than other manufacturers-...
22.	...affect our experience of the	body's	natural processes. We need also to...
23.	...his ear, That she repeals him for her	body's	lust; And by how much she strives...
24.	...intensity of exercise. Shape your	Body:	Shape your Life whilst you are...
25.	...encourage such intimacies. It was his	body	she cared for, nothing else. He...
26.	...screens and newspapers. Not the	Body	Shop. For Ms Roddick, a...
27.	...reduces tension in all parts of the	body,	so you are more responsive and...
28.	...later when the gray Chrysler K car--a	body	style so bland as to be noticeable--...
29.	...the edge of the bed beside his still	body	the gentle man who had been her...
30.	...Sexual Development in Boys Using the	Body:	The Effects of Physical Changes on...
31.	...by breaking down clay and adding	body	to light soils. At the same time it...
32.	...Scotland's capital has had a single	body	to represent it for 20 years. The...
33.	...you to let go of anger toward your	body,	to forget what you can't change and...
34.	...the entire musculature of the	body."	Tomatis draws a sharp distinction...
35.	...dose which irradiates the whole	body	uniformly, as determined using film...
36.	...left knee slightly and shift your	body	weight to your left foot. At the...
37.	...and then shot against Beeney's	body	when McAllister slipped, leaving him...
38.	...Advisory Service -- an independent	body	which receives government money says...
39.	...in the biochemical balance of the	body	which blurs the brain function, such...
40.	...in your feet, various organs of your	body	will respond, helping to reduce...

Figure 3 Random 40-token sample concordance for *body* from the COBUILD corpus

In the concordance, all we get in the way of context is a few words on either side. And already the set of full meanings of this apparently straightforward 'word' is multiplying. Imagine now that we had the entire concordance for *body* from the 45 million word COBUILD corpus, then for all the uses of the word in the entire English-speaking world from the last century. Then at least one complete sentence on either side of the word. Then the whole text of which the sentences form part. Then information about the purpose of each text, the characteristics of the audience and their relationship(s) with the writer or speaker, encyclopaedic knowledge of the subject matter, videotape of the circumstances of use, ... That's an awful lot of context, which would probably yield a mind-boggling number of different word-senses. And yet the human language faculty ensures that our knowledge of core word meanings is seamlessly integrated into contexts of use as the word forms are being encountered, and without us being aware of the problem. We'll take a look at how this happens in a little more depth in Chapter 7, where we see what happens when words are deployed in sentences and whole texts.

So what is a word?

We have seen that the traditional concept of a word as simply a name for a thing does not help us to break this part of the Language Spell. To say that it is a stored sequence of phonemes or letters linked to a core conceptual representation may be a better approach and is true in most cases, but not all (what does *of* mean in *Think of a number?*), and even then the definition gets us into problems. As we have seen, one 'word' might be linked to more than one concept, and vice versa: like *furniture*, it may refer to a category of concepts of the same 'type'; like *body*, it can refer to a group of concepts which share some more tenuous properties; or like *date*, it can be used to refer to completely unrelated concepts. What is it that holds in place the fluid relationship between words and things when we use them, saving us from utter confusion in our daily round of conversations and text events? What *is* a word, after all?

Words as lexical entries

Our use of the word *word* is at the root of the problem, and continues to frustrate our attempts to understand human lexical competence. You may have noticed that this is yet another case in which the Language Spell has unwelcome effects on the progress of linguistic science, by leading us unwittingly to assume that there is a unitary *thing*, which the word *word* names. Let's go back to basics for a moment. Many people, if asked, would say that a word is a name for something, in line with our discussion in previous sections. Others, quite reasonably, might focus on the form end, and report that a word is a sequence of letters surrounded by spaces on a printed page or computer screen. We see in these definitions the traditional notion of a word as a pairing of a symbol (a string of graphic shapes) which stands for (or represents) something else. Ferdinand de Saussure, one of the founders of modern linguistics, used the metaphor of a coin to illustrate this notion, with one side representing the form of the word (the signifier) and the other its meaning (what is signified).

When we briefly discussed modalities of language expression back in

Chapter 1, I argued that speech and text are the external manifestations of language, which itself exists uniquely in human minds. A sequence of printed letters, therefore, is not a word in the way linguists would wish to understand the notion: rather, it is a complex visual array existing in the external world, i.e. *outside language*. To become a word, the array must be perceived by the human visual apparatus (the eye, optical nerves and the input system wired into neural networks in the brain's occipital lobe) and then matched with a stored representation (a 'sign') in the lexicon. So *kfhrwoladwi* and *qjdqwi*, although sequences of letters surrounded by spaces, do not represent words, since they match nothing in our lexicons and are disallowed by our phonologies. So far, so good. Now how about the following forms?

- *hender*
- *empyema*

Well, they look more like words, especially the first one, but for most English speakers they have no matching entry in the lexicon, so should be ruled out. In fact, *hender* doesn't exist in anyone's lexicon, because I made it up, although it is pronounceable and follows English spelling patterns (it's a nonword). *Empyema* looks very odd, and yet will be recognized (i.e. successfully matched) by some, because it is a medical term for a collection of pus in the lung (sorry for the unsavoury example). So what is a 'word' for one person may not be a 'word' for another, and some 'words' seem more 'wordlike' than others.

Grammatical information

What makes *hender* more English-like than *empyema* is not only its resemblance to other known English words (e.g. *fender* and *hinder*), but also the fact that it ends in two phonemes which are used in other English words to build one word from another: see Chapter 6. The **suffix** form *-er* makes comparative adjectives from their simple forms (*pale-paler*, *slow-slower*) and also nouns with an 'agent' meaning from verbs (*ride-rider*, *farm-farmer*). So *hender* could refer to someone who *hends* or is more *hend* than his peers – if we only knew what *hend* meant. What's important here is that graphic (or acoustic) stimuli which don't match any full entry in our lexicons might still evoke partial recognition or a feeling of familiarity, and this might even (as in the case of the *-er* on *hender*) lead us to recognize a specific part of speech, like an adjective or noun. This reminds us that words are not just

ken signs connected to meanings, but also that they have
properties, such that some words behave as nouns, some
: as adjectives, etc. And some behave as all three:

now Bilbo's hair was beginning to **grey**   (verb)
he sky above Weathertop was ominously **grey**   (adjective)
(c)   ı he **grey** of Gandalf's beard had turned to white   (noun)

I call this grammatical information a word's '**frame**', because it tells
us where it can be deployed in sentences. In Chapter 7 we'll take a
closer look at the nature of parts of speech and the roles words can play
in sentences, but in the meantime, let's just look at a few examples to
explain the use of the term 'frame' here. The word *fun* is used only as a
noun by many speakers of English, appearing in frames such as the
following:

(12) (a) We had a lot of ___ at the Millennium party.
(b) Reading Chomsky is not my idea of ___.

Many, especially young Americans, use it as an adjective, as in:

(13) (a) It was really ___ to stay with you.
(b) We'd've had a ___-er time at Disneyland.

My English as a Foreign Language (EFL) students, on the other hand,
come up with sentences like the following:

(14) (a) We went to Acapulco to ___ on the beach.
(b) They wanted to ___ all night.

In (14) the word is obviously being used as a verb, and this is not
surprising, since the same concept is labelled in Spanish by a verb
(*divertirse*). If my students still employ subordinate lexical representations for English as their L2, then they'll attach the word form *fun* to
their lexical entry for *divertirse*, using it in the latter's frame, hence the
sentences in (14). The concept of 'fun' is not inherently, necessarily,
either nominal, or adjectival, or verbal (just as we saw with 'grey'), so
how it is used in a particular language will need to be specified in the
mental lexicon, along with its pronunciation and spelling.

A second example from English and Spanish should further clarify
why a word's 'frame' needs to be taken into account as well as its
form and meaning. In English, the word *put* must be followed by an
object (telling us what is put) and a phrase with a preposition like *in*,

on, or *under* (to tell us where it's put). The Spanish translation equivalent is the verb *poner*, and yet it does not always have to include the prepositional information, especially when the 'putting' is metaphorical. Hence, my Mexican EFL students can write:

(15) (a) She put some music
      (b) I'll put an example to show what I mean

Although the words mean the same thing, we can see that English *put* appears in the frame '[subject] ___ [object] + [prepositional phrase]', whereas Spanish *poner* has as its frame the simpler '[subject] ___ [object]', with the (implicit) location information understood from context (see Chapter 7).

Finally, within English there are word forms with single meanings which clearly have more than one frame. The word *near*, meaning 'close (to)' behaves as an adjective in (16a), requiring a preposition after it (like '*similar* to Denver', '*happy* about Denver' or '*close* to Denver'), but in (16b) it behaves like a preposition, with a simple noun following it (like '*in* Denver', '*through* Denver', '*above* Denver'):

(16) (a) The house was near to Denver
      (b) The house was near Denver

(We can also use *near* as a verb, as in (17):

(17) After an hour of travelling they neared Denver

But in this case we are adding the core meaning element {MOVE}, so it's not quite equivalent to the meaning of the adjective and preposition.)

Lexical triads

So a 'word' doesn't seem to be a unitary 'thing', nor even a thing with two facets, like a coin, but rather a 'triad' of three things at least: a physically externalizable form (phonological, orthographic for the literate, or signed), a syntactic frame and a meaning. Moreover, these three properties can be shared across different 'words', as we have seen repeatedly in this chapter. Figure 4 represents visually some of the possibilities we've discussed, using rectangles for word forms, ellipses for syntactic frames, and 'thought' clouds for concepts.

Notice how none of the triads correspond to a traditional 'word'. The form and meaning for *near* are shared by two frames. The form *grey* is shared by three frames with almost identical meanings. The

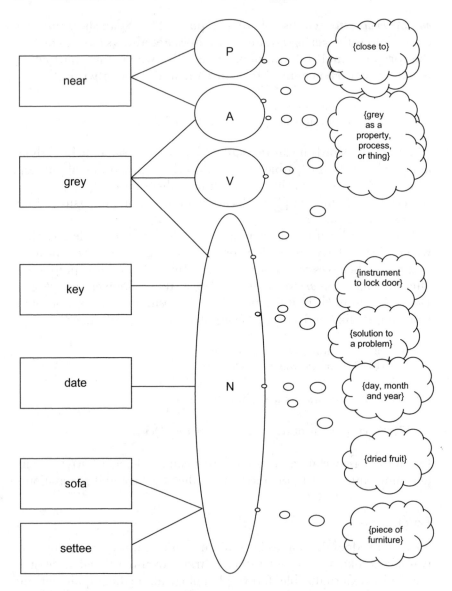

Figure 4 Network of interconnected lexical triads

form *key* is shared by two related, overlapping meanings (polysemy), whereas *date* has two entirely different meanings (homonymy). The concept of a 'sofa' leads to two separate word forms (synonymy). Not one is a unitary triad of form-frame-concept. In fact, *all* the words we know share at least parts of their form, their syntactic behaviour and their meanings with other words.

The three parts of wordhood are distinct, and lexical knowledge does not necessarily always involve a complete triad of all three. Sometimes the words themselves are 'defective', lacking one or more elements of the triad. Sometimes it is individual language users' knowledge of a word that may be incomplete, resulting in partial triads in their lexicons (but not those of others).

Let's look at inherently defective words first. Languages tend to have a 'core vocabulary' of words for common concepts, a stock of some thousands of words which are acquired in infancy and are known by *all* speakers, as full triads. These will include words for common entities (like *food, nose, truth*); processes, events and states (like *cook, rain, stay*); and properties of these (like *red, happily, evil*). Such words provide us with ways to express elements of conceptual systems, and are part of the staggering, potentially infinite, number of nouns, verbs, adjectives and adverbs which together are called **content words** (because they are seen as vessels filled with meaning, in tune with the 'transfer-of-meaning' view of language use).

But every language also has a common, finite set of normally short word forms which perform grammatical, rather than conceptual tasks, like the *of* in *Think of a number*. These are called **function words**, and include (in English) pronouns, articles, auxiliary verbs, question words and some prepositional particles (the *of* in *think of*, the *in* in *result in*, the *up* in *ring up*, etc.). Some do have minimal elements of meaning, of course, like the elements {MASCULINE, SINGULAR} in the pronoun *he*, but by and large they are conceptually empty, serving linguistic purposes only. These little words seem to be all form and frame, but little or no concept: the linguistic two-thirds of the lexical triad. Other words, like *hello, wow*, and *yes*, appear to be word forms with minimal conceptual content *and no syntactic frame*. Finally, in a previous section I pointed out that there are concepts without word forms (shoe lace ends, the runnel between lips and nose, the sound of a tree falling, etc.). Notice, though, that we can refer to these concepts linguistically, using pronouns like *it* and *them*: *I don't know what you call* **them**, *but* **they**'ve *come off and my laces are fraying;* **It**'s *between your lips and your nose;* **It** *was really loud*. This suggests that we know the frames their phonological forms would appear in if only they existed.

And lexical knowledge viewed as an aggregated sociocultural resource, across the members of a speech community, is a great deal more variable. Beyond the common 'core vocabulary' of content and function words, educated speakers of English may know well over a hundred thousand different triad combinations (i.e. 'words'), but no two speakers will have identical vocabularies. When readers come across the following lines in the English translation of Umberto Eco's novel *Foucault's Pendulum*, I'm sure most reach for their dictionaries (or, like me, hastily skip on to the next sentence):

> To each memorable image you attach a thought, a label, a category, a piece of the cosmic furniture, syllogisms, an enormous sorites, chains of apothegms, strings of hypallages, rosters of zeugmas, dances of hysteron proteron, apophantic logoi, hierarchic stoichea, processions of equinoxes and parallaxes, herbaria, genealogies of gymnosophists – an so on, to infinity.

But even Eco might not know what *empyema* means …

If we want to break the spell of words, therefore, we must ultimately consider individual lexicons in real human minds, or at least plausible approximations to them, rather than armchair ideals of *the* vocabulary of a language, or a lexicographer's painstaking but psychologically unreal collection of words from thousands of separate sources.

Now is probably a good time to eat humble pie and reveal some of the idiosyncratic contents of my own lexicon, to illustrate how words are spread rather messily across networks of form, frame and concept. I know the written word form *zeugma*, for example, and although I've looked it up before in the dictionary and I know it's a noun, I haven't successfully stored its meaning (I also incorrectly assumed it was pronounced 'zoigma' instead of 'zyoogma'). I draw an almost complete blank on ten more of the words in Eco's sentences, since I don't recall having encountered them before, although I could make some metalinguistic guesses (using my conscious knowledge of **cognates** and classical roots) and draw some conclusions about their meanings from suffixes I recognize (like *-ists*).

There are large tracts of fuzzy, partial, and – how shall I put it – *unorthodox* semantic knowledge in my existing triad combinations too: I know the word form *leeward* is a nautical term referring to one side of a boat, but I don't know which side it is or how it is defined. For many years I thought *egregious* meant the same as *gratuitous* (as in *an egregious insult*). I thought *gregarious* meant just 'jolly'. I have never been able to remember exactly what the legal term *tort* means, and I can't spell *diarrhoea*. I can also claim to have stored word meanings without word forms: I knew there was an adjective related to light energy, as *acoustic* is related to sound energy, but had to look in a thesaurus to confirm the existence of *photic* before using it in this chapter. This is a tiny, tiny selection of my lexical foibles. I suspect it's not unrepresentative of the population at large, in general tone if not in specific detail.

Words don't exist . . .

The Language Spell thus hides from us a number of important facts. One is that there is no fixed vocabulary of English (or of Spanish, Berber, Inuit or Ancient Greek). No one speaker knows all the words of a language, and not even the 20 volumes of the *Oxford English Dictionary*, citing past words of the language as well as present ones, includes them all (see the next chapter for more on dictionaries). Another fact is that a lot of the meaning of a word is contributed by its context in particular usage events, but that core meanings stored in our minds keep the form-meaning relation stable enough for us to be able to communicate with each other. Further, word meanings are not linguistic objects at all, but rather mentalese concepts in the part of the mind where we pool perceptual inputs from the senses, store our accumulating knowledge of the world, and act and react to this knowledge by forming and modifying beliefs, drawing inferences, making plans and decisions, moving our bodies, etc.

Finally, . . . *words don't exist*. At least in the traditional sense of unique pairings between names and things. Instead, people's minds contain complex, and often partial, overlapping networks of lexical entries (pairings of word forms and syntactic frames), connected with non-linguistic concepts.

This part of the Language Spell therefore binds (or blinds) us together as societies of speakers and hearers who can communicate with each other, by making us think that words are public entities like Saussure's coins, which we can exchange to buy the comprehension of our interlocutors. We have been concentrating so far in this part of the book on the economics of the system, i.e. what words are worth, semantically. The Spell tempts us to be most aware, however, of the 'minting' end of the word-as-coin phenomenon: their physical shape and texture, i.e. their surface form as phonological (or visual) objects, and how they came into existence. Hence the naive impression that words are Adamic names. In the next chapter we continue to reveal the workings of the lexical effects of the Language Spell, trying to find out how words get into children and thus into languages as shared community resources. This will allow us to examine how words appear to change over time, and so also reassess the perceived roles of dictionaries and writing systems as the ultimate repositories of lexical knowledge.

More information

George Lakoff and Mark Johnson's hugely influential book *Metaphors we live by* (1980; revised edition 2003) is a brilliant study of the pervasive role of **metaphor** in our daily lives and in our construction of experience and belief.

Ray Jackendoff's work has had a profound influence on my way of thinking about **language, meaning, and thought**. His most accessible work is Jackendoff (1993), but it's also worth looking at some of the essays in Jackendoff (1992) and (for really serious readers) his (2002) tour-de-force.

Jerry Fodor's seminal work *The modularity of mind* (1983) provides a cogent (and wittily expressed) argument for the 'computational' view of language and the senses, as modular **input systems** designed to deliver information to the central conceptual systems.

For a survey of issues in **vocabulary and meaning** which presents traditional semantic approaches as well as the more radical conceptual one adopted here, see Evelyn Hatch and Cheryl Brown (1995). This very readable book is written for language educators and also includes chapters on morphology, word formation and vocabulary usage.

The **bilingual mental lexicon** is discussed in several chapters of Janet Nicol's (2001) survey of bilingual processing. Although somewhat technical, there are excellent summaries of research on conceptual representation in bilinguals (by Judith Kroll and Natasha Tokowicz) and of the use of the priming technique (Kenneth Forster and Nan Jiang).

You can construct a short **concordance** for the word of your choice from the COBUILD corpus at www.titania.cobuild.collins.co.uk.

You can also perform a simple search for words at the British National Corpus website (http://sara.natcorp.ox.ac.uk/). It will give you a random 50-item selection of contextualized uses of the word from its massive database. David Lee's website at http://devoted.to/corpora is a fund of information and links about **corpora**.

4 Where Words Come From

> He learnt for the first time that there was no law of transmutation, as in
> his innocence he had supposed [...], but that every word in both Latin
> and Greek was to be individually committed to memory at the cost of
> years of plodding. [...] This was Latin and Greek, then, was it, this
> grand delusion! The charm he had supposed in store for him was really
> a labour like that of Israel in Egypt. What brains they must have in
> Christminster and the great schools, he presently thought, to learn
> words one by one up to tens of thousands!
>
> (Thomas Hardy, *Jude the Obscure*)

In this chapter we continue to challenge the public Spell-bound view
of language, again using words as our principal vantage point. We
begin by taking a first glimpse at how infants come to assume the role
of language users, zeroing in on the fundamental task of creating a
mental lexicon. In so doing we will begin to appreciate that words, and
language in general, are not just poured into the child's mind from the
outside, but develop also on the basis of internal, largely inbuilt,
cognitive mechanisms. The Language Spell leads us to believe also
that our language is principally our word stock, and that lexicographers are its guardians. In this chapter we reveal what's behind
'The Dictionary', and in so doing also expose and evaluate the
convenient fiction that languages exist as entities independent of the
brains of their users.

How children put names and things together

While writing Chapter 3 I learnt the words *empyema* and *zeugma*. Two
weeks later, I had forgotten the form of the first word and the meaning
of the second. Unlike the acquisition of grammar, which is all over bar
the shouting by the age of four, word learning goes on for as long as we
do. And I'm not just talking about academics, specialists and amateur
enthusiasts who need (or crave) new words in order to satisfy their
professional needs or indulge in their hobbies. All language users are

putting together, filling out, and connecting up triads of form, frame and concept, from infancy to dotage. Most English-speakers among the surging ranks of the world's centenarians have probably expanded their mental lexicons in recent years to include *spin* (in its new political sense), *euro* (the currency), *Viagra* (the virility drug), and many other nontechnical lexical novelties. And yet it is children who are the word learners *par excellence*, building up their lexicons with the raw materials needed by their developing grammars, as they celebrate their rites of passage into the speech communities which nurture them.

Children's word learning

Adults in rapidly changing social environments (especially in the world's educated elites and in the industrialized societies of the Northern Hemisphere) may well learn a few new words every year. But these accomplishments would show up as minor blips on the mind's 'lexometer' compared with the frenetic activity of young people aged between two years and the late teens (whatever their circumstances of birth and upbringing). According to one estimate, children between the ages of 18 months and 6 years learn, on average, one new word every 90 minutes! And the feat undertaken by children is not just quantitative in nature. When I put my mind to learning the word *zeugma*, it may seem like a chore, but I have a whole host of inbuilt aids which for the youngest infants are absent or undeveloped. These include:

- implicit knowledge that my fellow humans and I engage in interactions governed by social and cultural norms;
- a vocabulary full of other words;
- a grammar with which I can express and understand an infinity of word combinations;
- a vast encyclopaedia of concepts for things and things that can happen, learnt on the basis of what I have perceived with the senses, what I've been told by others, what I've inferred from both these sources, and what I've just imagined or plain invented;
- literacy: the ability to read, write and look things up in a dictionary (which, alone in this list, doesn't come along as an automatic benefit of species membership).

New-born infants have the *potential* for all this, in the form of neural circuitry set up to develop the requisite mental machinery. But they aren't born knowing it, and they don't get it taught to them by doting mothers and fathers, even in western societies where child-rearing is often abetted by pop-psychology gurus and guidebooks.

Since the Spell manages so successfully to hide from us the real nature of human language, and especially its great complexity, we tend to think that children's acquisition of language is a relatively simple process. In many cultures, parents and other caregivers celebrate their offspring's first words, delight in their linguistic 'errors' and inventions, ... and take credit for their ultimate success. And unlike many adult foreign language learners, such as Hardy's disillusioned Jude, children *do* routinely succeed, quite brilliantly, to master the linguistic system of the target language.

But they don't do it in the ways most people implicitly or explicitly believe. A common assumption is that language development happens through sloppy imitation, subsequently refined by parental intervention. First there are naming rituals ('Yeeeesss! It's a liddle doggy-woggy!!!'), then friendly coaching ('Yes love, you *broke* it: say *broke* for me, not *breaked*'), ... often followed pretty quickly by parental complaint ('No honey, it's not nice to say that'), until the child emerges into young adulthood – to his parents' eternal frustration – with the accent and patois of his *peers*. With luck, they fondly hope, the child will develop at least a minimal ability to exchange civil words with strangers, and enough expressive power to pass examinations and get on in the world.

This 'parentocentric' view overlooks an awful lot of what happens linguistically inside a child's mind during the first decade of life. Just as the Spell fools us into thinking that meaning is transferred from the speaker's head to the hearer's during conversation (like a birthday present being passed from one person to another), so it leads us to view acquisition as a process by which parents deliver 'the language' (say English, or Zulu, or Malay) to their children. We are aware that the metaphor is not quite accurate, since children don't know what the gift *is*, nor what to do with it once they receive it: hence the perceived need for parental instruction.

A little thought reveals the inadequacy of this explanation for the emergence of our linguistic competence. Not even the most regimental child-rearing environment has time set aside for drilling into its younger members the facts about vowel reduction in non-stressed syllables, auxiliary inversion in questions, or the kinds of complements taken by ditransitive verbs. An appreciation of the complexity of human language renders untenable the idea that parents are active artificers of their children's development as competent speakers and hearers. We've already seen that although all of us know at least one language, most of us (most language professionals and some linguists included) know as little *about* our language as we know about the functioning of the Internet. Not a very promising foundation for effective parental instruction, I'm afraid.

Is it just a matter of imitation and trial and error, then? Do children end up speaking and understanding like adults because they are surrounded (and cosseted) by adults, and simply proceed to parrot what they hear? Is this how toddlers learn their first words and how to string them together in appropriate phrases and sentences? It's clearly part of the story, since children do produce memorized, untaught expressions, including most of the words they know, and longer strings like *Time for bed*, *May the Force be with you*, and *Touch wood*. Individual words and expressions cannot possibly be encoded in their DNA, so they must, therefore, be picked up from the linguistic environment through repeated exposure.

Yet children are not merely precocious parrots, repeating back what they think they've heard, in what they think are the appropriate contexts, until their expressions acquire a high degree of acoustic fidelity and start to achieve their communicative objectives. Children's minds unconsciously store and analyse, hypothesize and experiment, process data and apply algorithms. We'll see in Chapter 8 how children do all this to fix the sophisticated paraphernalia needed for grammar and its effective deployment, but let's focus here on what *should* be the somewhat easier task of word learning. After all, they surely have enough time on their hands to learn the names of most of the things kids need to know, even some of the abstract ones? It's not as though we expect them to know *empyema* and *zeugma*, or even *accountant* or *prioritize*. There can't be much to learning words like *dog*, *apple* and *chair*, can there? ... Indeed there can, and again it's the Spell that makes us think otherwise.

Children of six from educated homes will know well over ten thousand words, and even the uneducated son of a goatherd in a remote part of Central Asia will know a good few thousand. Anyone who has studied a foreign language after puberty will know what a hard slog it is to master sufficient vocabulary to express oneself in a reasonably coherent fashion. Kids, though, are good at the difficult task of word-learning, despite the fundamental cognitive and linguistic differences between them and adults. Let's just consider some of those differences again, so we can see how instruction or imitation won't do as explanations for lexical development. New-born infants lack knowledge of the world, knowledge of social life and knowledge of the grammar of their language community. This means that initial mother tongue word learning is not just the infantile equivalent of getting out your vocabulary list or electronic dictionary and memorizing form-meaning correspondences. Children have to deal with a staggering set of challenges:

- They must learn the meanings to begin with (i.e. develop concepts of what they perceive around them and what they infer from those perceptions).
- They must understand that adults intend to communicate and get things done together through phonological sound (i.e. in a mode which excludes hand-clapping, sneezing, cooing, or other non-linguistic noises).
- They must come to know that certain sound strings arbitrarily represent conventional meanings (i.e. that there are words, that they are stored in the minds of the adults around them, and that they'll need to get these words into their *own* minds, rather than inventing their own personal vocabulary).
- They must learn to segment and extract the relevant sound strings from the speech stream (i.e. sort out where one word ends and the next one begins, and how word forms can change shape depending on where they appear in utterances, e.g. that *a* becomes *an* before vowels, and for some people (including me), *the* becomes *thee* in the same context).
- They must learn how to link these sounds with the right set of meanings (i.e. how *Pooh* refers to the animated bear, not the television screen he appears on; that not all bears are called *Pooh*; and that the word *he* can refer to any male creature, not just Pooh, his friends and Daddy).
- They must learn how the sound strings get strung together into longer stretches of meaning (i.e. learn each word's syntactic frame and how this allows it to get plugged into syntactic rules to build sentences).

Were we to cover all these mightily complex childhood accomplishments in the detail they deserve, this book would get dangerously heavy for the shelves. So instead, I'll serve up a brief description of one kind of study conducted with young children, to catch a glimpse of how their minds nonchalantly take up the challenges of building a mental lexicon, while they themselves get on with the real purposes of infant life.

Experimental evidence

Now it may appear rather obvious that a child will naturally and automatically map a new word (like *hender*) onto their concept of a new object (say a new toy) when the two are presented together; but the simplest, most obvious, explanations often turn out to be oversimplistic or plain incorrect. The philosopher Willard Quine first pointed out the complexity of the word-learning game. He argued that, logically, a field linguist (and we might add any 'civilian' second language learner) should find it impossible to infer the meaning of a word from an unknown language heard in a culturally appropriate context, unless they know its translation equivalent in their own tongue. As we saw in the last chapter, context is multiply ambiguous, and can be fickle. If the linguist's informant in the target speech community points to his friend and says *flimbu*, how are they to know whether the word is the friend's name, or means 'friend', 'goatherd', 'one who is always grinning', 'slow-witted', 'him' or a myriad other contextually possible alternatives? The eighteenth century French naturalist Pierre Sonnerat, on being shown a new species of lemur in Madagascar, thought that it was called an indri, since this is the word his local guides said as he encountered it. In fact, the Malagasy word *indri* means 'Behold!' (or possibly 'There it goes!') and the actual word for the animal is *babakoto*. But *indri* it is still called in French and English. This is essentially the same problem which faces the child when he hears a new word accompanying a new object.

It has been hypothesized that children don't guess wildly about which logically possible aspects of an object get linked to a new word form, but rather exhibit strong tendencies to assume, among other things, that:

- things only get one name (i.e. that words have isomorphic relationships with objects), so that if the object already has a name, then the new word must refer to some other aspect of it, such as a part of it, what it's for, or what it's made out of;
- words preferentially refer to whole three-dimensional objects bounded in time and space, rather than to parts or substances;
- words for objects which exhibit intentions and goals (especially human beings) are treated preferentially as proper names;
- words get extended preferentially to things of the same shape, rather than to things which coincide in function or substance.

The traditional way to find out about how children acquire their language is by watching them, listening to them, and keeping a detailed record of what they are saying, when they say it, and under what circumstances. There are a variety of rich longitudinal corpora of child speech, and they have yielded some sound scholarship. But it's hard to watch a child learn a word, since they may choose not to say it very often, or the opportunity to say it may not arise. Even if they do say it, it's not easy to tell how closely their surface token reflects an underlying, adult-like, triad of form, frame and meaning.

One way to infer aspects of the internal configuration of the child's developing lexicon and how it gets wired up is to design an experiment. It can't be like the priming studies we looked at in Chapter 3, with their unnatural tasks requiring computer familiarity and literacy, a good deal of concentration, and, frankly, a willingness to be bored out of their brains in the name of science (or additional course credit). It needs to be a child-friendly affair, involving toys and games and patient, smiley researchers. Imagine you want to know something about how 3- or 4-year-old children make connections between a new word and a novel concrete object, i.e. how they *map* a phonological form onto a meaning (the conceptual representation of the class of object). Since children vary greatly in the rate and order in which they learn words, researchers can't use existing objects and words for them (because they might already be familiar with one or both). But since there are many things and words that children have not yet experienced, researchers can invent both, and children will be none the wiser.

So, for example, you can set up an experiment in which the child is introduced to a new monster toy (assuming there *are* any left to be invented), and is told that 'This is *hender*.' If the monster has some prominent feature, like being covered in big spots, then it would be perfectly reasonable for the child to infer that *hender* means 'spotty'. After all, children do learn lots of adjectives, signalling properties of objects (like colour, shape and texture); and these will often be modelled by parents when their offspring are looking at objects with the relevant properties ('This is red', 'That one's furry', 'It's round, isn't it?'). In the experiment, then, you could present a second, identical, monster and ask: 'Is this one *hender* too?' The answer will help us understand how the child is mapping linguistic form onto experience. If he says no, then we can conclude that he is analysing the word as a proper name (*Hender*), belonging to one individual (the first monster). If he says yes, then he's interpreting the word as referring to a property shared by the two monsters (for example spottiness). Children overwhelmingly say no, in such contexts.

Experiments like these (pioneered by the psycholinguist Ellen Markman) reveal that children are predisposed to acquire word meanings in certain ways and not others. Their active contribution to word learning and language development in general gets seriously underestimated by most of us, enthralled as we are by their cuteness, lack of guile and apparent mental torpor. But this is the Spell at work again, blinding us to the rather obvious conclusion that baby minds, with a mere shrug of their synapses, grapple with and solve problems of language and thought of a magnitude and complexity which would reduce college-educated adults to despair.

The source of children's predispositions

Where children obtain these abilities is a matter of controversy in linguistics, philosophy and psychology – part of the great 'nature/nurture' debate that has dominated much of modern thought for many decades. As we shall see in greater detail in future chapters, most linguists now concur that children are not born as empty mental vessels into which intelligence is poured. The word *infant* is descended from the Latin *infans*, 'unspeaking', and although babies lack the sounds, words and structures of the particular language they end up speaking, it appears that they know more at birth than we might think. Some linguists (**nativists**, like Chomsky), believe that the brain is pre-wired specifically for human language; others hold that language skills emerge from more general genetic predispositions for complex mental activity. But however extensive and exclusive the dedicated pre-wired circuitry for language turns out to be in the human brain, all agree that nature plays as big a role as nurture in the remarkable metamorphosis of babbling baby into talking and listening child – of *infant* into *homo loquens*.

The arguments for a genetic predisposition for language were originally focused almost entirely on the domain of syntax (and we'll explore them more fully in Chapter 8), but the mental lexicon and the development of word meanings are providing fertile ground for further research on this topic. Experiments such as those discussed in the previous section suggest that virgin word learning requires, minimally, three interacting cognitive capacities:

- a *conceptual capacity*, which allows children to abstract away from perceptual experiences and construct concepts, which may then have words attached;
- an *inferential capacity*, which, among other things, allows children to

understand that people around them have i
intention to communicate their own thou
call a **theory of mind**); and

- a *linguistic capacity*, which allows childr
forms from the acoustic input they rec
such forms might mean from the v
morphological and syntactic contexts.

Put more plainly, to learn their vocabulary children n̲

- a conceptual system (things for words to mean);
- 'theory of mind' (the understanding that other people also mean);
- a grammar (to arrange word forms into meaningful combinations).

Research in this area is helping linguists to tease apart just how much of what we need to become a language user is uniquely linguistic in nature, how much of it is available to us, directly or indirectly, from our contact with the world into which we are born, and how much of it is not, and so must be coded in our genes.

It's hard to get one's mind around claims about mental abilities and ideas being encoded in genes. We're used to thinking of genes as instructional manuals for building arms and legs, livers and hearts, rather than for developing abstract traits like sexuality and aggression, musical ability or language. This again is a side-product of the Language Spell and its sister spells in other realms of cognition. Together they prevent us from understanding much about the parts of ourselves that we can't see or feel, or that don't have dissectible counterparts in other animals. Such invisible aspects of the human condition often only become tractable when viewed from the perspective of society, and yet, as we've seen, this often obscures their deeper biological nature. (Richard Dawkins' metaphors, which we came across in Chapter 3, cleverly use the language of the former to explain the latter.) Musical ability, for example, is viewed as a talent, sparsely and unevenly distributed across individuals in society. Western history in its long course has thrown up few musical geniuses of the stature of Bach or Bowie, Mozart or Miles Davis, and in each family across the world there are some who sing in tune, and some who don't. But in fact all human beings have an inbuilt ability to recognize rhythms, melodies and tone, even if they're 'tone-deaf'. This shared ability in the species seems to be independent of experience, i.e. is unlearnt, and so must come in the genes. More about this in the final chapter.

section we have dwelt on one small part of one area of
into early word learning. There is a great deal more involved
guage development than the attachment of lexical entries to
nings in conceptual systems, and we'll look at some of the recent
nking on some of these issues in future chapters. What we have seen
in this limited foray into children's minds, however, is that they are not
merely passive containers, into which words are shovelled by parents
or other carers, but rather active word-building machines, using a
dedicated inbuilt toolkit to construct permanent lexical triads out of
transient data from the environment.

Behind The Dictionary

The mental lexicon is a psychological construct that defies popular
credence. (Indeed, a research proposal I once submitted for
experimentation on lexical representation in Spanish-English bilinguals was turned down by a panel of evaluators on the grounds that
'there is no evidence for the mental lexicon'.) The evidence, though
different in nature from that collected in other fields, is abundant and
conclusive. And, in a way, unnecessary: where else are the collected
words of your language kept? Many non-linguists would answer
without hesitation that they are to be found in 'The Dictionary'. But
where do dictionaries come from? In this section we'll take a closer
look at the relationship between the mental lexicon and a printed
dictionary. This is a useful exercise, I think, because it crystallizes
many of the features which make the Language Spell so powerful, and
so allows us to tackle some fundamental folk conceptions of language
and its place in our lives.

Printed dictionaries are, for many, hallowed repositories of their
language and its history, but for me are quintessentially the *wrong*
place to look if we want to understand the true nature of this great
human endowment. They are revered so much partly because the
Spell deprives us of the opportunity to marvel at our own flesh-and-
blood version of lexicographical genius: the mental lexicon inside each
one of us. Don't get me wrong: I *love* dictionaries, and in my office at
work have over 20 of them in a row. Next to them on the shelf,
however, is a model of the human brain, spongy to the touch and
housed in a cut-away synthetic cranium. This juxtaposition is
coincidental (I ran out of bookends), but most appropriate, since the
brain contains the mother of all dictionaries: less erudite than its
printed offspring, exceedingly radical and very often vulgar, but
brilliant beyond measure.

Now of course this claim may seem wildly unfair to dictionaries, and as productive as comparing a box of matches with a microwave, or a paper aeroplane with a swift. But throwing into exaggerated relief the vast difference between the two kinds of word store is *precisely* my purpose here. People revere dictionaries but demean individual mental lexicons: even very highly educated people will defer to the authority of the OED when some lexical difference arises between them. Here I'd like to put individual vocabularies in perspective, and in so doing reveal the staggering immensity of the lexical prowess of children, Kalahari Bushmen and Oxford dons alike.

Substance, size and scope

Let's start with the most superficial difference. Most dictionaries are made of paper, glue and ink, from the cheap and ugly paperbacks favoured by schoolchildren, to sumptuous editions, exuding opulence, like that of the Spanish Royal Academy, with its stiff, cream, wallpapery pages held together by a red-and-gold tooled binding. More and more, dictionaries are appearing too in electronic format, on CD-ROM, websites and in handheld devices (used mostly, as far as I have observed, by old ladies on trains, to cheat at crosswords). The mental lexicon, on the other hand, is organic in substance, distributed in the tissue of the cerebral cortex. Aside from their physical manifestations, these two very different kinds of lexical repository vary in how many words they store. The first monolingual dictionary of English (Robert Cawdrey's *A Table Alphabeticall* of 1604) listed a mere 2,500 words, but the second edition of the OED has over a quarter of a million. The mental lexicon varies considerably more widely: from a single word (a baby's first), to perhaps 200,000 in a well-read adult.

A printed dictionary is public, a social artefact: it represents the collective lexical knowledge of a group of speakers, normally according to the language(s) they speak, but also (in more specialized works) where they live, their occupation, academic discipline, subculture, etc. Traditionally, it focuses on words typical of the written modality. It also often sets itself up as an authority and guide as well as a record, telling its users that *a phenomena* is incorrect, that *comprised of* is ungrammatical, and that *piss* is unacceptable in 'polite' society. There are thousands of monolingual and bilingual dictionaries, covering an astonishing range of fields of human activity. In a search for 'English dictionaries' on the Amazon website I found over 6,000 matches.

The mental lexicon, covering spoken, written and signed modalities without prejudice, is private, restricted to the lexical knowledge of individuals, but exhaustive within those restrictions: all the words you know are in your lexicon, even the really rude, crass, hackneyed, slangy and nerdy ones you'd never use yourself, together with all the ones peculiar to your own dialect, your secret childhood games, your occasional learning errors, and your conscious or unconscious inventions. It is morally neutral, judgement-free, and completely democratic. The mental lexicon obviously contributes to a level of *social* reality, beyond the confines of its owner's head, because to be useable its contents must coincide as closely as possible with those of other people. A massive overlap may be necessary for human language to make any sense, but the exact *degree* of overlap is not easily measured, and as we've seen, the coincidence will never be total. So, we can assume that there are over six billion different mental lexicons in operation on the planet today. And that's not counting multi-linguals (more than half the world's population), who carry around at least *two* interrelated lexicons in their minds, at no extra cost.

Shifting meanings

Perhaps the primary function of any dictionary, its owner will tell you, is to find the meaning of words. And yet as we've seen, a dictionary cannot contain meanings, only the external manifestations of word *forms*. Imagine that the family cat, kept inside all day while its masters are at work, and tired of destroying the sofa, decides to learn English so she can read the daily paper and combat the boredom of feline domesticity. Stretch your imagination further and assume she's managed to pick up the function words (like articles, pronouns, prepositions and conjunctions) and decides to work her way through the *Chambers Compact Dictionary* she finds on the bookshelf. Unaware of the conventions of the English writing system, she starts browsing from the end and, her eyes alighting on the attractive form *zeugma*, searches the entry for the word's meaning. What she finds are 42 further word **tokens**, representing 33 **types**, each with its own meaning:

> a figure of speech in which a word, usu an adjective or verb, is applied to two nouns, although strictly it is appropriate to only one of them, or it has a different sense with each, as in *weeping eyes and hearts*.

Undaunted, she looks up the first content word she doesn't know, *figure*, and finds a long entry with 15 nominal senses and three verbal senses. Scanning beyond all these further unknown words, in the hope of something familiar, she finds *figure of speech*, which she recognizes from the first entry she looked at. She reads:

a device such as METAPHOR, SIMILE, etc that enlivens language

Ten more words. Crestfallen, she realizes that the only way to find the meaning of *zeugma* is by already knowing the meaning of the 33 words in the original definition, and that looking for them in the dictionary will be as futile as chasing her own tail.

Human English speakers like us can find the meaning of *zeugma* in the dictionary because we already know the meanings of the words in the definition. The meaning, once distilled from the definition, gets stored directly (and non-linguistically, as we've seen) in conceptual systems. Now, pushing our imaginations to the limit, let's assume that somehow our resourceful feline internalizes the meaning of the word *zeugma* and starts to use it frequently in conversation. If she uses it in an off-hand way to the poodle next door, who asks what it means, the cat will be able to make a stab at explaining it, because her lexicon now stores a direct connection between the form and the *concept* itself. But if meanings are in minds, and nowhere else, the logical implication is that there can be as many different meanings of a word as there are mental lexicons which contain it. Say the poodle doesn't fully understand the cat's explanation, and decides that a zeugma is any expression that doesn't make complete sense. If he later uses the word, appropriately contextualized for his interpretation, in conversation with his offspring and less well-educated canine friends, then that's what the word will mean for them, no matter how much the lexicographers and scholars of rhetoric might object.

This is a frivolous tale, but it does illustrate a serious point: words mean what they mean only because of a tacit agreement to conventionalize their meaning. Dictionaries record these conventions, and for rare word forms used in literate societies, can serve to bolster the convention and remind users of it when memories have faded between usages. But most language users on the planet don't own dictionaries, and those that do rarely consult them, so in practice the conventions hold through use alone. 'Slippage' inevitably occurs, therefore, and conventional form-meaning pairings change with time.

Word histories and language histories

Many dictionaries include miniature histories of the words they list, like the note at the end of the *Chambers* entry for *zeugma*: '⏀ 16c: Greek, meaning "yoking together"'. Others, like the *OED*, go in for etymology in a bigger way. Here again is the potted history of *spell* cited in Chapter 1, from the *Shorter OED*:

> [OE. *spel*(1) = OS., OHG. *spel*, ON. *Spjall*, Goth. *spill* recital, tale :- Gmc. **spellam.* Cf. GOSPEL.] **1**. Without article: Discourse, narration, speech; occas. idle talk, fable. -late ME. **2**. A discourse or sermon; a narrative or tale -1653. **3**. A set of words, a formula or verse, supposed to possess occult or magical powers; a charm or incantation 1579. b. *transf.* and *fig.* An occult or mysterious power or influence; a fascinating or enthralling charm 1592.

The origins of the word are given as 'Gmc', i.e. Germanic, the hypothesized ancestral tongue of the extended family of speakers of English, Dutch, German, Norwegian and other north-west European languages (including Gothic, whose last speakers died in the Middle Ages). Germanic and its sisters, like Celtic, Italic and Indo-Iranian, diverged from their own **Indo-European** forebear over two millennia ago (more on this in Chapter 9). We cannot get much further back than Indo-European, believed to have been spoken some 7,000 years ago. And yet human beings like us have been around for perhaps half a million years, speaking with roughly the same kinds of extensive vocabularies and sophisticated grammars all along the way.

Word histories are the result of scholarship, and although the scholarship is superb, it has to rely entirely on written records (the earliest of which date from around 5,000 years ago), together with very clever, naturally *informed*, guesses. We can't track a word back before external, permanent traces could be left of it (i.e. before the age which embraces the Rosetta Stone and *Harry Potter* on audiotape), because the mental lexicon does not store historical data. Although some of us know or can guess parts of the recent histories of some words, and some erudite scholars have an extensive repertoire of such histories, this is part of our general encyclopaedic knowledge, not part of the lexical network in the language circuitry of the brain. If you've stopped to think about it, you will have noticed that *breakfast* was originally a verb followed by a direct object, '[to] *break* [one's overnight] *fast*'. But you *do* have to stop to think about it: most sane human beings don't invoke this concept when they come across the word on the back of a packet of waffles or a jar of marmalade. Human beings generally *think* words, in the mental lexicon, rather than *think about* them, in general-purpose conceptual systems.

This raises a very important point: if, as I have been relentlessly arguing, language is effectively locked into human heads, and even in speech and acquisition just gives the *impression* of being transferred from one head to another, then what does it mean to say that *zeugma* 'came to us' from the Greek in the sixteenth century, that English *spell* 'used to be' Germanic *spellam*, and that *breakfast* 'was originally' two separate words? The answer lies in the Fundamental Paradox underlying the Language Spell, which I talked about in Chapter 1: that language is socially motivated, but mentally realized. Given that it's so much easier for us to grasp the dynamics of our lives in society than to penetrate into the unconscious, psychological machinery that ultimately supports it, and given the overwhelmingly social motivation for language, it's hardly surprising that we have come up with fictions like the existence of a monolithic entity called English, roughly forged by Anglo-Saxons, refashioned by invading Normans, bejewelled by Shakespeare, steam-rolled around the world by the Victorians, and given a complete refit by the citizens of the USA.

Languages don't exist

This should have raised some eyebrows: *English, a fiction?* Well strictly speaking (and in a book on the *science* of language we must strive to speak so), the answer is *yes*: English is a fiction, albeit an extraordinarily convenient, indeed essential, one. I don't say this out of some Anglophobic desire to shock the linguistic inheritors of Bede, Chaucer, Austen, Churchill and Martin Luther King: *equally* fictional are the rest of the 5,000 to 7,000 'living languages' (and an unknown, greater number of 'dead' ones) which unite and divide the billions of human beings who live or have lived on this planet. Let me explain.

With some justification, we could argue that named languages exist only in the same way that nations exist: because some people *say* they do, and everyone else *believes* them. The existence of a nation, however, is built upon explicit socially constructed conventions and symbols, such as physical borders, recognized institutions, a head of state, membership of the UN and a flag. Nations require such paraphernalia not only to make them work, but also to make them *exist*, as they have no material substrate, no reflex in natural law or quantum physics, or in any other system outside of our own imaginations. Even though it serves a major social purpose, however, language *is* a physical entity, as we have seen: it is the set of structured components in each human being's brain which allows them to relate conceptual structures with phonological structures and thus share social meaning. Conceptual structures, phonological structures, syntactic structures and lexical structures must ultimately be woven from brain tissue before they can have any effect in our cultures and social lives.

So are there over 300 million Englishes, one for each English speaker's brain? This may be closer to objective reality. It's undeniable that the language in one brain is never the same as the language in the next person's, even if they speak the 'same' language. Take me and my brother Steven. We got linguistic input as infants from roughly the same set of people and in very similar circumstances: we were brought up together in the north of England, went to the same schools, share many of the same interests. We are still in constant (mostly electronic) contact. Is the English in my brain the same as the English in his? Certainly the contents of my language databases closely *resemble* his (and our syntactic competence is probably identical) ... but they also differ in certain respects, perhaps more so than our visual systems, our hearts, livers and other internal bits and pieces.

Here are a few of the differences. Steven moved to the South and adopted the characteristic long [a] sound in words like *class*, **bath**, and **aunt**. I crossed the Atlantic and my intonational patterns began to warp as I unwittingly mimicked those of US English speakers. Steven can converse at length about musical composition and interpretation using the appropriate technical vocabulary. I can't, but I can wield with some agility the jargon of linguistics and cognitive science. Further, Steven and I are never confused with each other when we speak on the phone to others: our voices are different enough to be unmistakable and instantly recognizable by people close to us both. And so on. Despite these phonological, lexical and vocal differences, however, all would concur that we're speakers of the same language, English. We speak the same **dialect** of English, although our individual 'voices', our **idiolects**, differ.

Let's look a little further in linguistic space. As an undergraduate, I shared a flat with Sam, an agricultural marketing student from Northern Ireland. It took a good few weeks for me to tune in to his accent of English, and even after a few years there were frequent miscommunications. Sam's spoken dialect differed greatly from mine, lexically as well as phonetically, and the two did not contain sufficient features in common for us to readily understand each other. And yet, like me, Sam is unequivocally labelled as a native speaker of English. We read and write in exactly the same ways (ignoring stylistic differences). Our underlying phonological systems must actually be almost identical too, despite superficial differences in pronunciation. But the fit is not exact, and what surfaced in our conversations was the phonetic equivalent of chalk and cheese.

Perhaps what makes Steven, Sam and me English speakers is the fact that we can at least understand one other without taking a foreign language course, by using the *common* parts of our linguistic competence. If this is so, then could English exist as the abstract set of commonalities of all its speakers? Might English and other languages exist in the same way that Singapore, Kenya or Canada exist, if we could only pin down the conventional factors, the necessary and sufficient conditions, which define them? This modest-looking hypothesis also turns out to be problematic, however. First, because the non-mutual aspects of linguistic competence – the bits that are unshared by all speakers – must still count as elements of language ... but of which? And second, because mutual intelligibility turns out not to be a foolproof test after all: not all people who understand each other are thought of as speakers of the same language, and not all people speaking the same language understand each other. Sam was bidialectal with regards to oral comprehension and production: he could understand my, more 'standard' dialect as well as his own more localized one, and could speak using both the UK's 'standard' dialect or his own Northern Irish variety (although his phonology, his accent, was tied only to his local dialect). I was shamefully monodialectal in *both* domains: for a while I failed to understand most of what Sam said to me, and couldn't, without parodying, converse with him in his own dialect.

But even if all 'English speakers' spoke a mutually intelligible, homogenous dialect with minimal differences in individual 'voice', this would still not provide sufficient foundation for a reasonable belief in the 'existence' of English as a monolithic entity which moves through history and spreads around the globe. Consider some close relatives of the English language. My friend Marc from the north of Belgium speaks Flemish; another friend Rob from The Netherlands speaks Dutch. Yet their 'different languages' are at least as mutually comprehensible as my dialect and Sam's. Flemish/Dutch is also very close to German in lexicon, phonology and syntax. Compare the following:

(1)   U zendt hem naar mijn vaders huis   [Flemish/Dutch]
       'You send him to my father's house'
(2)   Du sendest ihn zum Haus meines Vaters   [German]
       'You send him to my father's house'

If Marc or Rob wrote sentence (1) to my German colleague Ulli, she would instantly recognize sentence (2) beneath the Dutch/Flemish surface. Further, both (1) and (2) look remarkably similar to their English equivalent. Similarity means, inescapably, commonality of features: on the basis of just this one sentence, we observe that English, Flemish/Dutch and German share large amounts of lexical form. Table 1 shows some of these cognates.

Table 1   Some lexical cognates of English, Dutch/Flemish, and German

English	Dutch/Flemish	German
send	zendt	sendest
him	hem	ihn
my	mijn	mein
father	vader	Vater
house	huis	Haus

... And that's just scratching the surface. So to what language do *these* commonalities belong? And if they don't belong to any one language, just what *is* the degree of commonality that distinguishes dialects from languages and languages from each other? How do we decide where to draw the line so that Steven, Sam and I are judged to speak one language, Marc and Rob a third (or perhaps a third and fourth) and Ulli yet another?

Which brings us back again to the problem of word (and language) histories. Where are we to draw the historical lines between speakers of Modern English and Old English, and between Old English speakers and the speakers of the West Germanic language which preceded it? Some English history books state that the English language began in the British Isles in the fifth century, but then contradict themselves by also claiming that it was transplanted there by invaders from what is now north-western Germany, thus presupposing its prior existence. The speakers of these languages were real people, who started their linguistic lives receiving input from *their* parents, just like we did. There were no 'first' speakers of Old English. The first Angles, Saxons or Jutes born in Britain didn't baffle their parents by producing their first words in a brand new tongue. Likewise, the first utterances of children born immediately after the Norman Conquest in 1066 were not suddenly spoken in Middle English, heralding the end of the English of *Beowulf* and the new age of Chaucer and Malory.

Most present-day speakers of English would not recognize Old English as having any closer resemblance to the way they speak than do Dutch or German. In order for it to be intelligible, they would need to study it as they would a foreign language. Here is a small sample, taken from a letter by King Alfred (871–899), entitled *On the State of Learning in England*, see page 109 (I have simplified the spelling conventions to make it a little less frightening):

> Hie ne wendon thaette aefre menn sceolden swae reccelease weorthan ond sio lar swae othfeallan: for thaere wilnunga hie hit forleton, ond woldon thaet her thy mara wisdom on londe waere thy we ma getheoda cuthon.

Unintelligible indeed. Even Chaucer's English, some 400 years later, is hard to grasp completely without some scholarly support. Here are the first few lines of the General Prologue to the *Canterbury Tales*, see page 109 for details:

> Whan that Aprill with his shoures sote
> The droghte of Marche hath perced to the rote,
> And bathed every veyne in swich licour,
> Of which vertu engendred is the flour;
> Whan Zephirus eek with his swete breeth
> Inspired hath in every holt and heeth
> The tendre croppes, and the yonge sonne
> Hath in the Ram his halfe cours y-ronne;
> And smale fowles maken melodye,
> That slepen al the night with open yë –
> So priketh hem Nature in hir corages –
> Than longen folk to goon on pilgrimages,
> [...]

These extracts illustrate the difficulties associated with pinning down a language in time, as well as in space and speech community. And yet we would be loathe to give up the fiction that somehow Chaucer and King Alfred wrote in English. Just look at the Old English version of the Flemish/Dutch and German sentences we examined earlier, and see how close it looks to the same sentence as you or I would say it:

(3)   Thu sendest hine to mines faeder huse
       'You send him to my father's house'

Languages, then, have runny borders, both in space and time. What seems to hold a language together in the collective thought of a society is our *belief* that it must exist.

Perhaps, then, if English exists objectively it is the *sum* of all the language states in the brains of those whom society recognizes, now or in the past, as English speakers. But of course this argument, though probably the best we can come up with, is circular, boiling down to the claim that *English is the language that English speakers speak.* The belief in English, and other languages, is a product of the Spell, but one that we would be unwise to dispel too readily. Our belief in the objective existence of individual languages is more than convenient: it is an absolute necessity, part of the potent magic that saves us from a world of linguistic isolation – from the kind of brutal solitary confinement suffered by some autistic children and the unsupported congenitally deaf. We believe in the fiction because if we didn't, language would lack its social dimension, and so just plain wouldn't work: the Fundamental Paradox once more.

Internalized and externalized language

Let's pause and take stock for a moment. We've begun to see that a lexicon is the product of both nature (inbuilt cognitive predispositions) and nurture (exposure to contextualized speech). As we'll see in more detail in later chapters, children creatively construct a whole language for themselves using these resources. Since language is used for social purposes, however, one person's language must be as similar as possible to the languages of those people with whom they interact. The child's language acquisition device is designed, therefore, to produce as close a fit as possible with the inferred systems of parents, peers and others in the speech community. Hence we can abstract away from all these internal languages, and speak of an external language, shared by all its speakers, which we reify with a proper name like *English*, and record 'it' in dictionaries. It is almost impossible not to buy into the fiction, of course, and I certainly haven't managed (or even attempted) to do so in most of this book.

Noam Chomsky gives us a way to distinguish between the two uses of the word *language*, as internal mental capacity and as shared overlap between such capacities across speech communities and their history. The first, he calls **I-language** (for 'internalized language') and the second, **E-language** (for 'externalized language'). Ugly, I know, but English just forces us to resort to jargon here (Spanish has the rather more felicitous terms *lenguaje* and *lengua* to represent similar notions.) Chomsky holds that I-language is the proper object of study of theoretical linguistics, and may be explored in the same way that physiologists study the functioning of physical organs. Indeed, Chomsky calls I-language also the 'language organ'. He sees E-language as playing no role in a theory of linguistic competence (a characterization of our declarative knowledge of language). But just as physiologists extrapolate from data on individual organs, like human hearts and livers, to talk about *the* human heart, and *the* human liver, so Chomsky extrapolates from data on individual I-languages to talk about *English* and *Spanish*.

For some this is a category error, undermining the conception of language as a biological entity, since the equivalent of the human heart in linguistic terms should be the human language faculty, not an abstract social object like English. Linguists do buy into the necessary fiction of individual languages, but only as a methodological inevitability of the Fundamental Paradox, not as a philosophical contradiction. Here's why. Other cognitive systems, like vision, do not vary in the species. Cognitive psychologists can study any healthy eye and brain to understand how it works. Unlike our sensory equipment, however, the specific details of the language faculty in one person's mind must be tuned to those possessed by others in the same social group, so that communication can result. The specific state of an individual's I-language will then be determined by the society in which it must operate, and generations of I-languages will change almost as rapidly as the society itself does. In consequence, linguists cannot extrapolate from individuals to the species as a whole, but must be content with abstracting away to the fuzzy category of a social collection of I-languages, using individual language names like English as scientifically sloppy but convenient names for their object of study.

Thus Chomsky and the Oxford etymologists both abstract away from individual I-languages, but in very different ways. Chomsky works from the principle that language is an internal mental state, a configuration of the human brain, so may be studied using the techniques of natural science, on a par with enquiry into any physical organ. Many lexicographers work on the assumption that language is an external social construct, subject to the collective will of society and the authority of the literate. Since for Chomsky language is fundamentally about the shared properties of individual I-languages, he is not terribly concerned with historical factors. Similarly, a physiologist studying the functioning of the human heart need not normally be concerned with the hearts of the progenitors of the particular sample he has under the knife.

Babies as history-makers

But there must be a way to explain etymologies and other changes in E-language without abandoning the **mentalist** principles that

Chomsky, this book, and most modern scientists hold as beyond dispute. How *do* we account for the real impression that words have histories spanning millennia, if they are, as I have argued, entities bound within brain tissue, in an abstract I-language, for the lifetime of individual members of the human race? Actually, most of the pieces of this puzzle have already been put into place in this chapter. To see how they fit together, we must return to where we began: the development of language in babies. For words to have a history, they must have a way to jump from one generation to the next, as electrochemical charges leap the synapse in the human brain. This 'lexical synapse' works because of babies' rapid development of the conceptual, inferential and linguistic capacities I drew attention to earlier in the chapter.

To interact meaningfully with other people, children must first construct concepts of what they perceive around them: internal representations of things in the world and how they relate to each other, spawning representations of *categories* of things, types into which individual tokens in the world may be categorized (like 'finger', instead of lots of separate *bingers, zingers, hingers,* etc.). Once children have meanings, they must understand that these may be externalized, through language. This is where the inferential capacity acts, in concert with internal predispositions for language, such as how to deal with speech when it is directed to them by people in the external world (like parents). The inferential capacity – the child's development of a 'theory of mind' which allows them to infer that other people have intentions, including the intention to share meaning – is the key to the puzzle. Developing a theory of mind is perhaps best understood as learning to empathize: to understand that others may think, act and feel like you do. Without this, language would remain trapped inside: a complex, subconscious I-language with nothing to do.

Deployment of their inferential and linguistic capacities allows children to appreciate that speech directed to them reflects a communicative intention on the part of parents, older siblings and others. Since language has external effects, primarily in the acoustic domain (i.e. it makes a noise), then conscious *awareness* of it slowly emerges. Children's frustration at not being understood, and parental feedback concerning the child's language use, may add to this awareness. But the Spell wrought by evolution keeps the cognitive bulk of language hidden from view, leading to the inevitable assumption that language is of a kind with other external phenomena, like parental expectations of obedience, of respect for ownership rights (e.g. of siblings' toys), and of politeness in company – i.e. as part of the social code, belonging to the outside world. In other words, children come to share their parents' conception of the existence of an E-language. In the many human societies in which children regularly encounter speech in more than one language, this realization is presumably even sharper, although we must remember that it very rarely achieves much prominence in conscious thought: the Language Spell ensures that our appreciation of language is cloudy, and finds cohesion only in folk beliefs.

So the history of a word documents one small element in a massed, historical sequence of individual I-languages, which interact through the collective, Spell-induced, self-deception of E-language. But the interaction is necessarily indirect, *untelepathic*, mediated by the eddy and flow of air molecules between mouth and ear. As I keep stressing, language is not 'transferred' from speaker to hearer, with all its phonological, morphosyntactic and semantic features flagged. Children just hear noise, and must actively *reconstruct* speakers' intentions on the basis of contextual cues, inferences and their unfolding linguistic knowledge. For words this means a string of phonemes, a syntactic frame and a conceptual structure. And so, like a game of Chinese Whispers (or 'Broken Telephone'), what is received by the infant hearer is not necessarily what was intended by the adult speaker. When children's reconstruction of the input differs from adult interlocutors' output, but coincides in sufficient infant I-languages, then change in the E-language inevitably results.

This can happen at each of the three representational levels of the lexical triad. At the form level, for example, *mouse* and *house* used to rhyme with *juice* and *loose* in Chaucer's time. By Shakespeare's day they had gravitated through articulatory vowel space to roughly their current pronunciations. The *gh* spellings in words like *night* and *eight* reflect an earlier guttural consonant maintained in their modern German cousins *nacht* and *acht*. We also see words changing their syntactic behaviour, so that the Middle English adjective *round* (ultimately from Latin *rotundus*), began to be used as a noun and, in one of its most common manifestations nowadays, as a preposition (*round the corner, round the bend*). The verb *like* used to behave the same way as its cousin *please* in Shakespeare's day, so that the Bard's King John could say that *It likes us well* to mean *We like it well*. (The Spanish translation equivalent of English *like* (*gustar*) works the same way, causing occasional distress to both me and my EFL students.)

And we've already seen lots of examples of semantic change, often accomplished through metaphorical extension, but also through broadening or narrowing of meaning. My grandma Sybil, from

Newcastle upon Tyne in the north-east of England, could say (and often did) that she was *starving of cold*. This usage reflects the original sense of the word in Old English, when it meant 'to die (of any cause)', as does its modern German cognate *sterben*. During the course of many generations of word learning, it has come to be used in most dialects of English only for a narrower means of extinction (dying for lack of food). More common are cases of words which amplify their meanings, getting extended to broader tracts of semantic space. Thus, the popular adjective *nice*, that bane of the guardians of good usage, used to have the much more specific meaning of 'foolish' (it came from the Latin *nescius*, 'ignorant'). It forged its way into a series of related semantic fields ('simple', then 'tender' and 'delicate') until it conquered the whole conceptual ground of general agreeableness. (In modern Spanish, its cognate *necio* maintained its negative connotation, meaning 'silly', 'stupid', and now more often 'obstinate'). When this kind of creative reconstruction occurs across numerous linguistic structures, across whole communities of speakers, and over many years, then the 'language' itself changes, and West Germanic becomes Old English.

But this is not the only way that languages evolve. E-languages belong to groups of speakers, and speakers come into contact with other groups, so if the contact is sufficiently prolonged, then their languages will start to interact too. In my academic department in Mexico, most of the English native-speakers who have been around for a while now talk to each other about their *investigation projects* (from Spanish *investigación*, 'research'), about student *inscriptions* (from Spanish *inscripción*, 'registration'), and – before we can stop ourselves – about students *molesting* us (from Spanish *molestar*, 'interrupt, pester'). In the next chapter we look at this phenomenon, and more broadly, where our spoken and written word forms come from.

More information

 The richest discussion of **children's development of word meanings** is by Paul Bloom (2000). Although technical, it's a fascinating argument, and doesn't assume prior knowledge of psychology or linguistics.

Robert Stockwell and Donka Minkova's (2001) account of the **history of English vocabulary** and the kinds of phonological, morphological and semantic processes words undergo is both readable and erudite.

A classic text on the **history of English** was written decades ago by Albert Baugh and Thomas Cable. The fifth edition (2001) updates the account. A less stolid work, making the history of English come alive, is Robert McCrum, William Cran and Robert MacNeil's *The Story of English*, the companion book to their 1990s TV series of the same name, in a recently revised edition (2002).

Richard Hogg's (2002) introduction to **Old English** is an accessible account of the grammar of the language, which integrates examples from the scant text records available.

The classic translation of **Chaucer's** *Canterbury Tales* is by Nevill Coghill (Chaucer 2003). The original Middle English text appears in a 2005 edition, edited by Donald Howard.

 King Alfred's 'On the state of learning in England' may be found in the original Old English in Henry Sweet's (2003 [1876]) reader. A modern English translation is available online at www.departments. bucknell.edu/english/courses/engl440/pastoral.shtml, the site of Kathleen Davis's course on Medieval Authorship, at Bucknell University.

Chomsky gives his clearest explanation of the concept of **I-language** in his 2000 book, *New horizons in the study of language and mind*.

Douglas Harper's **Online Etymological Dictionary** at www. etymonline.com/, pooling the resources of many fine printed sources, allows you to look up word histories.

5 Forming Words

> Where were we? For the moment, a tangential observation. Strange how each of those three words encloses its successor, each shedding of letters echoing the sense of loss we always feel when casting the Orphean glance over the shoulder. A poignant diminution, once noticed.
>
> (Julian Barnes, *Love, Etc.*)

The 'poignant diminution' noticed by Julian Barnes in this chapter's epigraph is singular enough for its iconic ingenuity, but perhaps even more so because the author actually *noticed* it in the first place. I said at the end of Chapter 3 that the Language Spell 'tempts us to be most aware . . . of the "minting" end of the word-as-coin phenomenon: their physical shape and texture, i.e. their surface form as phonological (or visual) objects, and how they came into existence'. Well, I exaggerated: the Spell can be almost as powerful in the realm of form as it is in meaning, as this chapter will illustrate.

Word forms: speech and spelling

At the beginning of Chapter 3 I invented a fanciful scenario in which a group of our ancestors, at the Dawn of Language, invented word forms in an Adamic Convention. I imagined them coming up with vowel alternations, followed by consonants, and then stringing the two together in sequences to form syllables. Speech began somewhere in the region of 500,000 years ago. Only thousands of generations later did human beings start to make permanent records of their linguistic output, and only just over a millennium ago did English find a graphic medium using the Roman alphabet. Many thousands of E-languages have never evolved their own writing systems. Millions of existing I-languages have little recourse to the written word: in Sub-Saharan Africa, the Arab states and Southern Asia, at least a third of men and over a half of all women are functionally illiterate, according to UNESCO estimates. These millions of human beings, including the pre-literate sources of Homer's *Odyssey* and *Iliad*, the creator of *Beowulf*, the Aztec poets and the Emperor Charlemagne, have the same mental language faculty as the rest of us. Writing is not necessary for language. And yet among educated language users it is writing that is seen as the primary medium, dominating our linguistic awareness and assumptions, and colouring our linguistic knowledge and beliefs.

Of course, writing is one of the ways in which the privileged among us have been able to undo some of the Language Spell, by allowing us to make permanent, visible records of many facets of language use, and thus convert magic, song and myth into history, literature, science and philosophy. The invention of writing systems has changed our species. Although oral cultures can reach high levels of sophistication, it is literacy which provided the vehicle for the colossal cultural changes that have hurtled our species from the Bronze Age to the Internet Age in less than 2 per cent of the time that has elapsed since the Dawn of Speech.

The fact that full literacy is normally attainable only by those with access to sustained education, however, has meant that the liberator for many has become a captor for those who are excluded from its power. The Indian novelist Rohinton Mistry is well aware of bureaucrats' use of literacy to disempower his country's marginalized majority. In *A Fine Balance*, we follow the fortunes of two impoverished tailors, who have broken through the conventional bounds of their Dalit ('untouchable') caste by learning to read and write. The following exchange with a government rations officer illustrates how literacy is as much a caste-marker as a useful skill in many parts of the world:

> [The official] ... gave the tailors a ration-card application form. He said there were experts on the pavement outside who, for a small fee, would fill it out for them.
> 'That's okay, we know how to write.'
> 'Really?' he said, feeling snubbed. [...] The tailors' literacy was an affront to his omniscience. 'Complete it and bring it back,' he dismissed them with a petulant flutter of fingers.
> They took the form to the corridor to fill in the blanks, using a window ledge to write on. It was a rough surface, and the ballpoint went through the paper several times. They tried to nurse the pockmarked sheet back to health by flattening the bumps with their fingernails, then rejoined the line to face their interlocutor.
> The Rations Officer scanned the form and smiled. It was a superior smile: they may have learned how to write, but they knew nothing about neatness. He read their answers and stopped in triumph at the address portion. 'What's this rubbish?' he tapped with a nicotine-stained finger.

'It's the place where we live,' said Ishvar. He had entered the name of the road that led to their row of shacks on the north side. The space for building name, flat number, and street number had been left blank.

Literacy is more than just knowing how to externalize linguistic expressions through graphic characters. It is a matter of social status and power. Even knowing how to read and write is not quite enough for you to become a *full* member of the club. Filling out a government form can challenge the most educated amongst us (me included). We get judged also by the *way* we write: our handwriting and our knowledge of spelling conventions. And so much of the stuff of society is encoded in literacy. A street address, for example, is basically an orthographic code, and so even if Ishvar and Om the tailors know how to write, the location of their home has not been codified by literacy, and so their application is rejected.

This is something we should all be exercised about. It is a matter of urgency that the double-edged sword of literacy be wielded decisively to champion its acquisition by all members of the species in the shortest timeframe possible. Access to the printed word not only allows members of literate societies to deal with the day-to-day business of making ends meet, but also brings with it access to the thoughts of millions, far away in space and time, and allows individuals and communities to participate more fully in the doings of the species. Especially for marginalized cultures and groups, control of the written word can bring greater powers of self-determination and, in some cases, cultural survival itself. Here applied linguists have a central role, an issue to which we return in Chapter 10.

Mixing sound with spelling

More mundanely perhaps, but of great significance for modern humanity, an ability to write has on some levels also deepened the effects of the Spell, making it even more difficult for us to reflect on language in its natural medium. Take an apparently trivial example. A couple of years ago I came across the following in the corrections section of the *Guardian* newspaper:

> In a column by Thomas Castaignède, page 18, Sport, March 4, an error in transcription caused him to say: 'As we say over here, *ils se sont fait mangés* – they let themselves be gobbled up.' He actually said, '*Ils se sont fait manger.*'

The correction of the verbal ending from -*és* to -*er* does not change the *meaning* of the sentence, but in fact M. Castaignède said neither of them. What he 'actually said', was {eelsuhsõfaymõzhay}, or, if we pretend there are actual pauses between spoken words, the rather less unsettling {eel} {suh} {sõ} {fay} {mõzhay}. (For the moment I'll represent speech using crude spell-outs placed in braces –{zh} being my rendition of the *g* in *lingerie* or the *s* in *pleasure*, and {õ} a nasalized *o*.)

It so happens that French *mangé* and *manger* are pronounced identically, as {mõzhay}, despite their different endings in the orthography: the verbal endings are **homophones** represented by the sequence {ay} but not **homographs** (*-és* is different from *-er*). The *Guardian* says it got the quotation wrong because of 'an error of transcription', indicating that the wrong written form was used to render what the columnist had actually said. *Manger* is the infinitive form of the verb meaning 'eat' (as in *to eat*), and *mangé* is its past participle form (equivalent to *eaten*). We can say that the lexical meaning 'eat' is expressed by the stem *mang-*, the grammatical category INFINITIVE by the suffix *-er*, and the grammatical category PAST PARTICIPLE by the suffix *-é*. (More on these categories later.) The error in the sports column was that Castaignède presumably intended *mang-* plus *-er*, but was reported as having produced *mang-* plus *-é*. But here's the problem: you can't say *manger* or *mangé*. These are *written* forms. You can only say {mõzhay}.

Castaignède can only have *intended* with {mõzhay} to express the grammatical notion of INFINITIVE, and the only way anyone could know with certainty that that was what he was expressing, rather than PAST PARTICIPLE, is if he spelled the form out for them: with an 'r' at the end instead of an acute accent (') over the *e*. If we just look at the *meaning* of the sentence, independently of any knowledge of grammar, the past form *mangé* would look like an appropriate form, since the 'gobbling' happened in the past, and it is presumably this that led the transcriber to commit the error. Remember that the Spell blocks conscious access to the grammar of I-languages: French speakers don't deliberately pore over mental verb tables to select an appropriate grammatical suffix every time they open their mouths to speak, and yet the grammatical machinery they need to produce and comprehend language is there nevertheless.

An illiterate or under-educated speaker of French (including most French speakers who lived before compulsory education was introduced in France in the late nineteenth century) would not distinguish between the two phonological *forms*, though the syntactic frames and conceptual structures of the same lexical triads would differ slightly. There is nothing odd about French here: all that is going on is that two homophones happen not to be homographs, in the same way that English *they're*, *there* and *their* are pronounced the same but spelled differently. Similarly, many English speakers spell *have* as *of* when it is contracted to -*'ve* in contexts such as (1):

(1)   (a)   The dancers should of (should've) arrived by now
       (b)   Francis could of (could've) let me know

Since the two forms are pronounced {uv} and only writing distinguishes between them on the surface, this is unsurprising. For people that lack an ability to use written forms (or use them only infequently), homographs are purely academic. Writing is an optional extra for the human language faculty, so it follows that the grammar underlying the spoken output of illiterates (or those with low literacy skills) loses nothing in precision or communicative capacity as a result of their lack.

Linguists should not ignore writing, of course, as though it were just another way of rendering speech (or indeed as a confounding variable best put to one side because it obscures our view of the actual sounds of language). It is unfortunate that some scholars in the field betray precisely these prejudices. But if we are to understand human language fully, if the Language Spell is to be broken, we must also think beyond the written word, despite the allure of holy books, constitutions, dictionaries and literary lions, and the lure of shopping lists, benefit claims, legal contracts and email.

This is why it matters that *manger* is pronounced the same as *mangé*. The relationship between phonology and orthography is not completely equitable, even at the level of individual word forms. In language history, phonology actually forges ahead of writing, engendering dynamic changes in successive generations of I-languages, whereas sluggish orthography tends to get mired and mixed up in E-language conventions. Together, the near invisibility of speech and the confusion between words and things lead us to tacitly assume that in fact things are quite the other way round: that when we speak, we are simply naming written words. A consequence of this is that spelling skills get prized over rapping, and dialects fortunate enough to have provided the basis for writing systems become seen as the only correct varieties (see Chapter 10).

The primacy of the written word

Dictionaries, language academies, newspaper columnists and governments are often at the forefront of this unique respect for the written word, as they propose and support (and in the case of governments, often fund) reforms of the spelling system. The New Zealand Association of English Teachers ponders whether to allow students to use US spellings instead of British ones (the association's president 'is impressed by the "phonetic logic" of American spelling' according to a newspaper story, whereas the columnist who wrote it argues that from such a choice '[c]haos will naturally follow'). Languages with more 'phonetic logic' than English are not immune to this inevitable consequence of the Language Spell: another newspaper article informs us that the 1998 spelling reform for German 'reduced the number of spelling rules from 212 to 112, and the rules governing the use of commas – a particular bane of students – from 52 to nine'. (Unsurprisingly, the reform hasn't caught on, even after the publishing industry reportedly spent 200 million dollars on rewriting school textbooks.)

The German preoccupation with comma placement illustrates how punctuation is seen as being in need of particularly tight control. Many English speakers today complain about the gradual loss of the possessive apostrophe (me included when the Spell has me in its power). Yet it's a very recent convention in the language, more of a decorative graphic flourish than a significant aid to linguistic communication. The Immortal Bard's First Folio of 1623 is entitled 'Mr. William SHAKESPEARES Comedies, Histories, and Tragedies' and nobody complains about that.

Finally, consider the following quotation from an interview with the Director of the Royal Academy of the Spanish Language, when he was asked why the 'silent *h*' letter had been retained in their new spelling edict, even though it doesn't represent any sound in contemporary Spanish:

> [S]pelling should not only be fixed according to phonetic criteria (i.e. writing how we speak), but also on etymological grounds. That is, the spelling of a word can indicate how it relates with its source, its origin, [in the case of *h*] to tell us that we are speakers from the Latin cultural tradition. I like to say that the 'h' in *hombre* may not be pronounced, but [it] makes us brothers to all *hombres* of the Latin cultural tradition. If we were to suppress it, apart from causing mutual incomprehensibility, we would be denying that relationship.

A wag in a less reverential corner of the Mexican press, responding to this, asked whether Spain's 'brotherhood' with others in the Latin tradition wasn't compromised by the fact that that country's name

(*España*) should, on such etymological grounds, be *Hespaña*. He also pointed out that phasing out the *h* would remove one small cause of social stigma for the under-educated Latin American poor (many of whom are not *part* of the 'Latin cultural tradition'), who in writing often add an *h* where there shouldn't be one and omit it where there should be.

Sounds and phonemes

The crux of the problem is that spelling has become such a part of the fabric of our linguistic awareness and beliefs that we confuse the sounds of languages with the way they are written: phonemes with letters, intonation with punctuation. Linguists try to keep the two modalities clearly distinct by employing a special alphabet designed to represent speech sounds directly, rather than following phonologically-independent orthographic conventions. The International Phonetic Alphabet (IPA) provides a way of representing speech in graphic symbols, and IPA transcriptions are placed between square brackets to indicate that they are made of sounds, not letters. Imagine for the moment that such transcriptions are icons for computer speech files, and that clicking on them plays the pronunciation through your speaker system.

But even the IPA is 'contaminated' by orthography, relying as it does on conventional Roman letter symbols together with a few others, adapted from the Greek alphabet and other graphic systems. For example, the word *sixth* is represented phonetically as [sɪksθ] and *ease* as [iz]. Such a eurocentric system unwittingly invites lay users to identify some IPA symbols with the letters they resemble, and therefore with the sounds these letters conventionally represent in written words. In some cases it is easy to divorce the sounds from the letters, for example in some of the quirkier regions of the English orthographic system. The old chestnut *-ough* is probably the best example around, as the following sentence still doing the rounds on the Internet attests: 'A r**ough**-coated, d**ough**-faced, th**ough**tful pl**ough**-man strode thr**ough** the streets of Scarbor**ough**; after falling into a sl**ough**, he c**ough**ed and hicc**ough**ed.' In other cases, it's hard for beginning phonology students or EFL learners to see *six* as [sɪks] rather than [sɪx].

Nevertheless, the IPA provides a more accurate way to write (and *think*) about speech. Spanish *hombre* is transcribed as [ombre], not [hombre], and English *whole* and *hole* are both [hol]. But what exactly do the IPA symbols represent, if not the pronunciation of letters, characters or other orthographic units? I suggested earlier that we could try seeing them as icons calling up speech files, but this is inaccurate, since they are not tied to unique speech events (i.e. people actually talking). IPA transcriptions can't capture real utterances, since speakers have different voices, and every time they speak a word form, it will come out slightly differently. For the same reason, the word *phonetic* in the name 'International Phonetic Association' can be somewhat misleading, when the symbols it offers are used by linguists to represent not only **phonetic** sounds, but also **phonological** units. The difference between phonetic and phonological is a tough one, but it is crucial to an understanding of how words link meaning with sound.

At the end of Chapter 2 we sketched what it meant for an English speaker to know English. Part of Angela's repertoire of declarative knowledge was a phoneme inventory and a set of phonological rules for its use. Part of her procedural knowledge was (a) a set of articulatory routines for transforming sequences of phonemes into air molecule vibrations, using the vocal tract; and (b) acoustic analysis routines for converting those vibrations on the eardrum into strings of phonemes. This gives us at least two ways to think of the units of speech: as sounds *spoken* and sounds *heard*. Spoken sounds are describable in terms of articulatory gestures, i.e. the positions adopted by the components of the **vocal tract** (the space between the vocal cords and the lips and nostrils) and the patterns of resonance that result from air being forced up through them from the lungs. Heard sounds are describable in terms of acoustic signals, i.e. patterns of sound **amplitude** (loudness) and **frequency** (pitch), over time.

But since most human beings are both speakers and hearers (indeed, we can hear ourselves speak), then there must be something in our minds which ties together the motor signals shaping air flow through the vocal tract with the signals coming to the brain through the auditory nerve. It is this that distinguishes the phonetic (external) from the phonological (internal). To know that the word *body* begins with the unit /b/ is not just to know how it is pronounced, what it sounds like, or both of these together; it is a more abstract kind of knowledge, a single unit which underlies multiple instances of both production *and* comprehension (signalled by linguists with the use of slashes instead of brackets). In this way we can account for the apparent public nature of words, since we have the impression that the *same* word forms get both spoken *and* heard in social interactions. Without this impression language would be unusable.

So, apart from the phonetic procedural knowledge needed to make the sounds of language and sort them out from other sounds when we hear them, we have declarative knowledge of phonology, the abstract underlying system which mediates between speaking and hearing on the one hand, and meaning on the other. Crucially, also, phonological units allow us to 'remember' word forms when we're not using them, so that we can produce or recognize them the next time we need to, under new and different circumstances.

Form representations in the lexical triad can't be only memory traces of the shapes of the letters which spell a word, since you don't need to be literate to be equipped with a lexicon. Neither can they be simply a memory of the way words sound, since (a) they sound different on different occasions of use; and (b) memory of a sound on its own wouldn't be enough for us to produce it. We *do* store the sounds of speech in general memory, together with the sound of Big Ben's chimes, the crashing of waves in the sea, the first four notes of Beethoven's Fifth and a veritable cacophony of other memorized noise. The units of speech, however, unlike other remembered sounds, must also be stored in such a way as to permit (a) the motor system to *produce* them; and (b) the phonetic system to recognize *variants* of them produced by different vocal tracts under different conditions (on the telephone, in the shower, in a whisper, under the influence of alcohol, in a foreign accent, etc.). Finally, word forms can't be remembered only as sets of instructions to the articulators and lungs, since our auditory input systems don't get information about how sounds are produced, just how patterned clusters of molecules rattle against the eardrum. Indeed, we can recognize synthesized speech, which is produced by a computer program rather than a vocal tract.

The abstract word forms stored in the lexicon are best thought of, then, in terms of phonological units, called **phonemes**, which we can represent using the same IPA shorthand as is used to represent actual speech events. In a last effort to be more concrete, we might still try to define phonemes in phonetic terms, as the units of linguistic memory which link an acoustic signature with a pneumatic event in the lungs and vocal tract, but, alas, even this won't work, since the congenitally mute can develop perfectly functioning lexicons, and again we're faced with the problem that each event will be qualitatively and quantitatively *different*, both within and across speakers. We're going to have to accept the counter-intuitive conclusion that phonemes are not sounds, memories of sounds, or memories of speech events, but rather more abstract cognitive units which *underlie* our capacities to speak and hear word forms. Phonemes, then, are neither articulatory nor acoustic in nature.

Unfortunately, the Spell is reinforced here *for linguists* by the IPA and the phonologists, who define phonemes according to how they are produced in the vocal tract. The /b/ phoneme of *body*, for example, is described as a bundle of phonetic features including [VOICED], [BILABIAL], and [STOP]. **Voicing** refers to vibration of the vocal cords, and is what distinguishes words like *bat* and *pat*: [b] has vibration, [p] doesn't. (You can try this yourself by placing a hand over the vocal cords, or over your ears, and pronouncing each word in turn. Or better, try it with [z] and [s], since these sounds can be sustained without having to move on to a vowel, all of which are inherently voiced.) The feature [BILABIAL] refers to lip closure, and a [STOP] is a sound produced by a 'stoppage' or obstruction to the airflow in the vocal tract which causes pressure to build up, before being released suddenly. The lips provide the obstruction here, hence [b] and [p] are '**bilabial stops**'.

Phonologists have little alternative to the use of terms from speech production, because the Spell ensures that phonemes, like meanings, are pretty well hidden from introspection, finding their most concrete *expression* in the physical, dynamic, reality of the vocal tract. And we *need* a way to talk about phonemes. Only through talking about them can we link them on the one hand to the concrete world of physical events outside the mind, and on the other hand to our concepts of them, and the words and other linguistic units we use to communicate about them, stored *inside* the mind. (Indeed, only by talking and writing about them can phonology exist as one of the linguistic sciences!) The only other alternative to using articulatory phonetic terminology would be to talk about phonemes in terms of acoustic signatures, i.e. the effects of molecule displacement on the human eardrum, otherwise known as loudness, pitch and rate of input. This, as you may guess, is hard to pin down.

There *are* characteristic acoustic patterns associated with different vowels and consonants, which we can inspect in graphic representations known as **spectrograms** on a computer screen. (You've probably seen them in spy movies, when the technical whizz-kids transform one person's voice into another's, or match two recordings to establish whether they came from the same mouth.) But unlike the elastic vocal tract, nothing in the auditory system actually *moves* very much, and there are no discrete patterns anchored to observable entities like the tongue, the lips and vocal cords. Referring in a journal article or a lecture to the /b/ phoneme as a 'voiced bilabial stop' is clearly much more efficient than dictating a set of aggregate coordinates on a spectrogram.

The phonology of words in memory and in use

What then, does the form representation of the lexical triad look like? In most linguistic discussions of the lexicon it is left as a sequence of phonemes and an optional sequence of letters for the literate, but this is clearly just a short-hand for more complex structures. The orthographic representation is the simpler of the two, though is by no means a straightforward affair. For reading it must be abstract enough to be easily matched up with visual input corresponding to different kinds of handwriting, different print fonts, upper versus lower case and occasions where the input is degraded (a sign with letters missing, the miniscule smallprint in a contract, or a word mispelled, for instance). For writing it must be in a format which is readily interpretable in terms of motor signals to the arm and hands for the manipulation of a pen, a keyboard or a pointing finger to write in the air or sand, for example. Hence the notion of **grapheme**, to parallel the abstract and use-neutral phoneme.

The phonological representation is trickier. Written words for the most part retain their formal integrity in running text because they are blessed with the provision of blank spaces as buffers around them. Spoken words, on the other hand, get run together and sometimes, in fast speech, are reduced almost to nothing. A sentence like *I do not know*, for example, will normally get reduced to *I don't know, Don't know, I dunno*, or just plain *Dunno*. Since this expression is so frequent in the epistemologically blighted lives of most of us, it might become memorized as part of a fixed repertoire of commonly used utterances. As a memorized unit, it will be stored in the lexicon as an unanalysed whole – in effect as one long word. But fast speech does not just slur well-rehearsed utterances: novel ones too will be subject to predictable, rule-governed **phonological assimilation** and **phonetic reduction**. Take the following random example:

(2)   The transit police will arrest ten biologists for arson

It's almost certain that you have not encountered this sentence before, but if you speak it aloud now in normal, casual, rapid speech, the chances are that the final [t] on *transit* will get chewed up, the first vowel of *police* will disappear, *will* will be reduced to the single consonant [l], the [n] of *ten* will be tranformed into [m], and *for arson* will emerge as the single 'phonological word' *frarson*. There is, in other words, rampant reduction and assimilation in the content words, as their final phonemes merge with the beginning of the following one or get swallowed altogether, and severe contraction in the function words.

Clearly we don't want our mental lexicons to store all possible phonemic 'spell-outs' that their surface expression might take in different spoken contexts: that would be excessively profligate in terms of memory. Instead, any predictable modification patterns will be stored in the rules of the separate phonology component of our mental grammars. Take the word *ten*, which in its lexical representation ends with a consonant [n], made by touching the palate with the tongue just behind the teeth (giving it the feature [ALVEOLAR]) and allowing air to pass through the nasal cavity (the feature [NASAL]). The change of [n] to bilabial [m] before the following bilabial [b] of *biologists* will happen *every* time a word final [n] bumps up against a word-initial bilabial, except in extremely careful speech. So the lexical entry for *ten* will contain only the phonemes /t/, /e/, /n/, with [tem] being produced via access to a general phonological rule which turns its [ALVEOLAR] feature into [BILABIAL] in the context of a following bilabial. Hence *Zen Buddhist* is pronounced *Zem Buddhist*; *Can Peter?* as *Cam Peter?*; and *in Madrid* as *im Madrid*.

But there's more to a phonological representation than phonemes. Note that *biologists* has a different rhythmic beat than similar words of four syllables like *profitable, comprehension* and *tiramisu*:

- *profitable*:   **DUM**-dee-dee-**dum** (main stress on the first syllable);
- *biologists*:   **dee-DUM**-dee-dee (main stress on the second syllable);
- *comprehension*:   **dum**-dee-**DUM**-dee (main stress on the third syllable);
- *tiramisu*:   **dum**-dee-dee-**DUM** (main stress on the fourth syllable).

The stress pattern of the word must be listed in the lexical form representation, and for this to happen, the syllable structure must also be indicated. For some words, some or all of this may fall out naturally from general rules in the phonological component, but languages vary in how predictable word stress and syllable structure will be, so in such cases it must be marked in the form representation of the lexical triad.

Lexical stress must be kept separate from the stress patterns used in sentences for constrastive emphasis. The former, differentiating words like *re**fuse*** (the verb) and ***re**fuse* (the noun), is part of our declarative knowledge of word forms. The latter, on the other hand, are deployed strategically in language performance to mark the relative salience of the concept expressed. Writing does not always capture such nuances, as the following snippet from Ian McEwan's novel *Amsterdam* amply illustrates. The character Clive has written an angry message to his best friend Vernon, a newspaper editor, denouncing his publication of photographs which malign the memory of a mutual friend:

> What Clive has intended on Thursday and posted on Friday was, You deserve to be *sacked*. What Vernon was bound to understand on Tuesday in the aftermath of his dismissal was, You *deserve* to be sacked. Had the card arrived on Monday, he might have read it differently. This was the comic nature of their fate; a first-class stamp would have served both men well.

The inadequacies of writing as a faithful record of speech, abetted by the Royal Mail, lead to the unravelling of Clive and Vernon's friendship (... and, ultimately, to the two of them committing mutual homicide, no less).

Creating new lexical forms

So, phonemes arranged in syllables provide the raw materials from which words are built: but who builds them in the first place? When we recognize and produce known words in everyday use, we are *re*-building them, by matching the component phonetic units and stress patterns we've temporarily stored in short-term memory with stored phonemic representations in our (long-term memory) lexicons. But how are new words added to the lexicons of our speech communties so that the E-language has the resources it needs to allow communication of the new concepts that our societies are forever constructing? We know very little about the ultimate origins of lexical material, except to say that the likelihood of it happening via the deliberate, communal linking up of phonological substance to things in the world (Adamic naming) is quite remote.

Inheritance and borrowing

Rather than discovering ultimate origins, the techniques of historical linguistics lead us to *other languages* – either ancestor languages, whose lexical items have replicated themselves in successive generations until finding their current shape and usage in our own, or languages belonging to other communities altogether, whose lexicons have supplied ours with new material when their speakers have come into contact. The first source is often referred to as a language's **lexical inheritance**, and the second source involves a process known as **borrowing**, the source of **loan words**.

Unfortunately, this choice of terminology only aids and abets the Language Spell, by inducing us to treat words as 'things' (like coins) which 'belong' to groups, the ownership of which may be 'transferred' from one group to another, almost as though it's a volitional act of the parties involved. However, now that we've established in previous chapters that it's us who endow words with meanings, not the other way around, let's grit our teeth and accept these adapted, metaphorical meanings of the words *inheritance*, *borrowing* and *loans*. Thus, lexical inheritance is the process by which children's minds construct lexical triads which match those they infer to exist in the lexicons of mature speakers around them; and borrowing means the adoption in one E-language of lexical material from another E-language.

Languages in contact

Borrowing occurs when speakers of different languages come into contact, through population drift, immigration, invasion, trade relations, the transfer of knowledge through books or technology and even through holidays. The account I gave in the last chapter about lexical change perhaps gave the erroneous impression that linguistic systems are relentlessly fanning out through time and space (like Victorian Scots spreading around the globe and sundering their original family ties). But remember what has happened to my vocabulary and the vocabularies of my colleagues as the result of years of working in Mexico. Languages are also incestuous. The offspring and descendents of a single mother tongue can interbreed if enough of their speakers, after the original sundering, start to communicate again on a regular basis, leading to extensive cross-fertilization now between Spanish and English, both descended originally from a common ancestor tongue.

English and French provide a classic example from the past. The cataclysmic shift from King Alfred's Old English to Chaucer's Middle English was as radical as it was because of language contact, not generational re-analysis: the invasion of England by the French-speaking Normans in 1066 did much more to mould the present-day English lexicon than the language-copying infidelity of young children's minds. What happened in England at that time is that the entire governing class of the nation was essentially replaced by, or assimilated into, a francophone bureaucracy and a military, judicial and ecclesiastical power structure, owing allegiance to a French-speaking court. Although the ordinary people were naturally excluded from this new linguistic reality in the first instance, a bilingual state gradually came into being. When a new E-language has political, military and spiritual power on its side, the native tongue is bound to be affected. (French *culinary* power also had an effect – witness *mutton* from *mouton, beef* from *boeuf*, etc. – though when I was growing up this influence was much more detectable in the vocabulary than the kitchen...). During the Middle English period, over 10,000 words were 'borrowed' from French, and around three-quarters of them are still in use today.

I have often wondered what life must have been like during that phase of phenomenal social and linguistic upheaval in Britain. The process must certainly have been a slow one, but also a most extraordinary one, transforming the vocabularies of a nation from an essentially Germanic word stock in 1065 into an overwhelmingly Latinized one within 300 years. The intervening stages for ordinary folk, those burghers in the towns and peasants in the villages who had not received any formal instruction in Latin or the French of their new masters, must have resembled in some ways the experiences of Spanish-speaking immigrants today in the United States, or of slaves violently uprooted from their homelands in Africa and displaced to the Caribbean during the second half of the last millennium.

In situations where individuals are obliged to interact within groups which lack a common language, a **lingua franca** will often be adopted, in the absence of formal foreign language education. But the quint-essential example of human beings' indomitable will to communicate with their fellow men and women is to be found in the creation of **pidgin** languages. Pidgins are forms of language which have no native speakers, but that develop in the adult minds of members of interacting language communities as spontaneous E-languages which enable them to communicate in basic ways. Inevitably they are not as sophisticated as linguistic systems that have evolved over thousands of generations, and they therefore depend more on strings of content words than on grammatical devices for combining them together. But if the interacting communities stay in contact, and if, like slaves, they are denied any access to formal education, then their mental language faculties will inevitably elaborate on the system. Successive generations will creatively reconstruct what they hear around them, and gradually transform the pidgin into a **creole**, a fully-fledged system of I-languages which serves their purposes as well as the original languages of their forebears.

Pidgins do not arise out of the blue, as latter-day re-enactments of the apocryphal Adamic Convention, of course. Their resemblance to already existing languages is clearly evident. Their derivative nature is most noteworthy in the vocabulary, and most Caribbean creoles are described as English-, French-, Portuguese-, or Spanish-based, reflecting the tongues of the original colonial powers of the region. When you consider that the original pidgin innovators were adults with fully-equipped mental lexicons, but that the only common ground they had was the language used by the European slave-drivers, this should not be surprising. What seems miraculous is their offspring's rapid construction of complex creole *grammars* to use these words in ways that are as expressive as any E-language with a much longer pedigree. (More on this in Chapter 8.)

Here the Language Spell has often abetted racist prejudice, resulting in the common opinion that creoles are *incorrect* or simply *bad* versions of the European languages whose vocabularies they have adopted, without paying any attention to the facts of the language systems themselves. This may be attributable not only to beliefs in the unique 'correctness' of the home-countries' standard dialects in Europe, but also to the fact that most pidgins and creoles are spoken by people whose skin is darker and whose socioeconomic situation is lower than most Europeans'. It is salutory to think that the Anglo-Saxon race of the English must have undergone a similar process in the aftermath of the Norman invasion, so that our original 'Aryan' tongue is now forever Mediterraneanized.

Cross-linguistic influence and code-switching

What's happening in the minds of successive generations of language users as different E-languages jostle together in twelfth century England, in Mexican-American communities of the USA, or at thousands of other points of contact across the planet and through history? At first it must resemble what's going on in my mental lexicon and those of my English-speaking colleagues who live and work in Spanish-speaking Mexico. Although the power relations are going to be different in each scenario, and the eventual sociolinguistic outcomes will differ, the same pattern of cognitive events will unfold: linguistic features from the numerically and/or sociopolitically dominant language group will begin to seep into the I-language systems making up the minority language, as its native speakers are exposed to more and more input from the other group.

This phenomenon, called **cross-linguistic influence**, underlies all language contact situations, including the birth of pidgins and creoles, the development of multilingual communities, the process by which languages become extinct, and the learning of foreign languages through classroom instruction or individual study. In this last scenario the phenomenon gets played out in reverse, with learners' newly developing lexicons and grammars containing elements of the native tongue (as we saw with my EFL students in Chapter 3). Hopefully, these elements will diminish as proficiency increases, and the endpoint should be minds in which two languages peacefully coexist. In other cases, in authentic communities rather than artificial classroom environments, dominant languages displace minority ones, through the same process. This kind of **language shift** comes to pass because bilingualism often constitutes a transitory stage, rather than a lasting outcome of language contact.

As we'll see in Chapter 9, bilingualism is developed much more often in early infancy than in the classroom, in many thousands of communities all around the world. But this is the result of historical contact between what were originally monolingual groups, and way back then they had to have learnt each others' languages. So creole-speaking and bilingual communities have this in common: they both start out with an encounter between two (or more) monolingual groups of speakers, and end up with language-mixing, either completely in the case of creoles, or partially in the case of bilingual communities. As a result of both processes, new language varieties emerge, the result of cross-linguistic influence and the inbuilt linguistic creativity of the species.

A common phenomenon in bilingual speakers is the alternate use of both languages in daily interaction, even within a single utterance. This is known as **code-switching**, as when a Welsh-English speaker says *Come to the table. Bwyd yn barod* ('the food is ready') or when Mexican-Americans use what has come to be known as Spanglish. Code-switching is often viewed by monolingual outsiders as a sign of linguistic insecurity or ignorance, but in fact it obeys predictable patterns of social motivation and grammatically determined conditions on where the switch may occur. And in any case, code-switching is ultimately the mechanism by which cross-linguistic influence can introduce new words into a language, through language interbreeding. The Spell ensures that speakers will use *all* the linguistic resources at their disposal to do the job at hand, which is communication, not language apartheid.

Lexical recycling

Borrowing via contact is one of the two major ways that new word forms enter the lexicons of a speech community. The other is through reuse of the lexical material we already possess, by combining forms or shifting meanings. One thing is clear: very few words are invented through the creative fashioning of new word forms (i.e. by dipping into the phoneme inventory and arranging items from it into novel strings of syllables). Recapitulating the fictional labours of the Adamic Conventioneers is exceedingly rare, being found mainly in marketing, where names of new products are designed as carefully as their packaging and promotional materials. The pharmaceutical industry, for example, pays professional lexical innovators as much as £50,000 for names for its new drugs, but even here one can often find traces of other, existing words: *Zyban*, a drug to help people quit smoking, contains the verb *ban*; and *Viagra* evokes words like *vigour* and *virile*, ... perhaps blended with *Niagara*, for reasons I'll leave the reader to guess at.

We have already seen a number of cases where an existing word form is recycled to express new ranges of meaning: when word forms come to label more abstract concepts via metaphorical extension, like *body*, expand their meanings, like *nice*, or contract them, like *starve*, through generational reconstruction. Although the word form may not get substantially modified through the ages, the triad as a whole is reconfigured through its connection to the conceptual level, so these really are new words, given our definition of *word* as a lexical triad of mental representations of form-frame-concept.

Given this, we would expect that a word form could be reused in lexical coinages involving only reconfiguration of the *frame representation*, i.e. the range of possibilities for its syntactic deployment. There are indeed many such examples: the noun *access* is now commonly used as a verb (as in 'accessing the mental lexicon'); similarly, supermarkets *source* their vegetables from organic suppliers, and mobile phone users *text* their messages. The BBC World channel has even taken a verb (*to break*), converted into a noun (a *news break*), and turned it back into a verb again, when their announcers entone: 'Breaking the news every hour, BBC News is next.' (Conservative speakers who object to these 'modern' usages should probably think twice about *watering* their plants, *booking* their theatre tickets, and having their shirts *ironed*). This process of **conversion**, from one part of speech to another, is a rich source of new words, and although it occurs mostly between nouns and verbs, it's also possible between other parts of speech. Table 1 shows a selection of such alternations.

Table 1   Conversion from one part of speech to another

Source:	Used as:			
	Noun	Verb	Adjective	Preposition
Noun	–	she *wheeled* her barrow	*plastic* knives and forks	we decided to walk *back*
Verb	her *research* was funded	–	I'm getting rather *bored*	all *except* those two
Adjective	we saw the *last* of him	they *warmed* up their dinner	–	don't go *round* the bend
Preposition	into the *beyond*	and *downed* a pint of beer	I'm *through* with this book	–

Putting words together

The pool of word forms existing in the combined lexicons of a speech community at any given point is therefore always on call to serve new semantic and syntactic functions. If sufficient members of the community are in touch with another language, as slaves or masters, scholars or traders, then that second E-language too can be co-opted to enrich the lexicons of the first. Lexical triads can get reconfigured also without foreign intervention.

But actually, the most productive source of 'new ways to mean' is to *combine* memorized lexical triads into longer stretches of language. This can be done in two ways: first, building bigger words by adding two or more separate lexical forms together and memorizing the combination in the lexicon (through morphological word formation); and second, stringing words together in novel ways as needed, in order to make phrases and sentences (syntax). The next two chapters explore how we do both these things, and the nature of the relationship between them.

More information

    The International Literacy Institute (co-sponsored by UNESCO and the University of Pennsylvania) provides the **International Literacy Explorer**, a source of statistics and other information on literacy around the world, at http://literacy.org/explorer/index.html.

When I taught **English Phonology** a few years back, I found Heinz Giegerich's (1992) textbook to be an excellent, student-friendly

introduction. It covers the main standard varieties of the US, Southern England and Scotland.

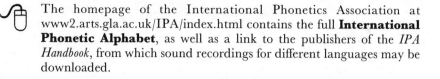 The homepage of the International Phonetics Association at www2.arts.gla.ac.uk/IPA/index.html contains the full **International Phonetic Alphabet**, as well as a link to the publishers of the *IPA Handbook*, from which sound recordings for different languages may be downloaded.

You can actually watch **voicing** happen in the vocal folds in glorious (animated) action, courtesy of the UCLA Phonetics Lab, at: www.humnet.ucla.edu/humnet/linguistics/faciliti/demos/vocalfolds/vocalfolds.htm.

Borrowing in English is addressed and illustrated in some detail in Stockwell and Minkova (2001).

John Holm's (2000) introductory textbook on **pidgins and creoles** covers their socio-historical origins, their development, and their grammatical characteristics. A briefer introduction may be found in Chapter 4 of Wardhaugh (2001).

Code-switching is discussed in Chaika (1994) as well as Chapter 3 of Wardhaugh (2001). See also Baker and Rhys-Jones (1998), discussed in the 'More information' section for Chapter 9.

Some nice examples of **neologisms** from UK newspapers, collected by researchers at the University of Central England, can be found at http://rdues.uce.ac.uk/neologisms.shtml.

Part III: Grammar

6 Morphology

Men, I want you just thinking of one word all season. One word and one word only: Super Bowl.

(attributed to Bill Peterson,
American football coach)

In Chapters 3–5 we examined words, the basic building blocks of human language, in considerable detail. Along the way we exposed several aspects of the Spell which governs people's folk understanding of language, and moulds their attitudes to it. We are now ready to move on to a quintessential property of human language, which the Language Spell hides from us even more successfully than it does the nature of words: the use of **combinatoriality** to enrich expressive power. It is our ability to combine linguistic units together in hierarchical structures that allows us to express an infinite variety of meanings. Yet the complex principles we use to do this are hidden from us, and take some coming to grips with, even for the practical and rugged morphologists and syntacticians who dedicate their lives to the cause.

Following on from our concerns in Chapter 5, we look first in this chapter at combinatoriality within the word, before moving on in the next chapter to syntax: the 'holy of holies' of human language for some linguists, but for others a technical problem which gets in the way of deeper understanding of how language works in the world. As always, we approach combinatoriality in words and between words first from the perspective of I-linguistic declarative knowledge, but then move on to ask how such knowledge changes through time and, in Chapter 8, how it is acquired by children and how we deploy it in actual communicative events.

Morphological combination

Combinatoriality within the word involves taking stretches of phonology from the lexicon which already have some meaning or function, and placing them in sequence to create a different word form. The minimal units so combined are called **morphemes** – minimal in the sense that they themselves are not the product of combination. *Body* is one morpheme, because it is formed by a combination of meaningless phonemes, whereas *slimy* is a combination of two morphemes: the independent word *slime* and a phoneme *-y* which, in this context, performs a conversion function, changing the part of speech of its sister morpheme from a noun to an adjective, and thereby relating a substance with a quality. The study of morphemes and their combination is called **morphology**, a term borrowed from biology, where it is applied to the study of the structural parts of plants and animals.

Most people are only aware of morphological combination through an interest in etymology and how different words relate together (for example that the Italian word which came to English as *infantry* actually *did* refer to a group of *infants*). For linguists, however, the primary interest of morphology is in its dynamic capacity, to be used on-line by speakers as they actively construct meaning. The most frequent dynamic use of morphology is when it is used on a daily basis to put words into the correct grammatical form when they appear in sentences (such as the French verbal *-é* and *-er* endings we saw causing so much bother to the *Guardian*). Less common, but more so than one would think, is the use of morphological combination to build brand new words. Here, for example, are two spontaneous creations of mine: *ex-Viagrans*, to refer to former users of Viagra, and (with apologies to Umberto Eco) *Ecoheads*, a new term for word nerds.

Of the 90,000 new words or new meanings of old words recorded in the OED for the twentieth century, around three-quarters involve combining existing morphemes together. That's over 600 a year! Glancing through a random copy of the *Sunday Times* in 2002, I came across the following word combinations which were new to me:

- *re-home* (of hounds who might lose their jobs due to a hunting-ban);
- *Diana-fanatic* (of an admirer of the Princess of Wales);
- *part-privatized* (of the UK air traffic control service);
- *Madonna-whore complex* (of Mahler's Eighth Symphony: don't ask);
- *Waffle-Warble* (of Tony Blair's public statements).

All but one of these examples are **compounds**, a fusion of two or more independent words. At least in English, these are the most common type of morphological neologism.

Compounds

A common way of combining existing lexical material to make new words is to just stick them end-to-end. This process is common in Germanic languages, especially Dutch and German, as well as others like Mandarin Chinese. The no-nonsense phonological concatenation of word forms which defines the compounding process is not, however, necessarily matched by a similarly straightforward summation of meanings. Sometimes the meaning of a compound is, roughly, the sum of the meanings of its parts. A *wolfman* is a fusion between a wolf and a man, for example. But a *trufflehound* is not the fusion of a truffle with a hound, but rather a hound that hunts out truffles; a *wolfhound* is not a cross between a wolf and a hound, nor a hound that hunts for wolves, but instead a hound that resembles a wolf; and a *wolftrap*, although most likely a trap laid by a human being for a wolf, could also be a trap laid by a wolf, or a trap that uses some wolfish trapping technique (what it can't be is a kind of wolf). And so on.

Given this apparent unpredictability of meaning, how can we ever use new compounds and be sure they are doing their communicative job? Take the novel compound *drughound*, used in the context of a recent addition to Heathrow security's canine unit (rather than metaphorically to describe a person who habitually takes or pushes drugs). If words could be added together in any old way, this new word *could* refer to a hound with ears shaped like cannabis leaves, a drug that makes you howl like a hound, or one of many other weird and wonderful canine/narcotic permutations. But most readers would probably hit upon my intended meaning without too much trouble (i.e. a hound that sniffs out drugs). This is because our interpretations of novel compounds are governed by two major constraints, one very general in scope and imposed by the nature of language as a social medium (we can call it the 'Social Constraint'), the other more restricted, and imposed by a rule in English-speakers' mental systems of morphological knowledge (the 'Right-hand Head Rule'). Taken together, they again reflect the Fundamental Paradox that 'language' is composed of many mental I-languages, but to be of any use these must be conceptualized as a single, social E-language.

The Social Constraint, touched on in Chapters 3 and 4, ensures that word meanings must be *conventional* in nature. Although word meanings are confined to individual speakers' heads, they are pretty useless if they are not matched by heavily overlapping meanings in the heads of potential interlocutors. So if we invent a new word, we have to be sure that our hearers will be able to understand it, otherwise it will provoke blank faces and we won't try it again. In certain circumstances, people do use words which they know are going to be new and incomprehensible to their hearers, in order to impress or bamboozle them (or, like Eco, to intrigue them). In such cases, blank faces are the goal; in lexical innovation, however, they are clearly not.

The meanings of new compounds that 'catch on' in an E-language must be at least *relatively* predictable, because speakers are in the main cooperative, and normally won't be willingly perverse. We are unlikely to come across the neologism *drughound* referring to the set of dogs which salivate when their owners smoke pot, or to the canine pets of those who argue for drug legalization (both perfectly logical, if odd, connections between dogs and drugs). Compound innovators (and that means all of us, potentially) don't combine words willy-nilly, despite the tendency of many compounds to mean more than the sum of their parts, and to be relatively unpredictable outside of a context of use. One way to ensure that new compounds will be interpretable to hearers is to model them on existing ones – in the case of *drughound*, English provides useful analogies in *foxhound* and *trufflehound*.

In addition to constraints imposed by the inherent civility of language users, we find that linguistic principles, represented in the morphological component of our mental grammars, will also limit innovators' use of lexical resources and listeners' search space for meanings. It so happens, for example, that new noun-noun compounds in English will normally use the first noun to say something about the second, rather than vice versa. A drughound has to be a type of hound, not a type of drug. The element that determines the type of entity the whole compound refers to is called its **head**, and in English, compounds are almost always right-headed. A blackbird is a kind of bird, not a birdy shade of black; a milkbottle is a bottle, not a type of milk; and a 'drughound kennel' would be a kind of kennel, not a kind of drug, a kind of hound, or a kind of drughound. The head also determines the part of speech of the whole compound, so that a blackbird is a noun, not an adjective.

Compounding versus other ways of combining words

What makes a compound different from other frequent co-occurrences of individual words? Why can't we say that in the novel form *drughound*, the noun *drug* has become an adjective, through conversion, and is used here to modify *hound*, in the same way that *hysterical* does in 'hysterical hound'? What makes the *Super Bowl* different from a *super bowl* (and so vindicates Bill Petersen's claim in this chapter's epigraph)? Why is the term *plastic surgeon* potentially ambiguous? The essential question here is, in fact, what makes some word pairs enjoy a morphological relationship (as a single compound word), and others a syntactic relationship (thereby retaining their separate word status)?

One possible response we can immediately dispense with is that compounds are morphological combinations because they are written with a hyphen, or with the space between the two elements occluded. It's true that some word combinations get this orthographic treatment. And then again others don't. My *Chambers Compact Dictionary* lists the following compounds starting with the noun *air*: *air bag, air-conditioning, aircraft, air-drop, air force, airgun*. Chambers may have a rule, but whatever it is, it's not part of general human linguistic competence. The spelling-together conventions certainly *reflect* people's feeling that the elements of a compound are somehow more closely related than elements of a syntactic phrase, but they don't *cause* the feeling. In fact, compounds must have existed way before writing systems were even dreamed of.

Compounds are different from syntactic phrases at each of the three levels of word structure – form, grammar and meaning – in the lexical triad. At the semantic level, we've already seen that compounds have meanings which cannot be calculated solely on the basis of the meanings of their parts (indeed, the meaning of unheaded compounds like *stalemate* would be completely impenetrable to a learner of English who only knew the words *stale* and *mate* separately). In syntactic constructions, such semantic unpredictability can't possibly occur, since the whole point of syntax in language is to allow us to go beyond conventional, stored meanings, to produce novel utterances with new meanings that don't result in blank stares from hearers. The semantics of sentences and other syntactic phrases must be **compositional**, i.e. recoverable as a direct function of the core meanings of the words of which they are composed. This, as we'll see in more detail in Chapter 7, is what allows human beings to be infinitely creative with the finite resources of the lexicon: the coining of a new word is an event (albeit a micro-event) in the history of human cultures, but a new sentence is more commonplace than a sneeze during the Moscow winter.

Memorizing by rote is the key to the difference between words and syntactic phrases. The connections between forms, frames and concepts in the mental lexicon specify a set of lexical items, and this set can be expanded, using our knowledge of morphology, by wiring up *new* triads from bits of existing ones. These then get memorized for future use. But normally we express new complex meanings *on-line*, by deploying memorized triads in new *syntactic* combinations. In everyday language use, we rarely need brand new words to get our meanings across, and normally our interlocutors recognize the words we produce because they've heard them before. Yet the sentences words occur in are not just prefabricated sequences, which have been rehearsed over and over until they get 'recognized' as familiar by hearers. On the contrary, both speakers and hearers actively *compose* and *decompose* brand new sentences all the time.

It can't be denied, though, that a lot of sentences get reused, and might become so frequent that they get committed to memory as though they were just very long compounds. Prefabricated phrases like *Speak of the devil!*, *Let's have a look*, *Here we go again* and *I love you*, might well account for a good deal of our output, but all human beings, whatever our daily drudgery, frequently express novel ideas. They may be as mundane sometimes as *I told you not to forget the butter I need for that cake* or *I expected Norma to have caught more fish than that after all her boasting*, or they may be lexically richer, like the sentences in a philosophical treatise, a Bob Dylan song or a novel by William Burroughs. Whatever their content, however, vast numbers of sentences are 'one-offs' (like most of the ones in this book), and language users don't have to try to recall the last time they heard or read them in order to find out what they mean. This, though, is *precisely* the way common compounds are routinely interpreted: by direct look-up in the lexicon, as memorized wholes. The meanings of *super bowl* and *stale mate*, therefore, are compositional, whereas the meanings of *Super Bowl* and *stalemate* are **non-compositional**.

Moving on to the level of syntactic frame, we can readily see that *blackbird* has one frame associated with it, whereas 'black bird' has two, one for *black* and one for *bird*. An adjective like *black* in 'black bird' needs its own frame so that it can be plugged into sentences like the following:

(1)   That bird is black, not grey
(2)   That's the blackest bird I've seen
(3)   Look at the black, scruffy-looking bird at the back of the cage
(4)   There's a light grey bird next to the very black one

When you slot the compound *blackbird* into sentences, on the other hand, the two elements work as one, resisting separation by other words as happens in (1) and (3) above, disallowing the addition of inflections like the superlative suffix *−est* in (2), nipping in the bud modification by intensifier words like *very* in (4), and ruling out substitution of the head noun by the pronoun *one*, also in (4). None of the following sentences can be construed as referring to blackbirds (as opposed to other birds which happen to be black), and they are ungrammatical under such an interpretation. (Linguists use an asterisk (*) to indicate a sentence which is not the product of our grammatical competence.)

(5)   *The -*bird* is a *black*-, not a sparrow
(6)   *That's the *blackestbird* I've seen
(7)   *Look at the *black*-, scruffy-looking, -*bird* at the back of the cage
(8)   *There's a light grey bird next to the very *black*- one

Finally, at the form level, compounds often get pronounced differently from their syntactic cousins. Nominal compounds, for example, regularly get their main stress on the first element, as opposed to the second, which is the pattern you find in normal pronunciation for a syntactic adjective-noun sequence. So *blackbird* is pronounced **DUM**-dee, whereas 'black bird' is dee-**DUM**; the bird *yellowhammer* is **DUM**-dee-**dum**-dee, whereas the unorthodoxly-coloured tool would be **dum**-dee-**DUM**-dee. When a compound gets entrenched in the E-language, and passed along through generations of I-languages, it ages faster than its syntactic counterpart, and if it's used frequently enough, its form can start to erode: hence *breakfast* is no longer pronounced as *break fast*, *half penny* became *hay-pnee*, and *Christ Mass* has become *Christmas*.

Affixation

So far, word formation through combinatorial morphology looks a lot like syntax, in that it combines elements from the lexicon into longer strings, but differs from syntax in that the elements so combined lose their independence, and the whole construction behaves phonologically, syntactically and semantically like one big word. But stringing together separate words is not the only way to make new words out of old lexical pieces – nor even is it the most common in the languages of the world. Much more extensive is the use of **affixes**: normally short phonological units called **prefixes** and **suffixes**, which get added to the beginnings and endings of words, respectively. Unlike the component parts of compounds, affixes cannot stand alone: they are **bound morphemes**, i.e. bits of meaningful phonology that don't get produced on their own (they are 'bound'). English has many of them, including the -*est* of *blackest*, the *non*- of *non-compositional*, the -*er* of *farmer*, and the *in*- of *ineligible*. Just like free-standing words, they are arbitrary combinations of form, frame and meaning, and therefore get their own entries in the lexicon. But unlike free words, they must be bound onto more substantial lexical hosts to achieve public expression: You can't point to a cage of black birds and ask 'Which is the -*est*?' or go to a farm and ask if the '-*er*' is at home.

Within and between the languages of the world, affixes come in many shapes and sizes. Some change their shapes, like chameleons change colours, to fit the host they get to hitch a ride on; others maintain their phonological integrity: compare *inelegant, impossible, ignoble, irregular* (*in-* and three massaged variants of it) with *uneducated, unpolished, unnatural, unrigorous* (*un-* invincible, throughout). Some can co-occur with thousands of potential hosts, others appear on only one or two (compare the suffix -*ness*, which can be popped on the end of almost any adjective to make a noun, and -*th*, which, conversely, turns only a few adjectives into nouns, such as *warmth, length* and *truth*). Some change the syntactic category of their hosts (*anti-war* is an adjective, whereas *war* on its own is a noun), others just fall into line (add *un-* to an adjective and it will remain an adjective). Some express hefty bits of meaning (like -*ify*, which adds (implicit) agency, causality and result to a quality, as in *purify*); others are semantic lightweights (-*ity* just makes a noun out of an adjective, affecting essentially only its syntactic frame).

Some languages have lots of affixes, especially suffixes. Turkish, Basque and Quechua (from the Andes) *only* have suffixes, whereas Thai and Navaho only use prefixes. Others, like Nahuatl and Aleut (spoken in Mexico and Alaska respectively), combine affixation with compounding to make *really* long words, which English-speakers would translate as whole sentences. Still others (e.g. Vietnamese and Chinese) use them very sparingly, preferring separate words to express different meanings and grammatical functions. Some languages allocate only one meaning or function per affix (like Turkish), whereas others get them to perform numerous tasks at once (like English -*s* on verbs, marking third person, singular number and present tense all at the same time). Chapter 9 gives more details.

If we're careful, however, we can see some overall method in this apparent morphological madness. The following five dichotomies have provided morphologists with particularly useful overlapping parameters with which to classify affixes and thereby begin to reveal what's possible universally:

- *Position*: **prefixes** are affixes that get attached before their host, whereas **suffixes** are affixes that follow the host;

- *Function*: **derivational** affixes make new words; **inflectional** affixes fit existing words into their syntactic frames;
- *History*: **productive** affixes are still used by speakers to make new words, while **unproductive** affixes define 'families' of existing words but don't get called upon any more to make new ones;
- *Form*: **phonologically transparent** affixes don't change their shape (or the shape of their hosts); **phonologically opaque** affixes blur the phonological boundary between the two elements;
- *Meaning*: **semantically transparent** affixes create compositional combinations (whose meanings are predictable); **semantically opaque** affixes appear in non-compositional combinations.

Let's see if we can use these dichotomies to unravel some of the mess that morphology appears to create for any clear conception of human language. Because, despite what looks like evidence to the contrary, morphology is not a smoke-screen thrown across human eyes by the artfulness of the Language Spell. Baroque as it all may seem to the innocent bystander, morphology is actually the perfectly natural consequence of the generational construction of I-languages by children (our fancy way of referring to language change). When 'unpacked', morphology can help us understand both how languages change through history and why they look so different from one another on the surface.

Where affixes come from

In the last chapter we addressed the question of where words come from, and how new words get created. But what about affixes? We know that the earliest forms of human language must have strung words together in basic syntactic combinations, but is it conceivable that affixes originated alongside the proto-word strings, in order to nuance basic lexical meanings, perform syntactic conversion, and provide the kind of syntactic glue we get with verbal and nominal inflections? Such a technical innovation would have been most improbable, I would have thought, at that rudimentary stage of language evolution.

An alternative view is that most affixes evolve *from* full words, as the latter appear in syntactic strings in the input to children, provoke the construction of new triads in infants' developing lexicons, and therefore occasionally get modified in form, frame and meaning, through successive generations of speakers. Historical linguists have detected many similarities between current affixes and coexisting or earlier, but now obsolete, lexical items. The hypothesis is that at some point in the evolution of human languages, a pair of frequently co-occurring words could be heard by a child as one single, complex word: a compound, presumably, which might subsequently get treated as a word plus a prefix or suffix.

Under what conditions might this happen, and why might one of the members of the pair be doomed to affixhood while the other maintained its lexical integrity and independence? It seems probable that this kind of **reanalysis** of a syntactic relationship as morphological is the result of a conspiracy between phonology and semantics. We've already seen that (E-)words can change their meanings from generation to generation, extending their concrete meanings to abstract domains through metaphor, like *body*, generalizing their meanings in cases like *nice*, and, more rarely, becoming more specific in meaning, like *starve*. Words can also change their shape through time, as each generation of learners fixes their phoneme inventory, phonological rules and word forms in the triad, on the basis of what they hear around them. Let's see how these two processes can result in the lexical enslavement of an independent word as a bound morpheme, doing service to a series of masters known as **roots**.

Word erosion

In order to fulfil its role as efficient messenger, speech accords more phonetic weight to more informative stretches of an utterance, so that greater stress falls on words that are less predictable, and less important words get de-stressed and therefore subject to more serious erosion. As we saw in the last chapter, fast speech causes consonants to be lost, especially at the ends of words, and in English and other languages, unstressed words can see their vowels all reduced to the primeval 'uh' that linguists call **schwa** and represent in IPA as /ə/.

This erosion, resulting in phonological opacity, is not caused by overuse, like the gradual degradation of banknotes, pencil lead or the toes of socks – the phonetic clothing of a word doesn't get *reused*: it's a new blast of air from the lungs each time. Neither is it the result of external forces, like a coastline receding under the pounding of the waves or part of a lawn disappearing under the constant tread of shoe-shod humans or their unshod animal cousins. Rather, it is a result of *lack* of force or use, given that naturally lazy humans expend as little effort as possible when they speak. This idleness cannot be viewed as morally reprehensible, however, since it increases speed of delivery, thus achieving the major goal of the Language Spell: to make language appear instantaneous, like telepathy. Of course, taken to extremes, fast speech would blur utterances to the extent that they were incomprehensible. There must therefore be give-and-take between the phonology and the semantics, sound and meaning, such that speakers expend as little effort as possible on encoding the physical form of the expression, whilst at the same time ensuring that enough meaning will be recoverable by the hearer for the communicative event to be successful. These are the 'push-me, pull-you' forces of **economy versus clarity**, which provide the dynamic tension holding together selfish I-languages as one selfless E-language.

With speakers indulging in this kind of selfish, but ultimately ecological, behaviour, it is no surprise that infants sometimes analyse the structures we've been looking at on the basis of what they *hear* rather than what was *intended* (as Chapter 4 suggested). Here's how. The dominant process of semantic generalization, if accompanied by phonological erosion in production, will conspire in certain cases to provide infants with input which suggests that two separate words are actually one. Children's minds are set up to detect co-occurrences of potentially meaningful bits of phonology in the input, and flag them as possibly significant. Evidence collected across many languages, by researchers like Dan Slobin, suggests that they pay particular attention to the margins of words, storing frequently recurring syllables at word beginnings and ends as separate units which may have special functions. Thus they pick up prefixes and suffixes.

But remember, the input they receive doesn't come with an instruction manual or any kind of linguistic labelling attached. Children can only identify some stretch of phonology as an affix by noticing a series of co-occurring cues in the input: a certain syllable may seem to express less semantic content than its neighbours in the speech stream; it may frequently follow sound sequences which appear to belong to a certain part of speech (like verbs); it may often co-occur with a certain modulation of the meaning of this class of words (past tense, for example); and it may always seem glued to them phonologically. Hence, any stretch of input might get analysed as a suffix if it fits this profile, even if it's a full word in the lexicons of the child's parents and older peers. And also vice-versa: although words like *timid*, *horrid*, and *torrid* ending in -*id* were originally analysed as suffixed, neither the roots nor the suffix are now semantically transparent. So the -*id* process is unproductive, and children will memorize the combinations it has produced in the past as unanalysed wholes, just like *elbow* and *banana*.

From word to affix

Let's look at a couple of concrete examples of affix evolution to see how the reanalysis process might work in practice. The English suffix *-ify* is added mainly to adjectives to transform them into **causative** verbs (verbs which include the meaning element of causation), taking *pure* to make *purify*, *plastic* to make *plastify*, *pax* to make *pacify*. This last example, together with others like *rectify*, *sanctify*, and *verify* (from *rectus*, 'right', *sanctus*, 'holy', and *verus*, 'true'), tells us that the process was in use in Latin, where many of the existing *-ify* verbs of English originate (mostly via the intermediary of French). The Latin verbs were actually *pacificare*, *rectificare*, *sanctificare* and *verificare*, and it is easy to see the separate verb *facare*, 'make' inside each of these words. So they started out as separate words, an adjective and a verb, combined in a syntactic relationship ('make right', 'make pure', etc.), which may later have become analysed as compounds (translating as *rightmake*, *puremake*).

In such a way, Latin-speaking children would hear the same verb, *facare*, cropping up continually after some adjective. They would note (unconsciously of course) that the verb wasn't exactly a deep well of lexical meaning, and decide (equally unconsciously) that the whole thing should get memorized in their mental lexicons as a single unit. Memorization in the lexicon means that the syntactic processing mechanism (our procedural knowledge of syntax) need not be invoked to see how the two elements fit together every time they recur. Subsequently, English speakers borrowed the forms, and through erosion at the end of the word, the original Latin *-i* + *facare* would gradually get eaten away until it became *-ify* (most often via French *-ifier*). Along the way, the newly coined suffix would get applied to brand new adjectives, producing occasional neologisms such as *plastify*, *gentrify* and *yuppify*.

Another example is the evolution of the future tense inflectional suffixes in Romance languages like French and Spanish, which illustrates the whole passage from contentful lexical item to affix. Cases of this kind are known as **grammaticalization**, since the outcome of the process is the creation of a new grammatical marker, in this case the inflectional suffix indicating tense. The Latin verb 'have' is *habere*, and its semantic evolution (described by the linguist Joan Bybee) is similar to the English verb with which it is cognate – the Old English form was *habban*. It started out as a verb indicating possession, among other things (English *have* was originally restricted to 'holding in one's hand'). In some contexts, *habere* was followed by an object noun which was modified by a clause expressing some kind of obligation, roughly equivalent to the English example in (9):

(9) I have [a job which needs doing]

Gradually, the construction started to be used with an infinitive in the modifying clause, as in the English (10):

(10) I have [a job *to do*]

In both these kinds of construction, the idea of obligation brought with it a sense of future time, since if someone is obliged to do something, it has not been done yet, and if done will be done in the future. In a subsequent development, *habere* began to be used with the infinitive directly, without an intervening noun, in sentences like (11):

(11) I have [*to sing*]

Latin word order allowed an infinitive like '(to) sing' to precede the verb, so children would get sentences like (12) in the input they received as they acquired the language:

(12) Cantare habemus
      [TO SING] [WE HAVE]
      'We have to sing'

This was in Classical Latin. By Late Latin, children were treating the pairing of verb + *habere* as compound-like constructions, instead of subordinate clause and main clause. Once the formerly free-standing lexical item had lost its fuller lexical meaning of possession, and was being reinterpreted as a marker of obligation with a strong future orientation, it didn't have far to go to reach its current form in Latin's Romance daughter languages. By Late Hispanic Latin, spoken on the Iberian peninsula a millennium ago, it had started to erode seriously, losing the central /b/, for example:

(13) Cantar hemos
      [TO SING] [WE HAVE]
      'We have to sing'

And subsequent generations then began to treat it as an inflectional future suffix, giving rise to a whole **conjugation** of forms for the different persons and numbers of the verb, as we see in Table 1.

Table 1   Evolution of the Spanish future inflections

	Latin	Late Hispanic Latin	Modern Spanish
Singular			
'I will sing'	cantare hábeo	→ cantar he	→ cantaré
'You will sing'	cantare hábes	→ cantar has	→ cantarás
'He/she/it will sing'	cantare hábet	→ cantar ha	→ cantará
Plural			
'We will sing'	cantare hábemus	→ cantar hemos	→ cantaremos
'You will sing'	cantare habétis	→ cantar heis	→ cantaréis
'They will sing'	cantare hábent	→ cantar han	→ cantarán

In such ways, lexical material gets massaged phonologically and semantically through generations of learners' active and creative analyses of the input, as they repeatedly forge their own I-languages – and the necessary illusion of a monolithic E-language unfolding over the centuries gets reinforced.

Since the reanalyses are normally imperceptible from one generation to the next, and linguists have documented so few of them, the unfolding is often taken to be unidirectional, from syntax to morphology. Often the instamatic snapshots historical linguists have been able to provide are taken as docudramas of a language's entire history: syntactic combinations become morphological combinations, word meanings get 'bleached', sloppy speech replaces careful articulation. The story that emerges seems to be one of inexorable decline, with literary ages of gold being replaced by contemporary shoddiness, impurity and solecism. Not so.

The loss of affixes

Taking the longer view, and divorcing languages from separate (but related) developments in the cultures they serve, we can detect vast cycles of change, as speech communities covertly shift the combinatorial power of their linguistic systems between the syntax and the morphology, as word forms eddy and flow, and zones of meaning expand and contract. For learners not only provide E-languages with new compound and affixed words by converting their parents' syntax into morphology: they can also *divest* their inherited tongues of morphological combinations, as the processes of phonological decay and semantic generalization lead them to reanalyse affixed words as simple ones, which can then, in turn, enter into syntactic liaisons with other simple words. The full circle, that is. We've already seen this with examples like *breakfast* and *timid*, and it also happens to whole systems of affixes, like the Old English inflectional systems. Here's how it happened.

Old English inherited a rich inflectional morphology from its West Germanic forebear. Inflections are a special class of morphemes, normally showing up as affixes, which convey grammatical functions like tense, number and person. Instead of building new words (*-ify* making *yuppify* out of *yuppie*, *un-* making *unxeroxed* from *xeroxed*), they put a word into the correct grammatical shape for use in a particular syntactic frame. Thus, *car* takes the form *cars* in the sentence frame 'He decided to sell one of his __'; and *crash* takes the form *crashed* in the frame 'He ____ his wife's new Jaguar yesterday.' Modern English has very few inflectional affixes. Apart from the plural *-s* in 'One of his *cars*' and the past tense *-ed* in 'He *crashed*', we have only:

- the homophonous past participle *-ed* in 'He has *crashed* again' (often *-en* in irregular verbs like *break/broken, be/been*);
- the progressive participle *-ing* in 'He's always *crashing*';
- the third person singular *-s* (homophonous with the plural on nouns) in 'He *crashes* daily';
- the comparative *-er* in 'This bird is *blacker* than that one';
- the superlative *-est* in 'This bird is the *blackest* in the cage'.

That's all. You'll often see the possessive *'s* added to this list, but it's not strictly speaking an inflectional suffix, since it gets added not to individual nouns but to entire nominal *phrases*: in the phrase *the Archbishop of Canterbury's beard*, the facial hair belongs only to the archbishop, not to the entire see of Canterbury.

Languages like Russian and Swahili have vastly more complex inflectional systems. Russian speakers, for example, must select one of up to a dozen different suffixes to place a noun in its appropriate grammatical form, and Bantu languages like Swahili can mark different classes of noun with up to 18 different suffixes. English *used to* resemble these languages more. Old English nouns and verbs had quite a respectable inflectional wardrobe from which to dress for grammatical outings. Here's a conjugation for the past and present tenses of the OE verb *lufian*, compared with its threadbare Modern English descendent, *love*:

Table 2 A comparative verbal conjugation for Old and Modern English

Person & Number	Old English		Modern English	
	Present	*Past*	*Present*	*Past*
1 SG	lufie	lufode	love	loved
2 SG	lufast	lufodest	love	loved
3 SG	lufaδ	lufode	loves	loved
PL	lufiaδ	lufodon	love	loved

Inflectional marking on the Old English noun was equally complex. In Table 3, I give the noun **declension** for *stan*, 'stone', showing **case** and **number** inflections. Case is an inflectional category that is marked morphologically in many languages, most often through suffixes, and it serves to indicate the roles that nouns play in sentences. **Nominative** case normally indicates nouns which are the subjects of verbs; **accusative** case marks direct object nouns; **genitive** case corresponds to the Modern English possessive, as in *the stone's colour, the colour of the stone*; **dative** case is used for indirect objects, as in *they gave* **the stone** *a lick of paint*.

Table 3 A comparative nominal declension for Old and Modern English

Case	Old English		Modern English	
	Singular	*Plural*	*Singular*	*Plural*
NOMINATIVE	stan	stanas	stone	stones
ACCUSATIVE	stan	stanas	stone	stones
GENITIVE	stanes	stana	stone's	stones'
DATIVE	stane	stanum	stone	stones

Now just because Modern English openly marks only a tiny fraction of the inflectional categories that it used to, this doesn't mean that the language is simpler overall. The key concept here is **overt marking**: the Language Spell ensures that vast tracts of the grammatical landscape of all languages are hidden from view. Human language is too complicated, and our communicative business too urgent, for all the pieces of our grammatical machinery to find expression in speech. This will become very clear in the next chapter, on syntax, where certain basic properties of linguistic communication are encoded in abstract principles which never see the phonological light of day. Here, however, let's concentrate on some of the grammatical functions most often expressed morphologically (via affixation in most languages), but which may also be **covertly marked**, i.e. there in your *head*, but not there in what the language requires you to actually *say*.

Covert marking and agreement

In many languages, for example Old English, and modern Spanish and German, nouns belong to arbitrary classes called **grammatical genders**. Membership of these classes rarely has to do with biological gender: Old English *wifmann*, 'woman' was masculine and *wif*, 'wife' was neuter; German *mädchen*, 'girl' belongs to the neuter class, and Spanish *barba* 'beard' is feminine; in Plains Cree, a language spoken in Canada, the genders are based on the distinction between 'animate' and 'inanimate'. Aristophanes (rendered here in William Arrowsmith's racy modern translation) made the point almost two and a half millennia ago in his play *The Clouds*, whilst at the same time taking a dig at a contemporary Athenian, Kleonymos:

STREPSIADES: *Basket* is masculine? But why?
SOKRATES: Because the ending *-et* is what in grammar we call a masculine termination. Like the *-os* ending of *Kleonymos*.
STREPSIADES: Wait. I don't see.
SOKRATES: I repeat: *basket* and *Kleonymos* are masculine in form and ending.
STREPSIADES: Kleonymos *masculine*? But *he's* feminine. Form and ending. Queer as they come. [...]

A word belonging to the masculine gender in one language may turn up as feminine or neuter in other languages: *unicorn* is masculine *unicornio* in Spanish, but neuter *Einhorn* in German, and feminine *licorne* in French; *shop* is masculine *magasin* in French, but neuter *Geschäft* in German, and feminine *tienda* in Spanish. In many cases, gender is overtly marked morphologically, so that in Spanish feminine nouns are marked with the suffix *-a*, and masculine nouns with the suffix *-o*. German doesn't have such a transparent system, on the other hand: all nouns are masculine, feminine or neuter, but very little in the phonology or the morphology will make this explicit (placing rather a burden on language learners!). And even in Spanish the marking system is not foolproof: the word for 'linguist', for example, is *lingüista*, but is masculine, as is *agua*, 'water'. In other cases the suffix doesn't show up at all: *paz*, 'peace' (feminine); *papel*, 'paper' (masculine); *flor*, 'flower' (feminine). In these cases, gender is covertly marked. I'll explain how we know this in a moment.

So if Spanish gender is not always predictable, and German gender rarely is, why bother with it at all? Why overtly or covertly mark nouns for membership of a group which is not even based on the semantic category whose name it borrows? One of the features of gender systems is that they extend temporary membership of their group to other words in the sentences in which they are deployed: a masculine noun will make its article also masculine; a feminine noun might require an adjective which modifies it to wear the same feminine suffix; a neuter noun may be referred to later with a neuter pronoun. Consider the following pair of examples from Spanish:

(14) (a) Compro per**a**s en vez de durazn**o**s, porque son más barrat**a**s

(a') 'I buy pears rather than peaches, because they are cheaper'

(b) Compro per**a**s en vez de durazn**o**s, aunque son más barrat**o**s

(b') 'I buy pears rather than peaches, although they are cheaper'

The English glosses are linguistically ambiguous out of context, because the pronoun *they* and the adjective *cheaper* could refer to either pears or peaches. It is, of course, highly likely that the speaker of (14a') buys pears to save money and the speaker of (14b') buys pears even though they can afford peaches, given discourse expectations and an appropriate intonation pattern. But the sentences *could* mean the opposite in the context of, say, one of Oscar Wilde's aristocratic ladies showing off to a less wealthy acquaintance in a letter: for her, (14a') might express the fact that she buys pears because they are more expensive, and (14b') that she buys pears despite the fact that they cost less.

In the Spanish sentences, however, the ambiguity cannot arise, whatever the context, since the adjective *barrato/a* is tied to the noun it modifies overtly, through what linguists call **agreement**. Agreement between one word and another in a sentence is very common in the languages of the world. Gender agreement is not the most common type: it occurs much more frequently with the inflectional categories **number** (singular/plural, for example, in the OE verb conjugation above) and **person** (1st, 2nd and 3rd in the same conjugation).

Agreement most often holds between a verb and its subject, but some languages also require agreement between the verb and its direct object. So agreement serves to link together parts of a sentence, and to this extent it is syntactic in function, although it becomes visible through morphological marking. The gender marking exemplified in (14) serves to link explicitly a property with the object it modifies. Covert gender marking, as in German, will, however, serve the same end, since noun genders will be represented in language users' minds in the lexical frames for nouns, even if there is no special affix to represent this information on the overt spoken 'surface'.

We must be cautious, however, about looking for a functional explanation for all inflectional categories. The gender marking in (14) would be of no help at all if the fruits compared were pears and apples, since Spanish *manzana*, 'apple', is also feminine. And as I implicitly acknowledged, non-linguistic context or other aspects of the linguistic system like intonation, or the pragmatic conventions for the use of the subordinating conjunctions *because* and *although*, would disambiguate the sentences in authentic utterance situations. On the other hand, gender systems are not the product of a post-Adamic Convention or some *ad hoc* committee of a national language academy, and languages do not evolve baroque embellishments just for the mischief of it. So it is likely that gender must have developed in groups of speakers' minds because it served *some* useful function in linguistic prehistory. Certainly, dividing up one's nouns into roughly equal groups of masculine and feminine can cut down potential ambiguities like those in (14) to a significant degree (i.e. every time an adjective might refer to either a masculine or feminine noun). Agreement between subject and verb also helps hearers to work out how the unfolding elements of a sentence fit together as a sentence is being uttered.

Inflection and word order

Getting back to our original concern, the loss of English inflections, two important questions remain: (a) did English lose its inflectional *markers* (i.e. the affix forms) or its inflectional *categories* (the bits of semantic meaning and grammatical function that the forms express)?; and (b) in either case, how did this affect the language's expressive power (i.e. was it rendered more open to ambiguity as a result)? With respect to the first question, as you may have guessed, linguists argue that the inflectional categories are still there, but marked covertly. We see this in the remnants of the English morphological case system, for example, which is visible now only in pronouns, for example *he/him/his*.

In (15) the subject (*the pig*) is nominative, and in (16), as the object, it is accusative, but this is overtly marked only in the pronoun versions:

(15) (a) The *pig* loves the farmer
      (b) *S/he* loves the farmer
(16) (a) The farmer loves *the pig*
      (b) The farmer loves *him/her*

Latin is a language that overtly marks case on common nouns. The translations of (15a) and (16a) would be:

(17) Porcus agricolam amat
      'Pig_{NOMINATIVE} farmer_{ACCUSATIVE} loves_{THIRD PERSON SINGULAR PRESENT}'
(18) Agricola porcum amat
      'Farmer_{NOMINATIVE} pig_{ACCUSATIVE} loves_{THIRD PERSON SINGULAR PRESENT}'

The usual place for the verb in Latin is at the end of the sentence, but word order is actually pretty free. All the following permutations of (17) are perfectly grammatical, and because of the case suffixes, they all mean that the pig loves the farmer, unlike their scrambled English equivalents – (15a) doesn't mean the same thing as (16a), that is!

(19) (a) Porcus agricolam amat
      (b) Agricolam porcus amat
      (c) Porcus amat agricolam
      (d) Agricolam amat porcus
      (e) Amat porcus agricolam
      (f) Amat agricolam porcus

So Latin is a **free word order** language, whereas modern English is a **fixed word order** language. Some languages are somewhere in between, like Spanish, one of the descendents of Latin, in which multiple orders are possible, but they carry with them different patterns of emphasis and focus:

(20) (a) El granjero ama al cochino
           'The farmer loves the pig'
      (b) Al cochino, el granjero ama [pero a la vaca nada más la tolera]
           'As for the pig, the farmer loves him/her [but as for the cow, he only tolerates her]'
      (c) Ama el granjero al cochino [pero no tanto que a la vaca]
           'The farmer *loves* the pig [but not as much as the cow]'

In fact, every permutation is allowable in Spanish, but since the order reflects a slightly different shade of meaning, linguists say that it has **pragmatic word order**.

You will have noticed the inverse correlation between fixed word order and overt morphological marking of case. And this answers our second question about the loss of inflections in the wake of the Norman Conquest: the expressive power of English was not reduced by the loss of case affixes, since the slack was taken up by word order. When morphology withdrew, syntax stepped in to take its place. (For Spanish, the loss of case-marking on nouns was compensated for, at least in animate nouns, by its overt marking on the article, *al* being an accusatively marked version of *el*, 'the'). So, although grammatical systems shift, the communication of meaning remains paramount, and grammar continues to subserve it, just as we would expect given the logic of the Language Spell.

In this section we have seen how morphological information interacts with syntax, the way words are put together in novel ways to create new meanings that don't need to be memorized, because they may never be used again. The next chapter provides a sketch of how this computational system works. As the most hidden and therefore unintuitive part of our language faculty, it will perhaps be daunting for some, and tedious to others. But I implore you to persevere: we are now at the very heart of language's magic.

More information

A comprehensive and readable presentation of the linguistic study of **morphology** is Francis Katamba's (1993) textbook, drawing on data from dozens of languages. A more recent introduction to morphology, but restricted to English, is Andrew Carstairs-McCarthy's (2002) textbook, written specifically for non-linguists.

Steven Pinker's book *Words and rules* (1999) discusses the fundamental distinction between **rule-governed combination and rote-learning**, using as a running example the English irregular verbs. It is amazing what he manages to conclude about the nature of language itself from this one small corner of English morphology.

Murray McGillivray of the University of Calgary explains the **Old English inflectional system** at the website which accompanies his course: www.ucalgary.ca/UofC/eduweb/engl401/grammar/index.htm.

Under every friendship there is a difficult sentence, that must be said, in order that the friendship can be survived.

(Zadie Smith, *The Autograph Man*)

Some syntacticians like to argue that their area of linguistics is at the very core of human language, since it is the only component of our mental grammars that directly interfaces with neither sound nor meaning, both of which lie *outside* of language: phonology connects sound with the lexicon; the lexicon and morphology mediate between sound, syntactic patterns and meaning; and semantics connects the lexicon and syntax with meanings in conceptual systems (Figure 1 in Chapter 2 summarizes this basic architecture). Only syntax is 100 per cent linguistic, they claim. But this isn't entirely true, since intonation patterns, for example, are sound structures which are directly sensitive to the patterning of sentences. Also, word order (determined by syntax) is sometimes the only thing telling us who did what to whom – resolving basic issues of meaning like the case of the pig-loving farmers and farmer-loving pigs of the previous chapter. Nevertheless, syntax is arguably still the most impenetrable and abstract component of human language, analogous with the hugely complex programming supporting friendly desktop icons on a computer screen, and under-standing it defies even the most ingenious Spell-breakers.

In this chapter I will take it slowly, and only talk about some of the basic aspects of syntax, concentrating on its major building blocks and the simplest ways in which it strings words together. I also try to relate it to meaning and language in use as much as possible, in order to make it more palpable to the syntactophobic reader. As a linguist whose eyes still rapidly glaze over in colloquia and conference papers on syntax, I understand only too well the sheer intellectual effort it takes many people to make sense of the topic. But to shamelessly mangle the quotation from Zadie Smith: 'Under every relationship between linguist and non-linguist, there is a difficult set of sentence structures, that must be presented, in order that the relationship can be survived.'

Syntactic combination

To most people, **syntax** is perhaps a vague aspect of 'good grammar'. But to many beginning linguistics students, it is a subject to be classed with calculus or alchemy: an arcane mystery shrouded in obscure formalisms and seemingly unconnected with the *real* world of language. Imagine the horror of an English Literature student who, thinking it would be interesting to know how Faulkner or Joyce produce such imaginative sentence structures, opens up one of Chomsky's books and sees the following:

α is locally bound by β if and only if α is X-bound by β, and if γ Y-binds α then either γ Y-binds β or γ = β

Yet syntactic knowledge, perhaps including scary stuff like this part of Chomsky's 'Binding Principle' for pronoun interpretation, is invoked by all human beings many times a day, with as little ado as sneezing. It is only the Language Spell that prevents us from seeing the Binding Principle as part of who we are as users of human language.

The word *syntax* comes to us through Latin, from a Greek word made from a prefix meaning 'with' and a verbal root meaning 'arrange' – hence, the combined term meant 'arranging [words] together'. Syntacticians study the ways in which language users can arrange words on-line into larger units, including full sentences with a subject and verb. For the uninitiated, the scientific study of syntax must appear to be a rather trivial pursuit: surely it can't be a terribly complex task to describe how to order words in English, or Japanese, or Malayalam? Isn't it all just a variation on the 'natural' theme of Subject-Verb-Object? In my first term as an English linguistics student, I remember puzzling about what it was that the department's syntacticians actually *did* in their offices, behind firmly closed, undergraduate-proof doors. What could it mean to 'do syntax'? Wasn't it all put down in grammar books many years ago?

In fact, human syntax ranks along with the structure of DNA as an example of enormous subtlety and power in naturally-occurring complex systems. And indeed, the human genetic code is likely to be cracked wide open before natural language syntax is fully understood (many genetic scientists are actually borrowing from modern theories of syntax in their descriptions of our species' genome). Researchers have come a long way towards understanding the basic principles of syntax over the past 40 years or so, but a full syntactic description, even of English, the most studied of all languages, is still far away. Governments and multinational corporations have spent indecent amounts since World War II trying to program computers to use human syntax, with extremely disappointing results (to the extent that many programmers trying to simulate human language on machines attempt to bypass syntax altogether). Arranging words together in sentences is not, then, as trivial as it seems.

Traditionally, the only conscious contact most people have had with syntax is when, as school children, they were exposed to the notion of *grammar*. 'Grammar' in this sense is assumed to cover both syntax and inflectional morphology. For modern linguists, though, the term *grammar* has been extended to cover all rule-governed aspects of individuals' I-language knowledge, including phonology, productive morphology, syntax and aspects of sentence semantics. The rules of syntax (and of the other grammar components) are not rules in the sense of social strictures or conventions (like public park regulations or the rules of etiquette), nor how-to instructions (like the rules of chess or of ballroom dancing). Instead, they are rules in the sense of *regularities* – the I-language principles underlying the way we express and comprehend meaning through word combination.

No school grammar book contains anywhere near all this knowledge. Indeed, what you find in school grammar books are greatly simplified attempts to describe only a very small fragment of what we know about an E-language. Normally the discussion of syntax is restricted to basic word order, parts of speech, verbal and nominal morphology, and rules of grammatical 'usage'. Program the 'rules' from one of these books into a computer and although it might not end sentences with a preposition, most of its output will be gibberish.

For human languages to work, they can't express meaning by just arbitrarily throwing together memorized sequences of phonemes (that is, their semantics can't rely only on phonology and morphology in the lexicon). The sentence in (1) has all these things, but it's not English:

(1)   *From guns hunted Miranda office rabbits sheriff's the with

People don't make sentences by ordering the words they need randomly (or alphabetically, as in this example). When we combine elements from the lexicon, the order in which they occur carries meaning. If it didn't, *the toad in the hole* would mean the same as *the hole in the toad*; and *Can pigs fly?* would be equivalent to *Pigs can fly*. Some languages have freer word orders than others, as we saw at the end of the last chapter, but even the most libertine impose some sequential limits.

The missing ingredient of (1)'s lexical spaghetti is syntax, and if we stir in a pinch we can get the more English-looking sentence in (2):

(2)   Miranda hunted rabbits with guns from the sheriff's office.

I don't know where I got this example from, and you may think that it needs a good dose of semantic and pragmatic context too to make it useable. But that's one of the marvels of human language design: syntax works (i.e. makes sentences seem *right* somehow) independently of any reasonable context of use, and even in the absence of interpretable meaning itself. Hence our inevitable attempts (and desperate but unfulfilled *need*) to interpret sentences like Lewis Carroll's '*Twas brillig, and the slithy toves did gyre and gimble in the wabe*' or Noam Chomsky's '*Colourless green ideas sleep furiously*'.

Syntactic ambiguity

But syntax is not just in the business of discovering the rules which account for linear word order. You may have noticed that sentence (2) is ambiguous, i.e. it has more than one possible semantic interpretation. For example, how do we know whether it's the hunter or the rabbits who have the guns? The sentence could refer to outlaw cottontails who've raided the sheriff's gun cupboard (i.e. *rabbits armed with guns from the sheriff's office*). Or, perhaps more reasonably in the absence of context, the guns from the sheriff's office could be what Miranda is using to hunt the rabbits with (i.e. *Using guns from the sheriff's office, Miranda hunted rabbits*). But if it *is* the rabbits who have the guns, how do we know whether they or the guns (or both) come from the sheriff's office? That is, they may be rodent deputies rather than outlaw bunnies (i.e. *rabbits from the sheriff's office, armed with guns*).

The sentence may be disambiguated in the absence of context if we know how the words are grouped together in the speaker's mind *within* the linear sequence. If the sequence *with guns from the sheriff's office* modifies the verb *hunted*, then the utterer is saying that Miranda is armed. If *rabbits with guns* is a single unit, modified by *from the sheriff's office*, then the rabbits could represent the law. If *guns from the sheriff's office* is a single phrase, modifying *rabbits* via the preposition *with*, then they could be outlaw bunnies. Figures (1) to (3) schematize these distinctions.

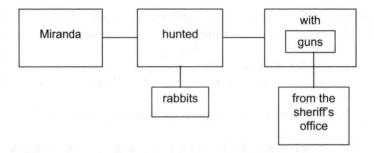

Figure 1   Rabbits getting hunted with the sherrif's guns

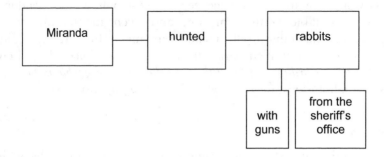

Figure 2   Armed deputy rabbits getting hunted

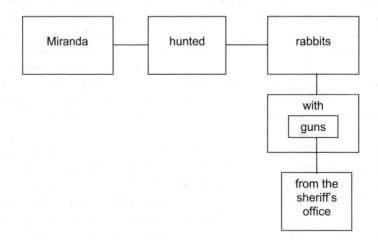

Figure 3   Armed criminal rabbits getting hunted

Ambiguity is rife in language, and this is a result of its combinatorial design. The system itself is made up of a finite set of phonemes and words in any one person's mind: this makes its vocabulary *learnable*. As we saw in Chapter 3, though, the words can normally be used to refer to more than one concept, and we are seeing here that they can be combined together in different ways: this makes language *maximally expressive*. Normally, and especially in context-rich spoken interaction, the ambiguities resolve themselves without us noticing (the Spell at work); sometimes, however, and especially in context-impoverished written texts, we can get caught out and 'led up the garden path' until our language processors work out which syntactic and lexical choices were intended by the writer. Here are some examples:

(3)   There's nothing dogs like more than charging birds
(4)   The 30-second advertisement features images of Mr. Kerry playing soccer with his daughters, in his military uniform and on the campaign trail...
(5)   He leaned on Emma's table and listened to Wilfred saw the fiddle
(6)   As bewitching as the news was the generosity with which it was welcomed by the older members of the staff ...

The sentence in (3), from Jonathan Carroll's novel *After Silence*, caused me to backtrack and read it again, because I interpreted *charging* as an adjective modifying *birds*, instead of a verb with *dogs* as subject (I was also momentarily – and ludicrously – waylaid by the lexical ambiguity of the verb *charge*: were the dogs demanding payment from the their avine fellows?). The example in (4), from a report in the *New York Times*, caused my colleague Patrick Smith to imagine John Kerry playing soccer not only with his daughters, but also while sporting army fatigues and shopping for votes. And in (5), from Annie Proulx's *Accordion Crimes*, I just couldn't stop reading *Wilfred saw the fiddle* as a separate subject-verb-object structure with *see* as the main verb in past tense. Finally, in (6), from V. S. Naipaul's *A House for Mr. Biswas*, I was enticed into interpreting *As bewitching as the news was* as a clause in its own right. In example (3), my problem was simply in activating the intended syntactic frame for one of the words in the sentence. In (4) to (6), however, it was also the syntactic *grouping* of the words which caused me and Patrick to get the wrong end of the semantic stick.

These different interpretations of the same linear sequence of words show how important syntactic knowledge is to us and our language. They also highlight the critical fact that syntax is about *hierarchical* structure as well as *linear* order: we combine words together into units that are smaller than whole sentences, and which in turn are made up of still smaller units – much like leaves on a tree, twigs on a branch and branches on a tree.

Hierarchical structure

To reveal their implicit hierarchical architecture, syntacticians use **syntactic trees** like those in Figures 4 to 6 instead of the friendlier-looking but unsystematic joined-up boxes of Figures 1 to 3.

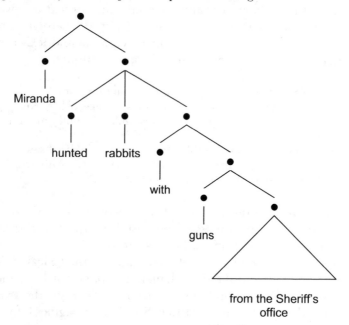

Figure 4   Rabbits getting hunted with the sherrif's guns (tree diagram)

Without for the moment bothering about why the branching goes exactly like it does, take a glance at the overall *shapes* of the trees. Such a cursory view immediately shows how sentences are not flat linear sequences, with the syntactic role of each unit defined only by its relative place in the lexical queue, but rather arboreal structures, where different branch attachments and leaf patterns can correspond to very different meanings.

Hierarchical organization plays a role throughout language structure (and probably in the mentalese structures of conceptual systems too). In phonology, for example, **syllables** exhibit hierarchical organization. Each syllable has a compulsory vowel, providing the essential blast of air from the lungs, which can then have consonants

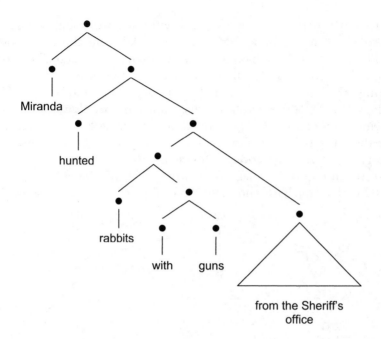

Figure 5   Armed deputy rabbits getting hunted (tree diagram)

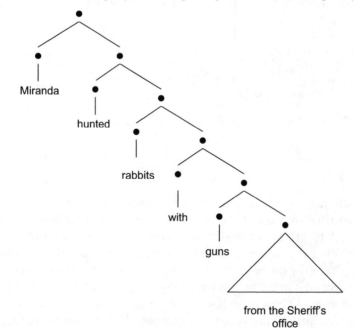

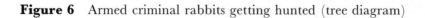

Figure 6   Armed criminal rabbits getting hunted (tree diagram)

added to it at either end – just as we saw with the apocryphal attempts of the Adamic Convention to find new ways to label the things around them. The vowel, as the obligatory element, is analogous to the head of a compound; consonants, therefore, modify the head vowel by 'colouring' the basic acoustic signal at its beginning and/or end. In phonology, the vocalic syllable head is called the **nucleus**, and the 'modifying' consonants are positioned on either side, as an **onset** (before the nucleus) and a **rime** (after the nucleus). The nucleus and rime together form the **coda**. This structure is illustrated in the syllabic tree in Figure 7 (where W = word, S = syllable, O = onset, C = coda, N = nucleus, and R = rime).

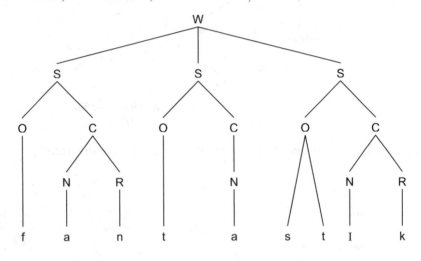

Figure 7   Syllabic structure for the word *fantastic*

Constituents

Each node in a tree represents a **constituent** of the whole structure. Some constituents, higher up the tree (closer to the trunk in real trees) correspond to groups of nodes, and represent in syntax the level of **phrase**; other constituents, at the bottom of the tree, are positions for individual words, labelled by their parts of speech. (Perversely, trees grow downwards in syntax and genealogy – perhaps they should really be called *roots*). These simplest constituents (the leaves of the tree), allow syntax to be connected up with the lexicon, by providing an interface with the frame representation of words. If a word's frame says simply that it's a P (preposition), then it can be used in any position marked 'P' in a syntactic tree. Many frames, however, also designate restrictions on the syntactic company which the word can keep in any particular tree (as we began to see in Chapter 3). So verbs, for example, are marked as **transitive** if they can take a direct object, and **intransitive** if they can't. More on this later.

Subject and predicate

Let's look at the major constituents of sentences and how they can be filled with lexical material. Starting with the division at the top of each tree in Figures 4 to 6, note that the **subject** *Miranda* is separated from all that follows. The intuition reflected in this division is that a sentence, at least an ideal sentence, says something about something else. The 'something' (here hunting) is the **predicate** and the 'something else' (Miranda) is the subject. Sentences, then, *predicate* something of something else. In our example, the sentence tells us that there's some hunting going on (predicate) and that it's Miranda who is doing it (subject). Here are some more examples:

	SUBJECT	PREDICATE
(7)	Knives	**cut**
(8)	The tortoise we bought last week	has **escaped** its cage
(9)	Tim	**gave** Jomo a present
(10)	A present	was **given** to Jomo
(11)	Jomo	was **given** a present
(12)	Some members of the team	**received** a stiff fine from the judge
(13)	She	**liked** the portrait of Henri
(14)	The portrait of Henri	**pleased** her
(15)	It	**snowed** the other day
(16)	That it snowed the other day	**surprised** everyone

These sentences are about situations in which some cutting, escaping, giving, receiving, liking, pleasing, snowing and surprising is going on. It is, of course, the verb that tells us this. The verb is really the head of the whole sentence, not only identifying the conceptual core of the situation described by the sentence, but also binding together the participants in the situation. The verb mediates between the **subject** on an 'aunt' branch and the **object**, if there is one, on a 'sister' branch (see Figure 8).

The subject is whatever fills the position in the tree which is sister to the predicate (to the left of it in English). It is not always the agent or

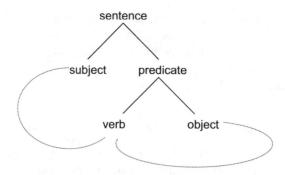

Figure 8 The verb mediates between subject and object

the 'doer' of the 'action' of the verb, as school grammars generally tell you. When the verb is in passive voice, for example, the undergoer of the verbal action appears in subject position, as in sentence (10) (I'll repeat the sentences as we need them, so you don't have to keep flipping back through the pages):

(10) A present was given to Jomo

Here 'what is given' is expressed in subject position, even though it more typically appears in direct object position, as in (9):

(9)   Tim gave Jomo a present

Sentence (11) shows us that **indirect objects** can also appear in subject position:

(11) Jomo was given a present

Here the subject expresses '*to whom* something is given'.

Notice what a disparate range of linguistic expressions can occur in the subject position. A subject can be as long (e.g. (8)) or as short (e.g. (13)) as we want, reflecting the amount of information we actually encode linguistically:

(8)   *The tortoise we bought last week* has escaped its cage
(13) *She* liked the portrait of Henri

Instead of *the tortoise we bought last week* in (8) we could say simply *the tortoise*, or *it*, depending on how much our interlocutors know of our current pet inventory. Similarly, instead of *she*, in (13), we could say

Ms Alison Chang or *the rich old lady from the big house on the corner who came for tea yesterday.*

Subjects differ in function, as well as form. They can be associated with a variety of semantic roles, including: **instrument**, i.e. something used to get something done (*knives* in (7)); **agent**, causing something to happen (*tortoise* in (8) and *Tim* in (9)); general **theme** (or **patient**), undergoing an action, state or process (*present* in (10) and *portrait* in (14)); **recipient**, receiving something (*Jomo* in (11) and *members of the team* in (12)); **experiencier**, experiencing some state of mind (*she* in (13)); ... or they may have no role at all (*it* in (15)):

(7)   *Knives* instrument cut
(8)   *The tortoise we bought last week* agent has escaped its cage
(9)   *Tim* agent gave Jomo a present
(10) *A present*theme was given to Jomo
(11) *Jomo* recipient was given a present
(12) *Some members of the team* recipient received a stiff fine from the judge
(13) *She* experiencer liked the portrait of Henri
(14) *The portrait of Henri* theme pleased her
(15) *It* no role! snowed the other day

And the kinds of expressions that occur in subject position can also occur in the positions of object, indirect object and object of a preposition, as in (17), (18) and (19), respectively:

(17) Have you seen [the tortoise we bought last week] object?
(18) I fed [the tortoise we bought last week] indirect object some lettuce
(19) Try not to step on [the tortoise we bought last week] object of preposition

Noun phrases

Subjects and objects typically refer to the key 'participants' in the situations we want to talk and write about. They are expressed syntactically as constituents that linguists call **noun phrases** (NPs). Like the main elements of compounds and syllables, the essential elements of NPs – nouns – are called their *heads*. Just as the heads of semantically transparent compounds determine the part of speech and semantic class of the whole unit (such that a *wolfhound* is a kind of hound and a *hunting rabbit* a kind of rabbit), so too do heads of NPs (such that *the tortoise we bought last week* in (8) refers to a kind of tortoise, not a kind of buying or a period of seven days).

The concepts which head nouns pick out may enjoy more explicit linguistic expression through the use of **modifiers**. Modifiers of nouns come in different shapes and sizes. In English, the **definite** and **indefinite articles**, e.g. *the* in (13) and *a* in (9), are the most lightweight, serving to express whether the noun reference is established in the current discourse context (in which case a definite article is used), or is being newly introduced (in which case the noun is preceded by an indefinite article):

(13)   She liked *the*_{definite} portrait of Henri
(9)   Tim gave Jomo *a*_{indefinite} present

Adjectives, like the *stiff* of *stiff fine* in (12), are content words which express further attributes of core nominal concepts, and may themselves be modified (e.g. *very stiff*). **Prepositional phrases** (PPs) may fulfil a similar role, using the function words we call prepositions to link a modifier NP to a noun, as in (13), where *of Henri* (in the NP *a portrait of Henri*) tells us *who* the portrait is a portrait of.

We can also use whole sentences to modify nouns: these are called **relative clauses**, and are often introduced by another set of function words like *which*, *who* and *that*. These are known as **relative pronouns** in traditional grammar, reflecting the fact that they substitute the modified head noun within the relative clause. Thus, in sentence (8), *that* is a function word which refers to the head noun of the NP (i.e. *tortoise*). If relative clauses are kinds of sentences, then they should have their own subject and predicate. And indeed they do: (20) shows how the sentence *We bought the tortoise last week* can modify the noun *tortoise* in the main sentence:

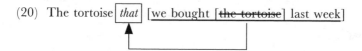

(20)   The tortoise | *that* | [we bought [~~the tortoise~~] last week]

The subject of the relative clause is *we*, and its predicate consists of the verb *bought*, the object *the tortoise*, and information about when the purchase occurred (*last week*). The object of the relative clause is identical with the *subject* of the main clause (about the tortoise escaping) and so is substituted by the relative pronoun *that* and displaced to the beginning of the clause to link it with the noun it modifies.

Pronouns (like *that* or *she*), lone common nouns (like *knives*), and proper names (like *Tim* and *Jomo*) all have the same distribution as NPs (i.e. can appear in the same positions as nouns accompanied by modifiers). We can thus conclude that they are all NPs. An odd case, which doesn't seem to fit this pattern, is the subject of sentence (16):

(16) *That it snowed the other day* surprised everyone

As with relative clauses, what we have here is a sentence within a sentence: the subject of (16) is a sentence in its own right, *converted* into a NP, just as we saw at the lexical level at the end of Chapter 5. Notice that this kind of clausal NP can also occur in object position, as in (21), where it functions in the same way as other object NPs, like (22) and (23):

(21) You said [that it snowed the other day]
(22) You said [many things]
(23) You said [it]

Thus, the amount of information we want to express about an entity participating in some situation we have mentally represented will be associated with a series of **syntactic categories** (parts of speech like nouns, adjectives and articles), which are arranged in linear and hierarchical order as NP constituents of a sentence.

Verb phrases

The situations that NPs find themselves participating in are expressed through predicates, which tend to get labelled by verbs, in **verb phrases** (VPs). VPs, as you have no doubt guessed, are constituents with head verbs. VPs, even more so than NPs, represent a many-splendoured class of syntactic expressions, displaying all sorts of exotic grammatical plumage. The form in which VPs surface in speech and writing depends in large part on an individual verb's selection of subjects and **complements** (modifiers on a sister node, such as direct objects). Subjects and complement NPs jointly contribute to the full meaning of verbs by fleshing out their participating elements, and are known together as the **arguments** of the verb (see Figure 9).

The complement of a verb is like the modifier of a noun, giving more specific information about the verb's conceptual structure. The typical complement of a verb is a direct object NP, as in *its cage*, object of *escape* in (8), and *a present*, object of *give* in (9) and (11):

(8) The tortoise we bought last week has escaped *its cage*
(9) Tim gave Jomo *a present*
(11) Jomo was given *a present*

Verbs sometimes require their objects to appear as PP complements, such as *dream* or *think*, which normally require a PP headed by *of* or

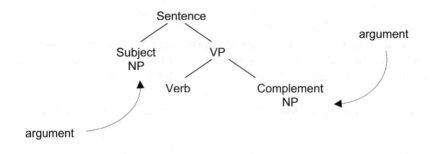

Figure 9   A verb and its arguments

about, although the prepositions here lack any semantic content. Other prepositions heading complement phrases, like the *from* after *receive* in (12), have more meaning (in this case marking a source):

(12)   Some members of the team received a stiff fine *from the judge*

Some verbs, intransitives like *snow* or *sneeze*, do not allow a direct object. Others can appear in both transitive and intransitive contexts, like *cut* in *Knives cut*, or with a direct object, as in *Knives cut butter*. Uniquely transitive verbs require a direct object NP (such as *surprise* in (16)):

(16)   That it snowed the other day surprised *everyone*

Yet other verbs use an indirect object as well as a direct object, as in *Jomo*, indirect object of the verb *give* in (9) and (10):

(9)   Tim gave *Jomo* a present
(10)   A present was given *to Jomo*

Thematic roles

We saw in our whirlwind tour of NPs that subjects could perform a number of functions. Arguments expressed in verbal complements have the same range of functions. These functions are known as **thematic roles**, and include AGENT, INSTRUMENT, THEME, RECIPIENT and EXPERIENCER (we'll use small capitals from now on for thematic roles of a verb's arguments). Take the subject NP in (13) and the object NP in (14):

(13)   *She* liked the portrait of Henri

(14) The portrait of Henri pleased *her*

Both fulfil the thematic role of EXPERIENCER, and indeed, *The portrait pleases her* means roughly the same as *She likes the portrait*. The only real linguistic difference (aside from questions of style) is the choice of verb form (*like* versus *please*) and the reversal of the thematic roles of subject and object position which this choice entails. (Recall from Chapter 4 that Shakespeare could use *like* in the same way as *please*, saying *It likes me well* for *We like it well*.)

Finally, not all NPs are verbal arguments with a thematic role. In (15), *to snow* is just *to snow*:

(15) *It* snowed the other day

Although *it* is in subject position, it doesn't label a participant. It is there merely because English requires there to be some lexical material in the subject position, even if it lacks any semantic content (hence the name **dummy subject** for this kind of structure). Languages like Spanish do not require overt subjects:

(24) Está nevando
'[It] is snowing'
(25) Organizaron una reunión
'[They] organized a meeting'

Such languages, marking subjects *covertly*, are called **null-subject** languages, and can be found all around the globe. Now it may have occurred to you that English speakers also drop subjects on a regular basis in informal speech. Couples often say *Love you* instead of the fuller *I love you*, for example. But as Julian Barnes' character Gillian makes clear in his novel *Love etc.*, this is a performance phenomenon, rather than an aspect of our grammatical competence:

> When did I last say it to Oliver? I can't remember. After a few years we got into the habit of dropping the 'I'. One of us would say, 'Love you', and the other would say, 'Love you too'. There's nothing shocking about that, nothing out of the ordinary, but one day I caught myself wondering if it wasn't significant. As if you weren't taking responsibility for the feeling any more. As if it had become somehow more general, less focused.

If Gillian were a Spanish speaker, her concern would never have arisen: *Te amo* will do just fine.

Getting back to the syntactic nitty-gritty, we notice that unlike dummy *it*, the NP *the other day* in (15) *does* have semantic content, but doesn't correspond to a verbal argument with a thematic role. Contrast the following sentences:

(15) It snowed the other day
(26) We enjoyed the other day

The other day is 'what is enjoyed' in (26), but *not* 'what is snowed' in (15). More precisely, the phrase *the other day* is a complement NP (direct object) of the verb in (26), but a non-thematic **adjunct** NP in (15). Adjuncts are 'optional extra' phrases, like adverbs, which do not fulfil obligatory roles in the clause. Thus, the sentence in (27) is ambiguous:

(27) She remembered the other day

Here, the phrase *the other day* could be an adjunct telling us *when* she does the remembering (e.g. *She (finally) remembered (her name) the other day*), or a complement telling us *what* she remembers (e.g. *She (fondly) remembered the other day (when they had so much fun)*).

System or chaos?

It might appear from all these examples that verbs go their own sweet way, blithely imposing all sorts of arbitrary restrictions on the expression of the NPs which label participants in the verbal action. Some such restrictions are obviously derived from a particular verb's meaning. The verb *hit* is transitive because there's always a 'hitter' and a 'hittee'; *sleep* is intransitive because you don't sleep things. But then again, snowing *is* just snowing: not even God can *snow*, and although we can be *snowed on*, *in*, or *under*, the meaning of the verb *snow* just doesn't require anything to be snowed (except snow itself, I suppose, but that would be a little redundant). So semantics doesn't explain why we need to express a subject, even a 'dummy' one like *it* in *It is snowing*.

In fact there's a great deal of verbal syntax which just can't be explained by appealing to what verbs mean. For example, if it's OK to say *She remembered*, without saying *what* she remembered, why is **She enjoyed* disallowed? If you can say *He melts the butter* and *Butter melts*, why can't you say **The government disappeared the dissident*, when you can say *The dissident disappeared*? (In Latin American Spanish, both are grammatical.) The other verbs we've looked at show similarly quirky restrictions. Unlike *remember*, *escape* is not fussy about its complement structure, making the object optional, and even allowing us to express it via the preposition *from*. And, as we saw, the major difference between the almost synonymous verbs *please* and *like* is that in the former the EXPERIENCER is in object position and the THEME is in subject position, whereas in the latter the positions are reversed. In other words, the difference is more syntactic than semantic.

What's going on here? Is a theory of syntax just a *list* of sentence parts in lexical entry frame representations – the linguistic equivalent of the parts-list for a self-assembly wardrobe kit? Must children memorize sequence after sequence of idiosyncratic nouns, verbs and modifiers, connected together in arbitrary tree structures? Although it may seem like some eccentric baroque device, assembling sentences from a random assortment of syntactic, lexical and semantic paraphernalia, syntax is actually closer to an iMac computer or a Jaguar XJS in its elegance of design and mastery of function. Let's step back a bit to see how.

Syntax and pragmatics: conventional meaning in novel contexts

The essential job of grammar is to turn complex, multidimensional meanings into discrete, linear patterns of sound, so that the meanings recovered from the sound resemble as closely as possible the meaning that the sound was originally intended to encode. Given that the number of messages we can convey is infinite, but our vocabulary at any one point is finite, this means that word forms from the lexicon, representing conventional core meanings, must be deliverable in *conventional* but *novel* arrangements which get the speaker's communicative job done. This job is shared between syntax and **pragmatics**.

Conventionally, syntax and pragmatics are studied independently (though some theories of syntax are more sensitive to communicative function than the one I am basing my account on here). This is because, as we saw with the Lewis Carroll and Chomsky sentences at the beginning of the chapter, the former is logically independent of the latter. But this isn't a conventional linguistics book, and I'm interested here in showing how combining words actually leads to language *use* in the real world. So I'll take the risk of alienating both the syntacticians and the pragmaticists by introducing pragmatics slap-bang in the middle of my chapter on syntax.

Our pragmatic knowledge provides a set of principles which govern the use of linguistic expressions in real communicative settings (and we'll explore it more thoroughly in the next chapter). A sentence can have many uses, independently of its compositional meaning, as we saw in Chapter 2 with Angela the English speaker's use of the following sentence:

(28) Might I suggest we open a window?

On their own, the lexical items and their syntactic arrangement suggest that Angela is asking whether she could make a suggestion about opening a window. But her communicative intention is probably rather different (to get her boss to refrain from smoking in her office, for example). Pragmatic knowledge is a powerful factor in language use, without which we would be doomed to engage in robotic discourse, devoid of the nuances of inferred meaning, blind to context, and insensitive to the range of social functions we call upon language to perform: Spock passing the time of day with Data on the Starship Enterprise. But pragmatic knowledge cannot be used at all without the presumption of an underlying compositional semantics, and this is determined by the core meanings of words and – crucially – their syntactic arrangement in sentences. So the essential function of syntax is to provide a shared framework for the combination of core lexical meanings into a compositional semantics for sentences: a common, context-free baseline for pragmatic interpretation. It can't, therefore, be just a hodgepodge of idiosyncratic lexical behaviours.

Syntax in action

Let's take a procedural view now, to bring things down to earth with an example of syntax in action. What happens when Spike, a speaker of English, wishes to convey a message to a hearer, Harry, about a specific situation . . .say a compliment on his choice of necktie? What happens in the minds of speaker Spike and hearer Harry? We'll take it step by step. First, before any linguistic activity, Spike must see Harry's tie. This, as we saw in Chapter 3, requires Spike's visual input system to activate his 'tie' concept in memory, together with his 'Harry' concept. (Obviously other things will be happening as well, such as an inference that if Harry is wearing the tie, then it probably belongs to him, but we can't possibly deal with all the details here.) An aesthetic judgement then ensues, followed by the formulation of an intention to compliment Harry. By now Spike will have activated in mentalese a series of core concepts in which {TIE}, {POSSESSED-BY}, {HARRY}, {SPIKE}, and {LIKE} feature prominently, together with a relation between them (remember, these are concepts, not words). The conceptual structure Spike is activating will therefore contain a THEME, the tie, related to a POSSESSOR, Harry, with a relation of admiration holding between the THEME and Spike as EXPERIENCER.

At this stage, there is no requirement to activate linguistic expressions for these concepts (recall that thinking is not just internal speech). Spike *could* express the compliment by feeling the cloth of Harry's tie between thumb and forefinger and then giving a thumbs-up gesture, or emitting a non-linguistic sound like 'Mmmmm!' with a rising-falling intonation contour. But if the compliment is to be expressed linguistically, then the mentalese concepts in their conceptual structure will need to invoke words and syntactic relations to bind them together in an appropriate way.

The language-neutral conceptual structure in Spike's mind will contain more information than can be, or need be, expressed linguistically. The interrelated concepts activated before language gets engaged form part of a more complex **mental model** encoding Spike's immediate perceptual experience, knowledge, beliefs, attitudes and intentions with regard to the situation. The model will contain information about the colours and patterns of the tie, about the situation in which the encounter takes place (as Harry sets off for a job interview, arrives home from work, …), about the relation between the two men (brothers, colleagues, friends, partners, …), about the sincerity of Spike's emotional state (does he *really* like the tie, or is he just being polite? Does he like the tie only on Harry or would he also wear it himself?), about the physical context (in an office, a place of worship, …), and so on. Spike must know (unconsciously of course) how much of the mental model can and should be expressed via language to achieve his goal.

The subset of information in the mental model that will be expressed linguistically is known as a **propositional structure**, and may be viewed as the core meaning of an utterance, in the same way that the core meanings of individual words like *body* and *egg* must be representable free of contextual information about specific instances of their use. One propositional structure corresponding to Spike's communicative intention may be represented as in Figure 10.

Note once again that the 'words' in Figure 10 are not yet actually words activated in Spike's lexicon, but are still just mentalese concepts: for this reason I have indicated his positive evaluation of Harry's tie as {+EVAL}, in an attempt to abstract away from particular words, like *like*, *admire* or *dig*. (If only there was a way to represent word meanings *without* using words!) Once the proposition has been activated,

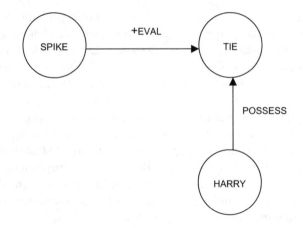

Figure 10   A propositional structure for Spike liking Harry's tie

however, it can be mapped onto linguistic expressions. There is a bewildering range of lexical items and syntactic structures that can be used to linguistically encode any conceptual structure, as the partial list in (29)–(37) illustrates for the meaning underlying the proposition in Figure 10:

(29) Spike likes Harry's tie
(30) I like/love/admire/dig your tie!
(31) Your tie pleases/delights me
(32) That tie looks good on/suits you!
(33) Your tie is (very/really) nice/smart/beautiful/lovely/great/elegant!
(34) What a nice tie!
(35) Nice tie!
(36) Nice!
(37) I like it!

These utterances encode different aspects of Spike's mental model in a number of ways, not all of which are appropriate for the specific context I have sketched. For example, the utterance in (29), although encoding the proposition, would be pragmatically inappropriate. If Spike refers to himself, he will do so using the first person pronoun *I*, rather than using his name. Equally, if he refers explicitly to the tie's owner, Harry, he will use the second person pronoun *you* when addressing him, and if he decides to express Harry's relation with the tie, he will use the possessive *your*, as in (30). (If he were reporting his aesthetic judgement to a third party, he might use the third person possessive pronoun *his* or the name *Harry*.) Utterance (31) is pragmatically inappropriate for another reason: conversational style no longer uses verbs like *please* and *delight*, except in jocular allusions to more formal times.

Note that Spike does not need to refer linguistically to himself or to Harry at all. In terms of thematic roles, utterances (32) and (33) dispense with any encoding of the EXPERIENCER (Spike). Utterance (32) does it by expressing the concept Harry as a kind of LOCATION role, with a verb which relates the THEME (the tie) with that LOCATION. Utterance (33) achieves the communicative goal by expressing Harry as POSSESSOR and modifying the tie THEME with an evaluative adjective. And even the THEME itself (the tie) need not be labelled: utterances (36) and (37) will suffice to express Spike's message if the non-linguistic context is sufficient to direct Harry's attention to his choice of neckwear.

Finally, Spike's intention may be made manifest by focusing on elements from the mental model which are not part of the proposition of Figure 8. Utterances (38) and (39) refer to the selection of the tie and its sartorial message, retaining the [+EVAL] feature through the use of adjectives:

(38) Good choice!
(39) A most eloquent statement!

How Spike selects the aspects of the mental model which will ultimately be expressed, and how he selects the content words that will label these conceptual aspects, represent tough challenges for cognitive psychology. But given that our major concern is to see how syntactic knowledge needs to be invoked to get the communicative task accomplished, I'll sidestep the issue. For although the pragmatic force of the message can be clear from non-linguistic cues (facial gesture, eye gaze, etc.), Spike's production mechanisms won't just pull out the appropriate lexical items at random and turn them into sound in the order in which they get activated. The choice of lexical items will in part determine the syntactic patterns used to link them together, but likewise, bits of syntactic patterning will also determine aspects of lexical selection. For example, the choice of the verb *like* will require the expression of the object (remember, a first person subject may be omitted in casual speech):

(40) *(I) like!
(41) (I) like it!

Similarly, the choice of an adjective such as *nice* or *lovely* to express the compliment will make Spike less likely to refer to himself as experiencier, making (42) more natural than (43):

(42) (That's a) nice tie!
(43) I think that's a nice tie!

And the choice of a verb like *please* or *delight* (unlikely as it may be), will require, as we have seen, the EXPERIENCER and THEME to assume different syntactic positions from those they would assume if Spike were to use a verb like *like* or *love*.

So far we have been concentrating on what goes on in the speaker's mind when he expresses a message linguistically. But Harry the hearer's mind is also hard at work as soon as Spike starts displacing the air molecules around him. Harry's mind has already set up a mental model of the overall situation which will correlate well with Spike's (including, perhaps, the knowledge that Spike is an inveterate tie-wearer and has a connoisseur's taste in the subject). But language understanding is not just a matter of pragmatic guesswork on the basis of contextual knowledge and hearing a few key words like *like* and *tie*. Spike could say all sorts of things using those words:

(44) I **like** that **tie**
(45) I don't **like** that **tie**
(46) I would **like** that **tie** with another shirt
(47) My Dad would **like** that **tie**
(48) My cat would **like** that **tie** (to play with)
(49) Do you **like** that **tie**?
(50) I'm not sure I **like** that **tie**

For Harry to get the message, he needs to recover its syntactic structure as well as identify the words used, whatever pragmatic and semantic motivations and choices may be activated in Spike's mind, and whatever expectations, cues from the context, or lexical items Harry activates. It's a complicated melange of semantic, lexical and syntactic contingencies, and yet we do it all without thinking, every time we open our mouths to speak or our ears to listen, every time we deploy our fingers at a keyboard or fix our gaze on a screen. For speakers and hearers, readers and writers, the success of the enterprise depends in large part on having shared norms, both linguistic and non-linguistic. The linguistic norms that correspond to our declarative knowledge of syntax are well hidden by the Language Spell, but let's see if we can dig a bit deeper and reveal some more of their intricacy and, why not, their *beauty*, in the next section.

Syntactic rules

To clothe our complex communicative intentions in conventional, compositional, linear arrays of words, syntax deploys a small number of rules and principles which determine how the words can hook up together and how the phrases that result correlate with chunks of meaning. All essentially revolves around the verb, as we have seen. But the core meanings of verbs only come to life when they contribute to the expression of situations in which actual entities are participating (weather verbs like *snow* being a rare exception). As we've seen, we normally label the participating entities as NPs, which can fulfil various different thematic roles in these situations, including INSTRUMENTS, RECIPIENTS, EXPERIENCERS and the like, drawn from a finite list.

Although the verbs we looked at before seemed rather flighty, they, like all words, are actually governed by a few key combinatory rules and principles, which we unconsciously invoke when we want to engage in linguistic communication. The different shapes that NPs, VPs and PPs take do not have to be listed in our lexicons for each word that may appear in them. Instead, the I-languages we have constructed as infants rely on a small number of rules which govern the ways different sentence constituents may be hooked together. To begin with, syntacticians make generalizations over what kinds of basic tree structures each language allows. One way of representing these rules is via initially off-putting (but soon pretty cool-looking) statements like the following:

I	S → NP VP
II	NP → (D) (A) N (PP)
III	VP → (AUX) V (NP) (PP)
IV	PP → P NP

These four rules work specifically for English, and between them describe an *infinite* number of English sentence structures (though only a small subset of the full range of possibilities). Rule I says that part of a syntactic tree can have an S (sentence) node with two branches, the one on the left labelled NP and the other VP. Rule II tells you what kinds of branches the NP can have, ranging from a single N (the obligatory head), to the head plus a variety of optional modifiers, three of which are indicated in parentheses. On the left of the head N we can find a D (for **determiner**, the technical term for the syntactic category which includes definite and indefinite articles) and A, an adjective (we'll ignore here adjective phrases like *really nice*). Following the N we find an optional prepositional phrase (PP). Rule IV tells us how the PP node branches: it has a P daughter on the left and another NP daughter (the object of the preposition) on the right.

Rules II and IV allow us to construct NPs such as the following:

(51) Ties
(52) The ties
(53) The silk ties
(54) Silk ties
(55) The silk ties in the drawer
(56) The ties in the drawer
(57) Silk ties in the drawer
(58) Ties in the drawer

The words in these phrases come from our lexicons, and we know they can be arranged in this way because the syntactic categories listed in their frame representations match the syntactic categories D, A, P and N included in the rules.

The NPs can serve as subjects of the verb via Rule I, and as objects via Rule III. If we build the partial tree structure allowed by Rule III, using all the options, including AUX for auxiliary verbs like *be* and *have*, we can get predicate VPs like:

(59) ... has put the silk ties in the drawer

The fact that NPs and PPs appear as both **mother nodes** (on the left of the arrows) and **daughter nodes** (on the right) captures the infinite creativity of our syntactic competence. Through what is called **recursion**, a simple, finite set of syntactic rules allows us to produce an infinite number of structures. Applying Rule I, for example, we get structures like the partial tree in Figure 11:

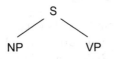

Figure 11   Applying Rule I

We may then expand the NP as a simple D N sequence, giving us Figure 12:

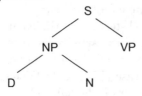

Figure 12   Applying Rule II

If we then expand the VP as a simple V plus an NP, we can insert a PP under the object NP, as in Figure 13:

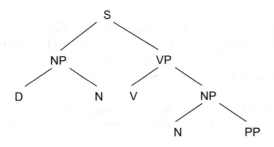

Figure 13 Applying Rule III and Rule II again

This PP has within it another NP, which we can then expand again as a D N PP sequence repeatedly, through recursive application of Rules II and IV (see Figure 14).

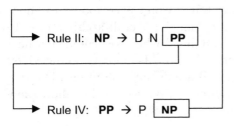

Figure 14 Recursive rule application

This recursive relationship gives us sentences like (60) (where, to save space on the page, I group constituents between square brackets):

(60) An owl flew into [the kitchen [**of** the house [**of** the sister [**of** my friend [**from** that area [**to** the west [**of** the Tower [**of** London]]]]]]]].

Perhaps this example sounds a bit artificial (it *is*), but it's still English, and it's processing limits, not syntactic rules, that keep real sentences shorter and sweeter. In languages which don't use much noun-noun compounding, syntax has to be regularly invoked to link strings of nouns together with prepositions. In Spanish, for example, you get long NPs with recursive PP structures (normally using *de* 'of') where English would use a multiple-noun compound N:

(61) Comité [**de** Reestructuración [**del** Programa [**de** Inglés [**de** la Universidad [**de** Momoxpan]]]]]
'Momoxpan University English Program Restructuring Committee'

Recursion is perhaps more common in English with relative clauses, which, remember, are of category S. If we modify Rule II to include an optional S after the head N, we can get, through recursive application of Rules I and II, sentences like the following:

(62) She was the one [who had made the argument [that the policy [which her own party had rejected] was actually popular with the public]]

Rules such as I to IV are known in syntax as **phrase structure rules** and capture the core set of combinatory patterns of languages. The ones we have looked at here have been much simplified, and are restricted to only some basic English structures. A richer phrase structure component of English is needed to capture the full facts of canonical sentence structure, but it won't need too many more rules. Furthermore, as we'll see later on, the overall architecture of phrase structure can be drastically simplified when we renounce a narrow E-language anglocentrism and delve into I-language knowledge shared by all members of the species. But let's not rush things. Before passing on to taste some of the full richness of syntax, we'll see how the various pieces we've discussed so far fit together.

Putting leaves on the tree

Although there are very productive, creative processes in morphology (such as compounding in English, Dutch and German), and although we can coin new words also phonologically by stringing together syllables which haven't been strung together before, most new meaning gets out into the world through the everyday use of a small set of phrase structure rules, plugging together material from our lexicons in multifarious ways. Syntax thus serves as an interface between meaning and sound: between conceptual structure represent-ing some communicable aspect of a mental model (the non-linguistic message) and the lexicon (chunks of phonology in form representa-tions). The thematic structure of verbs plays the pivotal role here, linking the situation and its participants (the propositional structure) with the lexicon via frame representations. These in turn allow words to be built into phrase structures through links with the rule component of the syntax.

When we looked briefly at lexical frame representations in Chapter 3, we saw that Spanish-speaking EFL learners sometimes use the verb *put* in non-native structures, because the Spanish equivalent *poner* does not take an obligatory PP complement. As a result, they produce sentences like:

(63) *She put some music
(64) *I'll put an example to show what I mean

We can schematize the difference between the two verb frames as follows:

put: V, [__NP PP]
poner: V, [__NP (PP)]

The information in brackets following the syntactic category (V) is called the word's **subcategorization frame**, and shows the complements that can or must appear in sister branches to the verb (the verb's position is indicated by '__'). Thus, *put* requires a NP and a PP, whereas *poner* requires only a NP (the PP, in parentheses, is optional).

Subcategorization frames such as these, however, provide both too little and too much information. The syntactic category of a verb's subject is given via Rule I, so doesn't need to be listed here, but its thematic role *ought* to be: remember that the main difference between *like* and *please* (apart from style) is one of thematic roles, changing the syntactic order of what fills subject and object position:

(65) (a) The portrait pleases Alison
      (b) Alison likes the portrait

Since this behaviour is unpredictable, a feature only of these verbs, it must be listed in lexical frames. Subcategorization frames don't cut the mustard here (both verbs would appear as [__NP]), ... but thematic roles do. Listing thematic information also, as I've suggested, allows the whole system of words, syntactic phrases, propositional structures and mental models to be coordinated.

Listing subcategorization frames in our frame representations would also be a bit redundant because they repeat information represented in the syntactic component of our mental grammars. The possible complements of verbs are explicitly represented in phrase structure rules. Rule III, remember, tells us that a verb may be followed by an optional NP direct object, followed by an optional PP. And thematic roles match up nicely with syntactic phrases: in a typical English sentence, the subject NP, to the left of the VP, is highly correlated with the role of AGENT, and the object NP, postverbally in the predicate, is highly correlated with THEMES and PATIENTS. INSTRUMENTS, GOALS, and SOURCES are often linked to verbs by prepositions (*cut* **with** *a knife, put ties* **in** *a drawer, receive a fine* **from** *a judge*). So, it's more likely that the syntactic company verbs like to keep, and the thematic roles their arguments adopt, are expressed mentally through **thematic grids** like the following:

put: V, [A__T G]
poner: V, [A__T (G)]

Here, A = AGENT ('the putter'), T = THEME ('what's put'), and G = GOAL ('where it's put'). These roles in the lexicon can then be linked with the phrasal syntax and with conceptual structure. This allows language users to connect strings of phonemes with their meanings in *meaningful arrangements*. The phoneme strings are memorized in the form representations of lexical entries. The meanings are stored in conceptual structures. The two get arranged together to make specific expressions via phrase structure rules in the syntactic component. And the syntactic component itself mediates frame information from lexical entries with propositional information in conceptual structure.

In Figure 15, I have drawn a picture of a tiny chunk of the linguistic and conceptual knowledge to be found in minds like Angela's and Spike's, yours and mine. The bits and pieces included underlie our ability to produce or comprehend sentences like the following:

(66) He put the ties in the drawer

Figure 15 may look a little intimidating, but it's worth a good look: remember, this is a tiny part of the vast network of linguistic knowledge that *all* English speakers have in our minds, and its counterpart in your mind and mine must be invoked for us to use language, so that we can shoot the breeze together, write poetry, ... and so that these pages can communicate something. The figure portrays part of the lexicon, part of the syntactic component and part of conceptual structure, with subscript numerals showing how different units are correlated ('co-indexed'). I've omitted phonological and morphological rule components altogether, so it doesn't look *too* scary.

At the top left, in the lexicon, we can see the lexical entry for *he*.

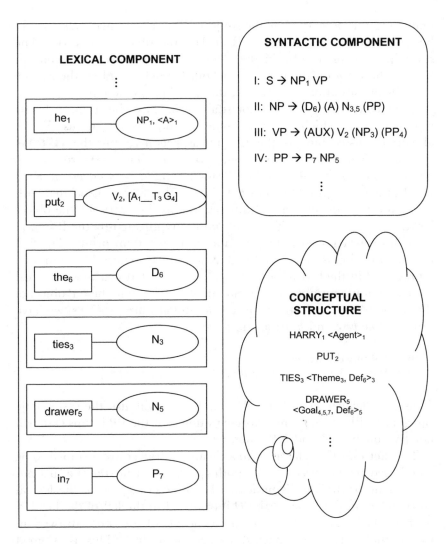

Figure 15   A small part of English and what it can mean

Although it's traditionally called a pronoun, it's really a pro-NP, since it can substitute a whole noun phrase:

(67) *Spike's friend from Boston*$_1$ smiled as *he*$_1$ put the ties in the drawer.

Hence the syntactic category of *he* is marked as NP, and its thematic role as AGENT ($<A>$). Both its form and frame are co-indexed, via the subscript numeral 1, with the NP of Rule I in the syntactic component, indicating that *he* is used as the subject NP of a sentence. (*Him* would be co-indexed with the NP in Rule III, the object of a verb.) The subscript 1 turns up also in the Conceptual Structure, on a concept labelled here *Harry* (the person to whom *he* refers), and on the role he plays in the situation (i.e. AGENT, the 'doer' of the action).

The next lexical entry, for the verb, has the richest frame representation, which by now comes as no surprise to us. We've already discussed most of the relevant aspects here, but the 'G' GOAL specification perhaps deserves more comment. The GOAL role is co-indexed via subscript 4 with the PP (used to build *in the drawer*) in Rule III. In the Conceptual Structure, however, the GOAL is associated with its counterpart in the verb's frame as well as the entry for the object location N (*drawer*) and the relative position indicated by the P (*in*). (I wish this was a PowerPoint presentation rather than print!) The fact that the location is mentioned with a noun in sentence (13) cannot be represented in the lexical entry for *put*, because that lexical entry must serve an infinite number of uses, not all of which name the NP object of the preposition. For instance, just as *he* and *him* are pro-NPs, we have pro-PPs like *here* and *there*, as in:

(68) He put the ties *here*
(69) But she has moved them *there*

Thus, the lexical entries for *here* and *there* will list their syntactic category as PP in the frame representation, but the PP in this case will not give birth to P and NP daughters.

The fact that the references to a tie and a drawer are assumed to be established in the discourse by both speaker and hearer (i.e. it's not any old tie or drawer) is indicated by the co-indexing of the lexical entry for *the* in the lexicon, the *D* introduced to the left of the head N by Rule II in the syntax, and the concepts of 'tie' and 'drawer' in Conceptual Structure, marked as *def*, 'definite.' (This is a good example of pragmatics expressed directly through grammar.)

Finally, a word about Conceptual Structure here. Although the contents of the Lexical Component and the Syntactic Component are portrayed as permanent databases in my picture, ready to be invoked for any language event, the contents of Conceptual Structure appear already configured to express one proposition associated with a particular mental model (Harry putting a tie in a drawer). This is just for convenience. Conceptual Structure is actually a hierarchical rule-system for combining concepts (as agents, instruments, paths, processes, etc.) which, like the syntactic and lexical components, must be independent of actual performance and stored permanently in long-term memory. Propositions are built from these rules on the fly, in short-term (working) memory, whenever language gets invoked. And mental models are either stored as memorized chunks of conceptual structure in long-term (episodic) memory, or are also built on the fly to represent situations as we are experiencing them. Linguists like Ray Jackendoff have begun the mammoth task of working out how Conceptual Structure – the syntax of thought itself – may be put together. But don't worry, I won't get into that here.

We've seen in this chapter (congratulations for surviving this far!) that it's our syntactic knowledge which allows us to be infinitely creative with the finite list of words we have memorized in our mental lexicons. It may all seem highly abstruse, but without it we would simply not be able to indulge in the luxury of real communicative acts. In the next chapter, I continue the folly of discussing two topics which normally appear far apart in introductory books on linguistics: the argument that syntactic knowledge is based on innate predispositions encoded in the genome, and the more hands-on observation that actual language use in discourse situations cannot possibly work without knowledge that goes way beyond syntax, lexicon and compositional semantics. Through this unlikely juxtaposition I want to highlight again the Fundamental Paradox underlying the Language Spell: that language is both biological and social at the same time, and can't be fully understood if one aspect of it is taken in isolation from the other.

More information

One of the clearest and most student-friendly introductions to **English syntax** is still, for me, Andrew Radford's (1988) *Transformational Grammar*, although it is now, I know, very dated. His clear style is maintained in a number of recent books which update the theory, the latest being Radford (2004).

A more elementary introduction to **English syntax** for the non-specialist is Linda Thomas (1993). For language teachers, I recommend Roderick Jacobs (1995).

On the construction of **propositions** and **mental models** in discourse processing, I recommend Rosemary Stevenson's (1993) book. For production, see Willem Levelt's monumental *Speaking* (1989).

One way to think about the complexity of the syntax of human languages is to consider whether a machine might be able to 'get it'. Some **Artificial Intelligence** projects on Natural Language Processing, for example Connexor at www.connexor.com/demo/syntax/, are pretty impressive: their demo allows you to type in or copy-paste a sentence and then sit back and watch as its syntactic structure emerges. (But unlike us, it doesn't know how to handle sentences like 'Fish sharks eat are usually small', and will only give you one analysis for 'I made her duck'.)

Ray Jackendoff's (2002) brilliant (and profoundly sensible) rethink of linguistics and the relationship between language, meaning and the world is bound to become a classic. It was written with the educated layperson in mind, although it will probably be challenging for many readers outside of academia.

Thank you madam, the agony is abated.

(Lord Macaulay, aged four,
after hot coffee was spilled on his legs)

We come into the world as *infants*, non-speakers, equipped with prodigious grammatical potential, but as yet incapable of passing the time of day with other members of our species. By the age of four we are using complex syntax, coupled with a mental encyclopaedia of implicit social knowledge, to accomplish a broad range of communicative goals in ways that are appropriate for diverse sociocultural contexts (although few of us are quite as precocious in our development as Thomas Babington Macaulay.) This chapter portrays the mental origins and social outcomes of our acquisition of sentence structures, from the genetic code to codes of linguistic conduct.

Acquiring the rules

In Chapter 4 we saw that the Language Spell causes us to see languages as monolithic social entities which change over time as they are handed down through history from one group of speakers to the next. Thus the Old English of King Alfred became the Middle English of Chaucer, which became the Early Modern English of Shakespeare, which a few centuries later became the Victorian English of Dickens, and arrived to our days as the contemporary English of J. K. Rowling and Snoop Dogg. We concluded there that this portion of the Spell may be broken by realizing that it is not *one* language that is handed down from group to group, but rather that *many* language faculties in the minds of *many* individual speakers are constructed anew during *many* infancies. This happens on the basis of a mixture of nature (innate capacities) and nurture (exposure to contextually supported language input). This view of language is called **innatist**, because it recognizes the role of an innate human disposition for language; mentalist, because it locates language squarely in the mind, rather than in behaviour (or in the vocal tract); and **generativist**, because Noam Chomsky, its principal architect, developed a theory of grammatical competence which he called a **generative grammar**, a computational system of combinatory rules which could (potentially) 'generate' (i.e. account for) all the syntactic structures underlying what people actually said in any language. Although the philosophical foundations of the approach lie in psychology, it was, interestingly, syntactic argumentation which provided the empirical impetus.

Structure dependence

Chomsky highlighted the fact that children seem to approach the language acquisition task already knowing certain facts about how syntax works. The kinds of facts he and other syntacticians uncovered about the structure of sentences are abstract and unexpected, a far cry from the kinds of prescriptive rules found in traditional grammar books, and much less easily observable than the English phrase structure facts we have been looking at up to now. And yet infants manage to master them without instruction, at breakneck speed, and without explicit cues in the input. Some scholars of language acquisition are not convinced by some of the more specific syntactic claims made by the generative school, but almost all agree that some syntactic constraints must emerge from the way the brain is hard-wired, and so must have its origins in the way DNA encodes our genome. (We'll leave the evolutionary and biological specifics until the last chapter.)

A basic constraint of this type is called **structure dependence**, which holds that syntactic rules in all languages will refer to hierarchically structured constituents, rather than the linear order in which words are deployed. The idea here is that if children have no prior expectations of structure dependence, and rely uniquely on the input they get from speakers around them, then they might be expected to formulate the simplest kinds of rules to guide their evolving syntactic competence and production. In many cases, the simplest rules would be based on permutations of linear order, and such proto-rules might work a lot of the time. But there would also be characteristic errors where structure dependence is violated. And here's the point: children appear never to produce this kind of ordering error, suggesting that, from the outset, they assume that syntactic rules *are* structurally dependent.

Take the following pair of sentences, for example:

(1)   (a) The guy next to Anna is yawning
      (b) Is the guy next to Anna yawning?

Children acquiring English detect that a yes/no question is formed in the E-language samples they are exposed to by displacing an auxiliary verb to the beginning of the sentence. The simplest hypothesis for them to entertain would be that the first auxiliary verb in the normal **declarative** version of the sentence is shifted to the beginning of the sentence, in a mere reshuffling of linear order. See Figure 1.

| is | the | guy | next | to | Anna | ____ | yawning |

Figure 1   Yes/no question formation

This linear re-ordering rule will work for most yes/no questions, especially the simpler kind that we may assume are more likely to be directed to children:

(2)   (a) Mummy is shopping
      (b) Is Mummy shopping?
(3)   (a) Felix has gone home
      (b) Has Felix gone home?
(4)   (a) Those men are laughing
      (b) Are those men laughing?

The trouble is that this simple rule won't produce the correct results for more complex kinds of sentences. Yes/no questions in English (**interrogative** structures) are actually formed not by simple linear re-ordering of words, but rather by displacement from one node to another in a syntactic tree. As we saw in the last chapter, sentence structures look more like mobiles hanging from the ceiling of a child's bedroom than the string of multicoloured beads around her mother's neck. Operations like the formation of a yes/no question in English require us to unhook a word from one branch of the mobile and hang it on an empty hook (normally higher up), rather than unstringing a word from a chain and putting it back closer to the clasp. And children all over the planet seem to expect this.

To get yes/no questions right, a child acquiring English has to recognize that it's the occupant of the auxiliary node in the VP of the main clause that must be moved, and its landing-site will be the node to the left of the NP subject. The rule is called by linguists **subject-**

auxiliary inversion. If kids always move just the first auxiliary in the string of words that make up the sentence, they'll sometimes make errors like that in (5b), derived from (5a):

(5) (a) The guy who is sitting next to Anna is yawning
     (b) * Is the guy who sitting next to Anna is yawning?

The problem here is that the first auxiliary belongs to the VP of a relative clause modifying the subject head noun *guy*, rather than to the main verb *yawn*. Figures 2 and 3 show simplified versions of the trees that correspond to these two sentences:

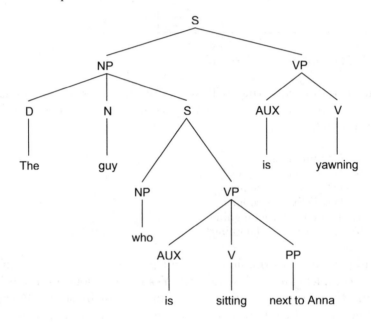

Figure 2   Tree structure for sentence (5a)

Structure dependence predisposes the child to understand that complex sentences related to simpler ones (like the interrogative formed from a declarative in (5)) will be related via abstract notions like 'subject NP', 'main clause VP', and 'empty sister node to main clause', rather than 'first occurrence of *be* or *have*', 'beginning of sentence', etc. Structure dependence and the machinery required for rules like subject-auxiliary inversion constitute facts about syntactic trees, rather than about the grammars of particular languages. Could children work it all out from the input they hear or must this tacit knowledge come from some other source?

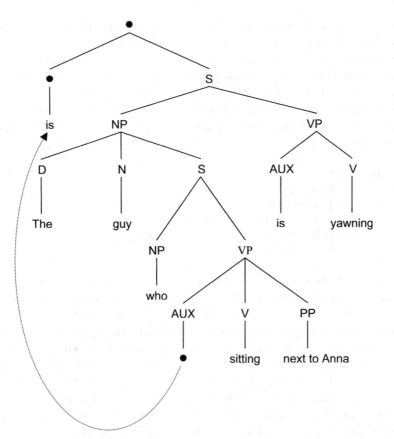

Figure 3 Tree structure for sentence (5b)

Isn't meaning enough?

We have established that children are not *taught* their native language, so we can dismiss at the outset any claim that parents sit their kids down and explain to them how to displace auxiliaries when they want to ask a question. (Lord Macaulay became grammatically competent independently of the fact that his family could afford expensive tutors.) But couldn't they work it all out from the *meaning* of sentences, i.e. from their propositional structure? Well, the problem here is that sentence (5b) is *ungrammatical*, not meaningless. Children, like all human beings, make meanings first and only then express them on the basis of the current state of their emerging linguistic system. For them to understand subject-auxiliary inversion from a purely semantic perspective, independently of structural aspects of sentences, they would need to identify something specific in the *meanings* of the word strings over which the auxiliary needs to be moved, for example that they were always expressions of the AGENT of some action. And yet psycholinguists have found that children don't seem to pay attention to the semantics of the subject as they acquire the rule. Subjects, as we have seen, may express quite a disparate range of conceptual entities. Here are a few:

(6) (a) Singing is fun
     (b) Is singing fun?
(7) (a) Jomo was given a present
     (b) Was Jomo given a present?
(8) (a) It is snowing
     (b) Is it snowing?

In none of these sentences does the subject express the agent of an action. In (6) the subject *is* the action, in (7) it's a RECIPIENT and in (8) it refers to nothing at all. Semantically, the subjects in (5) to (8) don't have anything in common. And yet children don't go through a phase of getting subject-auxiliary inversion right with some kinds of subject expressions and wrong with others: they get all of them right from the beginning. To confirm this, the psycholinguists Stephen Crain and Mineharu Nakayama conducted studies using techniques similar to the naming experiments I talked about in Chapter 4. They played a game with 3 to 5-year-olds in which a toy Jabba the Hutt (of *Star Wars* fame) responded to children's questions with yes/no answers. The question forms were elicited by the researchers via the phrase 'Ask Jabba if [declarative sentence]'. They used sentences with subjects of different semantic hues, like those in (5a)–(8a), and found that children uniformly applied structure dependence (i.e. got the question forms right), at all ages.

Thus, children as young as 3 years appear to know something about syntax as a structural system which is independent of the meanings it is used to express. It is the Language Spell which makes this so hard for us to appreciate, dooming us to forever confuse meaning with its linguistic expression. Only sophisticated grammatical analysis can save us from our doom. The linguist Ralph Fasold has captured the semantics/syntax distinction rather neatly, pointing out that '[Grammatical] principles keep language from being used to say things it would be very useful to say, while making it possible to say other things that are really not likely to be needed'. For example, I once noted down a sentence I had started, but couldn't finish grammatically, even though the meaning was perfectly clear. I was trying to explain that my new computer came with lots of free software, but that my partner and I didn't know what all this software was for. I said:

(9)   It's got 64 megabytes of software that we don't know what …

… and then I tried to finish the sentence with *does* or *it does*, both of which are sadly ungrammatical in this context. All I was trying to do was to modify the noun *software* in sentence (10) with a relative clause made from sentence (11):

(10)   It's got 64 megabytes of software
(11)   We don't know what the software does

But my rules of English wouldn't let me. And yet they *will* let me say things like:

(12)   That what Zyuganov called 'the Jewish question' has already come front and center this soon after Russia's collapse is arguably ominous

This is perfectly grammatical in English, but it is awfully hard to recover its meaning without reading it over a couple of times. (Ironically, I found it in an authentic reading from a textbook for learners of English.) Of course, given enough time, and the right pausing and intonation, we *can* interpret sentence (12), but grammar is not here fulfilling very responsibly its obligation to deliver meaning clearly.

On the one hand, then, meaning outperforms grammar (in the sense that there are ungrammatical sentences which are meaningful); but on the other hand, grammar 'overgenerates' structures (in the sense that it permits sentences which are at the very least semantically obscure). This means that children can't just *know* what's grammatical or ungrammatical in the language they are exposed to on the basis of whether sentences make sense or not. Sentence (5b) makes perfect sense by (the wrong) analogy with (1b), but children don't form yes/no questions in complex sentences by exploiting this analogy, even though it might appear to be the simplest solution.

The input isn't enough either

So if meaning doesn't provide the key, then what does? Perhaps the answer is just so obvious it hasn't occurred to syntacticians who do their research at their office computers rather than at a playpen in a nursery? Surely children don't produce sentences like (5b) because they never hear them in the input? Not so. Like so many 'obvious' accounts of the way language is, it is, alas, a fallacious product of the Language Spell, and the syntacticians' intellectual vantage point turns out to be as good as any. Children actually produce *lots* of linguistic expressions that they have never heard, and many do not conform to the adult grammar (remember, that's one of the main ways in which languages actually *change*). Take a look at the following samples of child speech (lifted from Sue Foster-Cohen's (1999) book on language acquisition):

- 2-year-old: 'That's she's Mom.'
- 3-year-old: 'What do you think what's in that box?'
- 4-year-old: 'Some women were arrested from the soldiers.'
- 5-year-old: 'He might have took it somewhere.'

It is through 'errors' such as these that we see children's active, constructive role in the acquisition process most clearly. Infants here are producing expressions they haven't heard before, extending rules they have constructed to new combinations of words and phrases. The 2-year-old, for example, has worked out that *she* can be used in the place of NPs referring to female animate entities, and that the inflectional category POSSESSION can be marked using a suffixed -*s*. She may have heard the form *she's* before, but not in the context of possession. The 3-year-old has realized that the identity of an object may be questioned in English by the use of the 'wh-' form *what* at the beginning of the sentence, with 'dummy auxiliary' *do* before the subject, but has not yet understood that English (unlike German and other languages) requires the *what* in its original position to be displaced, rather than copied, to the sentence-initial landing-site. The 4-year-old, meanwhile, has learnt that the preposition *from* can be used to mark a source, but not the source of an action (i.e. as an AGENT). Finally, the 5-year-old knows how to mark past tense on the auxiliary (*might*, past tense of *may*), but here marks it on the main verb *take* as well.

Chomsky and colleagues' 'armchair science' turns out to be vindicated after all, even in the absence of the patter of tiny feet.

Universal Grammar

So a child doesn't simply rely on the meaning of expressions or the availability of examples in the input in order to work out the syntax of the E-language to which she is exposed. What then guides her to the construction of an I-language which corresponds so well to the others in her community, even though they are invisible to her, enclosed in the neural nets from which community members' individual minds are spun? The answer proposed by Chomsky (and taken up by other innatists in linguistics, psychology, neuroscience and philosophy) is that the child is guided by an innate blueprint for human language, called **Universal Grammar** (or UG) – a property of the species, shared by all people, regardless of race, ethnicity, the century in which they were born or the place and circumstances of their birth and upbringing.

UG will not look like the grammars of individual E-languages (like English, Maori or Tibetan), nor will it resemble the I-languages of individual adult speakers (like my Auntie Mo, Dame Kiri Te Kanawa or the Dalai Lama). UG contains no phonemes, no words, and no phrase structure: only the potential for them, and restrictions on what form they can take. For example, it will provide a template for syntactic phrases which looks something like Figure 4:

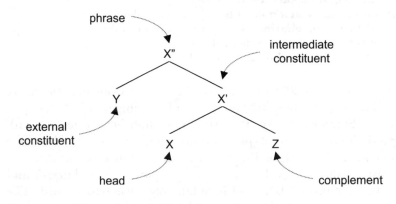

Figure 4   The universal 'X-bar' template for phrases

This template is known as an '**X-bar**' structure because the symbol 'X' is used to stand for any syntactic category (N, P, etc.), and 'bars' (X', X") are used to indicate hierarchical levels within the phrase which X heads. This template will allow the child to fix the particular phrase structure rules of the language to which she is exposed, without having to hear and memorize massive amounts of input. Once she has worked out which word in a group is the head, for example, her assignment of surrounding words to different syntactic categories and modifying functions will be delimited by the configurations she already 'knows' as part of UG.

Now, imagine again that the bit of tree structure in Figure 4 is a mobile, and the nodes can spin around, giving different linear orders for the words hung on the end of each branch. When combined with a **head-ordering parameter**, another aspect of UG which predisposes the child to expect the heads and complements of different kinds of phrases to line up on the left or the right, then the template becomes a powerful device for language acquisition. A child exposed to Spanish, for example, will begin to note that short words with little semantic content often precede conceptually richer forms, and will gradually assign them to the category of P (preposition). This will configure her system to expect heads to appear before their complements (as in Figure 4), and so to expect verb-object word order, as well as other correlated orders, such as relative clauses to follow Ns and As. And for Spanish (and English), these expectations will be met:

(13) Bailaron $_{PP}$[**en** la calle]
      'They danced $_{PP}$[**in** the street]'
(14) Mi amiga $_{VP}$[**come** muchos dulces]
      'My friend $_{VP}$[**eats** lots of sweets]'
(15) $_{NP}$[La **cancelación** de la fiesta] era inevitable
      '$_{NP}$[The **cancellation** of the party] was inevitable'
(16) Pepe es $_{AP}$[**orgulloso** de sus hijos]
      'Pepe is $_{AP}$[**proud** of his children]'

Now if the same child had been whisked away from her maternity ward in an Acapulco hospital and left as a foundling on the doorstep of a house in Fukuoka, Japan, then she might find herself dealing with **postpositions**, instead of prepositions. (This is exactly the same category as the Spanish or English preposition, but it occurs *after* the noun instead of before). This is because Japanese (like Turkish and many other languages) is a head-final language, whereas Spanish (like English) is head-initial. Children brought up in a Japanese E-language environment who work out that their language has postpositions will be predisposed to swivel the nodes of their phrase structure template until the head appears to the right of its complements, and this will aid them to fix their clause word order to object-verb, etc.

This does not, of course, mean that all or even most of the job of language acquisition is directed by UG: indeed, most of the grammatical nuts and bolts and all of the word forms of particular languages will have to be acquired using general learning strategies shared with other domains, such as sheer rote memorization, problem-solving and pattern-matching. Sophisticated detectors of statistical distributional patterns in the input and correlations with aspects of sociocultural, pragmatic and semantic meaning will also play a central role. But the possibility that an abstract notion like syntax has a biological base, and that human beings, from whatever language community, sociocultural background, or millennium, are all bound together by the same basic grammatical magic, is a very powerful antidote to some of the more insidious effects of the Language Spell.

Take pidgin and creole speakers again, who we last looked at in Chapter 5. They and their descendents have been maligned for centuries because their linguistic systems are seen as simple and child-like imitations of European imperial tongues. Remember that pidgins arise when speakers of mutually unintelligible languages need to understand each other, but they don't have the luxury of Berlitz institutes or UN interpreters. With natural human resourcefulness, they develop a new rough-and-ready linguistic system on the fly, which serves their purposes in the short term. But then here's the miracle: the children of pidgin speakers, deprived of the elaborate grammatically-structured input used by speakers of full languages, nevertheless begin to construct *bona fide* human languages, with all the grammatical frills attached. In fact, the creole languages they invent follow all the universal features we would expect of an established human language. This would be a remarkable coincidence if all that children brought to the task was the input they heard and general learning and problem-solving abilities. Derek Bickerton and others have suggested that the birth of a creole reveals UG at work *par excellence*, allowing children's minds to build a linguistic skyscraper when all they have been given by the environment is a few bricks. And the same thing happens with deaf children of non-signing (or non-native 'pidgin-signing') parents.

Yet language can't, of course, arise and operate in a complete vacuum: just as UG is no good for communication unless fleshed out with the phonemes, words and syntactic rules of a full I-language, so an I-language is of little use for sharing meaning without the contribution of contextual knowledge and shared norms about how to actually *do* things with words. So let's now take up again the vital role of non-linguistic context and social norms in the construction and delivery of linguistic messages.

Pragmatics: sentences in use

Forty years ago, Chomsky disturbed a lot of linguists, social anthropologists, psychologists and philosophers when he drew his distinction between linguistic competence ('the speaker-hearer's knowledge of his language') and linguistic performance ('the actual use of the language in concrete situations'). Perceived as particularly outrageous was his assumption, for the purposes of linguistic enquiry, of 'an ideal speaker-listener, in a completely homogenous speech-community, who knows its language perfectly and is unaffected by [...] grammatically irrelevant conditions [...] in applying his know-ledge of the language in actual performance'. Unfortunately, this notorious statement from his 1965 book *Aspects of the Theory of Syntax*, written before he had clarified things through his notions of I-language and E-language, was not properly understood by linguists and others working outside of his approach. His words were misinterpreted by many as sanctioning the contemplation of a community resource (e.g. an E-language like English) as something unaffected by sociocultural context ('grammatically irrelevant conditions'). What could it possibly mean to study 'an *ideal* speaker-listener['s] ... [perfect] knowledge of *the* language' [my emphasis], if 'the language' can only be defined as a group property, which must be inherently social?

The problem here was again that of the Fundamental Paradox: that language is socially motivated, but mentally instantiated. We have now seen that what Chomsky wanted to do was to explore and attempt to characterize the mental instantiation of language, i.e. I-language, especially the genetically-determined component responsible for syn-tactic combination. This doesn't entail a belief that 'ideal speaker-listeners' exist, or that performance factors don't: Chomsky is just an honest linguist, getting on with what he's good at. Clearly, however, a full picture of human language must go beyond his narrow goal, grasping the nettle of the Fundamental Paradox and explaining how I-linguistic knowledge is deployed 'in actual performance'.

In Chapter 7 I described the syntactic component of our mental language faculty as providing 'a shared framework for the combina-tion of core lexical meanings into a compositional semantics for sentences: a common, context-free baseline for pragmatic interpreta-tion'. A compositional semantics builds meaningful word combinations (syntactic structures) from conceptual information, via propositional structure. Propositional structure itself, however, must be embedded in a vastly richer conceptual network (a mental model) if it is to be relevant to us in the world. The study of linguistic pragmatics attempts to reveal and explain some of the ways in which propositions mediate linguistic structure and the non-linguistic perceptions, intentions and beliefs which lead to Dell Hymes' notion of communicative competence: our ability to use linguistic (grammatical) competence appropriately to share meanings in sociocultural contexts.

Beyond semantics

Let's look at a real example of language use to see how pragmatics approaches its task. I recently received via email a copy of an open letter addressed to Laura Schlessinger, a sometimes alarmingly intolerant dispenser of advice on US radio. The letter starts:

> Dear Dr. Laura,
>
> Thank you for doing so much to educate people regarding God's Law. I have learned a great deal from your show, and try to share that knowledge with as many people as I can. When someone tries to defend the homosexual lifestyle, for example, I simply remind them that Leviticus 18:22 clearly states it to be an abomination. End of debate. I do need some advice from you, however, regarding some of the other specific laws and how to follow them:
>
> 1. When I burn a bull on the altar as a sacrifice, I know it creates a pleasing odor for the Lord – Lev.1:9. The problem is my neighbors. They claim the odor is not pleasing to them. Should I smite them?
>
> 2. I would like to sell my daughter into slavery, as sanctioned in Exodus 21:7. In this day and age, what do you think would be a fair price for her?
>
> [...]

The letter, signed 'Your devoted fan, Jim', lists a further ten queries in the same vein. The words, syntactic structures and propositional semantics of this text will not on their own get Jim's message across. Indeed, Jim's message is *bigger* than any of the individual words or sentences he uses: taken as a whole, his letter 'means' something like the following:

> A literal reading of the Old Testament should not be used as a justification for contemporary condemnation of homosexuality, because consistent invocation of Old Testament injunctions would lead to the approbation of all sorts of absurd and nefarious practices.

Pragmatics goes beyond the deployment of words in sentences, to study the meaning of **texts** and **discourse**. A text for pragmatics is not necessarily a written document, like the Book of Leviticus in *The Bible*: it is any coherent stretch of language longer than a sentence. And discourse is not just conversation: it is any stretch of language constituting a single event, from a single word (e.g. when I growl

'Great!' on returning home alone to find the cellars flooded) to a long chain of sentences (e.g. one of Fidel Castro's four-hour speeches).

Ambiguity and presupposition

The text represented by Jim's letter to Dr. Laura has various levels of meaning, starting with the lexical level, where ambiguity will always be rife. Context already starts to enter the picture here by cooperating with the syntactic component to disambiguate homonyms. For example, although our syntactic competence tells us that *deal* in *a great deal* can't be a verb, it is contextual information from other parts of the sentence which leads readers to interpret the word as meaning 'amount', rather than 'bargain' or 'hand of cards'. Once reliable hypotheses about lexical meaning are reasonably supported, the propositional level of meaning can be constructed: this is the literal meaning of the sentences which make up the text. For example, Jim's sentence *I would like to sell my daughter into slavery* means, on this level, that he has a female child that he would like to exchange for cash. So far, this is straightforward semantics, constructed from core lexical meanings and syntactic rules.

On another level, however, the individual words activate (and are activated by) concepts which may convey certain **presupposed meanings**, such as the fact that one sells things that one owns. An implication of the sentence, then, is that Jim believes his daughter to be his property. As far as I can see, however, presupposed meaning has really nothing much to do with linguistic expressions per se, and everything to do with the (often socially determined) beliefs of individuals. A thief who sells stolen property, clearly does not understand the concept of selling as bearing the necessary implication that the goods sold are the property of the seller, unless of course his or her concept of property differs from that of 'society' as a whole.

Following some of the arguments developed in Chapter 4, however, there can of course be no such thing as a concept which belongs to 'society': in the end, concepts belong to individual minds, and so if a thief believes he is selling, then selling he is! If sufficiently overlapping concepts are represented in enough different minds, and the belief that they are shared leads to fruitful social transactions and norms· of behaviour, then to that extent they 'become' social . . . and we can get things done together as groups. Thus, presupposed meaning seems to be inherently pragmatic, separate from I-language: an extension of core lexical meaning, stored in people's conceptual systems, sometimes necessary from the point of view of logical objectivity, but generally a function of the ways individual minds create and store beliefs about the world and their patterns of interaction with it.

Intentions, implications and inferences

A further level of pragmatic meaning, even more clearly dissociated from the 'dictionary' idea of core lexical concepts, provides the key to Jim's overriding communicative intent. Because we are not Spock or Data on the Starship Enterprise, we know that Jim's letter is tongue-in-cheek: that what the writer says is not what he means. We know that he doesn't *really* want to sell his daughter into slavery, and indeed can surmise that he abhors Dr. Laura's beliefs about homosexuality. But how can we come to appreciate this level of meaning if there's no overt cue to it in the linguistic expressions he uses in the text? I know nothing about the identity of Jim, so my conclusion that he's dissimulating cannot be based on prior knowledge of his behaviour or publicly expressed beliefs.

There are, of course, some 'macro' cues which lie outside the text itself, for example the fact that the letter is an open message to a prominent media personality, posted on the Internet, and the inclusion of an anonymous introductory paragraph (redundantly informing us that the letter is 'funny, as well as informative'). A possible macro cue within the text is the use of the prefabricated phrase *End of debate*, which when spoken by someone in authority, like a parent or a police officer, presupposes that there *is* a debate, but that further engagement in it will not be tolerated, and when spoken by anyone else has come to conventionally signal the speaker's distaste for such intolerance. The use of the archaic word *smite* also alerts us to the letter's less-than-serious tone.

But even without such cues, most readers familiar with US religious culture would almost immediately 'get' the subtext, in the same way that anyone entering my flooded cellars with me would immediately appreciate the insincerity of my expostulation 'Great!' Human beings apparently *know* that words and sentences don't necessarily mean what the lexicon and syntax alone would suggest. And yet they need to know the literal meanings in order to understand the 'insincere' **implied meaning**. This is pragmatics *par excellence*, and is a *social* phenomenon through and through, since it relies on knowledge of culturally-based behavioural norms and expectations: we know that people no longer burn bulls on altars in their homes, or sell their offspring into slavery. We know to expect that there is a non-literal message lurking beneath these surface absurdities, because we engage in discourse (speaking, listening, reading, writing and signing) with a set of assumptions concerning the relevance of any linguistic expression to the communicative *goals* or *intentions* of the speaker.

The most well-known formulation of these assumptions is Paul Grice's **Cooperative Principle**, which is stated via four 'maxims':

- The maxim of **Quantity**, by which we all tacitly assume that speakers will express no more and no less than what they wish their hearers to understand.
- The maxim of **Quality**, by which we assume that speakers will express what they believe to be true.
- The maxim of **Relevance**, by which we assume that speakers will express messages which are relevant to the current (linguistic or non-linguistic) context.
- The maxim of **Manner**, by which we assume that speakers will express themselves clearly and economically.

Although these maxims capture the default settings of our pragmatic competence, the full richness of human linguistic communication reveals itself in their conventionalized *violation*. When we indulge in deceit (both white lies and black), rumour, gossip, sarcasm or fiction, we are not using language simply to report what we believe to be a true state of affairs, and yet it is the *presumption* of the Maxim of Quality which allows us to use language in such ways, to dissimulate, entertain, mislead, abuse, express contempt, etc. In most cases, the violation is conventionally recognized as such by the receivers of the message. Literature, for example, relies on this: Evelyn Waugh begins his novel *Brideshead Revisited* with the words ' "I have been here before," I said', but no reader will assume that the author is referring to himself. Similarly, people regularly ride rough-shod over the Maxims of Quantity and Manner when they use understatements and euphemisms, or when they tell jokes based on puns and *double-entendres*.

The Maxim of Relevance is invoked perhaps most often in this way. Sentences (18) and (19), for example, work as responses to the question in (17) because hearers make them relevant.

(17) So do you agree with the Board's decision?
(18) Is the Pope Catholic?
(19) Can pigs fly?

People can use clichés like (18) and (19) instead of a simple 'yes' or 'no' to make their response more emphatic, and hearers, instead of wondering what the Holy Father or domestic swine have to do with the decision of the Board, recognize by a series of inferences the speaker's communicative intent.

Linguistic interactions like Jim's email letter to Dr. Laura succeed because of tacit assumptions in the minds of language producers about what hearers already know, believe or can work out. If speakers don't calibrate their expectations about hearers' states of knowledge adequately, therefore, miscommunications can also result. Here is a passage from an article in the *Guardian* newspaper on racism in London's Metropolitan Police, which illustrates the sometimes fragile nature of these assumptions.

> **The only black member of the Stephen Lawrence inquiry**, which found the Metropolitan police to be institutionally racist, said **he** felt demeaned after an officer stopped **him** and asked to search his car. **John Sentamu, the Anglican bishop of Stepney in London**, said the officer could not justify his request.

For readers to correctly track references to the protagonist in this passage, they must go beyond its semantics, and make a series of inferences in order to link together the meanings of the linguistic expressions used. Nothing in the language employed explicitly links the identity of *John Sentamu* and *the Anglican bishop of Stepney in London* with *the only black member of the Stephen Lawrence inquiry* (although syntactic rules help us work out that *he* and *him* in the second and third lines refer to Sentamu, and not to Lawrence). Instead, readers must invoke the Maxim of Relevance, together with quite extensive cultural knowledge, such as the following:

- bishops are likely members of official inquiries in the UK (and yet few Anglican bishops are black);
- *Sentamu* is not a traditional last name for white Britons;
- Stephen Lawrence was a black teenager whose murder, by white youths, was improperly and inadequately investigated by the Metropolitan Police;
- in London, the police have used stop-and-search powers disproportionately on black members of the public.

Studies of corpora, those massive databases of language from real contexts of use that we saw in Chapter 3, have shown, predictably, that written discourse tends to explicitly encode much more of the language user's mental model and assumptions about shared knowledge than spoken discourse does. This is because the writer-reader interaction is normally 'displaced' in both time and space: writers never know for sure who will read what they have written, nor where they will be and when they will do it. The Irish poet Nuala ní Dhomhnaill may have had the written word in mind when she wrote her poem *The Language Issue* (translated here into English):

> I place my hope on the water
> in this little boat
> of the language, the way a body might put
> an infant
>
> in a basket of intertwined
> iris leaves
> its underside proofed
> with bitumen and pitch,
>
> then set the whole thing down amidst
> the sedge
> and bulrushes by the edge
> of a river
>
> only to have it borne hither and thither,
> not knowing where it might end up;
> in the lap, perhaps,
> of some Pharaoh's daughter.

Because of its displaced nature, writing tends to be more formal, with greater numbers of full NPs and fewer pronouns, with longer sentences, longer and less frequent words, more morphologically and syntactically complex structures and less ambiguity (Chapter 10 has more on this).

But judging one's (potential) interlocutors' state of knowledge and awareness of immediate context is not the only pragmatic homework that writers and speakers must do when they produce linguistic messages. Language is also used to register a great deal of information about the social relationships that hold among its users. This is especially so in face-to-face interaction, where tacit negotiation of topic, turn-taking, authority and purpose reflect the participants' perceived levels of power and degree of intimacy.

The art of conversation

The 'Helpful Hints' section of the operating instructions for my Panasonic telephone includes the following valuable advice: 'If you and the caller speak at the same time, part of your conversation will be lost. To avoid this, speak alternately.' Although we don't need instruction manuals or self-improvement guides to learn how to conduct conversation, this pre-eminently social activity is not as straightforward as it may seem on the surface. Dialogues in novels, plays, cartoon strips and TV soaps are written under the influence of the Language Spell, and so camouflage the intricate choreography of real linguistic interaction. But scholars in the field of **conversation analysis**, a speciality within **discourse analysis**, have helped reveal its hidden structure and codes. Real-life conversation is not just a simple matter of A speaking, then B, then A again, as in a Shakespearian drama. And neither is it haphazard free-for-all, divorced from the behavioural norms which govern other aspects of social life.

When two (or more) people talk together, they provide and pick up on subtle cues regarding the sequence of participation, the length of speaking turns and the objectives of the discourse. They also monitor the effect their participations are having on their interlocutors, and, as a default, attempt to 'package' their messages in ways which address their hearers' perceived current state of knowledge and reflect the degree of social distance or intimacy perceived to hold between them. When the social distance is considerable, or the talk is between strangers, the packaging normally includes ritualized expressions of politeness. Angela the English speaker, for example, might frame a request to a stranger with the words *I wonder if you would mind. . .*, as in *I wonder if you would mind closing the window*. It has been claimed that this kind of verbal packaging varies in length with the degree of politeness assumed to be needed. With an intimate, you can just say *Close the window*, i.e. express the propositional content of the message directly. But with a stranger, or someone perceived as more powerful than you (a customer if you're a waiter, a teacher if you're a student, a head of state if you're a minor civil servant), the polite packaging can receive more encoding than the message itself – to the extent that you can gesture towards the open window and say *I wonder if you would mind . . .*, leaving context to supply the meat of the message.

Here's an instructional case of real conversation between *two* heads of state, which allows us to see some of these strategies and cues in action. The dialogue took place between Vicente Fox, president of Mexico, and Fidel Castro, president of Cuba, in the spring of 2002. Fox was hosting a UN conference in which George W. Bush would be present, and at the last moment Castro advised his Mexican counterpart that he intended to be there too. This decision would cause potential embarrassment to Bush and to Fox, because of the tensions between the US and Cuba, and Mexico's desire to keep on good terms with its powerful northern neighbour.

Castro: Tell me, Mr. President, how are you?
Fox: Fidel, how are you?
Castro: Very well, very well, thank you. And you?
Fox: What a pleasure! Listen, Fidel, I'm calling about this surprise I got just a couple of hours ago, when I found out about your intended visit here to Mexico. But first, I'd like to make sure that this conversation stays private, between you and me, OK?
Castro: Yes, agreed. You got my letter, right? I sent it to you.
Fox: Yes, I got your letter just a couple of hours ago and that's why I'm calling you now.
Castro: Ah, good. They told me you went to bed early, and we sent the letter early.
Fox: Yes, I go to bed early, but this has kept me awake.
Castro: You don't say!
Fox: Yes, it got here ... It's 10 p.m. here now, it got here at 8 and actually we were here having dinner with Kofi Annan.
Castro: Ah!
Fox: But look, Fidel, I'm calling you first as a friend.
Castro: If you're calling me first as a friend, I hope you're not going to tell me not to come.
     [...]

This interaction, which I have translated as closely but as colloquially as I could, forms part of a dialogue which stretches over 40 column inches in the Mexican newspaper *La Jornada*. It is a consummate example of indirect speech acts and metalinguistic packaging, in which the two presidents attempt to achieve their aims or reach a compromise through the deployment of words which, on their own, convey little in the way of propositional content. Syntax and semantics provide the basic framework, but it is pragmatic convention which weaves the rich pattern of non-linguistic meaning around it.

Take, for example, the opening moves. Before they can touch on the matter at hand, they first go through the ritual **adjacency pairs** of greeting and expression of interest in the other's welfare – common opening strategies in all language communities, even if they do violate the Maxim of Quality (Fox's tacit recognition of the insincerity of the ritual is evidenced by his failure to answer Castro's repeated question regarding his welfare). Once the pleasantries are done with, Fox states the *theme* of his call (*Listen, Fidel, I'm calling about ...*), but he still hasn't stated his *purpose* when this extract finishes over 130 words later:

indeed, it takes a further 400 words or so before Fox's proposal finds expression. And even then, the route is somewhat tortuous:

Fox: [...] Look, let me make you a proposal.
Castro: Yes.
Fox: Yes?
Castro: Tell me.
Fox: I don't know when you intend to come, because you haven't told me, but my proposal would be that you come on Thursday.
[...]

Notice that the proposal itself (*you come on Thursday*) is not made directly, but rather using the **conditional mood**: literally, according to the grammatical encoding only, Fox is not making a proposal, but is telling Castro, hypothetically, what his proposal would be (if he were to make one). This is a conventionalized politeness ritual, and Castro recognizes it as such, proceeding as though the proposal had indeed been put. This is a good example of the way in which language is used to make requests indirectly, an exercise in **mitigation**, as though to *soften* the degree of imposition that any request inevitably entails (Penelope Brown and Stephen Levinson studied the expression of politeness in languages around the world, and found universal patterns which they explained on the basis of mutual 'face-saving' strategies).

Many languages also directly encode politeness grammatically. Spanish, for example, like German and French, uses two different second person pronouns: *tú* for intimates or those perceived as of lesser status (children, domestic employees, etc.), and the more respectful *usted* for strangers and those perceived as having higher status (teachers, elders, etc.). From the beginning, though, Fox and Castro fail to concur on the appropriate level of intimacy between them: Fox calls Castro by his first name and uses the informal *tú*, whereas the latter calls Fox *Señor Presidente* and sticks to the formal *usted* throughout. This pragmatic dissonance reflects the tension of the exchange, and highlights the different styles of each, an issue we take up in the following two chapters.

We have come a long way from the alphabet-book idea of language in which language expresses meaning by naming objects. This chapter and the last have shown how our shared systems for combining words allow us to express an infinite number of complex concepts and propositional meanings, and that children are genetically predisposed to acquire the rules by which these computational systems operate. But crucially, we've also seen how syntax and propositional semantics alone will not account for our ability to actually *use* language in real social settings. Here, we are seeing the Fundamental Paradox resolved in action, as our mental language mechanisms interface smoothly with social and cultural beliefs and practices, to the extent that we're not even aware most of the time of the seams that join them together. In the next couple of chapters we explore more fully the way mental I-languages emerge in human societies as group E-languages, in an attempt to further resolve the Fundamental Paradox, and so reveal more of the reality behind the Language Spell.

More information

 Stephen Crain and Mineharu Nakayama's paper on **structure dependence** in children (published in the journal *Language*) is discussed in Crain and Diane Lillo-Martin's excellent 1999 introduction to **UG** and its role in language acquisition.

 Susan Foster-Cohen's (1999) introduction to **language acquisition** provides a non-technical, lucid discussion of data and theory from the psycholinguistic perspective.

Pinker (1994), in passing, discusses the importance of **sign language** for an understanding of the role of our genetic inheritance in language acquisition. Derek Bickerton (1990) does so, in a broader context, for **pidgins**.

Virginia LoCastro's (2003) introduction to **pragmatics** for language teachers provides a clear and comprehensive review of the topic, especially its social dimension.

Conversation analysis hit the best-seller lists in the nineties with Deborah Tannen's *You just don't understand* (1992), about the differences between male and female conversation styles.

Part IV: Babel

... she could prattle on in Bombay's garbage argot, Mumbaiki Kachrapati baat-cheet, in which a sentence could begin in one language, swoop through a second and even a third and then swing back round to the first. Our acronymic name for it was Hug-me. Hindi Urdu Gujarati Marathi English.

(Salman Rushdie, *The Ground Beneath Her Feet*)

Although the basic computational architecture of human language is the same for all of us, emerging as it does from our DNA, it's probably the biblical story of Babel or its equivalent in other faiths that resonates more immediately and instinctively for most people. Spin the dial of a shortwave radio, glance through an issue of the linguistics journal *Language*, or walk down a street in Bombay, New York or Singapore, and it might appear that the only feature that links all language users is the use of the vocal tract (and even this isn't true, as we know from the existence of sign languages). Within communities speaking a single language, too, the diversity of linguistic form and function will stand out as sharply as the observed coincidences of phonology, lexicon, morphology and syntax.

This chapter and the next will explore (and celebrate) some of this diversity, and show how it is a natural consequence of the larger social diversity of our species. Developing some of the ideas first sketched in Chapter 1, though, I'll also be playing the pessimist once again, arguing that unless we combat some of the negative consequences of the Language Spell, this diversity will continue to be exploited or misunderstood. And also that this time there's a second, cultural, spell to deal with, the legacy of the emergence of the monolingual European nation state in the Renaissance. I'll try to show how many people, especially those of us acculturated in the Western European tradition of Britain, France, Spain, and their empires, make the inevitable association of 'one nation, one language', despite clear evidence to the contrary. The following passage, from a 1999 article in the *Guardian* on minority language rights in France, illustrates the staying-power of this prejudice:

> Chirac's refusal [to give even limited official recognition to France's seven regional languages] followed a recent verdict from France's highest court. It ruled that the European Charter on Regional and Minority Languages – which Paris signed in May after years of procrastination but has yet to ratify – posed a serious threat to 'the unity of the French people and the indivisibility of the Republic'. It also violated the French constitution, whose Article 2 states: 'The language of the republic is French.'
>
> [...] *Le Figaro*, the arch-conservative daily, said recognition of regional languages would threaten French, 'at a time when it is being bastardised by Anglo-Saxon words'. It also spoke alarmingly of linguistic freedom leading to separatist violence, and 'sooner or later to the dislocation of the French identity'.

We'll see how this tapestry of I- and E-language social psychology has conspired with sociopolitical factors to contribute to a world of language users scarred by considerable discrimination, abuse of power, and unfulfilled human potential.

We start, however, with a brief tour of the varied forms that language takes around the globe, and ask how it is that such spectacular diversity doesn't inevitably result in impenetrable voids of communication, at either local or global levels. We focus in particular on the astonishing fact of multilingualism in individuals, communities and nations. Then, in Chapter 10, we'll come to see that actually all speakers, even monolinguals, are linguistically diverse, commanding style repertoires which can be geared to a range of audiences and purposes. Our portrait of the world's linguistic cornucopia concludes with a discussion of what this diversity means for some of the 'language professions' and what kinds of effects their talk and text can have on us, their Spell-bound audiences.

Languages of the world

It is impossible to state with precision the number of languages spoken on the planet today. There are two main reasons for this. One is that we lack data, though in recent years valiant attempts at detailed documentation have begun, as linguists and the public at large become slowly more aware of the gradual but steadily increasing pace of language death around the globe. The other reason derives from the counter-intuitive notion I rather cavalierly introduced in Chapter 3: that languages as E-languages are actually only useful fictions, so are hard to pin down and quantify, as different groups of language users (including linguists) tell different stories about the status of one or another group's shared linguistic resources. Be this as it may, descriptive linguists have, with various degrees of confidence, counted between five and seven thousand language communities, i.e. groups of speakers who share more of their lexical, grammatical and communicative competences with each other than they do with others. This overlapping of linguistic competence is recognized, and indeed hallowed and ritualized, by the members of each community (and is codified in some cases also in grammar books and dictionaries). We can usefully suppose, then, that there are between five and seven thousand E-languages being spoken on Earth every day.

Some have just a handful of surviving speakers, others many millions. Some have a grim future (indeed their remaining native speakers will all die before this book appears in print), whereas others (like Mandarin Chinese, Spanish and English) will be around for a good few centuries (perhaps millennia) to come. The Ethnologue project (which can be explored at www.ethnologue.com), coordinated by the missionary group the Summer Institute of Linguistics, identifies 6,809 different languages in its 2000 edition, although some of them are extinct, and others may be viewed as dialectal variations of a single common E-language. The languages registered in Ethnologue have the following geographical distribution:

- Asia: 32%
- Africa: 30%
- Pacific: 19%
- Americas: 15%
- Europe: 3%

The figure for Europe perhaps explains why it comes as such a surprise to many speakers of European languages (especially Anglophones) that there are so many languages out there. The European tongues English, Spanish, French and Portuguese are the first languages of around 15 per cent of the world's population. Spanish counts as the largest, with 358 million speakers (the majority in the Americas). English comes second, with 341 million speakers in 105 countries (over 500 million if we include second language speakers). But spoken by more people than any other language is Mandarin Chinese, with a staggering 867 million users.

At the other extreme of the numbers game, Ethnologue reveals that of the nearly 7,000 languages identified, around 6 per cent are spoken by only a few elderly users. This percentage is set to rocket in the present century, with linguists predicting the loss of around three thousand languages by the year 2100. (That's an average of 30 a year, or 2.5 a month!) Table 1 illustrates the distribution of these almost extinct tongues, and gives a couple of examples for each geographical region. I chose examples which had relatively recent reporting dates, but by now of course the figures must have dwindled much further, and I imagine that one or more of these languages may now be gone forever from human minds and the communities they have helped construct.

Table 1   Almost extinct languages (total in Ethnologue = 417)

Region	Number of languages	Examples			
		Language	Country	Speakers	Date
Americas	161	Iñapari	Peru	4	1999
		Hupa	USA	8	1998
Pacific	157	Ura	Vanuatu	6	1998
		Kamilaroi	Australia	3	1997
Asia	55	Ainu	Japan	15	1996
		Arem	Viet Nam	20	1996
Africa	37	Bodo	C.Afr.Rep.	15	1996
		Luo	Cameroon	1	1995
Europe	7	Ter Saami	Russia	6	1995
		Pite Saami	Sweden, Norway	< 50	1995

How can we measure the degrees of variation between all the tongues spoken on the planet, and so get a feel for the different textures of their expressive power? This is an especially urgent task in many cases, given the speed of their demise. We owe much to the painstaking descriptions and analyses carried out by a small group of dedicated **field linguists**: the Vasco da Gamas and Neil Armstrongs, the Linnaeuses and Darwins, of linguistics. Field linguists travel the planet with tape-recorders and note-books, recording millions of phonemes, words and sentence structures and trying to make sense of the infinite number of combinations they can make. Equally, we owe a great deal to native speakers of languages spoken where linguistic science is unknown or underfunded, who serve as non-specialist informants. Increasingly, some of these informants are becoming skilled linguists in their own right, often motivated by a desire to document and save for posterity the tongues of their ancestors, and therefore part of their own cultural inheritance.

Using these data, linguists have been able to compare the ways we use our common language faculty, and have proposed linguistic **typologies** which enable us to get a handle on the multifarious expressions of Universal Grammar which have arisen across the millennia.

Historical typology

One way of appreciating linguistic diversity is to examine which languages of the world today are 'genetically' related to each other. This allows us to trace them back through time, to reveal their family trees, in the same way that biological taxonomists since Darwin and Linnaeus have done for the plant and animal kingdoms. The basic tools for this enterprise are **comparative analysis** and **comparative reconstruction**. The first refers to the grammatical legwork of comparing languages to see what kinds of phonological, lexical, morphological and syntactic resources they share. The greater the overlap, the more likely that they have descended from a common tongue. In order to get back into pre-history (i.e. before the invention of writing systems), linguists need to hypothesize languages for which we have no written evidence. This is done via comparative reconstruction: the use of data from languages for which we *do* have evidence to hypothesize a common parent and make some intelligent guesses about what it must have looked like.

These techniques mirror those of biological taxonomists. No-one has ever seen a dinosaur, and the fossils we have discovered present only partial evidence about their fleshier parts, and therefore their outward appearance. And yet the computer-generated images from *Jurassic Park* are probably quite close to the way the original beasts looked. Why? Because the scientists who have reconstructed them use information about the hides, eye balls, muscle tissue, wing shapes, tongues, etc. of animals still around today. This may be somewhat risky, but it's entirely reasonable, because we know that today's beasts have all evolved from earlier ones, maintaining large parts of their DNA, and that all animals are connected through some common stage in their past.

When comparing languages, historical linguists must follow the taxonomists in being very careful to identify linguistic resources which are *homologous*, rather than *analogous*. Although bats and birds both have wings which serve the same *function*, and are therefore *analogous* structures, they are not homologous: an analysis of their structural *form* reveals that bats' wings have more in common structurally with human hands (which cannot, alas, be used to fly with). A trivial linguistic example: Basque uses the vowel *a* to function as a determiner. So does English. Superficially, they are analogous in function and similar in form, like bats' and birds' wings. But a closer examination reveals that the Basque expression is suffixed, as *-a*, and is closer in use to the English definite article *the*. Thus they are unlikely to be homologous in structure. Similarly, when we notice hundreds of Basque words like *liburu*, 'book', *aireportu*, 'airport', and *eliza*, 'church', that are equivalent in meaning and similar in form to their Spanish equivalents (*libro*, *aeropuerto*, and *iglesia*), we should not rush to the conclusion that the languages are related (the similarity is the result of borrowing). Basque is actually an **isolate**, a language that has no known relatives.

Language families

One of the greatest scientific breakthroughs in historical typology occurred in the late eighteenth century when an English colonial judge, William Jones, noticed systematic correspondences between Greek, Latin, Gothic and Celtic in the west, and Persian (Farsi) and Sanskrit in the east. (Farsi is spoken in Iran; Sanskrit is the ancient language in which the sacred Hindu texts of the Veda were written around three and a half thousand years ago: it was described by Panini over two thousand years ago in his grammar, the *Astadhyayi*.) Following this discovery, historical linguists were able to show that most European languages were actually linked genetically with the languages spoken in modern Iran, Afghanistan and Northern India, through a hypothesized common ancestor called Proto-Indo-European (the *proto-* here comes from the Greek *protos*, 'first', and is used in historical linguistics to indicate reconstructed ancestor tongues). We don't know much about the original speakers of this language, but analysis of common vocabulary for elements of the landscape, combined with evidence of migration patterns, suggests that they might have lived over four thousand years ago in the Urals area of modern Russia. (This is an example of **linguistic archaeology**.)

Recall from Chapter 4 the words *vader* and *Vater*, the Flemish/ Dutch and German cognates of English *father*. Now take a look at the following list, this time for *mother*, to get a taste of the evidence for Proto-Indo-European:

Bengali	*ma*	Italian	*madre*
Bulgarian	*mayka*	Norwegian	*moder*
Catalan	*mare*	Pashto	*mor*
Czech	*matka*	Persian	*madar*
Danish	*moder*	Polish	*matka*
Dutch	*moeder*	Portuguese	*mãe*
English	*mother*	Romanian	*mama*
French	*mère*	Russian	*mat'*
German	*mutter*	Spanish	*madre*
Hindi	*mata*	Swedish	*moder*
Icelandic	*móðir*	Ukranian	*mati*

On the basis of this kind of comparative analysis of sound patterns and word forms, the Indo-European family was recognized, grouping over 400 languages on a variety of branches. Table 2 gives a sample of them, mixing family levels somewhat for the sake of simplicity.

Table 2 A selection of Indo-European languages grouped by branch

Baltic	Latvian, Lithuanian
Slavic	Russian, Ukranian, Polish, Czech, Macedonian, Bulgarian
Germanic	Icelandic, Norwegian, Swedish, Danish, English, Dutch, German, Yiddish, Gothic
Celtic	Irish, Scots Gaelic, Manx, Welsh, Breton
Italic	Latin, Portuguese, Spanish, Catalan, French, Italian, Romanian
Albanian	Albanian
Hellenic	Greek
Anatolian	Hittite
Iranian	Persian, Kurdish, Pashto
Indic	Romany, Urdu, Hindi, Assamese, Bengali, Marathi, Gujarati, Punjabi, Singhalese

Indo-European is one of over a hundred different families recognized by Ethnologue. By far the largest families are **Niger-Congo**, spoken in sub-Saharan Africa, whose ancestor tongue has left 1,489 descendents, and **Austronesian**, spoken in South-East Asia and the Pacific Islands, with 1,262 family members. The number of languages that we see today in each family doesn't necessarily reflect the number of their speakers or their geographical extension. The **Uto-Aztecan** languages of Mexico and the south-west of the United States number 62 in the Ethnologue count, but account for fewer than two million speakers. The 552 languages of the **Trans-New Guinea** family, spread across the islands of Papua New Guinea, are all spoken in an area less than the size of Spain. Basque, as we have seen is an isolate, a family of one. And neither does family membership necessarily entail the current physical proximity of its speakers: Hungarian, although completely surrounded by Indo-European languages, is actually a member of the Uralic family, which includes Finnish, Saami and Estonian way up in the north.

Formal typology

Languages are actually more diverse than historical typology alone would predict. Unlike animals and plants, the mutation process by which related human E-languages split from their siblings is largely social, rather than biological. For this reason, it also occurs at vastly greater speeds, measured in tens of generations rather than thousands. Organisms change *despite* reproduction, the gene replication process, because of 'copying errors' (a biological process). On the other hand, two dialects will drift as far apart as mutual incomprehensibility (i.e. become separate languages) as soon as their speakers stop *talking to each other* on a regular basis (a social process). Once this happens, the new languages will go their own sweet way, changing in unpredictable ways because of reanalysis and contact, as we have seen in previous chapters. Chapter 4, for example, explained how aspects of E-languages inevitably get modified because they are actually conglomerations of discontinuous I-languages, with parents *directly* transferring to their children nothing but the genes which encode Universal Grammar. And Chapter 5 revealed how contact between speakers of different E-languages can often result in drastic changes to their lexical and grammatical systems, in very short time-spans.

Take German and English. Despite their close genetic ties, they display some very obvious linguistic differences: German has grammatical gender and rich inflection; English doesn't bother with either of them any more. German ejects past participles to the end of the clause; English keeps them snuggled next to the auxiliary. German can invert any verb to form yes/no questions; English can only do it with auxiliaries. German has an *u* sound made with tightly pursed lips and the front of the tongue raised; English speakers can't pronounce it without lots of practice – but English has *th*, a sound zat German lacks. The list could go on and on. It's as extensive as it is because the Anglo-Saxons left their northern Germanic homelands a mere 50 generations ago, putting the North Sea between them and their cousins.

So another way to reveal the diversity of the world's languages is to look at the structures they use independently of their family history. This is the domain of **formal typology**. One of the features explored most thoroughly in this way is word order. Joseph Greenberg showed in the 1960s how the canonical order of subjects, objects and verbs correlates well with orders in other parts of the syntax, an insight which we saw exploited by the generativists in the notion of X-bar syntax. Thus, we can identify unrelated head-initial languages like Spanish and Hebrew, which normally place the verb before the direct object and have prepositions rather than postpositions; and unrelated head-final languages like Japanese and Hindi, which do the reverse. These orders are logically independent of each other, so there's clearly an underlying unity here. The correlations are not water-tight: Greenberg and later typologists have been very clear about the *statistical* nature of these universal tendencies, and exceptions are rife (although linguists like John Hawkins have been able to reveal deeper patterns through careful analysis).

Another area of formal diversity is to be found in languages' use (or not) of morphology. We saw in Chapter 6 how morphological systems come in as many different varieties as the products of the Heinz corporation, as the combinatorial power of languages ebbs and flows between heavy-duty fusion *within* words and broader liaisons *between* words in the syntax. A tripartite division is often made between **isolating**, **agglutinating** and **fusional** languages. The first (typified by Vietnamese and historically unrelated Mandarin Chinese) rely on syntax for their combinatorial power. Typically, each morpheme is housed within a separate word, so affixes are rare. The following example from Vietnamese illustrates this (I have simplified the orthographic conventions to make it easier on the eye).

(1)   Khi toi den nha ban toi, chung toi bat dau lam bai
       Literally: When I come house friend I, PLURAL I begin do lesson
       'When I came to my friend's house, we began to do lessons'

Agglutinating languages do the opposite, gluing together multiple morphemes within a word to get the communicative job done. Turkish is the example of choice here. For instance, *adam* means 'man', *adamlar* means 'men' (*man* + PLURAL), and *adamlarin* means *of the men* (*man* + PLURAL + GENITIVE). There are also super-agglutinating languages (**polysynthetic** languages) like Chukchi from Russia and Nahuatl from Mexico, in which so many morphemes can get glued together that one finds juggernaut words, represented by whole sentences in other languages. Here's one from Nahuatl:

(2)   ni-ki-n-tla-kwal-ti-s-neki
      Literally: I + him + PLURAL + eat + CAUSE + FUTURE + want
      'I want to feed them'

Finally, fusional languages like Russian, Basque and Spanish squish their morphemes into single affixes in the inflectional system, so that one prefix or suffix ends up carrying a lot of grammatical baggage all on its own. Here's an example from Spanish:

(3)   La niña cantará
      Literally: The/FEMININE girl + FEMININE sing + THIRD.PERSON/
      SINGULAR/FUTURE
      'The girl will sing'

But once again, the three typological classes have leaky borders: I don't think any language is 100 per cent isolating, agglutinating or fusional. They are ideal types, identified to help linguists understand the dimensions of language variation, and most languages lie somewhere in between. Take English. The three sentences below show features of all three types:

(4)   The soprano will sing in the choir
(5)   Books are getting cheaper
(6)   Mice are worse

In (4), English has an isolating feel, with each word except for two representing one morpheme (*will* has covert PRESENT tense, even though it carries future meaning, and *sing* is in the INFINITIVE). Sentence (5) shows some minor agglutination, with the plural of *book* added by a suffix -*s*, the progressive form of *get* marked by the suffix -*ing*, and the comparative of *cheap* indicated by the suffix -*er*. Finally, in sentence (6) the plurality of *mouse* is fused into the root; the plurality, third personality and present tense of *be* are fused together in an entirely different form; and the same thing happens with the comparative form of *bad*.

Languages display great diversity too in their use of speech sounds. As the part of language closest to the 'visible' surface, variation in phonology will come as no surprise to most people. It's not a complete free-for-all: all languages, for example, have variants of the so-called **point vowels** /i/, /u/ and /a/, which define the limits of vocal space in the mouth's resonating chamber. But anyone glancing at the examples and exercises in a typical phonology textbook will be immediately struck by the diversity, not the unity, of the sound systems described there. Here's a random sampling:

- Burmese has voiceless nasals (compare /n/ and /m/ in English, which you can tell are voiced by placing your hand over your Adam's apple as you pronounce them);
- Xhosa has 'click' phonemes made by forming a vacuum between the back of the tongue and the roof of the mouth and then pulling the tongue away (one is like the 'gee-up' sound made to horses, another is like the admonitory *tsk tsk* made with tongue against teeth);
- Some Australian languages don't have fricatives (like [v], and the consonant sounds in *other* and *thaw*);
- *Tftktst* is a pronounceable word meaning 'You sprained it' in Tashlhiyt Berber;
- In Spanish you have to add an [e] before word-initial [sp], [st], and [sk];
- [ps] in the syllabic coda becomes [sp] in Singapore English (e.g. *lips* becomes *lisp*).

All infants are born with the capacity to pronounce all these sounds, but the specific selection their language makes from the universal phoneme inventory rapidly becomes fixed, and their ability to pronounce the others just as soon fades. This is why people often speak with a foreign accent when they learn another language.

Phonological prejudice

Given the strength of the Language Spell, it is not surprising that variation in the *sounds* of language excite our prejudices more than morphological or syntactic differences. Take the reaction of Evelyn Waugh to the textures of Arabic: he asserts in his travel book *Remote People* that '[n]o sound made by mankind is quite so painful as the voices of two Arab women at variance'. And the languages of the European powers are not immune. Pink Panther fans will recall Peter Sellers' ridicule of the French vowel system – although for many it's the language of love. German, on the other hand, has an undeserved reputation for harshness: fans of the British comedy series Fawlty Towers will recall giggling sinfully at John Cleese's outrageous misuse of German consonants. (It's no accident that I have chosen examples from three British humorists, since their (our) gleeful prejudices about other languages are notorious, ... but I imagine that this kind of linkage between peoples and the linguistic sounds they make is global: ask Australians what *they* think of the plummy tones of upper class Limeys like Waugh, for example.)

Of course speech diversity is also rightly celebrated by more enlightened individuals (or the same individuals at more enlightened moments), giving the lie to sweeping judgements which link negative national or regional stereotypes with cacophony (or positive stereotypes with its opposite, *euphony*). Anyone who has delighted in the songs of the South African Miriam Makeba, singing with the click phonemes of her native Xhosa, or swoons at Dietrich Fischer-Dieskau singing Schumann's setting of Heine's *Dichterliebe*, will appreciate what nonsense negative stereotyping of foreign speech sounds can be. But it's also important to acknowledge that the nonsense is *unavoidable* (and that most linguists probably indulge in it too when our linguistic hats are off). This is because speech is the external manifestation of our I-languages, and therefore of our E-languages, so functions as a marker of group identity, worn like a badge, a regional costume or the sartorial trappings of a subculture (see the next chapter).

Let's now see what happens when you're in two linguistic gangs at the same time. In language, how can you dress simultaneously as Goth and disco queen, Wall Street broker and eco-warrior, devout Muslim and born-again Christian?

Multilingualism

If languages differ so much one from another, even when, as in the case of Basque and Spanish, their speakers live in very close proximity and share many cultural beliefs and practices, how is it that different language groups actually communicate with each other? In 1770 a royal decree proposed that Spanish should replace Otomí and Tepehua, the local languages of Tlaxco, Mexico, arguing that 'it is easier for two animals of different species to live together than two men speaking different languages'. The answer is that there are lots of people on this planet who speak more than one language. Salman Rushdie's characters (from this chapter's epigraph) speak five languages on a regular basis, and even mix them together within a single exchange. The four indigenous languages of their 'Hug-me' mix are among the fifteen official languages of India (the others are Assamese, Bengali, Kannada, Kashmiri, Malayalam, Oriya, Panjabi, Sanskrit, Sindhi, Tamil and Telugu), although the relationship between Hindi and Urdu is close to that between Flemish and Dutch. English, a colonial imposition but a lingua franca for many, has 'associate official' status. No Indian will be fluent in all sixteen tongues, but around 10 per cent speak at least two of them.

India, officially multilingual, actually has a low percentage of multilingual speakers from a global perspective. For the most part, speakers will get by with just one of the 398 languages spoken in the country. Many officially bi- or multilingual countries have more than one official language precisely because their political borders enclose different groups of monolinguals: Ireland, Canada, Belgium, Switzerland, Finland and India all have two or more languages listed in their constitutions for this reason.

On the other hand, officially monolingual nations like Ghana, the USA, Lebanon and the Philippines have high numbers of bilingual citizens, often over 50 per cent. As we saw earlier, there are vastly more languages than countries. Of the planet's almost 200 nation states (191 in the UN, plus a few others like Palestine and the Holy See), 120 have adopted English, French, Spanish or Arabic as their official language. Over 98 per cent of the world's languages are without official status. (It has always irked me that many websites, language-teaching institutes, and other multilingual organizations use national flags to indicate the languages they manage.) On the whole, countries are not quilts of isolated monolingual communities with no access to their nations' official tongue(s) or to those of their neighbouring communities. If we really want to see multilingualism in its full richness, we need to look not at nation states, but at individuals in their families and social networks. Linguists have estimated that between a half and two-thirds of the world's population speak more than one language: monolingualism is the exception, not the rule.

Individual bilingualism

The question I posed at the beginning of this section (how can different language groups communicate with each other?) thus starts to look a little odd from a global perspective, because it assumes that monolingualism is the norm. A visiting alien anthropologist from a distant galaxy might well be more interested in asking how come there are people that have only *one* language at their disposal. But this book is written for speakers of English, and most of us grew up, alas, as monolinguals (including, I bet, Evelyn Waugh, Peter Sellers and John Cleese). And, outside the European Commission in Brussels or the UN building in New York, many multilinguals undervalue their own linguistic resources, as we'll see shortly. So as realistic Earthlings, let's address the need to understand what it means to manage more than one language.

The problem is where to start. Defining bilingualism has vexed scholars, educators and politicians for many years now, especially in the English-speaking world, where the vantage point has always been overwhelmingly that of monolingualism. Which of the following would you consider to be bilingual, for instance?

- A 35-year-old Korean learner of English with a score of 470 on the Test of English as a Foreign Language (TOEFL). (Most US universities require a minimum of 550 for admission of non-English speaking candidates.)
- A student whose parents emigrated from Mexico to Arizona when he was a child, and who uses English at High School but Spanish with family and friends.
- A Beijing translator who learnt English at college and translates technical reports for the government, but who cannot translate literature or poetry, has had little contact with native English speakers, and has almost never used English for spoken interaction.
- The child of a deaf mother in Calcutta who has used both Bengali and Indian Sign Language since infancy.
- An Amish elder from Lancaster County in the US, who speaks Pennsylvania German at home and in the community, where he spends most of his time, and English elsewhere.
- A Lebanese taxi driver who speaks French and Arabic, like half of his fellow citizens, but never went to school.
- An educated Danish woman who excelled in English at school 30 years ago, but has hardly used it since.

This diversity of multilingual individuals highlights a number of issues in the definition of bilingualism. Does one need to be fluent in both languages for all situations of use (a **balanced bilingual**)? Is a bilingual someone who has acquired both their languages naturally, or can we count someone who has learnt one of them in an educational setting? Are bilinguals individuals who have developed at least a certain minimum level of competence in both languages? Does one have to *use* both languages on a regular basis, or is passively *knowing* an extra language enough? Are you a bilingual if you can only read and write in one of your languages (or in neither of them)? Are signers who also know a written language considered bilingual?

Psychologists would have a hard time coming up with a diagnostic profile for bilingual individuals (I bet manic depressives and serial killers are much easier). Hence the proliferation of terms for different kinds of bilingualism in the scholarly literature. The applied linguist Li Wei has counted 37 categories of bilingual, of which the following is a random sample:

- a *dormant bilingual*, who has moved to a new country and stops using his or her home country's language;
- a *receptive bilingual*, who comprehends but doesn't necessarily produce one of their languages;
- a *diagonal bilingual*, who speaks the standard dialect of one language and a non-standard variety of an unrelated language;
- a *subordinate bilingual*, whose second language is structurally influenced by their first.

So let's not define bilingualism. Instead, as a first approximation, try to think of it as a three-dimensional space in which we can plot anyone who knows more than one language, according to dimensions of age, competence and use. Figure 1 represents two different kinds of bilingual in this way:

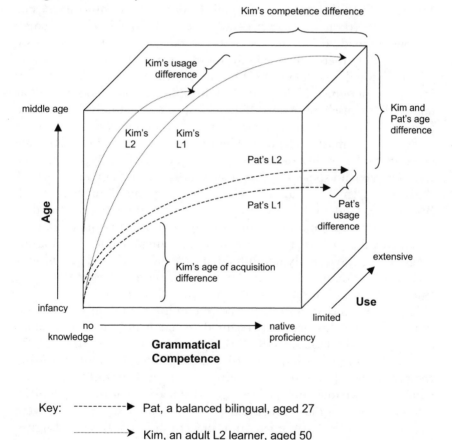

Figure 1 Dimensions of bilingualism

In Figure 1, I have plotted two hypothetical cases: Kim, a middle-aged salesman who learnt a second language when he was 20 for business purposes, and Pat, a 27-year-old balanced bilingual. Pat acquired her L2 at age 7, when her family moved to another language community, maybe that of one of her parents. Both grammars developed equally, though the original L1 was gradually used less, and so her L1 *communicative* competence probably suffered. Kim has an incomplete development of competence in the L2 (i.e. he never got very good at it), because he didn't use it as much as his L1. Readers could try plotting themselves into this 3D multilingual space ('middle age' may be replaced with 'centenarian' as appropriate).

Room for one language only?

My multilingual box is a simplified idealization, of course. For example, there's nothing in it to stop me from plotting ten languages for one individual, all in the native-proficiency and extensive-use corner. Surely there must be limits on the degree of *multicompetence* any one individual can develop? Or are multilingual speakers simply multiple monolinguals, *linguistically* schizophrenic but conceptually at one with themselves? Many bilingual speakers actually believe the former, sharing with monolinguals the idea that a jack of all linguistic trades can be master of none. The quotation from Salman Rushdie cited at the beginning of this chapter continues: 'Bombayites like me were people who spoke five languages badly and no language well.' I think this feeling is partly a consequence of the Language Spell. Because we tend to identify language with the thoughts it is used to share, and because most of us do not have multiple personalities, then we assume that the natural way to be is monolingual: one mind for one language. Consequently, multilinguals are often viewed as using a mental space designed for one language to represent *more* than one, thus resulting in imperfect competence in any of them.

This view has dominated received opinion and folk belief for much of recent history, and resulted in harsh practices in schools, especially in the US and UK during the nineteenth century and the first half of the twentieth. In order to stop bilingual children using their additional languages, mouths were washed out with soap, canes were wielded on backsides, and a variety of other penalties imposed and stigmas nourished. Native American children were apparently even kidnapped and placed in monolingual English boarding schools. One native Californian Pomo-speaking girl recalls being sent to the English-speaking Covelo boarding school in 1910 at age 11 (after her mother was induced to sign the papers by a government official):

> When I went to school at that time there were three girls there from Hopland. I already knew some of their language, it's a different dialect from mine. I couldn't talk the English language in the school at Covelo so I hollered to them when we lined up. Then one of the girls that was in my line reported me. They took me and strapped the heck out of me with a big leather strap. I didn't know what I got strapped for. Three days later those girls told me it was for talking the Indian language on the grounds, which I'm not supposed to do.

Some of the abusers probably considered themselves to be well-intentioned, since the research of the time, dominant until the 1960s and still influential in current educational and political thought, was suggesting that use of more than one language meant detrimental effects on thinking. But the social effects on minority language speakers around the globe were often devastating and long-lasting. The discrimination was also often abetted by political prejudices against the world communities of speakers of these additional languages. In the USA during the world wars, it went hand-in-hand with gross abuse of the human rights of German-Americans and Japanese-Americans.

What, then, is the truth about the minds of multilingual speakers? Well, it's a hard truth to discover, since the relevant scientific enquiry and its public dissemination have themselves been bedevilled by the combined effects of the Language Spell and implicit monolingual prejudice. One of the major problems concerns the appropriate standards of measurement, both of relative language competences and of the general intelligence with which it has been consistently correlated. The main stumbling block has been the use of inappropriate standards of comparison. For language competence, bilinguals have usually been compared with monolinguals, and have often been found wanting on this measure. For intelligence, standardized measures such as IQ have been used, and similar shortfalls have been detected in comparison to control populations.

Let's take intelligence first. There is considerable debate about what intelligence is and how it should be measured. Standard IQ tests tap into only a limited range of domains of intelligence (excluding, for example, the musical, spatial, emotional and kinaesthetic intelligences identified by psychologists like Howard Gardner) and, through their reliance on the medium of the printed word, confuse intelligence with literacy. IQ tests are also biased towards western, middle-class notions of intelligence, and the majority of bilingual speakers in the world are not born into the privileged families of 'official language' users. Indeed, many bilinguals have been obliged to acquire an additional (normally official) language because they or their parents moved to another country as economic or political migrants, or have been oppressed by foreign invaders. This means that many will not form part of the dominant, empowered, national majority (whom the IQ test designers have in mind). Finally, the IQ tests used to measure bilinguals have often been applied in the less dominant of the speaker's languages (the official one, of course).

When it comes to measuring their *linguistic* proficiency, bilinguals have been regularly compared with monolinguals (often with different socioeconomic and cultural profiles). Over the last few decades, however, experts have questioned this practice, arguing that speakers of more than one language should not be seen as serial monolinguals, but as speakers who have one *communicative* competence shared between different *grammatical* competences. The standard of comparison, then, should be *other* bilinguals for grammatical competence, and mono-linguals of a similar background for communicative competence. François Grosjean uses an athletic metaphor to make the point: a hurdler has two competences, jumping and running, though he probably can't jump as high as a high-jumper or run as fast as a sprinter. But as *athletes*, all three can win Olympic gold medals.

In order to appreciate this important point fully, we need to leave individual bilinguals for a moment and take a look at the typical social situations they act in and the communities they are part of. So far in this book we have traced most of the effects of the Language Spell to the Fundamental Paradox, and have tried to break the Spell by balancing our knowledge of the social life of language with a firm understanding of the mental life which supports it. In this case, we need to do the reverse, and carefully analyse the social life of multilinguals in order to understand how language is organized in individual minds.

The social life of multilingual speakers

Multilingual Bombayites like the characters in Rushdie's *The Ground beneath her Feet* might well 'swoop' from one language to another mid-sentence (the code-switching phenomenon we encountered in Chapter 5). But probably more frequently they will use each language for a different purpose, in different social situations, and with different interlocutors. Most bilinguals on the planet, for example, will use one of their languages for more informal interaction, with family and friends, and the other for more formal communication, at work, at worship or at school. Normally, the 'informal' language will have less social prestige in the community at large than the 'formal' language, which will often be an official language of the country they live in. This situation, a sharing out of linguistic resources along the 'use' dimension of my (increasingly too simple) 3D language box, is known as **diglossia**, a term introduced into English by Charles Ferguson, and deriving originally from the Greek word meaning *two languages*.

Ferguson's term refers to language communities, not individuals, and he used it not specifically for bilinguals, but for monolinguals who speak two different varieties (dialects) of their language, one a literary, standardized variety (the *High* or *H* variant), the other a local, non-standard variety (the *Low* or *L* variant). We'll see in the next chapter how this notion of diglossia brings together monolingualism and many types of multilingualism on a single continuum. For now, however, let's push ahead with our effort to characterize the multilingual individual from the point of view of their linguistic functioning in social settings. Joshua Fishman's extension of the term *diglossia* to bilingual situations is a key notion in this endeavour. Multi-language diglossia (the use of two languages for different social purposes) helps us to understand that the bilingual mind is *not* just two monolingual systems represented side-by-side in the brain. To see this, we'll look at one fictional inhabitant of the multilingual box, and modify her personal history a little.

Pat, the hypothetical balanced bilingual from the 3D box, moved from one monolingual setting to another, and so began to use her L1 in a gradually diminishing range of settings. Let's now re-cast Pat as Pavi, the bilingual Bengali-Indian Sign Language (ISL) user from Calcutta, and imagine that she lives in a thriving diglossic bilingual community of families with hearing-impaired members. Bengali will be her *H* language and ISL her *L*. She will use Bengali for some purposes, ISL for others: her *H* variant will be called upon for more formal situations which require literacy use, like school work and filling out government forms; her *L* variant will be used for chatting with her mother or planning a neighbourhood feast.

Now, we saw briefly in Chapter 8 how formal and informal discourse differ in the degree to which they utilize linguistic devices like pronouns and subordinate clauses, and how these differences correlate in part with writing and speech. Hence the *linguistic* devices Pavi draws upon for each social interaction will be drawn from each of her languages to different degrees. It is not hard to see, then, that any comparison of Pavi with a monolingual Bengali speaker or ISL user would be unjust: we need to take Pavi's entire communicative competence (i.e. her spread of appropriate linguistic knowledge across both languages) and compare it with the competence of a language user who employs only one grammatical system across a similar set of circumstances.

Talking across language borders

We've been concentrating so far on situations in which speakers grow up bilingual 'naturally', because of the language environment they are born into. But what about speakers who don't come into daily contact with other language communities, and so have not benefited from local multilingualism? And of course even natural bilinguals will be in trouble when they need to talk to some-one who speaks one of the *other* 6,807 languages on the planet (Ethnologue's count minus 2). What do politicians, merchants, tourists, conquerors, scientists, athletes and others do when they need to communicate with people who speak a language unknown to them? There are a number of possibilities. If there are enough speakers, and other assistance is not at hand, they might take the long road to constructing a pidgin, as we saw in Chapter 5. If they're on their own in the foreign language environment, and have the time and motivation, they may just buckle down and learn the language on their own.

I once met an elderly British merchant marine at a wedding party in a humble quarter of Mexico City, who in his twenties had fallen in love with and married a Mexican woman during shore leave at the port of Veracruz. He never returned to his home country, and now after so many decades spoke Spanish like a native. But he had never taken classes, and had lived the greater part of his life in a community of poor, monolingual Spanish-speakers. Using English was difficult for him, and his Geordie accent was tinged with Spanish phonemes and vocabulary from pre-war England. I will always regret not visiting him again with a tape-recorder!

More likely nowadays is that people who need to communicate with speakers of an unknown language will go to a language professional. They will learn a foreign language with the support of language teachers, textbooks, tapes and Internet sites. Or, if their need is more restricted, and they don't want to make such an investment of time and effort, they will obtain a translation from professional translators and interpreters (that's how I was able to read Umberto Eco and Orhan Pamuk while I was writing this book). Not too long ago, most human beings rarely strayed a few miles from their own villages, and so had no need for the skills of such language purveyors. But in the last couple of centuries, language teaching and translation have become mass endeavours (and big businesses). Since the invention of the aeroplane, the telephone, TV and the Internet, their work has become almost as commonplace as electrical power grids and running water.

Some language teachers and translators grow up bilingual, and decide to use their naturally acquired linguistic abilities to make a living, but most are themselves the product of formal language teaching in educational settings. Their work tends not to be appreciated as highly as it should be, especially in countries which celebrate monolingualism. Hanif Kureishi, in his novel *Gabriel's Gift*, places London's language teachers in less-than-flattering company when he tells how his father, a former rock guitarist fallen on hard times, finally starts to make money giving guitar lessons to the scions of the wealthy:

> Along with masseurs, drug dealers, accountants, personal trainers, language teachers, whores, manicurists, therapists, interior decorators and numerous other dependents and pseudo-servants, Dad had found a place at the table of the rich.

In many parts of the world, it's still the case that anyone who speaks English as a native can get a job teaching the language, despite the efforts of professional organizations like TESOL (Teachers of English to Speakers of Other Languages) and university departments of Applied Linguistics. I hope that the chapters so far will have convinced you that this is almost as daft as employing someone as a human biology teacher because they have a healthy working body.

Language teaching and translatability are successful enterprises nevertheless, despite the lack of proper public recognition of their importance. And together with the kind of natural multilingualism we have been discussing up until now, their success constitutes important evidence for the view of human language offered in this book, in at least two ways. First, they underscore the fundamental point made way back at the beginning of Chapter 1: that language is a separate system mediating between meaning and its external expression as sound or light energy. Learning a second language means setting up an additional linguistic system in order to produce and comprehend external energy patterns which code basically the same set of meanings that you express with your first language. Translating from one language to another involves comprehending external energy patterns using one grammar and then recoding the meanings they activate using the grammar of the second.

Of course it's not quite so simple (it never is). Multilinguals reading this may immediately object that languages rarely express exactly the *same* meanings in the same ways (if they do at all). As we saw in Chapter 3 with the bilingual priming experiments, abstract words are especially prone to differ in the details of the conceptual configurations that they express across languages. My Dad, a great lover of language, didn't study a second one until he and my Mum started travelling the world and generally enjoying themselves after their children had grown up and left home. I remember complaining about my French grammar homework as a young teenager. He told me he couldn't see what all the fuss was about: surely all I had to do was memorize the French translations for English words and then simply substitute one with the other, successively. All you needed was a bilingual dictionary. Thomas Hardy's Jude believed that even the brute task of word learning might not be necessary:

> ... Jude had meditated much and curiously on the probable sort of process that was involved in turning the expressions of one language into those of another. He concluded that a grammar of the required tongue would contain, primarily, a rule, prescription, or clue of the nature of a secret cipher, which, once known, would enable him, by merely applying it, to change at will all words of his own speech into those of the foreign one.

This is a perfectly natural way for monolingual speakers to approach the question of second language acquisition, and it's precisely because monolingualism propitiates the belief that one's language mirrors one's thoughts quite exactly. As the applied linguist Håkon Ringbom has put it: 'The learner tends to assume that the system of L2 is more or less the same as in his L1 until he has discovered that it is not.'

Multilinguals grow up 'knowing' that this is not the case: a Turkish-Spanish bilingual 'knows' that when speaking Turkish she must use an affix indicating whether she witnessed the event or situation described by the verb, but that when speaking Spanish no such affix is necessary. She 'knows' that when speaking Spanish, she can omit the subject, but in Turkish she cannot. And the point is that when speaking Spanish, she still *knows* whether she witnessed the verbal event or not and which participant would appear in subject position if she were to use it: it's part of the mental model underlying what she says, even if it doesn't get expressed overtly in the language she uses. So even though different languages use different **mapping** principles for expressing meaning, the conceptual structure is going to be the same, regardless of the bilingual's language choice.

If this were not the case, languages would be unteachable and untranslatable, and we'd be doomed as a species to lives of monolingual isolation. Languages may be learnt initially through direct connections to L1 grammars and lexicons, but once the L2 reaches a certain level of autonomy, translation occurs via the intermediary of conceptual structure: the common thought processes and knowledge that unites us as members of the same species, despite surface differences in the physical environments we inhabit and in the sociocultural beliefs and behaviours which have arisen due to our physical isolation one from the other.

The relative ease of language learning and translation also provide indirect support for the notion of Universal Grammar: if human language varied without limit, we would not expect them to be so learnable. Educated adults often find complex systems like calculus, computer languages, chess, musical notation and electronic circuitry exceedingly hard to grasp, and yet human languages, infinitely more complex than any of these, are learned to high degrees of proficiency by lots of people from all walks of life and all kinds of socioeconomic and cultural backgrounds. An underlying common design for language (UG) might explain how a speaker might be able to retune their L1 competence to that of an L2 with such facility.

... But hang on a minute. Isn't it true that foreign language learning is a major trial for many school kids, and that adults struggle even more? That the world's restaurant menus, hotel brochures, tourist guides and appliance instruction manuals are replete with (often hilarious) translation errors? That international relations, both personal and political, are often stymied or soured through (often unnoticed) derailings of interlinguistic discourse? Clearly learning a second language as an adult does not occur by the same super-efficient, lightning-fast, biologically-endowed processes that drive infant first language acquisition. Why is this the case if we have a built-in cognitive computer program designed specifically for successful language learning? Shouldn't UG provide the secret cipher that Jude the Obscure was hoping to find in his efforts to learn Latin and Greek?

The obvious differences between L1 and L2 acquisition have led some linguists to reject the claim that UG plays a role in the latter. The applied linguist Robert Bley-Vroman, for example, has argued for a 'Fundamental Difference Hypothesis', according to which L1 and L2 acquisition are run by different mental processes: the first by UG, the second by the kinds of general problem-solving capacities we use to learn how to play chess or read a map. Table 3 summarizes some of the main differences between the two processes, incorporating elements of Bley-Vroman's comparison.

Table 3 Some differences between L1 and L2 acquisition

	Infant L1 acquisition	Adult L2 acquisition
1	Often only one language involved	Always at least two languages involved
2	Age from 0 to puberty	Variable ages
3	Only UG available initially	Only L1 available initially
4	Underdeveloped cognition	Full cognition
5	Underdeveloped socialization	Full socialization
6	Consistent exposure to input	Variable exposure to input
7	Automatic processes	Voluntary/conscious processes
8	Goals predetermined	Variation in goals
9	Instruction irrelevant	Instruction often important
10	Correction normally unavailable	Correction regularly available
11	Affective factors irrelevant	Affective factors influential
12	Consistency in course and strategy	Variation in course and strategy
13	Consistency in success	Variation in success
14	Endpoint = stable adult system	Endpoint = variable proficiency

The features of L1 acquisition will be familiar from the discussions in Chapters 4 and 8. What characterizes the corresponding elements for adult L2 learning is the diversity of adult life: here we have fully socialized members of the species, with at least one full grammar and lexicon already in place, learning another language at different ages, under different circumstances, for different purposes, and with different levels of motivation, anxiety and enthusiasm. The last two characteristics in Table 3, concerning outcome, are the critical ones here. Bley-Vroman claimed that L2 acquisition is characterized by general failure, pointing out that few learners achieve a competence that is indistinguishable from native speakers, and that learners regularly construct only partial L2 systems, which often contain **fossilized**, non-target language elements. In other words, we often do things with the L2 that native speakers don't, and sometimes we repeat them so often that they stick.

The applied linguist Larry Selinker called such intermediate systems **interlanguage**. Interlanguage shares many characteristics with pidgins, since both are underdeveloped systems used for basic communication with speakers of other languages, although interlanguage is a property of individuals, not groups: each learner builds their own additional I-language, whereas a pidgin is shared between different language communities as a second E-language. Some aspects of interlanguage may be shared between learners, of course, such as the use of *put* without a prepositional phrase for Spanish-speakers, which we saw in Chapter 3. But many are personal, like one of my Mexican students' use of the suffix *-able* as an adverbial marker, in an essay in which a series of points were preceded by *firstable, secondable*, etc. This student analysed the phrases *first of all* and *second of all* as morphologically complex single words, an innovation he was led to by previous exposure to words like *readable* and *enjoyable* and the fact that the [b] in *-able* and [v] in *of all* are varieties of the same phoneme in Spanish.

Another critical point from Table 3 is No. 6, regarding exposure to input. Children acquire their native tongues, recall, on the basis of UG and the input from the E-language(s) surrounding them. If an adult gets sufficient L2 input, why won't their genetically-based UG kick in and allow them to develop native competence? Well, UG is a biological instructional manual for developing a *native* language, comparable to the part of the genetic code that builds human hearts. When its job is done, it goes into retirement. There is a good deal of evidence to suggest that access to UG declines around the age of puberty, since human beings acquire their native languages in childhood, not adulthood, and puberty is the stage of growth when the human organism reaches its steady, mature state. A famous, but tragic, case which supports this argument is that of Genie, described by the psycholinguist Susan Curtiss. Genie was kept by her parents in solitary confinement, and with almost no linguistic input, until she was 13-years-old, when she was rescued by social workers. She developed some linguistic abilities afterwards, but never attained anything like normal adult grammatical competence. UG cannot do its work without input from the environment, and that input must be available during the window of opportunity allowed for by our internal biological clock.

Finally, a word about affective factors. Children don't acquire their language(s) because they *want* to. They don't calculate costs and benefits, and they are not yet under the public influence of the Language Spell, so they don't accept or reject the learning task because they associate the language with a particular group of speakers, an intolerant teacher, or the economic advantages they might accrue as a result. In *Don Juan*, Byron wrote:

'Tis pleasing to be school'd in a strange tongue
By female lips and eyes
[...]
They smile so when one's right, and when one's wrong
They smile still more ...

Although there is a good deal of research on the role of child-directed speech and the ways in which carers, typically mothers in western families, might 'package' this input for their children, it is quite certain that the process is not dependent on the child's affective responses. Tender loving care from mother, lover, or mistress might motivate you to successfully learn a *second* language, but it wasn't necessary for your L1 acquisition. An infant Oliver Twist in a cruel, uncaring orphanage will have as little conscious motivation to acquire or resist the language(s) to which he is exposed as a spoilt child brought up by western parents versed in Dr Spock's child psychology.

Primatologists, who study the animal family that includes apes and us, tell us that early human beings started to spread around the globe from southern Africa around 100,000 years ago. As we'll see in Chapter 11, many scientists who study the biological evolution of the language faculty believe that these ancestors of ours had a version of UG already in their genes, and must have been speaking forms of language that resembled our own much more than they resembled the non-linguistic call systems of our primate cousins. We have seen in previous chapters how languages change rapidly and intermix freely, leading to the multilingual world our species has inhabited now for hundreds of thousands of years. UG and our irrepressible will to communicate ensure that we are not doomed to lead lives of verbal insularity. We acquire languages as children whether we like it or not, and with a bit of effort we can learn other tongues in adulthood. So despite our common biological equipment for language learning, we are clearly not language clones, even within our own speech communities. The next chapter complements this one by looking at linguistic diversity within single E- and I-languages. It concludes with an exploration of some of the ways in which the polychrome linguistic tapestry of nations has been handled by educators and politicians.

More information

A good introduction to our planet's **sociolinguistic diversity** (including the politics of it) is Nancy Bonvillain's (2002) book.

Ethnologue's site is at www.ethnologue.com.

Bernard Comrie's (1989) book is the classic text on **language typology and universals**.

 The website for IBM and National Geographic's 'Genographic Project' on human origins, which incorporates evidence from **linguistic archaeology**, is at www5.nationalgeographic.com/genographic.

Colin Baker and Sylvia Rhys-Jones (1998) assembled a stunning encyclopaedia on **bilingualism and bilingual education**. It is lavishly illustrated, both visually and linguistically, and is comprehensive in its coverage. Make sure your library has it. If you prefer a standard textbook, Baker (2001) is just as impressive.

 Jim Crawford's Language Policy Web Site and Emporium at http://ourworld.compuserve.com/homepages/JWCRAWFORD/ provides a wealth of information on the politics of **bilingualism and bilingual education**, especially with reference to the English Only movement and indigenous languages in the USA.

My favourite books on **second language acquisition** and its importance for language teaching are Ellen Bialystok and Kenji Hakuta's engaging 1994 work, and the award-winning basic introduction by Patsy Lightbown and Nina Spada (1999).

The **mapping problem** is clearly explained in Slobin's (1979) textbook on psycholinguistics.

'If you were born in New Jersey,' I said, 'and you were brought up in New York, how did you get that Southern accent?'
He grinned. 'I haven't got a real accent.' He looked at me. 'I went to reform school in the South. And then, later on, I used to go with this broad from Miami and I sort of put it on, you know, for her – she went for it – and I guess it kind of stuck.'

(James Baldwin,
Tell Me How Long the Train's Been Gone)

Chapter 9 sketched some of the vast interlinguistic diversity of our species, both in its I-language incarnations and its E-language manifestations. We now turn to the rich ways in which groups and individual speakers deploy a single language in different guises and for a variety of personal, social and professional ends (including impressing one's girlfriend, like Baldwin's character Christopher in the quotation). No single speaker has full access to the entire E-language resources of his or her extended speech community. And yet everyone commands a repertoire of styles and ways of speaking. In Chapter 4 I argued that each person constitutes a linguistic universe in their own right (there are over 500 million I-language versions of English, for example). And in Chapter 8 we began to see that the same language user will deploy different aspects of their competence in different circumstances and for different purposes. For example, Baldwin's character probably wouldn't use the word 'broad' when introducing his girlfriend to his mother, and would drop the conversational markers 'sort of', 'you know', and 'kind of' when writing to his bank manager for a loan.

There is also much variation between *groups* of speakers of the same language. Dialects, as we have seen, are a natural consequence of physical and social separation between speech communities. Within and across dialects there are also distinct linguistic varieties or styles, determined by your schooling, job, recreational pursuits, subculture, gender and sexuality, reading habits, mobility, political beliefs, age and ethnic group. In this chapter we explore this inner linguistic diversity, highlighting again some of the ways the Spell camouflages it, and the consequences this has for our daily lives. The chapter closes with a brief discussion of language diversity in the realms of education and politics, two professional arenas in which, I argue, the breaking of the Spell presents a special challenge, but a challenge that must be met if, as communities, we wish to create a more just world.

Styles and registers

There is a great deal of variety in the way English as an E-language is used on different occasions and by different speakers. This variety will be reflected at all levels of grammatical and communicative competence, including phonetic realization, phonological encoding, lexical choice, morphological complexity, syntactic patterning, semantic content, pragmatic force and discourse structure (i.e. the whole paraphernalia of language). The variables that take on different values at each of these levels will tend to correlate one with the other, so that, for example, for some situations of language use, simplicity of structure in one area of the grammar will often be accompanied by simplicity in the others. Recall Julian Barnes' character Gillian, in the novel *Love etc.*, reflecting on her use of the phrase *Love you* to her husband. The phrase is not only syntactically simple – a two-word sentence with no subordinate clauses and the subject dropped – but also phonologically, lexically and morphologically simple: two monomorphemic, high frequency word forms, one a pronoun, encoded in two syllables formed by just five phonemes, with the last vowel probably reduced to schwa. This is not a coincidence.

The elements of linguistic expression selected for particular situations of use are determined in part by a series of *non-linguistic* factors, including:

- the language user's identity, goals and psychological state;
- his or her knowledge or assumptions about the identity, goals and psychological state(s) of interlocutor(s);
- the medium through which the I-language externalizes the message;
- the external context in which the message gets expressed.

A pragmatically-challenged robot version of Gillian might have encoded her proposition using the phrase: *My husband, I wish to express the fact that I continue to experience an intense feeling of deep affection for you.*

But Gillian didn't do it this way, because as a sentient, social being, she knew that the situation in which the proposition was to be expressed called for a short, unelaborated, utterance: the relationship between them was intimate (but stagnating), the event called for immediate, not delayed, comprehension (i.e. through speech, not text), and the purpose was to fulfil a conventionalized parting routine (not to communicate new information).

The important point for us here is that Gillian is quite capable of using an expression like her robot alter ego's when the situation at hand calls for more complexity. In a letter complaining to a local council officer, for example, she may pompously type: *Dear Sir, I am writing to express the extreme dissatisfaction I continue to experience concerning the irregularity of the refuse collection services contracted by your department...* And, because her education has made her as comfortable in literacy as in phonology, she could do so perhaps almost as spontaneously as she would say *Love you* to her husband. It would be unconventional (and less effective) for her to express her annoyance by writing *Shift the bloody trash on time!*, although it may have conveyed her communicative intent more accurately.

An ethnographic view

What we are seeing here is diversity of individual linguistic expression, determined by different contingencies and conventions related to language users and use. Dell Hymes provided a handy mnemonic to catalogue the central ethnographic domains into which the relevant factors may be classified. His acronym *SPEAKING* provides an inventory of the components (a 'provisional phonetics') of communicative events. In the following examples, I have extended the model beyond speech to embrace all language use.

S   *Setting and scene*: the physical, cultural and psychological situation within which the language event happens (e.g. a meeting between university authorities and a student council; a risqué exchange in a singles' chat room; the negotiation of an international treaty at Versailles; the ritual invocation of a deity in a sacred grove; a glowing review of the latest Harry Potter novel in the local paper).

P   *Participants*: the language users and their roles in the event (e.g. a hectoring sergeant-major and his petrified raw recruits; an insistent pollster and indifferent respondents in a telephone survey; J.R.R. Tolkien's pre- and post-blockbuster readers; two deaf lovers signing during a romantic dinner; a psychiatrist and her client).

E *Ends*: the conventional goals of the event type and the personal goals of its participants (take a university lecture designed to impart knowledge and foment critical thinking, which features (a) a self-aggrandizing lecturer inviting hero worship and increased book sales, and his (b) bored or (c) enthralled students, the former just hoping for a passing grade, the latter seriously seeking enlightenment).

A *Act sequence*: the form and content of the language event itself (the phonological, lexical, morphological and syntactic structure of the discourse units; their semantic content, pragmatic formulation and interpretation).

K *Key*: the tone of the event (e.g. a sombre ritual like the enthronement of a pope; a relaxed, light-hearted, late-night reunion of friends in a smoky bar; an impassioned, emotional tribute at a funeral; a technical treatise on formal logic; a biting satire; a cosy chat over tea; verbal abuse directed at a member of a racial minority).

I *Instrumentalities*: the modality or channel selected to communicate with (e.g. a written legal code; graffiti on the wall of a public toilet; a Bombayite code-switching between Hindi and English; a poetry reading at a Cambridge college; a hearing signer interpreting between a deaf person and a non-signer).

N *Norms of interaction and interpretation*: the cultural conventions governing communicative behaviour (e.g. the obligatory leave-taking from absolutely everyone present at a Mexican party; the unself-conscious revelation of intimate autobiographical details by a Los Angeles matron within minutes of being introduced to a complete stranger; the volume of the chatter and degree of physical contact in an Egyptian coffee house; an embarrassed apology breaking the eerie silence in a packed English elevator).

G *Genre*: the type of conventional discourse associated with the event (e.g. a prayer, an election manifesto, a shaggy-dog story, a sonnet, a rap session, a lovers' tiff, a young child's monologue as she plays with her dolls, a telephone instruction manual).

Between them, the first three and last four of the factors of the *SPEAKING* mnemonic determine how a set of propositions will get encoded into one kind of linguistic expression rather than another by specific individuals on specific occasions of use, i.e. leading to the 'Act Sequence' (the fourth component).

Speakers do not, of course, make conscious mental calculations of linguistic coding possibilities for each component of the communicative event, just as they don't *wilfully* predetermine the phonetic value of each phoneme contained in the lexical entries of the words they are going to use. The on-line social calibration of discourse is one of the more impenetrable side-products of the Language Spell, and although we know quite a lot about the correlation between the ethnographic and linguistic factors involved, we are almost completely ignorant about the cognitive mechanisms which lead from one to the other in on-line performance. We're still awaiting the long-overdue collaboration between socio- and psycholinguists which would be required to show *how* language gets deployed in real time to mark aspects of social interaction. In the meantime, we must content ourselves with an appraisal of *what* marks *what*.

Style and register variation

The different forms of language that we use in different situations are known as **styles** and **registers**. Styles are defined by degree of formality, and registers by the *activity*, *topic* and *domain* associated with our language use. Of course, style and register often correlate. Many *topics* (like the latest developments in nanotechnology or the historical influences on the contemporary music of Michael Nyman) require learned terminology and are more often discussed in academic articles than chatted about over a beer. Other topics (like the new living room wallpaper or Uncle Jack's drinking problem) will call for an informal tone and normally won't be left for posterity in text version. Similarly, the *activity* you are engaged in will often require more or less formal language use: Internet chatting about job opportunities is different from sending in a job application online, and discussing the weather at the bus-stop is different from writing a meteorological report. Finally, the *domain* of a church wedding is more formal than that of a wedding reception, and the dock in a courtroom calls for a more formal style than does a prison cafeteria.

Because of these strong correlations, the terms *register* and *style* are often used interchangeably. Language modality is frequently aligned with them, so that *written style/register* is sometimes used instead of *formal style/register*, and *spoken style/register* for *informal style/register*. Certain words, for example, are almost *never* spoken, cropping up only in formal, written texts. The following anecdote told by the writer Robert Graves, from his spell at Oxford in the 1920s in the company of T. E. Lawrence (of Arabia), illustrates this rather nicely:

Professor Edgeworth, of All Souls', avoided conversational English, persistently using words and phrases that one expects to meet only in books. One evening, Lawrence returned from a visit to London, and Edgeworth met him at the gate. 'Was it very caliginous in the Metropolis?' 'Somewhat caliginous, but not altogether inspissated,' Lawrence replied gravely.

Despite the correlations between modality, style and register, though, the terms are logically independent. Table 1 illustrates this, using as examples the topic-defined registers of philosophy and pop music.

Table 1 Combinations of spoken and written registers and styles

Modality	Register	Style	
		Formal	*Informal*
Written	Philosophy	A treatise on St. Anselm's ontological argument for the existence of God, published by Continuum	An irreverent email exchange between philosophy students, discussing a homework exercise on aesthetics
	Popular Music	A post-structuralist analysis of a Peter Gabriel concert in *The New York Times*	A gushing tribute to the music (and good looks) of NSync in a teenage girl's private journal
Spoken	Philosophy	A radio interview with Chomsky about the influence of Plato's ideas on the development of linguistic theory	A heated discussion in a pub between drunken amateur philosophers, on the inheritability of criminal tendencies
	Popular Music	A business-like MTV board meeting discussing viewer complaints about the lyrics of an Eminem song	An emotionally-charged account of a Red Hot Chilli Peppers concert, in a fan's phone call to a friend who couldn't get tickets

Before going on to see exactly how languages reflect style and register in communicative events like these, it's important to point out that the concepts themselves are not inherently *linguistic* ones. An activity like greeting, for example, can be performed in different styles without language, depending on many of the same factors included in Hymes' *SPEAKING* list. On a continuum of decreasing formality,

Tony Blair might bow to the Queen at a state ceremony, nod curtly to the leader of the opposition on entering the House of Commons, shake hands with the Dalai Lama at the door of No. 10, wave to admiring crowds in New York, warmly embrace his local constituency agent, or kiss his wife Cherie on the cheek after a hard day's work. Similarly, the lawcourt 'register' requires a British judge to dress up in wig and gown, but a male member of the club might don tails and bow tie for a formal dinner, put on a red jacket and jodhpurs for a battle with fox-hunt saboteurs, and maybe wear jeans and a T-shirt when gardening or drinking a pint at the local pub.

Linguistic features

The language equivalents of bowing and kissing, of bow ties and T-shirts, are clusters of linguistic features, elements of our grammars which occur together and correlate with non-linguistic characteristics of the situation in which the talk or text is used. Research conducted over large amounts of text in corpora has revealed some of these feature bundles. Using a computerized collection of many genres of text (personal letters, interviews, academic prose, official documents, etc.), corpus linguists like Douglas Biber have identified sets of co-occurring lexical and grammatical elements which define different dimensions of register variation. Biber found, for example, that features such as first- and second-person pronouns (*I, us, you,* etc.), contractions (*won't, she'll,* etc.), emphatics (*so, really*), and Wh-questions (*What do you think about* ...), together characterize texts in which the language user is more personally involved in the situation, as in many cases of face-to-face interaction.

In narrative texts, on the other hand, third-person pronouns (*he, she, them,* etc.) are more common, together with past and perfect verb forms (*showed, have arrived,* etc.) and 'public' verbs such as *say* or *admit*. With large amounts of text in a broad range of genres, it's possible to plot such form-use correlations along a series of dimensions. The resulting generalizations are remarkably robust, and can prove very useful for applied linguists, in the design of authentic-looking foreign language teaching materials, or in forensic analyses of spoken or written evidence.

Let's look at a few fragments of real discourse, which I've taken from court transcripts and other documents related to the trial of Timothy McVeigh, the bomber of the Oklahoma federal building in 1996. They were selected rather unscientifically from the *Court TV* web archive, to represent spoken and written text within a single domain, and paired for length to allow for statistical comparison. (Transcripts from other domains of human interaction are not as easy to come by unless you have access to a text corpus. I chose this text genre since it's freely available on the Internet, so readers can try it themselves.) Here are the passages:

(1) (a) That the Government perceives the statements to be pivotal to its case is demonstrated by the Government's painstaking analysis of the statements in its letter to Counsel and the Court dated March 15, 1996 [...]

(b) The Court would like to advise you that there is a little bird family that is in this area. We have had the best minds in the institution to check it out, but they are chirping.

(2) (a) I certify that the foregoing is a correct transcript from the record of proceedings in the above-entitled matter.

(b) [...] why don't I hold it for you so you can show them what they're seeing. First of all, start with this metal fragment here.

Text (1a) is from a written legal brief requesting that McVeigh be tried separately from his co-defendant, Terry Nichols. Text (1b) is taken from the judge's introductory remarks to the jury at the preliminary hearing. Text (2a) is the stenographer's written declaration at the end of one of the session transcripts. Text (2b) is from the cross-examination of an FBI agent, in which the prosecuting attorney asks the agent to describe a photograph to the jury. We'll analyse these texts using the following linguistic features:

- length and complexity of sentences;
- length of words;
- morphological complexity of words;
- pronoun use versus full NPs;
- word frequency;
- Latinate versus Germanic vocabulary.

This is not an arbitrary selection of linguistic features: you may already have some inkling as to what we might expect from the textual analysis. We might hypothesize, for instance, that more formal, written text, such as (1a) and (2a), will use more complex structures than the oral (1b) and (2b), reflecting greater syntactic, lexical and semantic complexity. And, indeed, these predictions are largely borne out by the data, as we'll now see.

Length of expression and syntactic complexity

Although they are matched for number of words, text (1a), the legal brief, contains a single sentence whereas (1b), the judge's remarks, has two. Texts (2a) and (2b) are matched on number of letters (97 and 96, respectively), but the lawyer's request contains two sentences made up of 24 words, whereas the stenographer's declaration is a single sentence of 18 words. More formality, then, may imply lengthier expression overall. Note also the syntactic complexity of text (1a), with its use of a lengthy relative clause in subject position, a passive verb, and a double PP (also used in text 2a). It's important to appreciate, though, that syntactic complexity on its own is not restricted uniquely to formal, written texts: the syntactic tree for the first sentence in text (2b) is even more elaborate than (1a), combining together three separate clauses (headed by the verbs *hold, show* and *see*), whereas text (1a) has only two (headed by *perceive* and *demonstrate*). This observation allows a significant breaching of one corollary of the Language Spell, giving the lie to the common belief that spoken language is generally grammatically simpler than written text, and therefore, that literate languages and language users necessarily have more complex grammars than non-literate languages or language users. 'Simple' themes in 'ordinary' domains of use don't necessarily require less 'sophisticated' grammar.

A more reliable correlation between event and language use will normally hold at the *lexical* level: patently a situation involving more sophisticated concepts will require more words, and the greater variety of words you need, the more they are likely to show greater inherent complexity.

Lexical complexity

In Chapter 3 I imagined the Adamic Conventioneers constructing their first words out of single vowels, then adding consonants and moving from monosyllables to polysyllabic strings. But we can also measure the complexity of words in other ways. Length, as reflected in number of phonemes and syllables, correlates to a good degree with **word frequency** and conceptual complexity: the most frequent words in the language tend to be short ones (including most function words), and frequent words tend to be less conceptually dense (recall that function words normally perform more grammatical, than semantic, functions). Here are the 20 most frequent word families in the 100 million-word British National Corpus:

1	*the*	11	*I*
2	*be*	12	*to*
3	*of*	13	*they*
4	*and*	14	*not*
5	*a*	15	*for*
6	*in*	16	*you*
7	*to*	17	*she*
8	*have*	18	*with*
9	*he*	19	*on*
10	*it*	20	*that*

All are monosyllabic, the only exceptions being those members of verb families which carry the progressive inflection *-ing*, and the preposition *inside*, treated as a member of the *in* family. (*To* appears twice, first as the infinitive verb marker, second as the preposition: they're homophones.)

At the other end of the scale, long words tend to be associated with academic and technical registers, and are therefore much rarer in everyday language use. Here are the words I didn't know in the passage from Umberto Eco, cited in Chapter 3:

sorites	*apophantic*
apothegms	*logoi*
hypallages	*stoichea*
zeugmas	*parallaxes*
hysteron	*herbaria*
proteron	*gymnosophists*

... Not a god-fearing monosyllable among them!

For the historical reasons discussed in Chapter 5, English also has a typological distinction in the lexicon, which correlates well with register. Not only does Old English supply our vocabularies with high voltage four-letter words, but also with over 80 per cent of the 1,000 most common words of the language (including all the top 20 listed above). And although French gave us many new words (around 45 per cent of the 10,000 most frequent), it is Latin and Greek which have supplied English with the greatest number of 'learned' words (including Eco's dodgy dozen). Through the early Christian church, Latin had already come to dominate the discourse of religion and learning before the Normans became England's ruling class in 1066. But it was during the Renaissance and Enlightenment that Modern

English was born. During this period, roughly from Caxton's introduction of the printing press in 1476 to the American Revolution of 1776, vast numbers of our less frequent, more formal, scientific and cultural words were introduced.

These patterns are reflected in the lexical composition of our courtroom text fragments. Table 2 gives a summary of the characteristics of each fragment, showing the average length of words used (in number of letters and syllables), the approximate percentage of words with a frequency of less than 1,000 per 100 million in the British National Corpus, an index of morphological complexity (average number of morphemes per word), and the percentage of Latinate words.

Table 2 Lexical characteristics of four text fragments

	Average number of letters	Average number of syllables	Percentage of words with < 1,000 frequency	Average number of morphemes per word	Percentage of Latinate words
Written (1a)	5.1	1.7	59%	1.4	40%
Written (2a)	5.0	1.8	50%	1.5	50%
Spoken (1b)	3.6	1.1	41%	1.04	16%
Spoken (2b)	3.9	1.3	35%	1.05	4%

For more-or-less randomly selected text fragments, there is remarkable uniformity here. The more formal, written texts (1a and 2a) have higher indices of complexity than the more casual, spoken texts (1b and 2b), on each lexical measure. Moreover, within each modality, there is minimal variation in scores.

The importance of context

We saw in Chapter 3 that the interpretation of words in situations of use comes from two sources: (a) 'core' semantic representation(s), permanently linked to the lexical entry from conceptual systems; and (b) the information available from linguistic and non-linguistic context, which is normally required to recover the full, rich, communicative intention of the speaker or writer. The linguistic code itself is always ambiguous to some extent, but the Spell keeps us unaware of this fact, sealing off from view the sensitive 'context radar' we use to pick up on the environmental cues which allow us to select the most appropriate reading of the input. In casual face-to-face interaction, this works well, because shared context is rich and plentiful. We often know our interlocutors personally, the topic is generally familiar, and potential misunderstandings are either headed off in advance through the use of discourse markers, or are quickly cleared up through conventional repair and negotiation sequences. But in more formal situations, such as legal proceedings, where often people's liberty and large amounts of money are at stake, ambiguity must be minimized. To achieve this, information normally drawn from context must be *lexicalized* (put into words). This is especially true of written legal documents, which must, by their very nature, exist independently of Hymes' physical **S**ettings and **S**cenes.

One way that casual speech uses context to make communication fast and efficient is to refer to physically present people and things using *pronouns*. Pronouns are also used for people and things assumed to be currently focused in interlocutors' minds. Hence we see greater pronoun use in the spoken texts (1b) and (2b) than in the written texts (1a) and (2a):

Table 3 Use of pronouns versus full NPs

		Pronouns	Full NPs
Written	(1a)	2	8
	(2a)	1	4
Spoken	(1b)	4	5
	(2b)	6	1

Notice how the legal brief in text (2b) repeats the nouns *government* and *statement* instead of using a pronoun (*the government's painstaking analysis of the statements* instead of *its painstaking analysis of them*). Notice also how the meaning of the first sentence of text (2b) would be a complete mystery without the participants and the photograph to supply references for the six pronouns used. The use of the NP *The Court* instead of the pronoun *I* in text (1b) is a noteworthy anomaly in this respect. Legal convention elevates the judge to such a status that he or she comes to personify the institution itself, hence the implicit humour of this passage, with its incongruous juxtaposition of the ritualized self-reference with the prosaic topic.

Explaining the patterns

A look at the ethnographic components of each text situation reveals why the language in these texts patterns the way it does. Here are some highlights.

- *Setting & Scene*: Although all four texts are from the same judicial domain, texts (1a) and (2a) are legal documents, and so their use is tied to no single physical setting or scene (they may well have been written in legal offices, but could be read on the bus or in the bath). Although the spoken texts (1b) and (2b) occurred in the formal setting of a courtroom, the *Ends* of the discourse explain their casual tone (see below).
- *Participants*: The written documents were written by legal professionals following established convention, for the court and the public at large. The speakers of the other two passages (judge and prosecutor) have conventionalized roles of power over their respective hearers (jury and witness), but choose not to exercise that power explicitly through their language, which again the *Ends* factor explains.
- *Ends*: The legal brief tries to persuade the court to take a course of action, based on legal precedent, reasoned argumentation, and also some rhetorical effects. The stenographer's declaration is a formula designed to assure the public that the job was properly done. But although the spoken texts also have an immediate communicative purpose (announcing a potential source of acoustic interference and requesting the witness to explain a photo to the jury), each also has a psychological subtext: both judge and attorney clearly wish to put the jury and witnesses at ease in such a formal setting.
- *Key*: The written document fragments are sober and emotionally neutral. The spoken texts are warmer, with the judge invoking humour and the attorney exercising friendly engagement ('Why don't I hold it for you …').
- *Instrumentalities*, *Norms*, and *Genre*: Text (1a) is part of a lengthy written legal brief, following the conventions of the genre and using the expected vocabulary of the legal register. Text (2a), the stenographer's statement, is a frozen chunk, repeated word-for-word at the end of each transcript, serving as the textual equivalent of a wax seal. The oral texts (1b) and (2b) reflect the social shift in Western society away from Victorian linguistic propriety in the exercise of authority, towards more casual norms. (Although of course the register and style adopted only conceal the power

relations obtaining between the participants: the jury can't talk back to the judge, the witness may not refuse to comply with the prosecutor's friendly 'suggestions', and for both judge and prosecutor the courtroom register is second nature.)

I have spent some time on these examples because they illustrate quite effectively some aspects of the intralinguistic repertoires we all control to a greater or lesser extent. Registers from these repertoires are deployed effortlessly and often unconsciously, in the same way that multilinguals in diglossic situations deploy their separate languages for quite different purposes.

Dialects and accents

Our communicative purposes and the social conventions of language use we have internalized don't account for all the diversity within a single language, of course. Much more apparent, and perhaps of more social significance to us than registers and styles, are the different dialects and accents that we hear from our colinguals. This is because the way we sound and the words we use are perceived as markers of our social identities. In Chapter 1 we looked briefly at dialects as objects of pride and shame, or as instruments of identity and power. Now that we have explored some of the ways that language works behind the Spell, we can look at accents and dialects more dispassionately, and better understand why the idea of a 'correct' version of the language is linguistically untenable, even though it has played a major role in the development of the modern nation state, and continues to govern the ways in which we treat members of our own E-language groups.

Back to attitudes and beliefs

In Chapter 1 I tried to show how the Language Spell has led us to include speech patterns as an element in the complex of perceived traits which we use to categorize individuals into groups. The way we speak is seen as an inevitable part of who we are and where we belong, since the Spell encourages us to see language as an external object, which we wear like clothing. This is clearly a very useful ability, contributing significantly to the construction and maintenance of cohesive community bonds. Recognition of members of our own group, and pride in our collective heritage, can be positive outcomes of dialect detection. But unlike the clothes we wear, language is also seen as a direct expression of our thoughts. An implicit folk belief of many is that different E-languages were somehow 'devised', maybe through successive re-enactments of the original Adamic Convention, to optimally express the beliefs and identities of new cultural groups, especially, in recent centuries, *national* groups. The codified, 'standard', variety is assumed to be the 'right' way to encode the group's thoughts. It is an immutable, monolithic system which exists despite transient linguistic fashions (expressed through the slang and affectations of marginalized subcultures and cultural elites alike) and despite the barbarisms and solecisms, the quaintness and charm, of local dialects.

But the codified variety is linguistically 'standard' only in the sense that it has become 'the norm' for printed text, either because it was the dialect of the privileged class, or because it was selected for alphabetization by language planners (see below). Other senses of the term *standard*, such as 'basis or example', 'degree of excellence', 'unmarked case', or 'authoritative version', are applied to the dialect only on the basis of *non-linguistic* arguments or beliefs. Linguists should perhaps drop the term 'standard' altogether, and instead use terms like 'Educated Southern British English' (ESBE) for the UK's prestige spoken dialect and 'British Printed English' (BPE) for the non-localized written variety. I'll apply these terms where I can in the rest of this chapter.

Alongside the mix-up between 'standard' language and 'correct' language, regional and class dialects and accents have come to be appreciated and despised in the same way that some people will admire local costumes (though never wear them themselves) and frown on socks with sandals or jeans at the opera. The assumption of a default, 'accent-free', version of each language is one of the most powerful of our linguistic beliefs, and is highly resistant to the logical arguments proffered by linguists. This is because the judgements involved are not linguistic at all, but social: linguistic 'logic', like the damning of the double negative, is applied to members of racial or cultural minorities, like Speedy the black New York gang leader, but not to members of ruling classes, like Jacques Chirac or the King of Spain (whose languages allow them to double-negate without fear of public criticism). Such prejudices have a long history, and have only recently begun to be questioned by some more enlightened members of our societies, even in the so-called liberal West.

A couple of years back, a friend gave me a reprint of the English Dialect Society's booklet entitled 'A List of Words and Phrases in Every-day Use by the Natives of Hetton-le-Hole in the County of Durham', which was prepared by the local curate, the Rev. F. M. T.

Palgrave, in 1896. The subtitle reads: '... Being Words not Ordinarily Accepted, or but Seldom Found, in the Standard English of the Day'. The Victorian upper classes had a keen interest in local customs and practices, but their methodical and often celebratory accounts rarely led them to question the established social order. They read Dickens and Walter Scott rather than Marx and Engels. So Palgrave's unashamed assumption of social and moral, as well as linguistic, superiority comes as no surprise. This, from the preface, is his charitable view of the Hetton-le-Hole mining community:

> It is my opinion that, in spite of a rather congested population, the standard of morality is higher than in the South [...] There is a good deal of loud talk, exclusiveness and Pharisaism, amongst the miners as a class, but they cannot be called a degraded class by any means, not more addicted to their peculiar temptations than any other class. Soaking in public-houses on pay-Saturday is very general [...] But their home life compares well with that of men in any rank ...

The painstaking lexical analysis which follows is free of value-judgements, but the curate's underlying assumptions about the status of the dialect are clear.

The subtitle tells us that the miners' words are not 'accepted' in Standard English (which he later calls 'polite English'), and readers are informed that:

> Where the word 'fine' occurs in the text, it means something more refined than the dialect pure and simple, introduced in the presence of one more highly educated than the speaker.

The presence of such 'fine' elements in the community's speech reminds us also that its own members could be as conscious as the curate of the 'unacceptable' nature of their dialect.

The myth of dialectal 'unacceptability' continued throughout the twentieth century and has entered the new millennium almost unchallenged. A university professor in the 1970s is quoted as describing the Glasgow dialect as 'the ugliest one can encounter', and 'associated with the unwashed and the violent'. The *Oxford English Dictionary* was still explaining the use of the word *done* in *whodunit* as 'illiterate for did' into the 1990s. And in a 2001 piece in a US Internet discussion forum, a contributor writes:

> There are two kinds of people who use incorrect grammar. [...] Good incorrect grammar is used by those among us (you know who they are)

that don't know there is such a thing as grammar. [...] They say things like 'Ain't it a nice day?' 'You gave that money to who?' and 'He doesn't have no manners.' They don't bother us. [...] They don't make a big thing out of their bad grammar. They're unaware of it. Ignorance is bliss.

Then there are the bad incorrect grammar users. They've had some success in life through hard work, winning the lottery, being on the stock market [...]. They buy cell phones and other expensive toys. They drink designer coffee. And they try to improve their language.

They say things like
'Between you and I, Bud, this is a great football game.'
'Yeah, John, but whom is that guy who made that bone-crushing tackle?'
'I don't know, but I feel badly for that guy on the ground.'

It is this confusion of class, education, group membership, behaviour and morals that explains negative attitudes to non-standard dialects. The Spell effectively prevents us from appreciating this, and leaves us little option but to attribute our judgements to the linguistic facts of the dialect. It does this, as we saw in Chapter 4, by numbing our minds to the idea of language as a mass of I-languages, and warming us to the necessary fiction of E-language, through which we establish community ties and maintain group identities.

Changing attitudes?

But the Spell no longer has us all blinded equally. Greater public consciousness of the value of 'non-standard' accents and dialects may be emerging, at least in some countries. In line with my argument, though, it looks like it's being propelled more by changes in sociopolitical belief and the general erosion of class structure, than by linguistic revelation. David Ridley, who wrote a forward to the reprint of Palgrave's study a century after it first appeared, has a more enlightened view of language variation than many, noting that:

> [l]anguage constantly evolves with the adaptations of each generation and is never fixed, but [radio, cinema and television] have [...] functioned to standardise speech and marginalise dialect...

He is surely right about the role of the media in neutralizing a lot of dialectal variation, but I don't share his pessimistic view that local dialects have become more marginalized than in Palgrave's time. The linguistic attitudes of the UK establishment, for example, are finally emerging from their Victorian cocoons, I think, in spite of, or perhaps partly due to, the influence of mass media and the Internet.

During a sabbatical year in the UK a few years ago, I was surprised to hear so many Geordie, Irish and Scottish accents from newsreaders and continuity announcers on television, after decades of broadcaster worship at the shrine of 'BBC English'. Amongst other signs of incipient linguistic enlightenment, I was pleased to read that the Barnsley Health Authority had decided to give lessons in the local South Yorkshire dialect to doctors recruited overseas, so that they could better understand their patients. Moreover, on weekly trips to Durham University, where I was giving a course, I saw little sign of any move to ESBE amongst the local youth. (I didn't get to Hetton-le-Hole, unfortunately.) Although **dialect levelling** is occurring in current UK English, it's other 'non-standard' varieties that are the source of spreading linguistic features, rather than the 'proper' English of the traditional 'standard'. Instead of the **hypercorrection** to codified norms decried by the e-forum contributor cited above, the UK is witnessing what sociolinguists call **covert prestige**: the unconscious adoption of linguistic features associated with a group of speakers of a 'non-standard' variety.

But I suspect that any increase in the acceptance of local dialects is still quite superficial, extending only to accent, the phonological-phonetic aspect of a dialect, rather than embracing variation at deeper, more Spell-bound levels of language, such as morphology and syntax. This is because of people's deep-rooted, but largely unfounded, fear of Babel: the loss of mutual intelligibility between speakers of the same language. In Chapter 5, we heard the Director of the Royal Spanish Academy of the Language express this fear over the completely transparent case of the silent orthographic *h*. This was a patently absurd reaction, but is it possible that English or other tongues could split apart if we tolerate changes at the more fundamental level of *grammar*?

I honestly don't think we need to worry too much about grammatical variation within English. The double negatives of Speedy, the double modal verbs of Hetton-le-Hole miners ('They'll not can get any food'), the -*en* suffix of *gotten* in US dialects, and most other grammatical differences, are really quite trivial. They won't get in the way of communication, despite some people's irrational distaste for them. Talk of unintelligibility is normally completely unfounded, and when truly felt, often tends to border on the hysterical. Six months in multilingual Bombay or Nairobi might help such Babel-mongers see the issue a little differently.

International dialects

Dialects are not going to go away in global languages like English, even if the mass media succeeds in obliterating 'indigenous' ones. In the following passage from his novel *Gabriel's Gift*, Hanif Kureishi describes the emergence of London as a truly cosmopolitan metropolis in the latter decades of the last century:

> The city was no longer home to immigrants only from the former colonies, plus a few others: every race was present, living side by side without, most of the time, killing one another. It held together, this new international city called London – just about – without being unnecessarily anarchic or corrupt.

... But he's perhaps exaggerating just a little when he goes on:

> There was, however, little chance of being understood in any shop. Dad once said, 'The last time I visited the barber's I came out with a bowl of couscous, half a gram of Charlie and a number two crop. I only went in for a shave!'

As I argued in the previous chapter, we can no longer think of global languages like English as the property of individual nations, but rather simply as names we give to the language systems of groups of individual speakers, wherever they may come from. For English, then, dialect and accent studies can no longer restrict themselves to places like Durham, Sydney or New York: they must embrace all speakers of English, including those for whom it's an additional language. In Yann Martel's fabulous novel *Life of Pi*, the hero, a precocious Indian teenager, is marooned in the middle of the Pacific with Richard Parker, a Royal Bengal tiger (don't ask me how: read the book). In his delirious last days on the lifeboat, Pi 'hallucinates' a conversation with the tiger, part of which runs as follows:

> 'Why do you have an accent?'
> 'I don't. It is you who have an accent.'
> 'No, I don't. You pronounce *the* "ze".'
> 'I pronounce *ze* "*ze*", as it should be. You speak with warm marbles in your mouth. You have an Indian accent.'
> 'You speak as if your tongue were a saw and English words were made of wood. You have a French accent.'

English sawed up or spoken with marbles in the mouth is still English, and the more it gets learnt and used by new speakers, the more dialects and accents we will get used to hearing.

We should, I believe, learn a lesson from those communities that deal every day with different languages, rather than language-internal dialects: we saw in the last chapter that multilingualism is pretty much the planetary norm, and that diglossic situations are negotiated daily without any effort, by millions of language users across the globe. Things are not so different in monolingual situations: recall that the term *diglossia* was originally introduced by Charles Ferguson to describe speakers' joint use of 'H(igh)' and 'L(ow)' varieties of the same language, and only later applied to bilingualism by Joshua Fishman. Although I argued in Chapter 4 that my Northern Irish flatmate Sam was bidialectal on the receptive plane, he and all literate local dialect-users are really productively bidialectal too, since they write using the conventions of the 'H' variety, BPE. Given what we've seen about writing and speech situations earlier in this chapter, we can now appreciate that this is diglossia, pure and simple.

Linguistic diversity, education and power

The role of formal education is pivotal in promoting a diglossic approach to dialects, since it is literacy that generally gives L-variety speakers productive access to the H-variety, and literacy is a product of schooling, not of biology. But as teachers reading this know, educational practice is often subordinate to educational policy, formulated in cabinets, parliaments and think-tanks more than in teachers' conferences and classrooms. We are moving now into the domain of the language professionals: those, like teachers and politicians, who make a living, in part or entirely, from applying linguistic or metalinguistic knowledge. So let's end this chapter with a brief look at how the Spell, and the diversity it cloaks, affect the conscious manipulation and unconscious deployment of language by these two important groups of professional language users.

The Language Spell affects all human beings, even those who need to pay conscious attention to language and its use as part of their jobs, including linguists like me. As I pointed out in Chapter 2, not all language professionals are trained in linguistics, even 'language purveyors' like language teachers and translators, whose principal metier is language itself. It's still less frequent to find professional writers, politicians and lawyers with a background in either theoretical or applied linguistics (because, obviously, they need to know a lot more about their specific fields – such as literature, politics and economics, or the law). How, then, do their folk beliefs about language affect what they do? To what extent does the surface diversity of language, and our Spell-induced propensity for undervaluing or denying it, modulate the ways language gets used in professional settings? Massively, I think. And I'd like to suggest, in this section, that more sensitivity to the facts behind the Spell would help create healthier, fairer practices for both practitioners and clients/constituents alike. We'll look first at language in education, and then at language in politics.

Language in education

The previous section ended by suggesting that a more enlightened view of language-internal diversity would involve explicit recognition of the diglossic nature of all our monolingual speech communities, and, in general, a more global view of language variation. And yet language education, both for native speakers and learners, has traditionally been based on the fiction that the 'standard' variety *is* the language, implicitly or explicitly marginalizing 'non-standard' dialects and minority languages. Where the mother tongue is concerned, schools and curriculums often make no formal distinction between teaching the language and teaching its canonical literature. As a school subject, English in English-speaking countries tends to be associated largely with the reading of novels, plays and poems, and with the learning of spelling conventions, vocabulary and composition skills. Since the late 1980s, traditional grammar (i.e. prescriptive generalizations about the form and usage of varieties like BPE) has enjoyed a resurgence, after the libertarian sixties and seventies. (In most other language communities, I suspect that norms of grammar and usage based on the literary canon didn't fall into such disfavour in the first place.)

Although the National Curriculum of England and Wales recommends that students be taught about language variation, this seems to be largely restricted to appropriate styles and registers, rather than the use of other dialects. Teachers are told that:

[p]upils should be taught about how speech varies:
a) in different circumstances (for example, to reflect on how their speech changes in more formal situations)
b) to take account of different listeners (for example, adapting what they say when speaking to people they do not know).

The general guidelines state:

Pupils should be taught in all subjects to express themselves correctly and appropriately and to read accurately and with understanding. Since

standard English, spoken and written, is the predominant language in
which knowledge and skills are taught and learned, pupils should be
taught to recognise and use standard English.

The use of the word *correctly* here presupposes that, before instruction,
pupils may express themselves *incorrectly*. We have seen that this is an
unfounded assumption, one which is deeply-engrained in the popular
psyche. It holds sway in much of the educational establishment too.
We saw in the previous section how the idea of 'correct grammar'
springs from beliefs which are in essence deeply social: about society,
not language. It is this that makes the prescriptivist biases of many
educationalists and most of their political overseers so truculent. The
'great grammar crusade', which put traditional grammar back into
the UK curriculum in the 1980s, is, in the words of Deborah Cameron:

> ... a classic case where a bad argument, put forward by people who know
> little or nothing about language, nevertheless succeeds, because although
> much of its substance is nonsensical it engages with the underlying
> assumptions of its audience and therefore makes a kind of sense; whereas
> the opposing argument put forward by experts fails, because it is at odds
> with the audience's underlying assumptions and is therefore apprehended
> as nonsensical.

Now to be fair to the architects of the National Curriculum, they do
show some awareness of the importance of other ways of using
language, especially in pupils' lives away from school, affirming that:

> Teachers develop pupils' spoken and written English through [...]
> building on pupils' experiences of language at home and in the wider
> community, so that their developing uses of English and other languages
> support one another.

But are educationalists right in prioritizing 'standard' varieties like
BPE? I actually believe that they are, and I don't think this
undermines my arguments for the linguistic equality of other, spoken
dialects. In Chapter 4 I argued that the assumption of E-Language is a
necessary fiction and that the belief that language is socially embodied
is what makes I-language ultimately functional. The Fundamental
Paradox may only be resolved if we admit this balancing of biological
fact and social fiction. Over the last half millennium, small local
communities have been transformed into extraordinarily large and
complicated regional, national and even supranational networks. This
has been the product of political centralization, military conquest,
colonization, international trading routes, print technology and

latterly, the globalization of business, finance and communications. As a consequence, some E-languages have become incredibly diverse. Privileged varieties – the dialects of those who first wielded power over these larger E-language communities – have emerged. Over the past couple of centuries, the grammars of these power-dialects have become universally accessible through widespread literacy, bolstered by the mass media. In the UK, for example, the universal BPE emerged from ESBE, but when read aloud is no longer associated exclusively with the accent of the latter. The 'standard' dialects have a near monopoly on the printed word, and universal education has therefore inevitably produced generations of bidialectal citizens, the majority using a 'non-standard' dialect for everyday oral communication, and the 'standard' dialect for reading and writing. This is surely a good thing, if only we can get rid of the 'stigma' of the spoken variety.

Of course, there are no purely linguistic reasons to prevent the codification of any spoken dialect for text use, and as a consequence break ESBE's stranglehold on print in the UK, for example. Robert Burns wrote volumes of poetry in Lowland Scots in the nineteenth century, and Scotland's new parliament uses Scots as well as English and Gaelic as official languages. Political support is crucial, though, for the success of any such exercise. I know that some Scots reading this will be outraged at my classifying Scots as a dialect of English, rather than a separate language, with its own dialects spoken across the Lowlands and in Ulster. (Indeed, Ethnologue lists it as a separate language, with 100,000 native speakers and 1.5 million second language speakers.) But from a linguistic point of view, not a political one, it is hard to call it a separate language and at the same time deny the same status to African American English or the Durham dialect. Here is an extract from the Parliament's information leaflet, *Makkin yer voice heard in the Scottish Pairlament:*

> Ye can scrieve til a committee giein yer pynt o view anent an issue, a speirin or a Bill. They micht bid ye tae come alang an speak til the committee.

I imagine that most readers will immediately get the gist of this passage. The basic grammar of Scots differs from other dialects of English little more than they do from each other. It is largely vocabulary (like *speirin*, 'enquiry') which will make parts of it difficult for non-speakers to read, and accent which will make it hard to comprehend aurally – just as African American English might be hard for speakers of the Hetton-le-Hole dialect. Scots has the advantage not for linguistic reasons, but because it is associated with a proud national tradition.

Despite the limited success of national dialects like Scots, the fact is that very few spoken language varieties have codified written systems, and trying to get them accepted by the public-at-large and their representatives in government is an up-hill struggle, as the hullabaloo in California over Ebonics in the 1990s demonstrated. Many years will have to pass before this effect of the Spell has any chance of being eroded, and again, linguistic argumentation on its own will not be enough. Spell-breaking consciousness will have to work in tandem with lengthy communal deliberation and soul-searching on gnarly sociopolitical questions about identity, rights, and educational opportunities. In any case, the view I've been advocating in this book suggests that fostering diglossic *multicompetence*, for example in BPE and Geordie, or in American Printed English and African American Spoken English, is an appropriate objective of schools in the immediate future. A first step to true linguistic equality must be to divorce common written dialects like BPE from the privileged spoken dialects that spawned them, like ESBE.

Scottish schools seem to be moving faster than their southern cousins towards this kind of broader understanding of language variety, and thus the possibility of more rational discussion about 'correct grammar' and the role of the 'standard' dialect. Over a decade ago, the Scottish Education Department's *National Guidelines on English 5–14* was advising that:

> [t]he first tasks of schools are [...] to enable pupils to be confident and creative in [their] language and to begin to develop the notion of language diversity, within which pupils can appreciate the range of accents, dialects and languages they encounter. This will involve teachers in valuing pupils' spoken language, and introducing them to stories, poems and other texts which use dialect in a positive way.

I don't know to what extent Scotland's teachers follow these linguistically rather sensible guidelines, or whether their colleagues in England and Wales honour their National Curriculum's more lukewarm acknowledgement of the value of home and community language. But clearly the policy represents a significant advance towards linguistic equality in the public sphere: 30 years ago it would have been unimaginable for government to be dispensing this kind of enlightened advice. Let's hope that at least here, professional practice is actually following policy.

Language planning

History has witnessed many attempts by politicians to mould language practices in the states they govern, often in order to reinforce or extend their own hold on power. As the Spanish grammarian Antonio de Nebrija wrote in 1492, '[l]anguage was always the companion of Empire.' In more recent times, though, ideas from the applied linguistics field of **language planning** have been adopted by more liberal regimes, to provide greater access to civil life for the majority of citizens who are not speakers of the 'standard' language, in which much of civil life is conducted. Language planning has typically started with the *selection* of one language in a multilingual society (a legacy of empire), or one dialect in a language with no written system, to serve as the lingua franca and common written variety for national or regional civil purposes. Consequently, the variety must be *codified* – furnished with an alphabet, a descriptive grammar distilled from the actual grammars of its speakers, and the new vocabulary they will need for the new uses to which the language will be put. Decisions are made about both formal features of the linguistic system itself (**corpus planning**) and its role in the broader society in which it will be used (**status planning**). The fundamental belief underlying language planning is that conscious human action can change both language structure and language use. But language planners know that their proposals, and subsequent policy-making by politicians, will only be successful if they are *accepted* by a significant number of language users, especially those with influence, like community leaders and the socioeconomic elites.

The emphasis in language planning has been squarely on languages, rather than dialects – the UNESCO-supported Universal Declaration of Linguistic Rights, for example, focuses exclusively on language communities sharing a common E-language rather than a dialect of it. Even in cases of monolingual societies constituted linguistically by overlapping sets of oral dialects, the aim is to elevate one of them to the status of the 'standard,' and to educate other dialect speakers in the written use of this chosen variety. The language planning enterprise, then, is fraught with social risk, for the reasons we've been exploring in the latter part of this chapter. But it's a necessary prescriptive exercise if minority language users are to have any chance of making their voices heard beyond the borders of their local communities. Although grass-roots organizations and individuals play a vital role in the success of language planning (especially for the maintenance of minority languages), it depends inevitably, also, on the will and commitment of political leaders – which leaves the planners' work open, unsurprisingly, to distortion, manipulation and misuse.

The Soviet Union provides an interesting early example of large-scale language planning and its political implementation. Long before other large multilingual societies were to consider legal protection for minority language users, the new USSR, under Lenin, established the linguistic equality of all Soviet citizens, whatever their language or dialect, and embarked on an ambitious programme of codification and literacy education for the country's 130-or-so languages. In the 1920s and early 1930s, a small group of linguists worked on providing writing systems, based on the Roman alphabet, for the many languages with only an oral tradition, and the government attempted to provide mother tongue education for the entire linguistically diverse population. Largely due to the pioneering efforts of this time, illiteracy was almost eradicated in the country, and citizens were able to use their own languages in both speech and writing, however small their community.

The ideals of the Leninist language reformers were soon tempered, however, on the accession to power of Joseph Stalin. Stalin took a keen personal interest in linguistics, and actually wrote (or at least attached his name to) a booklet called *Marxism and Problems of Linguistics*, which was published a year after his death. The views expressed there, responding to a discussion in the state-run newspaper *Pravda*, formed part of an orchestrated public repudiation of the views of the linguist N. Y. Marr and his followers, and was designed to strengthen the role of Russian as a centralizing force and symbol of Soviet unity.

Some of the views expressed in Stalin's booklet have scientific merit from the perspective of current linguistic theory, although others (such as his vehement rejection of the possibility of fully expressive sign languages) would cause considerable disquiet among contemporary experts. And in any case, the political practice underlying his apparently informed and benign official 'policy' is a different story. Stalin saw the 'standard' variety of Russian as one of the major instruments of national unity and centralized control, just as the tsars before him had done. For him, local dialects were harmless, subordinate symbols of proletarian power, and upper-class dialects were insubstantial affectations. The separate languages of the Soviet satellite states, on the other hand, were soon viewed as a major threat, despite his booklet's celebration of regional variation and its affirmation that language was independent of cultural belief, including political ideology.

In the years leading up to the Second World War, Stalin's

government undid much of the work of the earlier reformers, imposing the Russian Cyrillic alphabet on minority languages, making Russian compulsory in all Soviet schools, and drastically curtailing minority language teaching and use in the republics. On the eve of war, local champions of minority languages – especially in the Ukraine and Tatar-speaking Crimea – joined millions of other citizens classified as threats to the Kremlin's power, and many, accused of collaboration with Nazi Germany, were imprisoned or killed. (Incidentally, Stalin's successors seem to have inherited some of his neo-tsarist linguistic views, if not, thankfully, his nefarious practices. When in 2001 Tatarstan decided to reimpose the Roman alphabet it had used prior to Stalin's imposition of Cyrillic in 1939, a Russian parliamentary commission called the move 'a threat to Russia's security'.)

Linguistic diversity has been perceived as a threat to nationhood throughout history and in all parts of the globe. President Chirac's refusal to contemplate official recognition of France's minority languages, official backing for the US English Only movement, and the stigmatization of the Sámi language in northern Scandinavia, are examples we have touched on in previous chapters. Nowadays, politicians' belief in national linguistic unity may be only tacit in our more multicultural societies, but it tends to run deep nevertheless. Here in Mexico, state governments are still implicitly minimizing the relevance and status of indigenous languages by referring to them with the term *dialecto*, even when their public policy is to champion indigenous language rights.

Language planning has its successes and its setbacks. The latter, I think, are in large part due to the kinds of social misperceptions and misuses of language diversity explored in this chapter and the last. Equally, its successes owe a good deal to the research of linguists and to applied linguists' attempts to break the Language Spell, despite the political forces and social pressures arrayed against them.

Language as power

Language plays a more subtle role in political life and policy-making, though, since politicians are also language professionals: not only do they make decisions about language in public life, they also use language as a principal work tool. Politicians are, as they like to tell us on election campaigns, ordinary folk, and as such are as much under the Spell as the rest of us. But Orwellian fears that language can be used by governments to brainwash, or at least to conceal, confuse, dissimulate and misrepresent, perhaps have some substance. For many, recent confirmation of this possibility was provided by the revelations of linguistic spin-doctory by the White House and Downing Street in their public justifications for going to war with Iraq.

The study of language use by politicians takes us beyond the identification of dialect, style and register, which reveal how language use essentially *reflects* or *represents* social elements lying outside language, to a level of linguistic enquiry which we may call discourse type or **genre**, where language is studied as situated social practice, especially in specific professional contexts. The primary concern of this domain of enquiry is to establish how institutionalized patterns of language use are perceived as constructing, or perpetuating, patterns of social belief and practice. Applied linguists have recently started to explore discourse in this way in a variety of professional domains, including doctor-patient interaction, scientific writing, dispute resolution, social work and news-reporting. Such studies take traditional pragmatics and discourse analysis into the realms of social policy, postmodernist thought and critical theory, where some academics have begun to assume the role of politically committed *actors* in civil debate, rather than as 'merely' objective observers and chroniclers.

One discourse issue that Western politicians pay close attention to, and that 'critical applied linguists' take a militant stance on, is whether patterns of lexical usage cause or perpetuate patterns of social exclusion. Under the guise of 'politically correct usage', this question has exercised the public imagination through extensive attention in the popular media. Does the generic use of *he* perpetuate sexist beliefs and practices? Should a committee have a *chairman*, a *chairperson*, or simply a *chair*? Is it better to use the relatively unknown word *Sámi* to refer to Lapps and their language (because they themselves prefer that name)? Why has the term *Mongol* been replaced by the more cumbersome 'person with Down's syndrome'?

The phenomenon of 'politically correct' or simply 'PC' language has figured prominently in academic and political discourse over the past 20 years. The term was first used in humorous self-parody by the New Left in the 1970s, before being co-opted by the Right, to mock what they perceived as their opponents' over-zealous efforts to fight inequality. Many English speakers have strongly held views on the topic, depending on their political inclinations and the degree of their resistance to the possibility of change in the established social order. Others are more pragmatic, gearing their linguistic practice to their current audience. One of my favourite examples of PC linguistic expediency comes from the psycholinguist Willem Levelt, who prefaced his book *Speaking* (1989) with the following note:

> I will contribute to the present chaos of person pronominalization in English by adhering to the following conventions: Speakers, whether male, female, or generic, will receive masculine pronominalization. Hearers or addressees will be treated as female. When there are two or more interlocutors (i.e. speakers/hearers), the first one will be male, the second one female, and so on in alternation. General use of these conventions in psycholinguistics will, given the bias for language-comprehension research, make most person reference female.

Levelt's cunning choice permits him to maintain the old default *he* and *him* as the most frequent pronouns used in his own book, which is about speaking, but enjoins the majority of his colleagues, who write about comprehension, to adopt the more radical *she* and *her*. A most principled strategy!

But the PC debate has a more serious strand, which touches on the very essence of the relationship between language use and political power, and derives, in part, from the Spell-driven identification of language with thought. Like Orwell, critical discourse analysts have stressed that language use in the public domain inevitably constitutes a sociopolitical act. Let's look at a concrete example, to see what they mean. In the 2000 election campaign for the London mayorship, the Conservative Party candidate, Steven Norris, promised to end the practice of what he called 'politically correct policing'. This commitment was made in the context of public response to the Stephen Laurence murder, touched on at the end of Chapter 8. The commentator Gary Younge, writing in the *Guardian* newspaper, had this to say on the subject:

> [The term 'politically correct'] has not become just a term of abuse directed at those who seek to extend equality and express it in their daily lives. It is also used to deride anything conservatives don't agree with [. . .] or simply don't like [. . .]. Its remit has become so wide it is virtually meaningless, an excuse for sloppy thinking aimed at anything that embraces or enhances diversity, or an excuse for thinking nothing at all.

> Take Norris's manifesto commitment. If he believes the Metropolitan police should continue to stop and search black people in massively disproportionate numbers [. . .] he should say so. To do so would alienate black voters whom he desperately needs. If he thinks the Met should be reviewing its procedures in the light of the Macpherson report [an official enquiry into the death of Stephen Laurence], he should say so. To do so

would alienate a traditional Tory base he also needs. So he pledges an end to 'politically correct policing', which no one can criticise because nobody knows what it means. And nobody knows what it means because it does not exist.

Younge's accusation was, in effect, that Norris and other conservatives were capitalizing on the changing semantics of the term 'politically correct' for electoral gain, as it was appropriated by the Right, and then by the popular press. The term 'politically correct policing' is a useful expression for a politician because it has no meaning, and therefore engages 'sloppy thinking' or no thinking at all. The 'Third Way' politics of Tony Blair and Bill Clinton has been the object of similar criticism: the strength of the concept is what it doesn't mean, rather than what it does (it's an alternative to both the right wing policies of Thatcher and Reagan, and to the militant socialism associated with the pre-Blair Labour party).

We are seeing two strategies here in political discourse. On the one hand we have the conscious employment of innovative expressions as instruments for social change, such as the use of *she* or *s/he* (where older usage would use the 'generic' masculine pronoun), or the Spanish email use of *amig@s* to stand for both male *amigos* and female *amigas*. On the other hand, we have the 'devious' use of expressions which do exactly the opposite, communicating less than the users actually know about the discourse topic, such as 'illegal combatants' for prisoners of war subject to the Geneva Conventions, or 'martyrs' for bombers who kill themselves in the process of murdering civilians.

But the use of language to provoke or conceal is not restricted to the political domain. All professional language users take advantage of the inexistence of telepathy. Consciously or unconsciously, they use the inherent power of poet over reader, advertiser over consumer, lawyer over witness, teacher over pupil, to package their message in ways which best achieve their different aims, exploiting the narrow wave band of human language to jolt, bamboozle, cajole, woo or abuse. And what language professionals do with language is not so different from the ways we all select varied lexical, grammatical and pragmatic encodings in our everyday language interactions, depending on factors like those in Hymes' *SPEAKING* list discussed earlier. That we tell little white lies to friends rather than insulting their new hairstyle or choice of partner, and talk of *cremating* the *departed* rather than *burning* our *dead* – these choices are not essentially different from those made by politicians when, for example, they call any soldier who happens to get killed in war a *hero* (even if they die as a result of *friendly fire* or *collateral damage*), or when they ritually violate Grice's Maxim of Relevance every time they're asked a straightforward question.

What the Spell induces us to overlook is that it's not language itself that is wielding some mysterious power to manipulate our minds in such cases, but rather its *users*. The only difference between language and other symbolic systems with a mission – from CD covers to wine bottle labels, from images of the Virgin of Guadalupe to the architecture of Norman Foster, from semaphore flags to computer icons – is that language has an unlimited communicative potential, and monopolizes the available channels for sharing meaning. This spectacular advantage has led, as we've seen, to the impression that language *is* meaning, but is also speech and text at the same time. Consequently we operate as though language actually embodies thought and carries it from one person to another. And hence the seductive idea that language is power, when in fact the power is in the social conventions and beliefs that govern its encoding and decoding, not in the code itself.

And so we've come full circle. In the first few pages of Chapter 1, I suggested that language is neither the thoughts or sociocultural processes it expresses, nor its external physical shape as speech, text or sign. In this chapter, we've explored its surface diversity and concluded that although it is used in many different ways by different groups and for different reasons, this is essentially a product of external sociocultural forces, rather than internal linguistic ones. In the last chapter, we'll strip language and culture to their biological core, making a final attempt to reconcile the Fundamental Paradox and so reach a deeper understanding of the Language Spell and its effect on our lives.

More information

 Bonvillain (2002) provides good explanation and exemplification of the **ethnographic** approach to language use, also using Hymes' *SPEAKING* factors as a starting point.

Doug Biber's ground-breaking work on the linguistic marking of **register and genre variation** using computer corpora is reported in Biber (1988). He and colleagues Susan Conrad and Geoffrey Leech (2002) have produced a student grammar of English incorporating findings on register and usage from the Longman corpus.

A great source for **word frequency** information on English words is Leech, Rayson and Wilson (2001). It includes information on frequencies in different genres/registers. The companion website at www.comp.lancs.ac.uk/ucrel/bncfreq contains plain text versions of the frequency lists in the book.

Jennifer Jenkins' 2003 book on **World Englishes**, presented in the same interactive format as Field (2003), is a great place to start exploring English as a global phenomenon.

The **National Curriculum of England and Wales'** levels and attainment targets for English can be found at www.ncaction.org.uk/subjects/english. **Scotland's** guidelines for English language education can be found at www.ltscotland.org.uk/5to14/guidelines/english-language/index.asp.

The Scottish Parliament's website in **Scots** is at www.scottish.parliament.uk/vli/language/scots/index.htm.

William Labov's testimony given at the US Senate hearings on **Ebonics** can be found at www.ling.upenn.edu/~wlabov/L102/Ebonics_test.html.

An authoritative, clear, and realistic look at the practices and outcomes of **language policy and planning** is provided by Bernard Spolsky (2004).

The **Universal Declaration of Linguistic Rights** was approved by over 100 NGOs in 1996 at Barcelona. Information and the text itself may be found at www.linguistic-declaration.org/index-gb.htm.

For more on **critical applied linguistics**, see Alastair Pennycook's (2001) highly influential and accessible introduction. (Pennycook dubs his topic 'Applied Linguistics with an Attitude'.)

Cameron (1996) has a good discussion of the phenomenon of **politically correct language**.

11 The Spell Unbroken

> Again Gandalf approached the wall, and lifting up his arms he spoke in tones of command and rising wrath. *Edro, edro!* he cried, and struck the rock with his staff. *Open, open!* he shouted, and followed it with the same command in every language that had ever been spoken in the West of Middle-earth. Then he threw his staff on the ground, and sat down in silence.
>
> (J. R. R. Tolkien, *The Lord of the Rings*)

Gandalf the Grey, Tolkien's polyglot wizard from *The Lord of the Rings*, was stumped. He had to open the gates to the Mines of Moria, so that the Fellowship could continue on their epic quest to prevent the One Ring from falling into the hands of the Dark Lord. The trouble was, the gates were protected by a spell, which Gandalf couldn't break, even after trying all the counter-spells he knew, in all the major tongues of elves, dwarves and men. The spell that keeps human language under wraps turns out to be similarly recalcitrant. As a first-year undergraduate, when I wasn't lost in Middle Earth or downing pints of Exhibition Ale in the local pub, I remember being quite baffled about the things I was hearing in my linguistics classes. Gradually, though, I began to 'get' it, and soon, like a sorcerer's apprentice, I was smugly celebrating my new-found knowledge. I carried around a little notebook, and showed people syntactic trees and phonetic transcriptions of what they had just said. Emboldened by the initial interest provoked by these tokens of knowledge, I pompously debunked the myth of correct English to anyone who would listen, and glibly belittled the importance of the written word. At first my family at home and my friends at the pub humoured me, but pretty soon concluded that linguistics was unrelated to reality, and heeded me no more. The spell of folk belief was too strong. Like Gandalf and his wizard's staff, I threw my notebook on the ground, and sat down in silence.

I'm not looking for sympathy. The plain fact is that my arguments from linguistics have generally been met with puzzlement or outright rejection. As a professional linguist, I get consulted about whether you should say *different from*, *different to*, or *different than*, and whether Spanish is hard to learn. On the fundamental question of what language *really* is, few people seem to want to know. Of course, as I've admitted more than once in this book, we linguists also operate under the Spell most of the time. I harbour many covert linguistic prejudices myself, which regularly pop out in conversation when I'm not wearing my professional hat (I opened the Preface with an example). So can the Language Spell be broken after all? Should we even try? Is the popularization of linguistics an arrogant, irrelevant or futile enterprise, doomed to failure? In *The Lord of the Rings*, the answer to the Moria spell turned out to be much simpler than Gandalf had thought (in fact, it was staring him in the face), ... but when the gates finally did open, what the Fellowship found was a vast network of dark caverns, occupied by powerful forces which ultimately proved to be Gandalf's undoing.

In this last chapter I'll try to get down to the nitty-gritty of the Fundamental Paradox, which, like the enchanted gates to the Mines of Moria, presents the main stumbling block for a deeper public interest in, and understanding of, human language. I'll suggest that the Spell is actually relatively easy to break, but that breaking it won't automatically change our attitudes and beliefs. My approach will be to sketch what linguists, neuroscientists and others have discovered or surmised about the biological facts of human language and how it has evolved in the species as a tool of cultural transmission. Finally, I'll grapple with the linguists' equivalent of Gandalf's plight, asking whether an attempt to break the Language Spell constitutes public service or academic folly.

Language biology

Throughout the book, I have claimed that our inability to appreciate the essential cognitive reality of human language is the result of biological evolution, leading to a fundamental paradox: that although language exists objectively only in individual human brains, it becomes most real for us *socially*, in the public arena for which it has evolved. Because this impression is so palpable, we often act as though language existed principally *outside* of us, in abstract entities such as cultures, jokes, conversation and song. In Chapter 1 I tried to give a flavour of the essentially *cognitive*, internal, nature of the language faculty by comparing it with mental apparatus which automatically steers us around physical terrains like supermarkets. In Chapter 2 I presented linguistic knowledge as 'knowing what' and 'knowing how': a declarative 'database' coupled with procedural mechanisms we employ when language is actually put to use. In Chapter 3 we explored how language is similar to the five senses, delivering information from external sensory stimuli to our central conceptual systems, and, in the other direction, encoding non-linguistic thought in the physical manifestations of speech and text. Chapter 4 tried to convince you that particular languages, like English and Spanish, are necessary fictions – 'E'-language extrapolations from our mental 'I'-languages, residing not in dictionaries or academies, but in our collective minds.

Then, after describing some of the nuts and bolts of our I-languages in Chapters 5–7, I made the crucial claim in Chapter 8 that our ability to build and use I-language derives from three sources: our DNA, the speech of others and the non-linguistic physical and social contexts in which language is always embedded. I'm sure many readers found my patchy treatment of the biological basis of language most unsatisfactory here. What could it mean that language is encoded in DNA? If language is biological, and Chomsky talks about a 'language organ', why did I then insist on presenting it chapter after chapter in the abstract metaphors of cognitive psychology, rather than the more concrete stuff of brain tissue and chromosomes?

The short answer to this latter disquiet is that we just don't yet know enough about how linguistic knowledge is represented and processed at the neurological level. (We know even less about how the brain handles aspects of communicative competence such as code-switching, conversation strategies, and the like). Another reason for highlighting the psychological and downplaying the neurological is that the former provides a better view. From a psychological perspective we can see much more clearly how language *functions*. The 'big picture' provided by psycholinguistics also makes it easier to reveal the ultimate connection between language as biological entity and language as social phenomenon. In contrast, the view from neurolinguistics is still rather misty. It's not yet possible to localize Swahili inflectional morphology or Spanish politeness strategies in the grey matter of the human brain.

So the emphasis on mind over brain was inevitable. But how come the cognitive facts so rapidly faded from view once I began to stress the social significance of language in Chapters 9 and 10? Wasn't I implicitly acknowledging that the Fundamental Paradox is irreconcilable? Well, I don't think so, though unlike the Spell itself, it's a tough nut to break. We'll try in this final chapter to see how brain, mind and culture are all equally implicated in the workings of human language, and indeed, that they are essentially just different views of the same human landscape.

I think it's time now to take a look at what neurolinguists *have* been able to reveal about language biology, for although the details may be sketchy still, the overall picture is quite astounding, and will help us tackle some of the thorny issues which lie ahead.

Language in the brain and mind

The human brain is the crowning glory of biological evolution. This is not just anthropocentric smugness: the organ on top of every human body, protected by its cranial armour, is the most complicated chunk of matter in the known universe. Together with its vassal nerves in the peripheral system (which reaches around the whole body, so we can wiggle our toes when we want to), the system contains ten to twelve billion **neurons**. Neurons transmit electro-chemical impulses to other neurons, through synaptic connections, and so as we engage in mental activity (all the time, even as we sleep), different patterns of neurons are getting 'activated'. One pattern of neuronal activity will correspond to the process of thinking about wiggling one's toes. Other neurons will be activated when we form a desire or intention to wiggle them. Another pattern will correspond to the motor command which actually makes the toe muscles contract. And yet another will correspond to the activation of the word *toe* if we want to tell someone what we're doing ('Look! I'm wiggling my *toes*!').

The neural circuitry controlling language and other higher order thought processes involved in perception, coordination and motor control, is mostly spread across the **cerebral cortex** (the 'grey matter'), a thin layer of tissue (around half a centimetre deep) which covers the convoluted surface of the brain's two hemispheres. The system is colossally dense. A single neuron can influence the activation of up to 4,000 others, and many millions of neurons may be activated simultaneously. If you think about it, this mammoth complexity shouldn't be surprising, since everything we know and experience, desire and fear, say and do, is somehow built out of patterns of neuronal activation. Neurons are the ultimate building blocks of our perception of reality, our self-knowledge, our consciousness and awareness of the world around us, our intentions and actions, our beliefs and dreams. Crucially also for an understanding of human language, they are the material substrate underlying the construction and perpetuation of cultures, ways of life, and social networks.

Everything from architectural styles and economic systems, to religious beliefs and fear of 'the other', are the product of individual brain states, which also serve to form and encode our impressions of the brain states of others around us.

It's extremely difficult to get one's mind around this (remember, we're 'designed' not to have conscious access to the machinery which runs us). See if the following analogy helps. Imagine a black and white photo on a low-resolution computer monitor. If you look very closely at one portion of the image (or use the zoom-in tool), you'll lose sight of the entire picture and see, instead, patterns of illuminated points called pixels (users of an old drawing application called Superpaint will be very familiar with this close-up view). Neurons are like pixels: taken individually they are simple, meaningless units, that can be 'on' or 'off' (black or white), or can be activated to a greater or lesser extent (different shades of grey). But in combination with many others, viewed from afar, they can reveal a complex, meaningful pattern.

This analogy should help to clarify the relationship between neurolinguistics and psycholinguistics, between 'language in the brain' and 'language in the mind'. The essential difference between brain and mind is one of perspective. Here's another analogy: the White House in Washington D.C. can be seen as a physical structure, made up of blocks of limestone, cement, wood, glass and gallons of white paint. But this perspective doesn't let us see its importance as the US president's residence and the seat of the federal government. At this level of abstraction it even lends its name to the government itself, as when we're told, for example, that the White House has (or hasn't yet) announced a new Middle East peace initiative. 'Mind', therefore, is 'brain' viewed from a distance, bringing into focus its higher-order design and function, rather than the bricks and mortar of its physical substance and operation.

Let me indulge in one more metaphor to convince you that the cognitive emphasis of this book is more fruitful than a neural view, given our objective of reaching a fuller understanding of human language and the spell it casts over us. My laptop computer is built out of plastic, metal, silicon and other physical materials. I have no idea how, when supplied with electrical current, its physical properties interact to allow me to create documents, surf the Internet and upload photos from my camera. If something goes wrong, I know I can't open it up and fix the problem. I take it to a qualified technician, who has been trained using materials and techniques developed by an applied scientist. In turn, the applied scientist, who has a hand in the design of the machine in the first place, ultimately depends on computer scientists in the universities and corporations for the fundamental knowledge required to build it. Analogously, for language it is the brain which constitutes our linguistic hardware, and if we experience some linguistic problem, like the need to learn a foreign language or translate a text, we go to a 'language technician': a language teacher or translator. If we're lucky, our technician has been trained in applied linguistics, itself informed by linguistic science and other disciplines. But unless the problem is specifically neurological, like aphasia suffered as the result of a stroke, we don't need to consult a neurolinguist. As this book has shown, it's the language *software* that we must attempt to understand in order to break the Language Spell.

Language hardware

But even though we can generally ignore the physical properties of language, we shouldn't do so completely, for the same reason we need to know that *someone* cares how computer software is built out of material substances. Like the ghost in the machine, Microsoft Word *is* resident in my laptop. The scientists know that it is actually embodied in a vast series of electronic microswitches that can be 'on' or 'off'. (The status of these switches is represented by the symbols '1' and '0' in patterns of binary code.) Similarly, although no exercise in brain dissection, microscopy or magnetic imaging will reveal syntax, phonemes or the lexicon, they *are* there, built out of circuits containing neurons in various combinations of connectivity and levels of activation. Unlike computer scientists, though, the neurolinguists didn't design the circuitry, and are only slowly beginning to understand how it might function and where in the physical brain it might be located.

One way we know that language is in the brain at all, rather than in the vocal tract or in books, is because we can observe how brain damage can cause people to speak ungrammatically, to have problems coordinating their speech, and to forget what things are called. Such language deficits are called **aphasias**, and affect millions of human beings. Aphasia can be caused by injuries to the head, strokes, dementias like Alzheimer's and perhaps even by genetic inheritance. Often, people with aphasia are otherwise perfectly healthy, with unimpaired intellect and cognitive functioning. This fact helps us to appreciate not only that language is biological, but also that it has a separate biological existence from other mental faculties: that the box labelled 'Linguistic input/output system' in the egg recognition diagram from Chapter 3 corresponds to specific portions of our neural spaghetti. Given the vast complexity of the neural network, though, the bits of brain involved in language will not necessarily be bundled up in neat physical locations in the brain – they're more likely to be spread messily over different regions, from the cortex to the basal ganglia deep within, like the tangle of cables, hubs and transformers behind your average desktop computer and its peripheral devices.

It was through cases of aphasia that neurosurgeons first established where language mechanisms are concentrated in the brain. In the early 1870s, Paul Broca identified an area of the left cerebral hemisphere involved in handling outgoing speech, and a few years later Karl Wernicke pinpointed another nearby which appeared to be central to speech comprehension. These regions of the cortex, now known as **Broca's** and **Wernicke's areas**, are located on either side of the Sylvian Fissure, a deep crevice in each hemisphere's surface which separates the frontal lobe from the temporal lobe (roughly parallel to imaginary lines running from each temple back up above the ear).

In something like 98 per cent of the population, language is concentrated in the left hemisphere, which specializes in temporal and spatial sequencing and analytic processes. The right hemisphere deals with more holistic processes, such as navigation, music and face recognition. Oddly, the left hemisphere controls the right side of the body, and the right hemisphere controls the left side. Left-handers, some 10 per cent of the population, are right-hemisphere dominant for many tasks, but around 70 per cent of them still have language in the left hemisphere. Furthermore, 70 per cent of injuries to the left hemisphere result in language deficits, compared with only 1 per cent of injuries to the right one. Broca first showed that lesions in the area named after him, close to the motor cortex controlling body movement, typically lead to problems related to language production. The speech of Broca's aphasics is slow and pronunciation is slurred. Sentences, uttered in a monotone, are short and syntactically simple, with few function words. In comprehension, though, they tend not to have problems. Conversely, Wernicke found that damage to the area named after him regularly led to problems in language comprehension, coupled with fluent, grammatically complex, but often vague and nonsensical production.

Studies of these aphasic syndromes have provided dramatic, but heart-rending, evidence that the physical localization of our declarative and procedural knowledge of language is primarily the **perisylvian region** (around the Sylvian Fissure). Broca's and Wernicke's aphasias, for example, suggest that different portions of the brain's language circuitry are involved in comprehension and production (the input and output arrows in the egg diagram). In the last few decades, new technologies using radio and gamma waves have been developed, allowing neurolinguists to measure the flow of blood to Broca's and Wernicke's areas in normal brains. The speed at which blood is pumped to a brain area reflects the degree of activation of the neurons there, since neurons are fuelled by oxygen carried in the blood cells. Techniques like these have shown enhanced neural activity in the areas affected in aphasia during language tasks like reading aloud or naming pictures. Taken together, the evidence from aphasia studies and brain imaging are leading to the development of detailed maps of the brain's linguistic terrain. Figure 1 shows the main highlights.

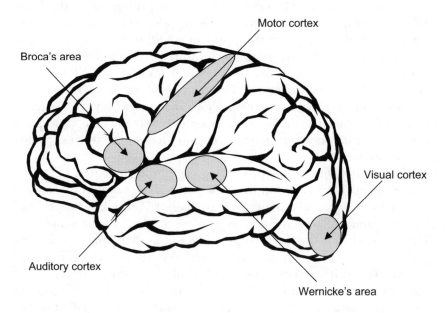

Figure 1 Language and related areas in the left cerebral hemisphere (side view with the front of the head on the left)

In addition to Broca's and Wernicke's areas around the Sylvian Fissure, we use the neural circuitry of the **auditory cortex** to process incoming sound, so when it's speech we're hearing, we can subsequently recover its phonological structure. The **visual cortex**, at the back of the brain in the occipital lobes of each hemisphere, is where images from the retina get processed, and it is on the basis of initial neural activity here that we can recover orthographical or manual structure from incoming light patterns that correspond to writing and sign. In production, the language areas need to activate neurons in the **motor cortex**, on the top of the brain, to tell the vocal tract and hands which muscles to contract and in which order to do so, allowing us to turn strings of phonemes, graphemes or 'signemes' into speech, writing or sign.

The thorny question of where in the brain we store conceptual structure, where our episodic, social and encyclopaedic memories are encoded, and where we formulate 'messages' and recover meanings and intentions from incoming language, is still unresolved. The cognitive scientist Lorraine Tyler tells me that the current evidence from damaged and normal brains is suggesting that it's distributed across various sites, predominantly in the left hemisphere. An explanation of language representation and processing in the brain will be incomplete until we have a better idea about this end of the equation. And yet to crack this problem would be to bring us close to penetrating the greatest mysteries of humankind: the biology of 'the soul', of the seat of consciousness, the human 'essence'. (We'll not try to grapple with the neurology of the meaning of life here. Instead, I'll continue fudging with the metaphorical terminology of cognitive psychology, speaking loosely of 'conceptual systems' and 'conceptual structure', and drawing another cop-out diagram featuring clouds, boxes and arrows.)

Significantly, but not surprisingly given our argument in this book, sign language is processed in the same parts of the brain as spoken and written language, and a signer with Broca's or Wernicke's aphasia will lose the same kinds of abilities as hearing aphasics of the same type. This suggests that the essential properties of human language are not tied to the vocal tract, i.e. to speech, but to the 'computational' machinery which takes some subset of conceptual structure (a 'meaning' or 'message') and turns it into a format which can be output via motor activity (be it the vocal tract or the hands). The fact that sign language develops in infants, and breaks down in aphasia, in essentially the same order and at the same rhythm as hearers' languages, supports this 'modality-neutral' view of human language.

We can now fill in some detail on the abstract flowchart I used in Chapter 1 to depict the claim that language exists separately from the mental representations of the meanings and physical expressions it mediates. Figure 2 shows the processes of language comprehension and production once more, but now referring to physical components of the human body, in the form of dedicated neural circuitry. (Again I should stress that the brain regions mentioned in each box indicate only the principal ones involved, not all.)

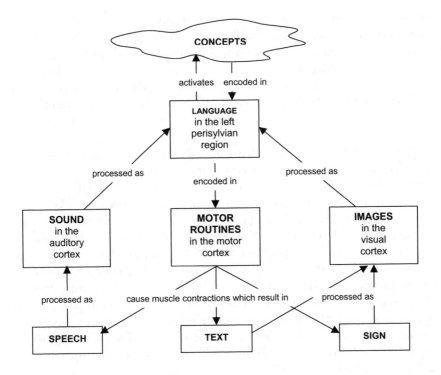

Figure 2 Language processing in the brain

The next question is: how do the neural circuits for language get there? Is the brain at birth like a basic computer platform, onto which we have to install software downloaded from the Internet or bought on CD-ROM? In other words, is the mind-brain a blank slate, a new empty building, a jug waiting to be filled? Or does the human computer come with some of the software already installed, with settings ready to be configured on the basis of the input it processes once it's switched on? If the latter, then how did this software come to exist, in the absence of a divine computer programmer or visitors from a technologically superior planet?

Language evolution

We don't yet have complete answers to these questions, but the available evidence strongly suggests that the child's brain is already 'language ready' at birth, at least to some extent. The relevant neural circuitry corresponding to the adult system is therefore the joint product of information encoded in the genes and information from the environment processed by the sensory input systems: neither nature nor nurture alone. Debate still rages about whether the relevant genetic information is specific to language, or is shared with other cognitive or social abilities 'prewired' in human DNA. But few scientists now believe, as the behaviourists did, that a newborn's mind is a completely blank slate onto which the individual's identity is uniquely written by external forces in the social and physical environment.

Let's start by considering learning, the process through which we acquire new brain states – new configurations of neural circuitry which represent knowledge, abilities, beliefs, etc. Learning is itself a complex cognitive ability, with its own structures and processes. The route between the outside world and our inner conceptual systems isn't some superhighway down which 'information' flows unimpeded until it reaches the epistemic parking lot of the mind. For a start, the 'information' out there in the world is not neatly packaged into byte-sized bundles, ready to be harvested by our senses and merely delivered into mental storage. The world we experience is jam-packed with data, most of it irrelevant to our current concerns at any given moment. It must be itemized and prioritized, and a lot of it must be ignored – otherwise, our minds would implode or seize up with the effort of dealing with it all.

Take vision. Just look up from this page for a moment and take in the scene around you. How many separate objects can you see? How many edges does each one have? How many different colours can you distinguish? How many of the objects are partly occluded by others? Despite the benefit of years of life experience, socialization and schooling, I guarantee you won't come up with hard numbers, even if you happen to be in the lounge of a brutally minimalist apartment. All visual scenes are extraordinarily complex when you take a good look at them – especially if you're asked to make an inventory of what you see. And this futile thought experiment is based on *one* scene which may already have changed dramatically, if you're reading this in a Starbuck's or on the bus, say. If as a baby you had to 'learn' *every* possible bit of information from *every* visual scene spread out in front of you, you'd be driven bonkers within ten minutes of first opening your eyes. ... And then of course there are sounds, smells, textures, temperatures and tastes. All this is potential 'information', a permanent sensory tsunami relentlessly crashing over our minds, flooding our neural networks over and over again during every waking moment.

'Learning' is patently not the same as receiving information. It is both more, and less. *Less*, in the sense that we sift the information, filtering out what we consider irrelevant or already learnt; and *more*, in the sense that we also *interpret* and *connect*, finding out what things are for, how they work, and how they relate to other things. Further, vast amounts of what we come to know are not there in the physical environment to begin with: they are deduced, inferred, imagined, intuited, hypothesized ... and may not even be true. A blank mind, suddenly awash with swirling data from the senses, wouldn't be able to learn at all. Learning can't explain how children come to know things unless *it itself* is explained. So how does the newborn child learn how to learn? The only reasonable answer to this chicken-and-egg quandary is to assume that children are born with some mental apparatus already in place in the brain, giving them a sneak preview of the kinds of data out there that could be significant, and laying down some of the basic neural circuitry for dealing with them. In other words, children are born *already knowing how to learn*.

If this is so, then the design of the brain circuits involved in the first learning experiences must be pre-specified in the chromosomes, along with instructions for the development of all the other bits and pieces that make up a human being, from the circulatory, lymphatic and digestive systems, to the ears, nose and toes. A further question, though, is whether the relevant genes lead to the development of a single all-purpose learning device, like a Swiss army knife, used for everything from grasping objects to grasping ideas, or whether it develops a suite of dedicated tools and, crucially, whether a language acquisition device or Universal Grammar is one of them. The data from aphasics and the arguments from child language acquisition discussed in Chapter 8 suggest the latter. More on this anon.

The genetic inheritance

Clearly, some parts of the human body, in the brain and vocal tract, are particularly well adapted for language use, and we inherit them from our parents. This means that they evolved in the species, typically because they helped to solve some adaptive problem that our ancestors faced in the past. Many complex properties of living things, like the eye of a cat or the wings of a bird, are so spectacularly good at what they do that one is tempted to think they've been designed by cosmic engineers. But the reality, though no less miraculous, need not appeal to any external agency: biological attributes like these are evolutionary solutions to adaptive problems, and they arise through the process of natural selection. We inherit from our parents a suite of genes, molecules which regulate our development from fertilized ovum to adult organism. The genes are the chemical agents responsible for perpetuating a species, building new organisms out of the copies of parental DNA. But the copying fidelity is not perfect, and the existence of genetic variation gives rise to minor differences between parents and offspring in each generation. If this genetic variation positively affects reproduction rates – perhaps by increasing the likelihood that the organism (or more of its sibling group) will survive until reproductive age – then the adaptive trait will spread in the species, as those individuals who have it produce more offspring, and those that don't gradually die out.

This process, mapped out in large part by Charles Darwin a century and a half ago, will be familiar to most readers, in the context of our own species' past, and also perhaps as an explanation for 'exotic' animal attributes like peacock tails, bat wings, and elephant trunks. (I assume that if you have read this far you probably don't believe in the creationist myths of Christianity and other religions.) Fewer readers, however, may be familiar with the idea that language and other mental-social abilities may have evolved via the same genetic mechanisms that have led to the *physical* shape and functioning of contemporary animals and our component parts. The idea (studied by **evolutionary psychology**) may be unfamiliar, but it shouldn't appear shocking in any way: the brain is a physical organ too, and cognitive capacities and processes (together with emotional moods and responses, and other mental functions) are ultimately embedded and played out in the neuroanatomical structures of the brain. Behaviour evolves, because it's caused by minds in interaction with the environment, and *minds* evolve, because, as we've seen, they're the same thing as brains. And the brain is the seat of language.

Since our contemporary brains and fundamental aspects of our behaviour must have evolved from more ancient brains and behaviours, we should be able to find homologues of them in related species. The human brain is larger and more complex than that of our closest relative, the chimpanzee, and although it does lots of fancy things a chimp brain can't (like develop a moral code or argue about football), both have evolved from the brains of a common chimp-human ancestor, between six and twelve million years ago. The possibility that other animals 'have language' has always intrigued us, leading both to folk belief about talking to beasts, and to scientific data on birdsong, bee dances and, above all, ape language. There's a good deal of controversy in this area, both inside and outside academia, which (luckily in my view) we don't have space to get into here.

Nevertheless, I imagine everyone will agree that *human* language occurs naturally only in human beings.

This is surely hardly surprising. No-one would deny that other animals have communicative abilities, but it may not be very useful or worthwhile to use *our* species' language faculty as the measuring stick. Although there is certainly cross-species communication, no pet-owner can honestly claim to have had a conversation with the family dog or parrot, like Vicente Fox did with Fidel Castro. No ethologist or naturalist has ever observed nonhumans using systematic negation rules, like Speedy, or function words, like the McVeigh case prosecutor. Let me flaunt some of the particularities of our own communication system in the following, very human, interrogative structures: why should we expect other species to have a complex representational, expressive and interpretive ability characterized by phonological, morphological and syntactic combinatoriality featuring hierarchical structure, recursive potential and semantic compositionality, and why imagine they might need a massive lexical network and the capacity to express and interpret intricate social meanings and an infinite range of interconnected propositions? It's a very anthropocentric view.

Human mind-brains, although built from the same ancestral template, are different from chimp mind-brains, both quantitatively and qualitatively. They are 'better' at some things (like language) and 'worse' at others (like the coordination of tree-gymnastics). They have evolved to perform specific functions within our evolutionary niche, not just to provide 'general intelligence' or 'memory' which adapts to our experiences after each of us is born. The human eye and the eyes of other primates are structurally not that different, but a generic primate eye plugged in to a neural blancmange of 'general intelligence' will not yield our species' characteristic visual perception traits and abilities. The brain of a newborn child or chimp is not like the hollow shell of a new building, with empty rooms awaiting plumbing and power, furniture and fittings. Instead, it is already cabled for electricity and hooked up to the Internet, with some spaces pre-assigned for cleaning staff, security and management, and others for offices, cinemas and shops. It's just waiting for the interior decorators, and for the staff and the public to come in and make it their own.

Language sources

The previous section has argued that mental functions evolve, and that language is part of evolution's legacy to contemporary human minds.

But minds on their own can't speak or hear phoneme strings. To operate in the non-telepathic real world, language-capable brains with enhanced Broca's and Wernicke's areas need to be attached to a delivery system (for humans, the motor system coupled with a vocal tract) and to detection and decoding equipment (the auditory system). They also need to have something to say (i.e. creative conceptual systems). So, given that complex adaptive traits don't arise in a vacuum, we may attempt to identify in these older, related systems some possible sources for language in our evolutionary past, sources which may have led to the ultimate specialization of neural mechanisms for language learning and language use. Further, given that half of the evolutionary equation is provided by the *environment*, which determines the biological fitness of random copying mutations, we must look also at the ecological niches into which our forebears strayed. A number of exciting new possibilities have been proposed by language scholars in the past couple of decades, and although each is pitted against the others in scientific journals, I think we can recover from them a plausible scenario. I paint it in the following pages in very broad strokes, amalgamating some of current researchers' most compelling insights rather than representing any single one of them faithfully.

Perhaps first came something to talk about. Around four million years ago, our ancestors began to walk on two legs instead of four, thus freeing up hands for tool design and use a couple of million years later. Their bipedal existence also led to the formation of collaborative groups on the savannahs, replacing their more self-reliant foraging existences in the trees. While this was going on, they would also inevitably be exploiting (recent) increases in brain size to develop richer conceptual systems. As briefly mentioned in Chapter 1, these early people, ranging across broader tracts of land which lay way beyond their immediate sensory experience, would need to keep track of their own customary routes and terrains, of the movement patterns of animals they were hunting or being hunted by, and the best places for shelter and water in different seasons of the year. This means storing mental maps and cognitive logbooks.

Those individuals who kept slightly better records and accessed them a little bit faster, would be biologically fitter than their peers, and so might leave more offspring, better prepared to withstand the ravages of the new bipedal environment. These more adapted members of the species would gradually permeate the population, filling it with more skilled mental modellers, rememberers, predictors and planners. Similarly, those generations of individuals who developed an adaptive trait which resulted in the fashioning of more sophisticated tools (for example, close-range visual acuity, a more precisely controlled prehensile grip, or better mental images of the outcomes of manual motor routines), would participate in the same cognitive boom, filling out their available neural circuitry with more and more dedicated mental applications. Such individuals would thus develop knowledge: concepts that they were aware of knowing, and would come to want to share. Language evolution, then, would require the conceptual system to get hooked up to a symbolic system capable of bridging the gap of physical space between individuals.

Enhanced motor programming ability would clearly affect the delivery end of the language chain, bringing more complex sequencing routines to gesture and sound and so laying the basic brain cabling for the amodal language faculty which allows the deaf to acquire a natural language too. But speech became privileged, as a medium which may be broadcast at 360°, can be transmitted in the dark or from behind obstacles like trees, and which frees the hands up for other purposes. So our ancestors were soon also expanding their proto-phoneme inventory, so that what they had to say could be matched by ways to say it. Before standing upright, early hominids would be using vocal calls for some basic communication tasks, just as chimps do. As a result of their novel upright posture, the shape of their vocal tracts was reconfigured, and this may have led to a more sophisticated resonating chamber, allowing for the development of a broader repertoire of vocalizations based on the three universal point vowels (briefly mentioned in Chapter 9) and an embryonic syllable structure. Philip Lieberman has argued strongly for the central role of speech in language evolution, demonstrating how apes and Neanderthals alike lack the capacity to produce the expressive range of syllables that *Homo sapiens* build words out of.

We have very little idea of how or when the two systems of conceptual meaning and phonological structure got hooked up in the systematic ways which underlie modern human language, but along the way, the system must have gone through a phase in which it was short on grammar but long on random word-chaining. As Derek Bickerton has observed, we glimpse a similar sort of 'proto-language', as he calls it, in pidgins, human infants under two and the performance of human-taught apes. Bickerton hypothesizes that this precursor of UG lacked some of the essential features of modern grammar, such as complex verbal frames, grammatical items expressed through function words or inflectional morphology, and recursive rule application. But once this lexically-based proto-language was forged, complex syntax would be the inevitable next-generation software development. Before syntax, human language was just 'bigger' animal language, a souped-up primate call system, limited by the 'naming' mentality of our Adamic Conventioneers' counterparts in real prehistory.

As we saw in Chapter 7, words strung together like beads on a string have limited expressive potential. The power of contemporary human language comes from its hierarchical structure, characterized by X-bar syntax and the rich argument structure of verbs. These innovations allowed densely hierarchical thought to be output in serial strings of phonemes, by weaving it into syntactic trees corresponding to a predictable compositional semantics. Now, hierarchical structure is observable also in the syllable (at the sound end of the language equation) and in conceptual structure (at the meaning end). Which might have been the source for the new syntax? Andrew Carstairs-McCarthy has argued that the X-bar template of UG derives from the kinds of hierarchical syllable structure we saw briefly at the beginning of Chapter 7. Others, like Ray Jackendoff, argue that it was Conceptual Structure, touched on at the end of the same chapter, that spread over into language and gave it new recursive ingenuity.

Whatever the order of events and the relative contributions from each potential source, the selection for a modern Universal Grammar would then trigger a spiral of mutually reinforcing expansion. Your great-to-the-n^{th}-power grandmother's new concepts and ideas would need new expressive power to be shared with others, and the new ideas of others could in turn only enrich her conceptual systems if she had the necessary linguistic biotechnology to decode the language structures which externalized them. The current state of the spiral is a massively powerful language system linking a phenomenal conceptual database and sociocognitive calculator at one end, with a spectacular pair of input-output devices at the other. Some, like Steven Pinker, argue that the language system, UG, may have been directly selected for and coded in the genes (including maybe FOXP2, a gene associated with inherited grammar deficits in a family studied by Myra Gopnik). Others, like Philip Lieberman and Noam Chomsky himself, believe that the evidence points to language being an emergent property of the mind-brain, riding piggy-back on other evolutionary processes. Alas, we're still at the level of informed speculation, and it may well be that we'll be kept in the dark for some time to come. But whatever the ultimate sources and current genetic specificity of language, it's a hell of a show!

Language, biology and culture

We are now getting closer to reconciling the Fundamental Paradox. Language is clearly a biological entity. Just like the physical bits and pieces of a human being, it evolves gradually in the species, develops on the basis of interaction with the environment during infancy into an adult form, and breaks down as a result of damage or old age. But unlike the tongue or toes, language couldn't evolve or grow at all without engaging with its counterparts inside the brains of other individual members of the species – that is, without having other people to talk to. The whole reason for language being language and not just cranially imprisoned conceptual structure is that human beings live in social groups, held together by the nebulous but potent forces of culture. At the same time as our ancestors began to run around, think a lot, and design axes, they were elaborating more culturally sophisticated social groups and networks, providing a larger number of potential interlocutors.

Culture shares with language three fundamental properties:

- It is extraordinarily complex.
- It has no objective existence outside of individual human brains.
- It doesn't get invented anew by each newborn child.

Its complexity, coupled with the rapidity with which it's acquired by children, suggests that culture too must be the product of biological evolution. This doesn't mean, of course, that specific cultural beliefs and practices, like those of contemporary Mexico or Japan, are inherited through the genes. A Mexican-born child whisked away in early infancy to Japan will acquire not only the Japanese language, but also Japanese culture; any vestige of Mexican heritage, linguistic or cultural, will immediately evaporate. It is as though we have a kind of 'Universal Culture', a genetically determined cultural capacity which, like UG for language, provides a blueprint for cultural learning. Just like language, cultures are perceived as monolithic entities by laypeople. But in fact they have runny borders and betray shared elements throughout time and space: there is no single Mexican or Japanese culture, just as there is no single Spanish or Japanese language. This is because both language and culture depend on local input interacting with a common brain plan.

Language and culture are inextricably linked, not only conceptually but also causally. The human cultural capacity depends on minds which can boast at least three fundamental psychological capacities:

(a) a language faculty; (b) learning mechanisms; and (c) theory of mind. Theory of mind, our ability to see beyond external behaviour to inner intention, was last encountered in Chapter 4 as one of the major prerequisites for language acquisition in children. It was surely the development of a more sophisticated theory of mind which first allowed our ancestors to suspect that their peers may have something interesting and useful to share with them. Through theory of mind, our remote ancestors apprehended that others possessed thoughts and exhibited behaviours which were similar to, but independent of, their own. They would then be ready to develop patterns of behaviour and belief which might become hard-wired in the species ('Universal Culture'), but leaving a lot of room for local variation ('I-culture' and 'E-culture') too.

Presumably, the cultural capacity arose originally because it was adaptive. Individuals would observe specific behaviours at work in others around them, and, if they appeared useful, would learn them. They would have to do this through imitation, not only of the other's external behaviour, but also the inferred *motivations* and *intentions* which their theory of mind attributed to them. Ultimately, we have this capacity to acquire a culture because our ancestors found it useful, because cultures tend to encode winning strategies, like personal hygiene and an incest taboo, and because you're safer as a member of a gang than out on your own (especially once the gang has invented trade, money, the rule of law and other recent cultural objects).

This cultural capacity must have played a central role in the development of language. One proposal about language evolution, offered by Robin Dunbar, is that it arose as a function of increased group sizes, as a primitive version of modern-day gossip, substituting the compact grooming circles which gave social coherence to smaller communities. This account, unlikely as it might seem at first glance, has the merit of explicitly recognizing the central *social* purpose of language, a feature often ignored or sidelined in other scientific proposals. The hypothesis also rather nicely captures the essential link between language and group membership. As we saw in Chapter 1 and then in more detail in Chapters 9 and 10, language or dialect are principal ways in which people covertly and unconsciously signal which group they belong to, rather than serving only as a conduit for the transmission of propositional content.

At the same time, though, language is also the most outstanding tool we possess for sharing information, and thus must have contributed mutually to the development of the cultural capacity. By pooling knowledge into a common culture, we increase our biological fitness as a species. In Chapter 4 I spent a few pages explaining a complicated but rather delightful experimental technique called *bilingual translation priming*, which suggested that the learning of abstract word meanings is dependent on language to a greater extent than the learning of concrete word meanings, which can be learnt via direct sensory experience. Since much cultural knowledge is spun from the most abstract of meanings, from entities that have no direct sensory counterparts or physical referents (sanctity, hospitality, honour, debt ...), we can readily appreciate that language will be the primary and essential mechanism for its transmission. Cultures, like E-languages, only exist because we believe in them. They are perpetuated in the species through a combination of innate predisposition (i.e. dedicated neurological structures built according to genetic instructions) and information from the environment, which is largely linguistically modulated.

Living under the Language Spell

In the integrated kind of linguistics I believe language specialists ought to be fashioning, there should be no great conflict between the culture-and-use-oriented (functionalist) and mind-and-representation-oriented (formalist) views of human language described in Chapter 2. It's hard to deny or ignore that culture and language are interwoven, as we've seen throughout the book. According to this kind of linguistics, there is no contradiction between recognizing the central sociocultural reality of language and at the same time claiming that both culture and language are biologically encoded and biologically driven. This is because, ultimately, biology powers minds and minds engineer both culture and language, resulting in seamlessly interwoven linguistic and cultural interaction between individuals. And so it becomes clearer: the Fundamental Paradox is another illusion. Language can be, and must be, simultaneously both biological and sociocultural, because that's its job: to link separate biological organisms through a channel which allows them to share thoughts and feelings, and so build an individual identity that is also integrated into a series of culturally-defined groups.

The result of this remarkable evolutionary process is that, through culture and language, human beings now transmit information from generation to generation in a way that was, before this biological innovation, only possible through the genes. Like language, the genes transmit information from one individual to another. But these individuals must be related, and *uni*directionally at that (parent to offspring, not vice versa). Unlike the genes, modern human language allows infinitely varied kinds of information to be transmitted, between kin and non-kin, and in *any* direction you want. With the advent of writing and subsequent technological breakthroughs, such information may stay around for millennia, and be accessed from anywhere in the world. In this way, linguistically-mediated culture beats the genetic code at its own game.

The story that has been slowly emerging in these pages is that we can reveal what's behind the Language Spell if we take a close look at the nature of the biological language faculty and how it is used by individuals in society. This has meant covering some apparently very disparate topics in linguistics and trying to see how they all fit together into one coherent tale. I have been claiming throughout that the Spell has kept us blinded to the unitary and unifying nature of language, by closing off from view its inner workings, and throwing into relief only its sociocultural profile. Now I think we can appreciate that it's not a question of 'either/or' (psychological versus social, nature versus nurture, internal versus external), but rather *always both simultaneously*, and so the magic finally becomes more transparent – more Wizard of Oz than Gandalf the Grey.

But will an understanding of the Language Spell necessarily help us become more open-minded, caring, decent folk? Many sceptics would say not. Let's say the spell is broken, the gates to the Mines of Moria swing open, and the Fellowship passes through ... but to what? The Mines are a gloomy place, and Gandalf's spell-breaking performance brings little illumination. Breaking the Language Spell leaves us in a similar predicament. We'll take up the evolutionary telescope again to see why. Richard Dawkins has argued that the most accurate way to think about evolution is not at the level of the organism, but rather of the individual gene. Genes, according to him, are the ultimate 'replicators', inhabiting body after body through the millennia, like the supernatural villains of Gothic horror stories. Through reproduction, genes from the father and the mother get mixed together, and a unique new individual is created. But all his or her genes came from one parent or the other (every cell in your body contains an almost exact copy of half your Mum's chromosomes and half your Dad's, 23 from each). In this decidedly unsexy view, the bodies of organisms just provide temporary housing for genes on their eternal self-preservation trip. This is the essential insight of Dawkins' 'selfish gene' theory.

Dawkins' concept of the 'selfish gene' helps to explain why many species live in mutually supportive family groups. Around half of your genes will be found in your siblings, and more or less an eighth in your first cousins. Since you share genes, helping your brother or cousin to survive helps copies of *your* DNA to survive. According to this story, it is adaptive for an individual to look out for itself *and* its kin, and groups will initially be kin-based. Human communities, however, have increased way beyond the confines of kinship relations, as Robin Dunbar and others have pointed out. So if selfish genes are running the show, why did our ancestors start to identify with people who didn't necessarily share any of their genes, defining loyalties and mutual support networks at the level of culture, rather than just kin?

It's not just a matter of strength in numbers, though clearly that's part of it. Human beings *do* have a natural tendency to help one another, even though aggression and war are also part of our nature. The evolution of our capacity to be nice to non-kin, known as **reciprocal altruism** (or less fancily, 'mutual back-scratching'), has been studied in depth by evolutionary psychologists, game theorists and others. Through computer modelling and psychological experimentation, their studies have shown that cooperation is a better strategy for long-term individual gain than cheating or greed. Reciprocity is common too in other species, from mice to fish, and the research suggests that this is yet another product of natural selection.

As human groups grew in size, advancing beyond the web of genetic ties, language must have begun to serve as a major identifier of who is in the group and who represents 'the other'; who is your friend and who is your enemy; who will be likely to cooperate and who will be more liable to cheat or betray you. As we've seen in previous chapters, groups with distinct phonologies, lexicons and grammars arise because speakers of the same original language reach some critical mass and then divide. One band goes to live over on the other side of the hill, another along the river closer to the sea, and a third across the mountain range. If they don't stay in contact, dialects may then become separate E-languages, and at the same time cultural practices and beliefs will diverge even further. One in-group becomes a network of in- and out-groups. This must be, on a much larger time-scale, how *Homo sapiens* originally spread out from southern Africa around 100,000 years ago, carrying to all contemporary brains not only speech and UG, but also the potential for endlessly different E-languages serving endlessly different cultural arrangements.

And this is where we are now: the way people speak not only binds us together in the reciprocal fiction of E-language, but also erects barriers that keep us apart, especially once different ways of speaking are associated with different cultural groups, be they classes, tribes, castes or nations. Accents, dialects and languages, like the round-helmeted heads of the Roundheads or the red coats of the Redcoats, serve to distinguish friend from foe, in-group from out-group. Chapters 1, 9, and 10 provided numerous examples. As I've tried to show, the language prejudices highlighted there are rooted in the evolutionary spell of language, which cloaks the mental machinery of grammar so it can optimally do its job. But ironically, by keeping itself under wraps so well, language got hijacked by our cultural capacity to construct group identity and so help ensure mutual in-group support. The problem for us now is that this general niceness is based on reciprocal altruism at the level of communities, rather than the whole species. We tend to be nice to people who are like us, and intolerant and suspicious of those who are not. People 'like us' have to be superficially similar: same skin and eye colour; same shape of eyes, nose and lips; same clothes and body ornaments; same accent and same language . . . being human is no longer enough.

Hence the mismatch between our linguistic knowledge (the internal machinery of grammar) and our linguistic folk beliefs, between the egalitarian potential of Universal Grammar and the collective shame of monolingual imperialism and linguistic exclusionism. If we tacitly believe, as the Spell causes us to do, that our dialect or language defines our world, that concepts and the words we use to refer to them are indistinguishable, that thought is language, and that some kinds of language are better than others, then inequality between linguistically different groups is the inevitable and natural result. We believe these things because the effects of the Language Spell sit so well with our culturally-determined 'us-and-them' nature. The Spell appears to be aided and abetted by another, stronger spell: the spell of culture itself.

In the relationship between language and culture, culture is the dominant partner, as we've seen time and again. Language is simply the thread that holds the quilt of culture together. So breaking the Language Spell will not break the 'Culture Spell' it subserves: Gandalf may have got into Moria, but he is defeated by the more ancient spells that are unleashed against him there. In the longer run, our selfish genes, working for their own short-term replication rather than long-term benefits for their carriers, also appear to guarantee that both spells will remain unbroken, since they favour both optimal language design (relative invisibility) and group identity (fortified through reciprocal altruism).

Is, then, a conscious understanding of language worthwhile after all? Should we not accept our biological destiny, reconsign linguistics to the obscure groves of academe, and go about our business as usual?

Emphatically *no*. The view of language and culture presented here clearly entails that we can *change* our destiny and free ourselves from biological determinism. As Dawkins states in his book, *The Selfish Gene*, 'We, alone on earth, can rebel against the tyranny of the selfish replicators.' Through the emergence of cultural, moral and ethical codes, the human species long ago transcended the narrow goal of procreation and perpetuation of the genes. Not completely, of course, because we can't rewire the brains we've inherited; we can only overlay the ancient seams with the more enlightened networks of culturally constructed beliefs. (And, just as obviously, it would be foolish naivety to conceive of culture as uniquely a force of goodness and light: think of slavery, the Nazi gas chambers, female circumcision, apartheid, the Inquisition, ...!) But linguistic interaction, spread ever wider in our recent history through the technologies of writing, telecommunications, trade and travel, can transport the good ideas as well as the bad, and reach an ever greater number of individuals from vastly different cultural groups.

In essence, what this means is that an understanding of the Language Spell, of the biological realities behind language, gives us a chance to *move on*: to recognize the constraints of our biology and then set them to one side, so we can open our eyes to more of the liberating potential of language. In this way, linguistics can make the Spell yield momentarily, allowing us a brief glimpse of the marvels behind it, but then it will inevitably roll back again, allowing us to continue the pretence that language is telepathy. ... Only now, perhaps, a little more wary of the cultural spell which we *do* have the power to break.

Maybe this is not quite the spectacular revelation you were expecting (in *Lord of the Rings*, Gandalf the Grey rises from the infernal depths to be reborn on the mountain top as Gandalf the White). But the magic of language is commonplace, and linguistics needs no pyrotechnic flashes, bangs or disappearing acts to reveal its secrets. If we can get people to peer behind the Spell for a moment, just long enough to see what's there and reflect on what it implies for their attitudes to, and beliefs about, themselves and others, then surely that's more than enough.

Linguistics in action

In Chapter 1 I made a distinction between three mental domains in which language is implicated:

(a) *Linguistic knowledge*: This is the language faculty itself, stored permanently in long-term memory as grammatical and lexical competence, and deployed in actual events as pragmatically-modulated and socioculturally-mediated performance. This knowledge is of such complexity that theoretical linguists, psycholinguists, sociolinguists and others will have their hands full trying to describe and explain it for many decades to come. Underlying the surface diversity is a common groundplan, the product of evolutionary mechanisms which gave rise to our particular configuration of language, mind and culture. This discovery, given special impulse by Noam Chomsky over the past half century, should make linguists' work easier … and yet it is still very much an up-hill battle, given the power of the Language Spell.

(b) *Linguistic awareness*: This refers to conscious *attention* to our permanent linguistic knowledge and to specific language events. It is exceedingly limited in scope, shallow in analysis and fleeting in duration. Our linguistic awareness has these features because it's in our best interests to concentrate instead on the two domains which language allows us to *bridge*: the inner domain of our thoughts and intentions, and the outer world of social and perceptual experience. We are only really ever aware of the front-end and back-end of the system: the sounds and other physical manifestations that non-telepathic language requires, and the semantics which funnels our thoughts into strings of word forms. A consequence of this is that language, lying in between, seems invisible most of the time, and when visible merges in our consciousness with the domains it is designed to bridge: words are confused with the meanings they label, and speech or spelling are seen as transparent manifestations of our identities.

(c) *Linguistic belief*: This is the result of our limited awareness: a folk system of knowledge which is generally useful on a day-to-day basis, but has some unwelcome consequences. Given that beliefs do not normally arise in a vacuum, but are the complex outcomes of cultural inheritance, experience and personal reflection, and given that the universal nature of language is hidden from view by the Spell, we end up believing things about language which are based more on our cultural capacity and world view than on the underlying facts.

I have argued that through knowledge of the fields of linguistics and applied linguistics we can temporarily, partially, break the power of the Language Spell – in other words, we can set aside for a while our linguistic *beliefs* and increase the boundaries of our *awareness* to reveal in some small degree the splendours of our actual linguistic *knowledge*. The big question, then, is what real service this knowledge could provide in our daily lives: of what practical use is linguistics to the non-linguist? Let me close this book with a few modest proposals.

First, at the level of the individual. We are not slaves to our biology, nor to the supreme achievement of culture to which our biology has led us. We can use the increased awareness of language that linguistics provides to change, or at least moderate, some of our fundamental beliefs. Every time we wince at a foreign or local accent, or criticize a grammatical 'error', we can pause and reconsider: it is not the phonological system underlying the speech we hear that causes our distaste, but rather the associations we make between those speech patterns and our beliefs about the identities of the *users* themselves. Dialect and accent do not reflect, like a mirror, the belief systems, intelligence, attitudes or moral systems of the individuals who use them. It's simply not the case that African American English speakers have illogical minds because they use double negatives, or that Germans are cold and harsh because they use 'guttural' phonemes. Equally, we shouldn't judge groups of speakers because of their levels of literacy or their multilingualism: the few remaining monolingual speakers of Mexico's indigenous languages don't have more primitive minds because the languages they speak might lack a writing system, and Mexican Americans don't have confused or schizophrenic thoughts because they glide from Spanish to English and back again in conversation.

Another way in which linguistic knowledge may allow individuals to combat prejudice and appreciate the equal potential of all speakers and all languages is to reflect on the status of their own languages and how they have been assigned values by self-appointed custodians such as academies, educators, politicians and newspaper pundits. Next time we ask or are asked whether a word exists, we could look to its *use*, not whether that use has been recorded and approved in a dictionary. Next time we bemoan the gradual loss of the apostrophe in English possessives, we might remember that punctuation is a social convention imposed upon the language's written representation, rather than being part of English itself (and we might come to realize that its continued usage will depend on *social consensus*, rather than linguistic logic: remember, Shakespeare didn't need the apostrophe). And next time we compare our own language to others, we could bear in mind that English often looks as exotic and strange to speakers of other languages as theirs might appear to us (indeed, to a speaker of Old English, the version we speak wouldn't look like English any more: it would appear closer to Old French, and our ancestors would probably find modern German or Dutch more familiar).

At the level of social groups, communities and nations, we can jointly use linguistics to reappraise the way we perceive and construct our communal identities, and the way we implement our social and educational policies. A starting point would be to question the notion of 'one nation, one language'. If we believe that all of a nation's citizens have equal rights, and at the same time realize that the languages they know and use are the principal channels through which they can access and exercise these rights, then we may draw the conclusion that the governments which represent us *must* take the appropriate measures to safeguard the rights of our minority language speakers. Also, if we value cultural diversity and the unique richness of different languages as mechanisms of cultural transmission, perpetuation and transformation, then we might consider lending our support to grass-roots movements for language maintenance, or lobbying for effective government action to halt the death of viable tongues. Perhaps we could be more vocal also in questioning our politicians' fondness for yoking the national language with patriotism, so that we might influence their deployment of it as a weapon to control troublesome minorities. At the same time, governments and communities might be better convinced of the need to ensure that all speakers have legitimate access to the written modality, and to the mainstream languages and dialects in which national affairs are conducted. These urgent actions require us to be aware of the support and advice available from applied linguists (in the areas of language policy and planning, second language teaching, bilingual education and literacy), so that these rights transcend declaration-signing ceremonies and actually get implemented on the ground.

As members of unequal communities, global and local, some of us might be provoked by research from linguistics to reflect on the consequences of our language use as an unconscious tool of domination. The languages of the European colonial powers in general, and English in particular, have gradually become the principal channels for the planet's linguistic activity over the last half millennium. Local languages have been replaced to a lesser extent also by Mandarin Chinese, Arabic, Hindi-Urdu, Bengali, Indonesian and other powerful regional tongues in many parts of the globe. Although I've tried to make clear in this book that language hegemony is really cultural hegemony, we cannot deny that the languages of the powerful are amongst the principal instruments through which this power is wittingly or unwittingly exercised. I don't think sociolinguistic engineering will resolve the cultural conflicts of empire to which we are heirs, but I do believe that linguistics can sensitize us to some of the issues, and help us to understand which potential routes to greater understanding may be worth following or not. A useful first step might again be for speakers of dominant languages to recognize the reality that, on a global level, their languages have been effectively decoupled from the notions of state and ethnicity they were originally identified with. English, Spanish, French and the other postcolonial tongues are now forming dynamic elements in the cultural capital of millions of ethnically non-European speakers, whether native speakers or not, from Singapore to Bombay, from Pretoria to Mongolia. This should have profound effects on the ways we approach many different spheres of human activity, from language teaching to publishing, from international relations to global business. It carries with it the potential for both mutual benefit and further inequality.

These are just some of the ways in which linguistics in action can make a difference. And yet the Spell will remain completely unbroken for most until linguists are heard and read more widely. As I suggested in Chapter 2, linguists themselves bear some of the responsibility for their almost complete absence from the newspapers, magazines and TV screens. But the real reason for our shadowy existence is the Spell itself. Because language is so present and yet so invisible in our daily lives, we need a helping hand. The only way this can happen, to my mind, is if education departments and school districts allow us a place in their curriculums. As you've experienced in this book, linguistics touches on human biology, psychology and culture at every turn. It also inevitably teaches aspects of history, computer science, geography, philosophy, anthropology, civics, political science and a wide range of other fields too. Isn't it positively scandalous that our children are being denied this knowledge in the classroom? I invite teachers and educational experts to recommend how this may be achieved, but I believe that a very strong case could be made for offering language and linguistics as a specific course in both secondary school and teacher education curriculums.

I hope this book has shown you that what linguists do is not only fascinating in itself (as well as being rather good fun) ... but moreover that it is absolutely, urgently, *practical*. What human attribute is more essential in our communal lives than our capacity for language, and yet what aspect of our nature and behaviour do most of us know less about? The Language Spell serves us well as a species; but I firmly believe that linguistics can help us live a little better as individuals and members of local and global communities. I hope I've left you at least partly convinced.

More information

 Loraine Obler and Kris Gjerlow (1999) provide a lucid and concise introduction to **language and the brain**, covering neurolinguistic anatomy, organization and, especially, different kinds of language impairment.

Princeton University hosts a great site on **brain and language** at www.molbio.princeton.edu/courses/mb427/2000/projects/0008/brain.html. It has sections on technology, anatomy, impairment and the social impact of **neurolinguistic research**. Nice visuals too.

Websites offering information and practical advice for **aphasics** and their carers include Speakability at www.speakability.org.uk/index.htm in the UK and the National Aphasia Association in the USA at www.aphasia.org.

The authors cited in the sections on **language evolution** vary in their degree of accessibility to the non-expert. Steven Pinker (1994), Derek Bickerton (1990), and Robin Dunbar (1996) are the most readable. Philip Lieberman (1984), Ray Jackendoff (2002, Chapter 8), and Andrew Carstairs-McCarthy (1999) are rather more difficult, especially the last one. (It's worthwhile pointing out that there have been important developments in the thinking of some of these scholars since these works were published, and that the ideas of some are expressed in greater detail in other, more technical, publications. An extensive and up-to-date bibliography is maintained at www.isrl.uiuc.edu/amag/langev by Jun Wang of the University of Illinois at Urbana-Champaign.)

Dorothy Bishop (1997) provides a readable discussion of **Specific Language Impairment**, the study of which has led to claims about a 'grammar gene'.

Steven Pinker (1994) discusses the idea of '**Universal Culture**' in a non-technical way. His 2002 book reproduces a list of 'Human Universals' identified originally by Donald Brown.

Richard Dawkins' *The selfish gene* (1989) is the second edition of his classic 1976 popular science interpretation of Darwinian theory and its application to the biology of culture. A beautifully written work, with a lot of new material in this edition, including responses to his many critics.

 Visit http://www.psych.ucsb.edu/research/cep/primer.html to download '**Evolutionary Psychology**: A Primer', written in 1997 by Leda Cosmides and John Tooby, the leading lights of this new discipline.

Henry Plotkin's 1998 introduction is very readable, as is Pinker (2002), although his ideas may be too tendentious for those that are not already convinced (like me) by his essential arguments.

Hidden away at the bottom of the 'Recent and forthcoming papers' link of Ray Jackendoff's website at http://people.brandeis.edu/ ~jackendo/ is the handout for a talk he gave in 2003 as president of the Linguistic Society of America entitled '**The structure of language: Why it matters to education**'. Worth a look.

Sources

Note: Full references for academic sources are given in the Bibliography.

Preface

xi   The spelling mistake is from *The Herald* (Mexico section), 12 August 2004, p. 8.

xii   The quotations from *The Tempest* are from Act I, Scene II.

1. The Spell

1   The epigraph is from McEwan, Ian (2002), *Atonement*. London: Vintage, p. 37.

6   Pamuk's invocation of colour is from Pamuk, Orhan (2001), *My name is Red*. London: Faber and Faber, p. 225.

8   The definitions are from the *Shorter Oxford English Dictionary*. (1973, 3rd edn). Oxford: Oxford University Press.

12   The Kaqchikel testimony is quoted in Fishman (1997, p. 240).

13   The Sámi testimony is quoted in Marainen (1988, p. 185).

13   The Ainu testimony is quoted in Fishman (1997, p. 183).

13   King Juan Carlos' comments were reported in *La Jornada*, April 2001, p. 56.

16   The article on the Queen's English appeared in the *Guardian*, 13 June 1999.

17   An example of Labov's 1970s work is Labov (1972).

18   The Kinyarwanda reference appeared in *The Economist*, 26 July 2001.

23   The language and philosophy quotations are from Wittgenstein (2002 [1953], p. 41).

24   Language as thought control features in Orwell, George (1949/1990), *Nineteen Eighty-Four*. Harmondsworth: Penguin.

24   The linguistic bigotry quote is from Cameron (1995, p. 12).

25   The Kenyan example is from Ngugi wa T. (1987), *Detained. A writer's prison diary*. London: Heinemann.

2. Linguistics

28   The epigraph is from Haiman (1998, p. 191).
39   Prince Hippolyte appears in Tolstoy, Lev Nikolaevich (1865–77/ 1993), *War and Peace* (trans. L. Maude and A. Maude). Ware: Wordsworth Editors, Book 1, Ch. IV, p. 16.
41   Communicative competence is discussed in Hymes (1972, pp. 269– 93).

3. Names, Words, and Things

49   The epigraph is from *War and Peace*, Book XI, Ch. IX, p. 686.
53   Lok finds metaphor in Golding, William (1955/1997), *The Inheritors*. London: Faber and Faber, p. 194.
54   The abstract words are from Roy, Arundhati (1998), *The God of Small Things*. New York: Harper Perennial, p. 3.
56   The *rings* letter appeared in *Guardian Weekly*, 8 November 1998.
59   The quotation is from Byatt, A. S. (1996), *Still Life*. New York: Simon and Schuster, p. 176.
61   The quotation is from Byatt, A. S. (1996), *Still Life*. New York: Simon and Schuster, p. 187.
62   Charles asks about the 'tender runnel' in Murdoch, Iris (1978/1999), *The Sea, the Sea*. London: Vintage, p. 42.
63   The 'thought in the larynx' idea is from Watson (1913, pp. 158–77).
70   Weinreich's typology is discussed in Weinreich (1953).
75   The COBUILD sample concordance is from www.titania.cobuild. collins.co.uk.
76   The 'word as coin' idea is from Saussure (1986).
82   The quotation is from Eco, Umberto (1988), *Foucault's Pendulum*. London: Vintage, p. 25.

4. Where Words Come From

85   The epigraph is from Hardy, Thomas (1895/1998), *Jude the Obscure*. Harmondsworth: Penguin, pp. 30–31.
90   The word learning problem is discussed in Quine (1960, p. 29).
90   The *indri* example is from the *Shorter Oxford English Dictionary*.
103   The Alfred quotation is from Sweet (2003 [1876]).
103   The Chaucer quotation is from Chaucer (2005).

5. Forming Words

110   The epigraph is from Barnes, Julian (2000), *Love, Etc.* London: Picador, p. 17.
111   The literate tailors appear in Mistry, Rohinton (1995), *A Fine Balance*. London: Faber and Faber, p. 176.
112   The French error is corrected in the *Guardian*, 9 March 2002.

115   The New Zealand spelling reform story is from the *Guardian*, 30 May 2000.

115   The German spelling reform story is from *Guardian Weekly* (originally in the *Washington Post*), 17–23 August 2000, p. 29.

115   The Spanish *h* problem was reported in *El Financiero*, 21 September 1999, p. 62 (my translation).

115   The less reverential wag is 'Nikito Nipon' writing in *La Jornada*, 6 August 2000, pp. 8–9.

122   Clive and Vernon do battle in McEwan, Ian (1999), *Amsterdam*. New York: Anchor Books, p. 161.

6. Morphology

133   The epigraph is from an anonymous email message.

137   The compound spellings are from the *Chambers Compact Dictionary* (2001), Edinburgh: Chambers.

144   The history of *have* is described in Bybee & Pagliuca (1985, pp. 59–83).

146   The history of Spanish future inflections comes from Resnick (1981, p. 100).

149   The quotation is from Aristophanes (1962), *The Clouds*. In *Four Plays by Aristophanes* (trans. W. Arrowsmith). New York: Dutton Signet, p. 73.

7. Syntax

154   The epigraph is from Smith, Zadie (2003), *The Autograph Man*. New York: Random House, p. 318.

155   The Binding Principle is from Chomsky (1981, p. 184).

157   The 'slithy toves' are from Carroll, Lewis (1872/ 2004), *Through the Looking-glass*. London: Puffin.

157   'Colorless green ideas' first appeared in Chomsky (1957, p. 15).

159   Sentence (3) is from Carroll, Jonathan (1993), *After Silence*. New York: Doubleday.

159   Sentence (5) is from Proulx, Annie (1997), *Accordion Crimes*. New York: Simon and Schuster, p. 191.

159   Sentence (6) is from Naipaul, V. S. (1969), *A House for Mr. Biswas*. Harmondsworth: Penguin, p. 486.

169   The 'love you' quote is from Barnes, Julian (2000), *Love, Etc*. London: Picador, p. 158.

173   Mental models are discussed in Johnson-Laird (1983).

8. From DNA to Discourse Community

187   The epigraph is quoted in Trevelyan, G. O. (1876/1978), *Life and Letters of Lord Macaulay*. Oxford: Oxford University Press, Ch. 1.

192   The Jabba the Hut experiments are reported in Crain & Nakamaya (1987, pp. 522–43).

192   The quote from Ralph Fasold is from Fasold (1990, p. vii).
195   The original work on X-bar syntax can be found in Jackendoff (1977).
196   On the head-ordering parameter, see Pinker (1994, pp. 111–12).
197   The creole-UG connection is discussed in Bickerton (1990).
198   Chomsky's notorious statement is from Chomsky (1965, p. 3).
202   The Cooperative Principle is described in Grice (1975, pp. 41–58).
202   The quotation is from Waugh, Evelyn (1945/1980), *Brideshead Revisited*. Harmondsworth: Penguin, p. 23.
203   The racism and the police quotation is from *Guardian Weekly*, 27 January–2 February 2000.
204   The poem is from Ní Dhomhnaill, Nuala (1990), *Pharaoh's Daughter* (trans. Muldoon, P.). Oldcastle, Ireland: The Gallery Press.
206   The Fox-Castro conversation was quoted in *La Jornada*, 23 April 2002, p. 3 (my translation).
207   The politeness research is in Brown and Levinson (1988).

9. Interlinguistic Diversity

211   The epigraph is from Rushdie, Salman (1999), *The Ground Beneath her Feet*. London: Jonathan Cape, p. 7.
212   The French languages story is from *Guardian Weekly* 1–7 July 1999, p. 5.
219   Word order typology is discussed in Greenberg (1966, pp. 73–113).
219   Deeper typological patterns are discussed in Hawkins (1995).
221   Arab women are maligned in Waugh, Evelyn (1931/1985), *Remote People*. London: Penguin, p. 78.
224   The sample of bilingual categories is from Wei (2000).
227   The Pomo testimony is quoted in Hinton (1994, p. 176).
227   Multiple intelligences are discussed in Gardner (1983).
228   The athletic analogy is from Grosjean (1985).
229   Monolingual diglossia is discussed in Ferguson (1959).
229   Bilingual diglossia is discussed in Fishman (1980).
231   Language teachers are maligned in Kureishi, Hanif (2001), *Gabriel's Gift*. New York: Simon and Schuster, p. 168.
232   The quotation is from Hardy, Thomas (1895/1998), *Jude the Obscure*. Harmondsworth: Penguin Books, p. 30.
232   Learner's assumptions are discussed in Ringbom (1987, p. 135).
233   The 'Fundamental Difference Hypothesis' is proposed in Bley-Vroman (1989).
234   Interlanguage is discussed in Selinker (1992).
235   Genie's case is discussed in Curtiss (1977).
236   The quotation is from Byron, Lord George Gordon, (1970 'Don Juan'. In Jump, J. (ed.), *Byron: Complete Poetical Works* (revised edn). Oxford: Oxford University Press, Canto II, CLXIV.

10. Diversity Within

238   The epigraph is from Baldwin, James (1968/1998), *Tell Me How Long the Train's Been Gone*. New York: Vintage International, p. 447.

242   The Lawrence of Arabia story is told in Graves, Robert (1929/1981), *Goodbye to All That*. London: The Folio Society, p. 260.

245   The McVeigh transcripts are from www.courttv.com/archive/casefiles.

253   The dialect study quotations are from Palgrave, F. M. T. (1896/1997), *A list of words and phrases in every-day use by the natives of Hetton-le-Hole in the County of Durham* (reprinted as *Pitmatic talk 100 years ago*). Gateshead: Johnstone-Carr Publications, p. v.

254   Ridley's view of language variation is from Ridley, D. (1997), Forward to Palgrave (1896/1997), p. iii. See previous note.

255   The Barnsley initiative was reported in the *Daily Telegraph*, 3 May 2003.

256   Cosmopolitan and multilingual London is brought to life in Kureishi, Hanif (2001), *Gabriel's Gift*. New York: Simon and Schuster, p. 15.

256   Pi and Richard Parker disagree in Martel, Yann (2003), *Life of Pi*. Edinburgh: Canongate Books, p. 248.

259   The 'great grammar crusade' is evaluated in Cameron (1995, p. 81).

259   The National Curriculum quote is from www.ncaction.org.uk/subjects/english/.

260   The Scottish Parliament quote is from www.scottish.parliament.uk/vli/language/scots/index.htm.

261   The Scottish Education Department quote is from www.ltscotland.org.uk/5to14/guidelines/englishlanguage/index.asp.

263   The text of Stalin's paper 'Marxism and Problems of Linguistics' can be found at www.marxists.org/reference/archive/stalin/works/1950/jun/20.htm.

264   The Russian reaction to the Tatarstan orthographic reform was reported in *Guardian Weekly* (originally in the *Washington Post*), 26 April–2 May 2001, p. 33.

266   The pronominalization strategy is from Levelt (1989), p. xvii.

266   Gary Younge was writing in *Guardian Weekly*, 24 February–1 March 2000.

11. The Spell Unbroken

270   The epigraph is from Tolkien, J. R. R. (1954/1974), *The Lord of the Rings*. London: Allen and Unwin, p. 325.

285   Sources for the work on language evolution are given on p. 298.

286   The 'language gene' is discussed in Pinker (1994, chapters 10 and 11) and Pinker (2002, Ch. 3).

286   The inherited grammar deficit is discussed in Gopnik & Crago (1991).

Bibliography

Aitchison, Jean (1998), *The Articulate Mammal. An Introduction to Psycholinguistics* (4th edn). London: Routledge.

Baker, Colin (2001), *Foundations of Bilingual Education and Bilingualism.* Clevedon, UK: Multilingual Matters.

Baker, Colin and Rhys-Jones, Sylvia (1998), *Encyclopedia of Bilingualism and Bilingual Education.* Clevedon, UK: Multilingual Matters.

Baugh, Albert and Cable, Thomas (2001), *A History of the English Language* (5th edn). Englewood Cliffs, NJ: Prentice Hall.

Bialystok, Ellen and Hakuta, Kenji (1994), *In Other Words. The science and psychology of second-language acquisition.* New York: Basic Books.

Biber, Douglas (1988), *Variation Across Speech and Writing.* Cambridge: Cambridge University Press.

Biber, Douglas, Conrad, Susan and Leech, Geoffrey (2002), *Longman Student Grammar of Spoken and Written English.* London: Longman.

Bickerton, Derek (1990), *Language and Species.* Chicago: Chicago University Press.

Bishop, Dorothy (1997), *Uncommon Understanding.* Hove, UK: Psychology Press.

Bley-Vroman, Robert (1989), What is the logical problem of foreign language learning? In Gass, S.M. & Schachter, J. (eds.), *Linguistic Perspectives on Second Language Acquisition* (pp. 41–68). Cambridge: Cambridge University Press.

Bloom, Paul (2000), *How Children Learn the Meanings of Words.* Cambridge, MA: MIT Press.

Bonvillain, Nancy (2002), *Language, Culture, and Communication: The meaning of messages* (4th edn). Englewood Cliffs, NJ: Prentice Hall.

Brown, Penelope and Levinson, Stephen (1988), *Politeness: Some universals of language usage.* Cambridge: Cambridge University Press.

Bybee, Joan and Pagliuca, William (1985), Cross-linguistic comparison and the development of grammatical meaning. In J. Fisiak (ed.) *Historical Semantics, Historical Word Formation,* pp. 59–83. The Hague: Mouton.

Cameron, Deborah (1995), *Verbal Hygiene.* London: Routledge.

Carstairs-McCarthy, Andrew (1999), *The Origins of Complex Language: An inquiry into the evolutionary beginnings of sentences, syllables, and truth.* Oxford: Oxford University Press.

— (2002), *An Introduction to English Morphology.* Edinburgh: Edinburgh University Press.

Chaika, Elaine (1994), *Language, the Social Mirror* (3rd edn). Boston: Heinle and Heinle.

Chaucer, Geoffrey (2003), *The Canterbury Tales* (translated by Nevill Coghill). Harmondsworth, UK: Penguin.

— (2005), *The Canterbury Tales* (edited by Donald Howard). Harmondsworth, UK: Penguin.

Chomsky, Noam (1957), *Syntactic Structures*. The Hague: Mouton.

— (1965), *Aspects of the Theory of Syntax*. Cambridge, MA: MIT Press.

— (1981), *Lectures on Government and Binding: the Pisa Lectures*. Dordrecht: Foris.

— (1988), *Language and Problems of Knowledge. The Managua Lectures*. Cambridge, MA: MIT Press.

— (2000), *New Horizons in the Study of Language and Mind*. Cambridge: Cambridge University Press.

— (2002), *On Nature and Language*. Cambridge: Cambridge University Press.

Comrie, Bernard (1989), *Language Universals and Linguistic Typology* (2nd edn). Chicago: Chicago University Press.

Cook, Guy (2003), *Applied Linguistics*. Oxford: Oxford University Press.

Crain, Stephen and Nakamaya, Mineharu (1987), 'Structure dependence in grammar formation'. *Language, 63*, 3, 522–43.

Crain, Stephen and Lillo-Martin, Diane (1999), *An Introduction to Linguistic Theory and Language Acquisition*. Oxford: Blackwell.

Curtiss, Susan (1977), *Genie: A linguistic study of a modern-day 'wild child'*. New York: Academic Press.

Dawkins, Richard (1989), *The Selfish Gene* (2nd edn). Oxford: Oxford University Press.

Dunbar, Robin (1996), *Grooming, Gossip, and the Evolution of Language*. Cambridge, MA: Harvard University Press.

Fasold, Ralph (1990), *Sociolinguistics of Language*. Oxford: Blackwell.

Ferguson, Charles (1959), Diglossia. *Word, 15*, 325–40.

Field, John (2003), *Psycholinguistics. A resource book for students*. London: Routledge.

Fishman, Joshua A. (1980), 'Bilingualism and biculturalism as individual and as societal phenomena'. *Journal of Multilingual and Multicultural Development, 1*, 3–15.

— (1997), *In Praise of the Beloved Language: A comparative view of positive ethnolinguistic consciousness*. Berlin: Mouton de Gruyter.

Fodor, Jerry (1983), *The Modularity of Mind*. Cambridge, MA: MIT Press.

Foster-Cohen, Susan (1999), *An Introduction to Child Language Development*. London: Longman.

Gardner, Howard (1983), *Frames of Mind: The theory of multiple intelligences*. New York: Basic Books.

Giegerich, Heinz (1992), *English Phonology. An Introduction*. Cambridge: Cambridge University Press.

Gopnik, Myra and Crago, Martha (1991), 'Familial aggregation of a developmental language disorder'. *Cognition, 39*, 1–50.

Greenberg, Joseph H. (1966), 'Some universals of grammar with particular reference to the order of meaningful elements'. In Greenberg, J. H. (ed.), *Universals of Language* (pp. 73–113). Cambridge, MA: MIT Press.

Grice, H. Paul (1975), 'Logic and Conversation'. In Cole, P. and Morgan, J. L. (eds) *Syntax and Semantics 3: Speech Acts* (pp. 41–58). New York: Academic Press.

Grosjean, François (1985), 'The bilingual as a competent but specific speaker-hearer'. *Journal of Multilingual and Multicultural Development, 6, 6,* 467–77.

Haiman, John (1998), *Talk is Cheap. Sarcasm, alienation, and the evolution of language.* Oxford: Oxford University Press.

Hatch, Evelyn and Brown, Cheryl (1995), *Vocabulary, Semantics and Language Education.* Cambridge: Cambridge University Press.

Hawkins, John A. (1995), *A Performance Theory of Order and Constituency.* Cambridge: Cambridge University Press.

Hinton, Leanne (1994), *Flutes of Fire: Essays on California Indian languages.* Berkeley, CA: Heyday Books.

Hogg, Richard (2002), *Introduction to Old English.* Edinburgh: Edinburgh University Press.

Holm, John (2000), *An Introduction to Pidgins and Creoles.* Cambridge: Cambridge University Press.

Hymes, Dell (1972), 'On Communicative Competence'. In Pride, J. B. and Holmes, J. (eds), *Sociolinguistics* (pp. 269–93). Harmondsworth: Penguin.

— (1996), *Ethnography, Linguistics, Narrative Inequality.* London: Taylor and Francis.

Jackendoff, Ray (1977), *X-bar Syntax: A study of phrase structure.* Cambridge, MA: MIT Press.

— (1992), *Languages of the Mind. Essays on mental representation.* Cambridge, MA: MIT Press.

— (1993), *Patterns in the Mind. Language and human nature.* New York: Harvester Wheatsheaf.

— (2002), *Foundations of Language. Brain, meaning, grammar, evolution.* Oxford: Oxford University Press.

Jacobs, Roderick A. (1995), *English Syntax. A grammar for English language professionals.* New York: Oxford University Press.

Jenkins, Jennifer (2003), *World Englishes. A resource book for students.* London: Routledge.

Johnson-Laird, Phillip (1983), *Mental Models: Towards a cognitive science of language, inference and consciousness.* Cambridge: Cambridge University Press.

Katamba, Francis (1993), *Morphology.* London: Macmillan.

Labov, William (1972), *Sociolinguistic Patterns.* Philadelphia, PA: University of Pennsylvania Press.

Lakoff, George and Johnson, Mark (2003), *Metaphors We Live By* (2nd edn). Chicago: Chicago University Press.

Leech, Geoffrey, Rayson, Paul, and Wilson, Andrew (2001), *Word frequencies in written and spoken English based on the British National Corpus.* London: Longman.

Levelt, Willem (1989), *Speaking. From intention to articulation.* Cambridge, MA: MIT Press.

Lieberman, Philip (1984), *The Biology and Evolution of Language.* Cambridge, MA: Harvard University Press.

Lightbown, Patsy and Spada, Nina (1999), *How Languages are Learned* (2nd edn). Oxford: Oxford University Press.

LoCastro, Virginia (2003), *An Introduction to Pragmatics. Social action for language teachers.* Ann Arbor, MI: University of Michigan Press.

McCrum, Robert, Cran, William and MacNeil, Robert (2002), *The Story of English* (3rd edn). New York: Penguin.

Marainen, Johannes (1988), 'Returning to Sámi Identity'. In Skutnabb-Kangas, T. and Cummins, J. (eds), *Minority Education. From shame to struggle.* Clevedon: Multilingual Matters.

Nicol, Janet (ed.) (2001), *One Mind, Two Languages. Bilingual language processing.* Oxford: Blackwell.

Obler, Loraine and Gjerlow, Kris (1999), *Language and the Brain.* Cambridge: Cambridge University Press.

Osherson, Daniel (ed.) (1995–1998), *An Invitation to Cognitive Science* (Vols 1–4; 2nd edn). Cambridge, MA: MIT Press.

Pennycook, Alistair (2001), *Critical Applied Linguistics. A critical introduction.* Mahwah, NJ: Lawrence Erlbaum.

Pinker, Steven (1994), *The Language Instinct. How the mind creates language.* New York: Harper.

— (1999), *Words and Rules.* New York: Basic Books.

— (2002), *The Blank Slate. The modern denial of human nature.* New York: Viking Penguin.

Plotkin, Henry (1998), *Evolution in Mind. An introduction to evolutionary psychology.* Cambridge, MA: Harvard University Press.

Quine, Willard V. O. (1960), *Word and Object.* Cambridge, MA: MIT Press.

Radford, Andrew (1988), *Transformational Grammar. A first course.* Cambridge: Cambridge University Press.

— (2004), *English Syntax: An Introduction.* Cambridge: Cambridge University Press.

Resnick, Melvyn C. (1981), *Introducción a la historia de la lengua española.* Washington, DC: Georgetown University Press.

Ringbom, Håkon (1987), *The Role of the First Language in Foreign Language Learning.* Clevedon, UK: Multilingual Matters.

Saussure, Ferdinand de (1986), *Course in General Linguistics* (trans. R. Harris). La Salle, IL: Open Court.

Schmitt, Norbert (ed.) (2002), *An Introduction to Applied Linguistics.* London: Arnold.

Selinker, Larry (1992), *Rediscovering Interlanguage.* London: Longman.

Slobin, Dan (1979), *Psycholinguistics* (2nd edn). Glenview, IL: Scott, Foresman and Company.

Spolsky, Bernard (2004), *Language Policy.* Cambridge: Cambridge University Press.

Stevenson, Rosemary J. (1993), *Language, Thought and Representation.* Chichester, UK: Wiley.

Stockwell, Robert and Minkova, Donka (2001), *English Words. History and Structure.* Cambridge: Cambridge University Press.

Sweet, Henry (2003 [1876]), *An Anglo-Saxon Reader in Prose and Verse.* London: Kegan Paul.

Tannen, Deborah (1992), *You Just Don't Understand*. London: Virago.

Thomas, Linda (1993), *Beginning Syntax*. Oxford: Blackwell.

Wardhaugh, Ronald (1999), *Proper English. Myths and misunderstandings about language*. Oxford: Blackwell.

— (2001), *An Introduction to Sociolinguistics* (4th edn). Oxford: Blackwell.

Watson, John B. (1913), 'Psychology as the Behaviorist Views it'. *Psychological Review, 20*, 158–77.

Wei, Li (2000), Dimensions of bilingualism. In Wei, L. (ed.), *The Bilingualism Reader* (pp. 3–25). London: Routledge.

Weinreich, Uriel (1953), *Languages in Contact: Findings and Problems*. New York: Linguistic Circle of New York. (Reprinted by Mouton, The Hague, 1974.)

Wittgenstein, Ludwig (2002 [1953]), *Philosophical Investigations: The German text, with a revised English translation* (trans. G. E. M. Anscombe). Oxford: Blackwell.

Glossary

abstract words are words which refer to CONCEPTS which don't have associated visual or tactile representations, i.e. are not objects we can see or touch. They are typically words referring to ideas, states, actions, processes, events, properties, or manners in which things happen.

accusative refers to the grammatical CASE of nouns (or pronouns) when they function as objects of verbs, e.g. *book* in the sentence *Jocelyn wrote a <u>book</u> about butterflies*.

acoustic phonetics is the subdiscipline of linguistics which studies the nature of the speech signal and how it is processed by the human auditory system. Its practitioners are amongst the few linguists who are trusted with expensive technical equipment (see SPECTROGRAM).

adjacency pairs are fixed utterances which conventionally co-occur in conversation, like A: *Hi, how are you?* B: *I'm fine thanks, how are you?*

adjective (A or Adj) is the SYNTACTIC CATEGORY of a word which serves as the HEAD of an adjective phrase (AP or AdjP). Adjectives typically modify or specify the meaning of a noun and occur within the noun phrase (e.g. *a rather odd definition*) or after a verb such as *be* or *seem* (e.g. *that definition is rather odd*).

adjunct refers to the type of optional MODIFIER phrase which is not an ARGUMENT of a verb, such as *the other day* in *Dianne celebrated her birthday the other day*.

affix is a term used to refer to PREFIXES and SUFFIXES together. Thus, *unhealthiness* has three affixes, of which one is the PREFIX *un-* and the others are the SUFFIXES *-i* and *-ness*.

agent is the THEMATIC ROLE of an ARGUMENT of a verb, an animate being who instigates some process or action, such as *Isela* in *Isela prepared pigs' trotters for dinner*.

agglutinating languages are those which form morphologically complex words by stringing together sequences of AFFIXES before and/or after a ROOT MORPHEME. Think glue.

agreement is the MORPHOLOGICAL phenomenon by which two words in a syntactic relationship are jointly marked for some INFLECTIONAL category (NUMBER on a subject and verb, GENDER on an ADJECTIVE and noun, etc.). There is agreement even in the sentence *The linguist begs to differ*. (Both *linguist* and *begs* are SINGULAR.)

amplitude in ACOUSTIC PHONETICS is the relative loudness or intensity of some stretch of the speech signal. It is measured in decibels ('dB').

anthropological linguistics is the subdiscipline of linguistics which studies the ways in which language reflects, mediates or constructs the patterns of beliefs and practices of distinct cultural groups.

aphasia is a condition involving impairment or loss of linguistic knowledge or ability. It may be due to congenital or acquired brain damage.

applied linguistics is the sister discipline of linguistics which studies and proposes solutions to practical issues and problems related to language use in political, educational, social and professional settings. Some prefer the term *Applied Language Studies*, to avoid the implication that applied linguists merely 'apply linguistics' rather than having original and innovative ideas of their own, with inputs from different fields.

argument refers to any of the entities labelled by NOUN PHRASES which participate in verb meaning. They assume different THEMATIC ROLES, such as AGENT or INSTRUMENT. A verb like *give* is associated with three obligatory arguments (the giver, the recipient and the thing given), whereas *cut* is associated with two obligatory arguments (the cutter and what is cut) and an optional one (the instrument used).

articulatory phonetics is the subdiscipline of linguistics which studies the manner in which the speech signal is produced by the lungs, larynx and vocal tract.

auditory cortex is the area of CEREBRAL CORTEX in the brain where sound input is processed. It is adjacent to WERNICKE'S AREA.

Austronesian is a language family which groups together the historically related languages spoken in Southeast Asia and some of the Pacific islands.

balanced bilinguals are speakers whose two languages are roughly equivalent in terms of COMMUNICATIVE and GRAMMATICAL COMPETENCE.

bidialectal refers to a speaker who controls two different dialects to roughly the same degree.

bilabial speech sounds are those which involve lip closure, such as [b] and [m].

borrowing is the process by which a word in one language is used in another language, often assimilated to the pronunciation of the receiver language and sometimes with a modified meaning. Borrowed words are seldom returned.

bound morphemes are MORPHEMES which don't occur on their own, including all AFFIXES and some ROOTS, such as -*mit* in *submit* or -*couth* in *uncouth*. Thus, the *un*- in *Prometheus unbound* is bound.

Broca's area is a region of CEREBRAL CORTEX above the Sylvian Fissure associated with language production.

case is the system which classifies or encodes the grammatical functions of nouns and pronouns as SUBJECTS, objects, etc. The system may be overtly expressed, as in Latin, where all nouns carry suffixes which indicate their case, or it may remain abstract, as in the case of English case.

causatives are a type of verb which involves a cause-and-effect process, such as *enrich uranium* or *resurrect the dead*. Some languages employ INFLECTIONAL affixes (equivalent to English *en-* in *enrich*) to productively build causative verbs.

cerebral cortex is the scientific name for the 'grey matter' of the brain, the thin outer layer responsible for most higher-level cognitive processes.

coda is the consonant (or string of consonants) that follows the vowel in a syllable, e.g. [nts] in *pants*. In a hierarchical syllable structure tree, it is sister to the NUCLEUS, and together they form the RIME. The word *coda* has two syllables but no codas.

cognates are words in different languages which share the same, or similar, form and meaning (like *rose* in English and French, *rosa* in Spanish), or words of the same language which derive from the same historical source word (like my last name *Hall* and *hell*, both descended from a term meaning 'covered place', derived from the Proto-Germanic form **xal-* or **xel-*, 'cover, conceal').

combinatoriality is the fundamental principle by which linguistic rules combine elements to create more complex structures. For example, SYLLABLES, MORPHEMES, and words are combinations of phonemes; morphemes can be combined into words; words are combined into PHRASES; and phrases combine to make sentences. *Com-bin-at-or-i-al-ity* is an excellent example of what combinatoriality can combine at the morphological level.

communicative competence is our ability to use language appropriately and effectively in communicative acts. Please write to me at cjhall@mac.com if you think I need help with this.

comparative analysis is the method by which HISTORICAL LINGUISTS explore the genetic relationship between words and structures in different languages. The technique has also been used to predict error patterns in second language learning, with mixed results.

comparative reconstruction is the method by which HISTORICAL LINGUISTS recreate the form and structures of languages for which we have no historical record.

competence in linguistics is our permanent, DECLARATIVE KNOWLEDGE of language and how it may be used. It is contrasted with PERFORMANCE, the PROCEDURAL KNOWLEDGE and events involved in contexts of actual use.

complements are those syntactic phrases which occur as obligatory or optional sisters to major SYNTACTIC CATEGORIES in SYNTACTIC TREES. For example, a transitive verb like *sing* can take an optional NOUN PHRASE complement such as *a requiem* as one of its ARGUMENTS, and adjectives such as *fond* require a PREPOSITIONAL PHRASE complement such as *of beer*.

compositionality in SEMANTICS is the principle by which the meaning of the whole equals the sum of the meaning of the parts, such that the compound *puppy dog* is a dog which is a puppy, but *hot dog* is not a dog which is hot. Similarly, the VERB PHRASE *shoot the breeze* doesn't refer to a ballistic attack on the wind, whereas *shoot the sheriff* does refer to such an attack on a law enforcer.

compound refers to a combination of one or more lexical ROOTS. *Language spell* is a compound noun, as is *compound noun* itself.

compound representations are postulated representations in the bilingual MENTAL LEXICON in which two word forms in different languages are independently associated with a common concept or meaning, such as *cigar* in English and *puro* in Mexican Spanish.

computational linguistics is the subdiscipline of linguistics which uses computers to solve language problems, such as the analysis of large bodies of text, or for the testing of theoretical hypotheses about language structure.

concepts are the stored mental representations of what we experience, know or construct about our universe. Linguistic meanings constitute that subset of our concepts which are expressible through language. Many concepts are formulated and/or accessible via non-linguistic means, such as vision, hearing or taste (e.g. those expressed by the words *tree, melodious,* or *sour*). Some (like 'magic' or 'God') are constructed internally, without any external sensory experience. Others (like 'thing' or 'move') are probably INNATE.

conceptual systems is the 'central' part of the mind where CONCEPTS are mentally constructed and represented.

concordancers are computer programs which search a CORPUS of TEXT for some word and produce a list of its occurrences, together with a portion of preceding and following context. Such lists are useful for seeing how words are actually used, either by a single novelist or poet, or across a massive range of speakers and writers in different GENRES.

concrete nouns refer to CONCEPTS which have an associated visual or tactile representation, i.e. objects we can see or touch. The noun *concrete* is a particularly good example of this class (except when it's used ABSTRACTLY, as in *concrete noun*, that is).

conditional mood is the grammatical mode by which a verb indicates contingent possibility, as in *If I were elected president I would reduce taxes*. It is also often used as a PRAGMATIC tool, to express MITIGATION, as in *Could you move your car, please*?

conjugation refers to the set of INFLECTIONAL variants taken by a verb to indicate different NUMBER and PERSON values.

connotations are semantic values conventionally associated with the CORE MEANING of a word. Churchill used the phrase *terminological inexactitude* of a fellow member of Parliament, to avoid the negative connotation of *lie*, a term which parliamentary etiquette forbids.

constituents are units in a hierarchical structure: nodes in a syntactic, morphological, or syllabic tree (see MOTHER NODE and DAUGHTER NODE).

content words are words which serve to express CONCEPTUAL content rather than perform grammatical functions (see FUNCTION WORDS). This class, comprising all the nouns, verbs, adjectives and adverbs, is potentially infinite (through NEOLOGISM).

conversation analysis is a subfield of linguistics which studies the structure of conversations, including ADJACENCY PAIRS, the social roles of interlocutors and their associated 'rights' (e.g. adults versus children), and the functions of different conversational elements, such as attention-getters like *Guess what?*, turn-taking markers such as *So, anyway* (to end a turn), and topic-changers like *So what about ...*

conversion is the grammatical phenomenon whereby a single WORD FORM is used as two or more SYNTACTIC CATEGORIES, e.g. *snow* as a verb and *snow* as a noun. It is also used to refer to the historical morphological *process*, by which a word used in one syntactic category comes to be used in another. In some cases (such as *convert* the verb and *convert* the noun), there is a difference in STRESS placement too.

Cooperative Principle is the term Grice used to refer to the set of default assumptions (or maxims) underlying all human linguistic interaction. The assumption that we are generally cooperative is the rule that proves the exception, as we see in the widespread *conventional violations* of Grice's maxims in real conversation.

coordinate representations are postulated representations in the bilingual MENTAL LEXICON in which two translation equivalents are either represented as having separate meanings (Uriel Weinreich's original rather unlikely proposal) or as having *overlapping* (similar but not identical) conceptual representations (my reformulation).

core meanings are the central, prototypical aspects of the meaning of a word that have to be permanently attached to an entry in the MENTAL LEXICON. The meaning a word may actually express in *use* will depend on how its core meaning is deployed in both linguistic and non-linguistic context.

corpus refers to a massive computerized collection of authentic language, often drawn from different GENRES and, increasingly, from the spoken as well as written modality. Corpora are used for the analysis of grammatical patterns in *usage*, as well as the calculation of WORD FREQUENCY and the frequency of word combinations or grammatical structures. The results are useful in literary analysis, language teaching and other applied domains.

corpus planning is the kind of LANGUAGE PLANNING which makes decisions about, and sets objectives for, the codification of a previously uncodified language or language variety in terms of its vocabulary, grammar, writing system and norms of usage (contrasted with STATUS PLANNING). It has nothing to do with a CORPUS, although corpora may be useful tools for the enterprise.

covert marking 'happens' when a grammatical property is not expressed through sound or spelling, such as [SINGULAR] in *the linguist* or object (ACCUSATIVE) CASE in *He loves a linguist*.

covert prestige is the phenomenon in which aspects of a regional or non-mainstream accent or dialect spread to speakers of other varieties, including the mainstream (prestige) variety. Covert prestige blossomed in the 1960s in the UK, as working-class Londoners adopted features of the Liverpool accent of the Beatles, and posh Londoners took on some of the vowel qualities of Michael Caine and other celebrated cockneys. It is now booming throughout the UK, leading to DIALECT LEVELLING.

creoles are human languages which started life as less expressive PIDGINS, but developed the status of full language systems on being acquired as native tongues by children, who endowed them with complete grammars and more extensive vocabularies.

cross-linguistic influence is the process by which the form, structure or semantic MAPPING used by one language can affect the learning, use or loss of another language. It is also known as *transfer* and, often unfairly, *interference*.

dative is the grammatical CASE of nouns used as INDIRECT OBJECTS, often when they refer to the beneficiary of an action or a state, as in *Gaby gave the book to Tom*.

daughter nodes are the CONSTITUENTS of a hierarchical tree structure which share the same MOTHER NODE at the next level up (a daughter node may be an only child).

declarative knowledge of language is the permanent linguistic COMPET-ENCE we all store in long-term memory. It and our PROCEDURAL KNOWLEDGE of language together constitute an individual's language faculty. THEORETICAL and DESCRIPTIVE LINGUISTS study the nature of speakers' declarative knowledge of language(s).

declarative sentences are those with a tensed verb in the basic word order (Subject-Verb-Object for English). They do not necessarily have a declarative *function*: the declarative sentence *This train goes to Edinburgh* may be a question if it is spoken with rising intonation.

declensions are classes of inflectional affixes on nouns, often listed in tables. They normally mark NUMBER and CASE information.

definite articles are function words (*the, this, that, these, those*) used to designate nouns whose reference has been established in a currently activated DISCOURSE or MENTAL MODEL. So I can now refer to *the nouns* mentioned in the previous sentence. See DETERMINER.

derivation is the kind of morphological combination which creates (or has created in the past) new AFFIXED or COMPOUND words. It is distinguished from INFLECTION, which doesn't create new words. The word *derivation* is derived from the combination of morphemes *derive + ate + ion*. The complex word *derivation rule* is a compound derivation.

descriptive linguistics is the branch of linguistics which describes the grammar and lexicon of particular languages or dialects.

determiners are the class of FUNCTION WORDS that in GENERATIVE linguistics include the DEFINITE and INDEFINITE ARTICLES (*the, a*), the demonstratives (*that, those*, etc.) and the so-called 'possessive PRONOUNS' (*her, their*, etc.). They are all lumped together into a single group because they all occur in the same SYNTACTIC TREE positions (before a HEAD noun and its immediate MODIFIERS) and they cannot co-occur.

dialects are varieties of a language which may differ at all levels of the grammar and lexicon, and are spoken by groups defined by region, socioeconomic class, etc. Some dialects are called languages, because they are associated with powerful (often national) groups, like Dutch and Flemish, Hindi and Urdu. Some languages are often called dialects for the opposite reason, especially indigenous languages in countries with a colonial past, such as Mexico.

dialect levelling is the SOCIOLINGUISTIC process by which different dialects become more similar to each other. This homogenization has been observed recently in British English, where elements of the dialect spoken in and around London are spreading northwards.

diglossia is the phenomenon in which a community or individual employs different languages, DIALECTS or REGISTERS for different purposes or contexts of use. For example, a Muslim cleric from Egypt might use Classical Arabic in the mosque and Colloquial Arabic at home, and a Mexican American may watch the TV news in English but email friends in Spanish.

discourse is a level of language which goes beyond the syntactic or the literal semantic, encompassing the interlocutors' intentions, the context of use, and the organization of sentences into more complex units. The word is also used to refer to a 'chunk' of language at this level, which may vary in length from a single word (*Move!* yelled by a gridlocked motorist) to a lengthy conversation or a 600-page novel.

discourse analysis is the subdiscipline of linguistics which studies the DISCOURSE level of language and its relationship with sociocultural contexts, language users' roles and intentions, and ideological aspects of language use in different domains.

dummy subjects are subjects which don't refer to anything. They have to be there in languages which are not NULL-SUBJECT. In English, they include the *it* in *It's about time* or the *there* in *There's not much time left*.

economy versus clarity refers to the tension between the speaker's inclination to be brief and the hearer's need for enough information in order to understand the message. This tension can account for some of the ebb and flow of historical change, the dynamics of DISCOURSE, and the differences between written and spoken MODALITIES (where differing amounts of context can determine how economical the speaker/writer can be).

E-language is Chomsky's term for the concept of language as an External phenomenon: the product of individual or group PERFORMANCE in the social world. The term has been extended (as in this book) to the idea of 'a language' as a communal system.

ethnographic domains distinguish different aspects of the sociocultural events studied by ethnographers. Ethnography is a methodology used in the social sciences to explore and understand such events from the participants' point of view.

etymology is the (study of the) history of WORD FORMS and WORD MEANINGS. According to the *Oxford English Dictionary*, for example, *etymology* can be traced to Greek *etumos*, meaning 'true' and *-logos*, 'word'. It came into English from Latin, via Old French.

evolutionary psychology is an approach to cognitive psychology which studies the genetic origins of the mind and behaviour, including language. It has tended to get a bad press, largely because its findings have been mistakenly interpreted as moral claims about INNATE differences between the races and the sexes. In fact, it departs from the premise that all human beings are born with equal capabilities, the product of our genetic inheritance.

experiencer is the name given to the THEMATIC ROLE of nouns which, not surprisingly, do the experiencing in the context of verbs like *love, enjoy, fear*, etc. James, in the sentence *James experienced great pleasure on smoking his* *first cigar*, fulfils the role of experiencer as an ARGUMENT of the verb *experience*.

faculties, in Fodor's sense, are the different parts of the mind we use to experience reality and thus form knowledge of, and beliefs about, the world. They include the five senses, language, and perhaps others (see INPUT SYSTEMS). Hence the adage that 'deans don't grow old – they just lose their faculties'.

field linguistics is DESCRIPTIVE LINGUISTICS practised *in the field*: collecting and transcribing data on unstudied or understudied languages from the speakers themselves in the places where they are spoken, and then rigorously describing them.

fixed word order is exhibited by languages which don't allow much variation in the sequencing of the major constituents of a sentence (like SUBJECT, VERB and COMPLEMENT). English has fixed word order: You can't say *Fixed word order English has*, for example (unless you're Yoda from *Star Wars*).

formal typology is the linguistic comparison and categorization of languages according to the kinds of structures their grammars allow. So, for example, English and Spanish are typologically similar because they both have basic subject-verb-object word order, but are typologically different because English requires a subject to be expressed, whereas Spanish does not (see NULL SUBJECT). *Historical* typology is different, because it groups languages according to common ancestry, and this is no guarantee of formal similarity (on this measure, English and Spanish are of the same type because they both belong to the INDO-EUROPEAN family).

fossilization is the phenomenon by which learners of a second (or subsequent) language acquire some INTERLANGUAGE form or structure which doesn't match what native-speakers or successful learners do, and which remains as a permanent part of the developing system.

frame is the term I use to refer to the unpredictable, idiosyncratic, mostly grammatical information which we know about words. As lexical knowledge, frames form part of entries in the MENTAL LEXICON. In PSYCHO- and APPLIED LINGUISTICS, frames have not been given as much attention as WORD FORMS and WORD MEANINGS.

free word order is basically the opposite of FIXED WORD ORDER. In languages with free word order, anything goes/goes anything.

frequency in ACOUSTIC PHONETICS refers to relative pitch (the cycles of vibration of the air molecules in the speech stream). It is measured in units called 'hertz' ('Hz'). Not to be confused with WORD FREQUENCY.

function words are words which serve to perform grammatical functions rather than to express semantic content (see CONTENT WORDS). Function words are basically syntactic glue, allowing us to string together content words in grammatically complex ways. They include DETERMINERS and PREPOSITIONS, and belong to a finite list, resistant to BORROWING and NEOLOGISM.

fusional languages are those which express different grammatical functions simultaneously via a single AFFIX, rather than assigning each function to

its own affix (AGGLUTINATING languages), or its very own word
(ISOLATING languages).

gender in linguistics is a grammatical system for grouping together arbitrary
sets of nouns. The system is called gender because in some languages the
subgroups have been traditionally termed masculine and feminine (and
sometimes also neuter). In other language traditions, sexual gender terms
are not used to describe the system. There is often AGREEMENT between
the gender of a noun and the ADJECTIVE(S) and/or DETERMINERS that
modify it.

generative grammar refers (sometimes indistinctly) to: (a) mentally
represented grammatical competence; and (b) an explanatory theory of
this competence. It is particularly associated with Chomsky's approach to
grammar, although there are now a number of competing theories. Such
grammars were originally called *generative* because the aim was to produce
rigorous and exhaustive accounts of competence using rules which *generated*
all possible sentence structures and disallowed all ungrammatical strings.

generativism is the school of thought in linguistics which grew out of
Chomsky's original work on GENERATIVE GRAMMAR. It embraces a
MENTALIST approach to language and mind, and has been extended to
other areas of cognitive science. It represents a reaction to earlier
behaviourist and structuralist approaches to language and mind, which
concentrated on external behaviour or abstract structure. Generative
approaches explore the nature and limits of the mental-biological
knowledge underlying the behaviour, and attempts to explain the
emergence of structural knowledge from external experience and INNATE
predispositions.

genitive refers to the grammatical CASE of possessed nouns, e.g. *ring* in
Camilla's ring. Possession is not restricted to proprietary ownership: the
genitive is also apparent, for example, in *the shape of my heart* (marked by
the preposition *of*), *the president's husband* (marked by *'s*), and the Latin
sanctum sanctorum, 'holy of holies' (marked by the suffix *-orum*).

genre is a conventional type of DISCOURSE or TEXT in which linguistic
structures and functions are highly correlated with a particular context of
usage.

grammaticalization is the historical process whereby a free-standing word
(normally a CONTENT WORD) comes to serve a purely grammatical
function (and hence may turn into a FUNCTION WORD, or reduce to an
INFLECTION).

graphemes are the written versions of PHONEMES. A grapheme is therefore
the smallest unit which can make pairs of written word forms contrast in
meaning, like *s* and *c* in *site* and *cite*. Like phonemes, graphemes are
abstract mental units which may surface in different shapes: site, SITE,
site, site.

heads are elements of syntactic phrases or morphologically complex words
which determine the SYNTACTIC CATEGORY of the entire unit. The
concept normally correlates with the 'semantic head', so in the NP *the entire
unit*, *unit* is the head noun, and is also the semantic head, because the
phrase refers to a type of unit.

head-ordering parameter is a generalization about the limits on word order variation in languages. It is one of a series of hypothesized sets of structural options contained in UNIVERSAL GRAMMAR, which help to explain how children acquire their grammatical competence so swiftly on the basis of experience of erratic and relatively uninformative contextualized speech strings. This particular parameter states that HEADS of different PHRASES are likely to line up either before or after their COMPLEMENTS (i.e. head-initial or head-final).

historical linguistics is the branch of linguistics which describes and explains how language and languages change through time.

homographs are words which share the same written form, but not the same phonological form (pronunciation). For example, *lead* (the metal) and *lead* (the verb).

homonymy is the phenomenon by which two or more words happen to share their phonological and written form. See HOMOPHONE and HOMOGRAPH.

homophones are words which share the same phonological form, but not the same written form (spelling). For example, *their* and *there*.

hypercorrection is the SOCIOLINGUISTIC phenomenon by which speakers of a regional or non-mainstream accent or DIALECT tend to adopt features of the mainstream accent or dialect in linguistic contexts in which speakers of those accents or dialects do not actually use the feature.

hyponymy is the lexical phenomenon by which one word (the *hyponym*) refers to a concept which is a subcategory of a larger concept labelled by another word. *Horse*, for example, is a hyponym of *animal*.

idiolects are the personal linguistic systems of individual speakers. Most variation between idiolects that belong to the same DIALECT group will be at the levels of vocabulary size and voice quality. Languages, then, are abstractions from groups of dialects, and dialects are abstractions from many individual idiolects.

I-language is Chomsky's term for the concept of language as an Internal (also Individual) phenomenon: our mentally represented COMPETENCE.

implied meaning is meaning or speaker intention which is not expressed explicitly in the actual linguistic content (the PROPOSITIONAL STRUCTURE) of an utterance. We use our PRAGMATIC COMPETENCE to reconstruct this meaning or intention. A colloquial formulation of this idea is the notion of 'reading between the lines'.

indefinite articles are FUNCTION WORDS used to designate nouns whose specific reference has not been established in a currently activated DISCOURSE or MENTAL MODEL. The 'discourse or mental model' just referred to wasn't a specific one, hence the use of the indefinite article *a*. See DETERMINER.

indirect objects are nouns with DATIVE CASE, sometimes marked in English with the preposition *to*, as in *give a bone to a dog*, and sometimes by word order, as in *give a dog a bone*. In other languages they may be marked by an inflection, as in Latin *pax hominibus*, 'peace to (all) men'.

Indo-European is a language family which groups together the historically related languages spoken originally from Europe to Iran and northern

India. It has now spread (largely through colonization) all around the globe, from the Americas to Australasia.

inflection, the counterpart to DERIVATION, refers to the kind of morphological combination required by some languages to use a CONTENT WORD in a particular linguistic structure with a particular function. Inflection is normally expressed through AFFIXES (in INDO-EUROPEAN languages overwhelmingly SUFFIXES), and the most typical inflectional functions are NUMBER, AGREEMENT and TENSE.

innatism is the philosophical or scientific position which holds that aspects of our mental life (including language) are only possible because they derive from knowledge encoded in our genes. Chomsky rejected earlier empiricist and behaviourist views of language, which assumed that children's minds were 'blank slates', and proposed instead a return to rationalism, which argued that not all ideas are the unique result of experience of the external world.

input system is the term used by Jerry Fodor to refer to the INNATE systems of the mind responsible for the processing of sensory input, like sound and light. He extended the notion beyond the five senses to other subsystems like language, and possibly music and mathematics, which like the senses process input and deliver it to the mind's CENTRAL SYSTEMS.

instrument is the THEMATIC ROLE associated with nouns used to express the means by which something happens. In the sentence *The piano killed Harold instantly*, the piano is the instrument of Harold's death.

interlanguage is the term introduced by Larry Selinker to refer to the system underlying a learner's current knowledge of a non-native language. The *inter-* in interlanguage reflects the fact that learners are at a stage *in between* zero competence and native competence. Alas, most foreign language learners (including me) tend to stay there.

interrogative sentences are those which exhibit structures associated with the asking of questions, such as *Did you dance at the wedding?* and *What did you wear?* But interrogative sentences don't always ask questions: *Can you be quiet?* and *Who does she think she is?* have quite different functions. See PRAGMATICS.

intransitive verbs are verbs which don't take a direct object, like *stay, flop* or *die*.

isolating languages are those which tend to express INFLECTIONAL and DERIVATIONAL functions as separate words, rather than as AFFIXES. Such languages are short on MORPHOLOGY and big on FUNCTION WORDS.

language planning is both a subfield of APPLIED LINGUISTICS and a professional activity. It involves decision-making about the teaching, use, status and content of languages and DIALECTS, especially in situations where they come into contact and policies must be devised and implemented.

language processing is what the mind does when it produces and comprehends speech, writing, or sign. Language is 'processed' in that input representations are transformed into different output representations, with perhaps many other ones being computed in between. In reading, for example, GRAPHEMES are identified on the basis of visual input from letter shapes, and these are used to recognize word forms, which activate word meanings. In speech, ideas are transformed into word meanings, which activate word forms, which activate PHONEMES, which make the muscles of the vocal tract move.

language shift is the process by which a politically or numerically dominant language displaces a less dominant one, in both individual minds during their lifetime and whole communities over history.

lexical inheritance is the vocabulary of a language that comes down to its speakers from previous generations, rather than as a result of BORROWING from the word stock of speakers of another language.

lexical selection is the phase of LANGUAGE PROCESSING in which words are selected to express the message or intention of the speaker. It is normally a completely unconscious process in speech, but in writing it regularly involves deliberate search and choice.

lexical triad is the term I use to characterize the essence of wordhood as a set of three connected mental representations: the WORD FORM and FRAME in the MENTAL LEXICON, together used by language to express a WORD MEANING.

lexicon is the component of a language system which contains information about words. The term on its own is mostly used in the context of THEORETICAL or DESCRIPTIVE LINGUISTS' accounts of the language system, but is also commonly used to refer to the actual component of the mind where words are represented, i.e. the PSYCHOLINGUISTS' concept of the MENTAL LEXICON.

lingua franca is a language used by two or more groups of speakers of different languages as a means of communication. The term originally referred to a pidgin language used for Mediterranean trade in the Middle Ages.

linguistic archaeology is an application of HISTORICAL and TYPOLOGICAL LINGUISTICS to the tracking of migration of human populations, using COMPARATIVE ANALYSIS and RECONSTRUCTION.

linguistic awareness is our conscious *attention* to permanent linguistic knowledge and to specific language events. It is exceedingly limited in scope, shallow in analysis and fleeting in duration. In other words, language 'happens' mostly below the level of our awareness.

linguistic belief is the result of our limited AWARENESS: a folk system of knowledge which is generally useful on a day-to-day basis, but has some unwelcome consequences.

linguistic knowledge is the language faculty itself, stored permanently in long-term memory as grammatical and lexical COMPETENCE, and deployed in actual events as PRAGMATICALLY-modulated and SOCIO-CULTURALLY-mediated PERFORMANCE.

linguistics is the integrated branch of the cognitive and social sciences that studies human language. The word is first attested in English in 1855.

loan words are words that have entered a language through BORROWING. Neither *loan*, nor *word*, are loan words, both being part of our Anglo-Saxon LEXICAL INHERITANCE. Both *lexical*, and *inheritance*, however, were originally loan words, the first from Ancient Greek and the second from Old French.

mapping is the process by which languages correlate features of linguistic expression (like word order or INFLECTION) with meaning. Different languages 'map' meaning onto linguistic expressions differently, hence the 'mapping problem' for child acquirers, who must establish how their language does it, and for second language acquirers, who must work out how the new language maps similarly or differently from their native language. Like conventional maps of geographical terrain, linguistic expressions provide only a partial, schematic representation of underlying CONCEPTUAL structure.

mental grammar is our mentally represented linguistic COMPETENCE, as opposed to traditional (school) grammar or DESCRIPTIVE or THEORET-ICAL LINGUISTS' accounts of E- or I-LANGUAGE grammatical systems.

mental lexicon is where the mind stores knowledge of WORD FORMS, FRAMES, and their connections with WORD MEANING. See LEXICAL TRIAD.

mental model is Phillip Johnson-Laird's term for representations of situations in the mind. They are constructed on the basis of sensory and linguistic input, general knowledge and beliefs, attitudes and intentions. They are important for language because they are the starting point for when we want to say or write something, and the endpoint when we hear or read something. They involve far more detail than can be MAPPED onto linguistic expressions in production and, through inferencing, contain more information than the linguistic expressions we decode in comprehension. See LANGAUGE PROCESSING and PRAGMATICS.

mentalese is the 'language' of thought. Verbal language serves to translate sounds into meanings and meanings into sound, but the meanings themselves cannot be represented in this externalizable format: there is no homunculus ('little man') listening to the language we hear and telling us what it means, or telling us what to say when we wish to speak.

mentalism is the philosophical approach which explains behaviour (including linguistic behaviour) on the basis of mental states or representations in the mind. It is closely associated with NATIVIST accounts. (The term is also now used, to the chagrin of mentalist philosophers I imagine, to refer to a popular branch of magic.)

metalinguistic concepts, terms and processes are those which are used when language is being used to talk about or describe language (i.e. as a consequence of LINGUISTIC AWARENESS, LINGUISTIC BELIEF or doing LINGUISTICS).

metaphor is when a word form with one CORE MEANING (often CONCRETE) is extended to refer to another core meaning (often ABSTRACT), on the basis of some perceived similarity between the meanings. Originally a term from poetics, the process it refers to is now seen as a fundamental organizing principle of human thought, and perhaps played an instrumental role in its evolution.

mitigation is the DISCOURSE phenomenon through which speakers seek to minimize any imposition on their interlocutors. Hence, for example, speakers tend to *ask* if they may make a request (*May I ask where you bought your hat?*), or play down their own knowledge when in fact they know they are right (*I'm not sure, but I think that's my umbrella*).

modality is the channel used by language to externalize and internalize the meaning or message it encodes: speech, sign or written text.

modifiers are words or PHRASES used to modify (specify) the meaning or usage of a HEAD. They are CONSTITUENTS of a phrase which occur as sisters to the head they modify. Typical modifiers include the direct object NOUN PHRASES of verbs, PREPOSITIONAL PHRASES on nouns, and ADJECTIVE phrases on nouns.

monodialectal speakers have only one DIALECT. In today's global village, such speakers are becoming progressively fewer, at least with regard to their receptive knowledge.

morphemes are, strictly speaking, the smallest elements of linguistic meaning or grammatical function. They may be expressed as words or AFFIXES. More than one morpheme may be expressed by a single word or affix form: the word form *men*, for example, expresses the meanings 'man' and [PLURAL]; and the *-s* on *the man sings* expresses the functions singular NUMBER, third PERSON, present TENSE. The term is regularly used to refer to a minimal (unanalysable) word or affix *form* (as in BOUND MORPHEME), but a more accurate term for this is 'morph'. Hence, it is morphemes but not morphs which separate the men from the boys (*men* = one morph, two morphemes; *boys* = two morphs, two morphemes)

morphology is (the study of) the internal structure of words: how morphs (ROOTS and AFFIXES) are combined to express combinations of MOR-PHEMES as COMPOUNDS or affixed words.

mother node is the term used to refer to any node in a syntactic tree which, unsurprisingly, has one or more daughters.

motor cortex is the region of the CEREBRAL CORTEX involved in muscle control. It dedicates a massive amount of neural circuitry to the musculature of the speech organs.

nativism is the school of thought in philosophy and psychology which holds that parts of the mind may be INNATELY prespecified. Chomsky is the main proponent of nativism in linguistics.

neologisms are new words.

neurolinguistics is the branch of linguistics that studies the biological organization and functioning of language in the brain. (It has *nothing whatsoever* to do with 'Neuro-Linguistic Processing', an approach to psychotherapy.)

neurons are the cells of the brain, transmitting nerve impulses to each other and around the body through the synaptic interface.

Niger-Congo is a language family (the largest, according to Ethnologue) which groups together the historically related languages spoken in large parts of western, central and southern Africa.

nominative is the grammatical CASE of nouns (or pronouns) when they act as subjects of verbs, e.g. *books* in the sentence *Books about butterflies can be most edifying*.

non-compositionality is the opposite of COMPOSITIONALITY. *Hot dog* is a non-compositional compound because the sum of the meanings of the parts does not tell you what a hot dog is. The non-compositionality of word strings suggests that they must be stored in the MENTAL LEXICON separately from their parts. This has led to a method of foreign language vocabulary teaching which stresses the recognition and learning of lexical 'phrases' or 'chunks'.

noun phrases (NPs) are syntactic CONSTITUENTS which have a noun as head.

nucleus is the term used to refer to the essential vowel in syllables (see HEAD). If it doesn't have a nucleus, it's not a syllable.

null-subject languages are languages which do not have to phonologically express the subject of a sentence. They often indicate subject information through INFLECTIONS on the verb. See DUMMY SUBJECT.

number is an inflectional category that may be marked on verbs and nouns and which has the values [SINGULAR] and [PLURAL] (and in some languages also [DUAL]).

onsets are the consonants that appear before the syllabic NUCLEUS.

orthography is the equivalent of PHONOLOGY in the written domain.

overt marking occurs when a grammatical property is expressed through phoneme or letter strings, as in [PLURAL] -*s* and [PROGRESSIVE] -*ing* in *Marc was telling jokes.*

parsing is the technical term used in PSYCHOLINGUISTICS for syntactic processing during comprehension. Oddly, it is pronounced with a [s] by speakers of US English and a [z] by speakers of UK English.

patient is the THEMATIC ROLE of animate noun phrases which undergo some action or process, as in *the patient was anaesthetized before his operation.*

performance is the actual deployment of linguistic COMPETENCE in situations of use. The term is used to refer to both PSYCHOLINGUISTIC and PRAGMATIC processes, such as memory and LANGUAGE PROCESSING limitations in the case of the former, and contextual and social factors in the case of the latter.

perisylvian region is the area of the CEREBRAL CORTEX on either side of the Sylvian Fissure, a deep crevice separating the frontal and temporal lobes of the brain.

person is the inflectional category marked on verbs and coded in pronouns which distinguishes the speaker or a group which includes the speaker ([1ST PERSON]), the addressee(s) ([2ND PERSON]), and others ([3RD PERSON]).

phonemes are the abstract mental representations of speech sounds, or the descriptive units used by PHONOLOGISTS to describe our knowledge of these speech sounds.

phoneme inventory is the term used to refer to the phonemes we know.

phonetic categories and processes are those which are involved in the production and reception of speech sounds. See PHONOLOGICAL.

phonetic reduction is the process by which speech sounds are shortened, underarticulated, or lost during casual speech.

phonological categories, rules and principles encode our abstract knowledge of the sound system of our language, including its PHONEME INVENTORY, intonation patterns, SYLLABLE structure, principles of stress placement, rhythmic features and PHONOLOGICAL ASSIMILATION rules.

phonological assimilation is the predictable phenomenon, captured by phonological rules, by which speech sounds change their value under the influence of the speech sounds they co-occur with in running speech.

phonological opacity is the feature of MORPHOLOGICAL combination whereby one or more of the combined elements is pronounced differently than when it stands alone (in the case of ROOTS) or when it is used PRODUCTIVELY (in the case of affixes). For example, the vowel and final consonant of *opaque* undergoes radical change when the suffix *-ity* is added.

phonological transparency is the opposite of PHONOLOGICAL OPACITY: what you hear is what you get (e.g. *hope* + *-ful* = *hopeful*).

phonology is (the study of) our knowledge of the mental system underlying the ways speech encodes lexical and grammatical structure. The term has recently been extended to the signing systems of SIGN LANGUAGES. See PHONOLOGICAL.

phrases are syntactic CONSTITUENTS headed by nouns, verbs, adjectives, adverbs and prepositions.

phrase structure rules are statements which represent our knowledge of how syntactic CONSTITUENTS may be combined into grammatical strings. Each rule is like a piece of Lego, allowing bits of sentences to be fitted together to make a SYNTACTIC TREE.

pidgins are the basic linguistic systems which sometimes emerge in situations in which speakers of different languages find themselves in frequent contact and need to communicate. If a pidgin is given the chance to grow up, it becomes a CREOLE.

polysemy is the phenomenon in which a single word form has expanded its original CORE MEANING to express related or more specific concepts. A fine example is the verb *get*, which means 'acquire' in *Luz got a new hammock*, 'become' in *David got wet*, 'fetch' in *Alejo got my umbrella*, 'understand' in *Patrick didn't get the joke*, etc., etc.

polysynthetic languages express through MORPHOLOGICALLY complex words what other languages express through SYNTACTIC combination. This means that they have very long words containing multiple AFFIXES, and also resemble COMPOUNDS by, for example, incorporating direct objects into the verb (*Maggie groceryshopped* instead of *Maggie shopped for groceries*).

postpositions belong to the same SYNTACTIC CATEGORY as PREPOSITIONS, but occur after the NOUN PHRASE rather than before. English actually has a postposition: *ago* (compare [for [many years]] with [[many years] ago]. Together, PREPOSITIONS and postpositions are called 'adpositions'.

pragmatic competence is that part of our linguistic COMPETENCE which allows us to code and decode linguistically expressed meanings in socially and contextually appropriate ways. See PRAGMATICS.

pragmatic word order languages allow variation in the order of phrasal CONSTITUENTS in a sentence, but each given order corresponds to a different PRAGMATIC intention or emphasis.

pragmatics is the field of linguistics which studies how speakers express and interpet meanings in actual contexts of use. This means looking at how languages express elements of social interaction (such as politeness), and how hearers use non-linguistic knowledge and inferences to interpret non-literal or implied meaning. The former phenomenon tends to be studied from a SOCIOLINGUISTIC perspective, and the latter using the conceptual tools of PSYCHOLINGUISTICS.

predicate is the term used to refer to the part of a sentence expressed by the main VERB PHRASE, i.e. everything except the subject NOUN PHRASE. Predicates state something about the SUBJECT.

prefixes are AFFIXES (BOUND MORPHEMES) which occur before a ROOT. In the sentence *Prefixes are in pre-root position, pre-* is a prefix.

prepositional phrases (PPs) are sentence CONSTITUENTS which have a preposition as a HEAD. This may seem counter-intuitive, since they are FUNCTION WORDS, but the fact that they are heads (obligatory elements of a phrase) can be seen in sentences such as *Arantza swam [(right) under (the boat)]*. The modifiers *right* and *the boat* are optional parts of the verbal COMPLEMENT.

presupposed meaning is meaning that is implied by the CORE MEANING of a word or the PROPOSITIONAL meaning of a sentence, rather than by the context in which the word or sentence is used. It thus derives from our permanent, long-term knowledge of the world.

priming is the PSYCHOLINGUISTIC phenomenon in which prior exposure to a word (the 'prime') results in faster RECOGNITION TIMES for subsequently experienced words which share some aspect of their form or meaning. The phenomenon has been exploited by psycholinguists as an experimental technique used to measure just how, and to what extent, representations of words are connected to each other in the MENTAL LEXICON, and share elements in CONCEPTUAL SYSTEMS.

procedural knowledge of language is the knowledge contained in the suite of mental mechanisms that deploy or exploit DECLARATIVE KNOWLEDGE (LINGUISTIC COMPETENCE) in actual comprehension and production events, i.e. for LANGUAGE PROCESSING. It is thus the province of PSYCHOLINGUISTICS and PRAGMATICS.

productivity in MORPHOLOGY is the measure of the frequency with which morphological elements are used to create new linguistic expressions. A fully productive morphological element (such as INFLECTION through AFFIXATION) will be part of our linguistic COMPETENCE. An unproductive process will be effectively 'dead', perhaps used as a kind of cataloguing system for word storage in the MENTAL LEXICON, but otherwise a matter of ETYMOLOGY.

pronouns are linguistic expressions (function words like *him, it, they*) which refer to (without naming) entities in a DISCOURSE. Since they can refer to whole NOUN PHRASES, not just particular *nouns* (as in *When I saw the old house I immediately recognized it*), maybe they should be called 'pro-NPs'.

propositional structure is the level of mental representation at which the literal meaning of linguistic expressions are encoded. Hence the sentences *Mark has addressed the issue* and *The issue has been addressed by Mark* both have the same propositional structure. Our PRAGMATIC COMPETENCE allows us to get from the propositional level of meaning to the actual *intended* meaning. Thus, in our example, the speaker's IMPLIED MEANING may be that the issue is no longer open to debate (since Mark has addressed it).

psycholinguistics is the subdiscipline of linguistics (or the intersection of the fields of psychology and LINGUISTICS) which studies language as a mental phenomenon. Its major areas are language acquisition, LANGUAGE PROCESSING, and the mental representation of language and meaning.

reanalysis is the phenomenon in HISTORICAL LINGUISTICS in which a particular linguistic expression or structure is subconsciously analysed by speakers in a different way than it was in previous I-LANGUAGES (or E-LANGUAGE abstractions). Thus, for example, at the phonological level, the word *orange* started out in Persian as *narang* and lost its initial /n/ before being borrowed into English from Old French. This change may have been due to a reanalysis of the NOUN PHRASE *une orenge*. *Noranges* occur in Shakespeare (cf. also *nuncle*), so the reanalysis may have worked backwards in the minds of some early Modern English speakers.

recipient is the thematic role associated with NOUN PHRASE ARGUMENTS which function as – guess what – *recipients* of some process labelled by a verb, for example *lover* in the sentence *The rich industrialist left her lover everything*.

reciprocal altruism is the behavioural principle, discussed by EVOLU-TIONARY PSYCHOLOGISTS and others, by which an organism performs a 'good deed' which is subsequently 'repaid'. An example would be grooming practices in primates. The interesting question (especially in the context of Dawkins' 'Selfish Gene' theory), is how this principle could evolve in a species, given that the repayment is delayed, or, in the case of cheats, may not occur at all.

recognition time is the time it takes to recognize a word in incoming speech, writing or sign. It may seem instantaneous in terms of our LANGUAGE AWARENESS, but techniques in PSYCHOLINGUISTICS allow researchers to measure the process in milliseconds (and normally words *are* recognized in much less than a second).

recursion is the phenomenon in SYNTAX in which part of the output of one PHRASE STRUCTURE RULE is the input for another, permitting a potentially endless cycle of rule application. In practice, of course, recursion has to stop somewhere, because otherwise we'd get bored, fall asleep, or die (technically: PERFORMANCE factors would limit the deployment of our COMPETENCE).

register is the term used in SOCIOLINGUISTICS to refer to speakers' knowledge and use of linguistic expressions appropriate for different DISCOURSE types and GENRES. Knowledge of register is part of our PRAGMATIC COMPETENCE.

relative clauses are sentences contained within sentences which serve as MODIFIERS of some noun within the main sentence. This means they have their own (implicit) SUBJECT and PREDICATE. For example, in the sentence *The book I was looking for wasn't in the library*, the NOUN PHRASE *The book I was looking for* 'contains' the sentence *I was looking for the book*.

relative pronouns are (in traditional grammar) the FUNCTION WORDS used to introduce RELATIVE CLAUSES. So in the sentence *The thesis that Connie wrote about individual learner differences became a best-seller*, the word *that* is a relative pronoun, introducing the relative clause corresponding to the sentence *Connie wrote a thesis about individual leaner differences*.

rimes are the CONSTITUENTS of SYLLABLES which include the NUCLEUS and (if there is one), the CODA. In the monosyllabic word *ticks*, therefore, the rime is /Iks/. Any resemblance between the word *rime* and the poetic term *rhyme* is purely *un*coincidental.

roots are the lexical elements (normally CONTENT WORDS) which are phonological hosts for AFFIXES, or are combined together to make COMPOUNDS. In some languages, like English, roots can typically stand alone (e.g. *walk* in the affixed word *walker* and the compound *walkway*), but in other languages, like Spanish, they are normally BOUND MORPHEMES (e.g. *caminar* 'walk (verb)' and *camino* 'walk (noun)' – the root here is *camin-*). English also has some bound roots, such as *-couth* in the word *uncouth*.

schwa is the vowel in the word *the*, or the first vowel in *about* or *photography*. Vowels in unstressed syllables tend to be pronounced as schwa in English due to PHONETIC REDUCTION (cf. *ph**o**tograph*). The name comes from the Hebrew word for 'emptiness'.

semantic interpretation is the phase of LANGUAGE PROCESSING in which PROPOSITIONAL STRUCTURES are built for incoming language. This means getting the literal meaning from the words we encounter, and establishing their roles and relations in the specific syntactic structures we encounter them in.

semantic opacity is the feature of MORPHOLOGICAL combination whereby one or more of the combined elements means something different from its CORE MEANING when it stands alone. So *government* is SEMANTICALLY TRANSPARENT because the CORE MEANING of *govern* and the nominalizing function of the SUFFIX *-ment* are maintained in the combination. But in the semantically opaque combination *department*, the element *depart-* is meaningless on its own. See COMPOSITIONALITY.

semantic planning is the phase of productive LANGUAGE PROCESSING in which some part of the contents of our mind (a MENTAL MODEL) is encoded as a unit of meaning (a PROPOSITIONAL STRUCTURE) which may be expressed linguistically. See MAPPING.

semantic transparency is the opposite of SEMANTIC OPACITY. So, for example, in the morphological combination *unclear*, the *un-* suffix gets added to the root *clear*, in exactly the same way that it gets added to the root *able* to produce *unable*, and the result is the transparent summation of the negative meaning of the prefix *un-* and the meaning of the root (*clear* or *able*). See COMPOSITIONALITY.

semantics is (the study of) the ways in which language encodes meaning (i.e. the CORE MEANINGS of words and the PROPOSITIONAL STRUCTURE of word combinations). For many linguists, semantics is still not considered a MENTALIST enterprise. But according to CONCEPTUAL semantics, meaning must transcend language, and therefore becomes, essentially, a problem of PSYCHOLINGUISTICS.

sign languages are human languages which use the manual and visual systems as channels for linguistic communication, instead of the oral and auditory systems used by spoken languages.

sociolinguistics is the subdiscipline of linguistics which studies language as a social phenomenon. It is thus concerned with socially-conditioned variation between and within individuals and groups, the social functions of language, and how language determines and reflects speakers' social roles and relationships.

spectrograms (used in ACOUSTIC PHONETICS) are graphic images of the distribution of acoustic energy in speech, made by instruments called spectrographs. The energy is visually represented as shades of grey (showing AMPLITUDE), with FREQUENCY plotted on the y (vertical) axis and time on the x (horizontal) axis.

speech perception is the phase of LANGUAGE PROCESSING in which incoming speech is recognized as such and the sounds (PHONEMES) are separated out and identified so that WORD RECOGNITION can take place.

speech production is the phase of language processing in which the word forms activated through LEXICAL SELECTION, and assembled in sequence through SYNTACTIC PLANNING, are externalized as a string of speech sounds.

standard dialects are the varieties of a language which enjoy greatest prestige, are used in education and official contexts, and generally form the basis for writing systems. They are often associated with wealth, status and power, and are taken by many people (standard and 'non-standard' dialect speakers alike) to constitute the 'correct' version of the E-LANGUAGE.

status planning is the process, informed by APPLIED LINGUISTICS, in which norms are selected during LANGUAGE PLANNING.

stops are speech sounds like [t], [g] and [p] which are characterized by a sudden release of breath following complete blockage (*stoppage*) of the vocal tract by the lips or tongue. They are also called 'plosives' – think ex*plo*sion

structure dependence is a governing principle of human language, according to which linguistic units operate not just as linear sequences (required for SPEECH PRODUCTION), but as hierarchical groupings of CONSTITUENTS. Thus, no language will have a SYNTACTIC rule which forms the passive by reversing the linear order of the words in the active sentence, or a MORPHOLOGICAL rule which expresses second PERSON by placing the second phoneme of the verb at the end of the word.

style is the term normally used in SOCIOLINGUISTICS to refer to the degree of formality associated with linguistic expressions used in different domains of DISCOURSE. The issue of 'good style' and 'bad style' is a separate issue, confused by prescriptivist dogma, and probably better approached from the perspective of ease of LANGUAGE PROCESSING (as Steven Pinker suggests in his book *The Language Instinct*).

subcategorization frames are ways of representing speakers' knowledge of how individual words (especially verbs) may be deployed in syntactic phrases, specifying the range of COMPLEMENTS they may take. THEMATIC GRIDS, however, represent the same information and more.

subjects are NOUN PHRASE ARGUMENTS of a verb which occur outside PREDICATES. They often correlate with the THEMATIC ROLE of AGENT, but not always: in a passive sentence like *The book was attacked (by the critics)*, for example, the agent is demoted (or lost) and the object of the active sentence (*book*) appears in subject position.

subject-auxiliary inversion is the grammatical phenomenon in English and other languages whereby INTERROGATIVE sentences are formed by taking an auxiliary verb (like *can* or *is*) and placing it before the SUBJECT.

subordinate representations are postulated representations in the developing bilingual MENTAL LEXICON in which a lexical entry from a second language is connected to the lexical entry of a presumed translation equivalent in the native (or previously learned) language. Thus, when an L2 WORD FORM represented subordinately is encountered, it must be 'translated' into the L1 in order for the WORD MEANING to be identified.

suffixes are AFFIXES which occur after ROOTS, like the -*s* on *roots*.

syllables are units of speech which contain a vowel as NUCLEUS and may be modified by consonants in ONSET or CODA position. Syllable boundaries don't necessarily correspond to word boundaries in running speech: the phrase *start up*, for example, has the same syllabic structure as *star tup*.

synonymy is the lexical phenomenon in which two WORD FORMS express the same WORD MEANING.

syntactic category is the linguist's term for 'part of speech'. It is preferred because they are more relevant to SYNTAX than to speech. And of course, SIGN LANGUAGES have syntactic categories too.

syntactic planning is the phase of productive LANGUAGE PROCESSING in which the WORD FORMS activated on the basis of the speaker's intended message are placed in a syntactic structure, together with any required FUNCTION WORDS and INFLECTIONAL MORPHOLOGY.

syntactic trees are the diagrams syntacticians use to show the hierarchical CONSTITUENT structure of PHRASES and sentences. Combinatorial possibilities are constrained by a language's PHRASE STRUCTURE RULES (which are in turn constrained by the X-BAR template specified in UNIVERSAL GRAMMAR). Syntactic trees grow upside-down.

syntax is the (study of) speakers' subconscious knowledge of how words are combined to make phrases and sentences. As a subdiscipline of THEORETICAL LINGUISTICS, syntax has been a driving force of linguistic thought since Chomsky's revolution in the 1950s.

text in DISCOURSE ANALYSIS and PRAGMATICS is a unit of DISCOURSE which combines two or more sentences. It is not necessarily written.

thematic grids are representations of the linear order and SEMANTIC function (THEMATIC ROLE) of a verb's ARGUMENTS. Some classes of verbs share grids, because they have similar CONCEPTUAL structure (like *give*, *grant*, *lend* and *cede*). Thematic grids are stored in a word's FRAME representation in the MENTAL LEXICON.

thematic roles are the semantic roles of NOUN PHRASES expressing the ARGUMENTS of a verb and including AGENT, RECIPIENT, THEME and EXPERIENCER. They are also known in the trade as θ- (theta) roles.

theme, perhaps confusingly, is one of the THEMATIC ROLES assumed by NOUN PHRASE ARGUMENTS of VERBS. It covers the traditional grammar notion of 'patient' (animate receiver of some action or process), but also includes other semantic functions not covered by the other roles.

theoretical linguistics is the subdiscipline of LINGUISTICS which studies and theorizes about the structural properties of language, including PHONOLOGY, MORPHOLOGY, SYNTAX and SEMANTICS.

theory of mind refers to humans' (and perhaps other primates') INNATE knowledge that the minds of other members of the species have intentional states, including beliefs and desires. A recent explanation of autism suggests that children with this neurological condition lack (or have damaged) theory of mind. Hence their apparent egocentrism, reflected in difficulties comprehending that others may not know something, or may think differently from them.

tokens in lexical analysis are actual occurrences of word forms in some text. Thus, there are two tokens of the word *in* in the previous sentence. See TYPE.

transitive verbs take direct objects. *Take* is a transitive verb: you can't just say *Verbs take*.

Trans-New Guinea is a family of languages spoken in the Pacific islands of Indonesia and Papua New Guinea.

types in lexical analysis are categories of word, rather than the actual TOKENS we come across in speech, writing and sign. Thus, there are two tokens of the type *in* in the previous sentence. Similarly, in phonology, PHONEMES are types, of which the individual speech sounds we produce or hear are tokens. At a different level entirely, NULL-SUBJECT languages are a type of which Spanish and Italian are tokens. See TYPOLOGY.

typology is the subdiscipline of linguistics which classifies languages according to their structural TYPE, thus identifying some of the constraints on structrual variation in human language and, accordingly, the occurrence of universal patterns. Word order typology, for example, identifies subject-verb-object (SVO) and subject-object-verb (SOV) as the most common types.

Universal Grammar (UG) is the name given by Chomsky to the INNATE human biological endowment underlying our capacity to acquire language. Its properties include STRUCTURE DEPENDENCE and, it is thought, limited parameters of variation (such as NULL- versus expressed SUBJECTS, and HEAD-ORDERING in SYNTAX).

Uto-Aztecan is a family of languages spoken (regrettably by ever-fewer speakers) in Mexico and in some southern US states.

verb phrases (VPs) are the syntactic CONSTITUENTS which express the PREDICATE, and are headed by verbs.

visual cortex is the region of CEREBRAL CORTEX at the back of the brain (in the occipital lobes) which is involved in visual perception (and is therefore important for reading and comprehending SIGN LANGUAGE).

vocal tract is the name of the anatomical region in which speech sounds are made, from the larynx (where the vocal cords are) up to the oral and nasal cavities.

voicing is a quality of all vowels and some consonants, produced by vibration of the vocal folds (cords) in the larynx.

Wernicke's area is a region of CEREBRAL CORTEX below the inner end of the Sylvian Fissure, which plays a major role in language comprehension.

word forms are representations of the physical expressions of words as strings of PHONEMES and/or GRAPHEMES in spoken languages, and as signs in SIGN LANGUAGES. See FRAME and WORD MEANING.

word frequency refers to the number of times you (are likely to) encounter a particular word or string of words. Calculations of word frequency (often made using a CORPUS) are useful for assessing actual usage of language and, in the APPLIED LINGUISTICS domain, for making decisions about vocabulary learning and teaching in foreign language courses. Frequency is also a major dimension in the organization of the MENTAL LEXICON.

word meaning (at least according to the conceptual SEMANTICS assumed in this book) is the CORE MEANING expressed by a particular WORD FORM and its paired syntactic FRAME. Thus, word meanings are part of our permanent knowledge, stored in CONCEPTUAL SYSTEMS and linked to entries in the mental lexicon through SEMANTIC connections. Word meanings may expand (or contract) in actual use due to the role of context, which is analysed during LANGUAGE PROCESSING on the basis of our PRAGMATIC COMPETENCE.

word recognition is the phase of language processing in which incoming words are identified. The PSYCHOLINGUIST William Marslen-Wilson has posited that in spoken word recognition, numerous candidate WORD FORMS (a 'lexical cohort') will be activated in the MENTAL LEXICON in the early stages (say the first 100 milliseconds), because they match the acoustic input. Further input, together with previous context, will then rapidly converge to deactivate all candidates apart from (hopefully) the one you are hearing.

Subject Index

Note: Index entries defined in the Glossary are indicated with the letter **G**. Whole chapters are indicated in **bold**. References to the 'Further information' sections and to the 'Sources' section are in *italics*.

Scholar Index

Note: References to scholars mentioned in the 'Further information' sections and 'Sources' section are in *italics*.